William Styron's

The Confessions
of Nat Turner

A Critical Handbook

William Styron's

The Confessions of Nat Turner

A Critical Handbook

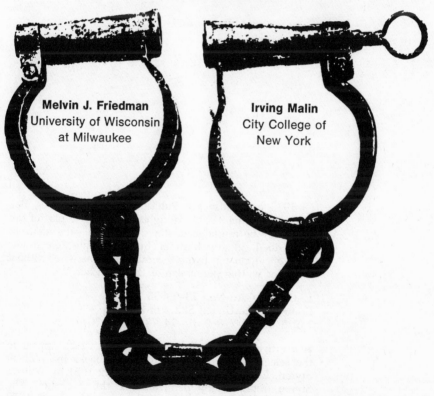

Melvin J. Friedman
University of Wisconsin
at Milwaukee

Irving Malin
City College of
New York

Wadsworth Publishing Company, Inc.
Belmont, California

L. C. Cat. Card No.: 73–99035
Printed in the United States of America
1 2 3 4 5 6 7 8 9 10–74 73 72 71 70

Illustrative quotations of unusual length which appear in the selections are from the following books by William Styron: *Lie Down in Darkness,* copyright 1951 by William Styron, reprinted by permission of the publisher, The Bobbs-Merrill Company, Inc.; *The Long March,* © 1952 by William Styron, reprinted by permission of Harold Matson Co., Inc.; *Set This House on Fire,* © Copyright 1959, 1960 by William Styron, and *The Confessions of Nat Turner,* © Copyright 1966, 1967 by William Styron, both reprinted by permission of Random House, Inc.

PREFACE

We believe that William Styron's novel *The Confessions of Nat Turner* will be read and discussed for many years. It portrays the most disturbing question faced by Americans—the relationship of the races —and, consequently, it has provoked and will continue to provoke both thoughtful and extreme reactions. The questions of black versus white, art versus history, and "fact" versus "fiction" are the guiding relationships of this casebook.

Our casebook is arranged in a simple manner. Part 1 contains background materials: the "original" confessions of Nat Turner (a work of fiction?); an autobiographical portrait of Styron and the South; and three interviews with Styron following the publication of his novel. Part 2, a critical discussion of Styron's novel, poses significant unanswered questions. For example, the eight reviewers disagree about the ultimate worth of the novel—some consider it a simplistic propaganda tract; others praise it as a literary achievement of great merit. The novel's language, symbolism, characterization, and public importance are discussed from these opposing viewpoints. Ernest Kaiser's essay from the collection *William Styron's Nat Turner: Ten Black Writers Respond* provides a valuable black perspective.

In an attempt to broaden perspectives, we include in Part 3 an early and not previously reprinted story of Styron and five long essays on all of his works (Two of these—Roy Arthur Swanson's "William Styron's Clown Show" and Karl Malkoff's "William Styron's *Divine Comedy*"—have not been previously published.) These essays help us to understand the relationship of *The Confessions of Nat Turner* to Styron's earlier novels of crime, punishment, and redemption.

Although Part 4 does not deal directly with *The Confessions of Nat Turner*, it helps us understand Nat Turner as an historical figure and as a slave. The selections include poetic, journalistic, and fictional portrayals of Nat Turner; a chapter from the autobiography of Frederick Douglass; a description of slavery just before the Civil War by a moderate white Northerner; and an essay, written by a white Southerner in the 1930s, looking back on the institution of slavery.

At the end of the book we have posed questions for study, discussion, and writing in the hope that these will help the student to confront the various selections, *The Confessions of Nat Turner*, and his own American heritage. We have also included a full bibliography by Jackson Bryer and Marc Newman, which has not been published before. This bibliography points the way for the student who wishes to further explore and evaluate *The Confessions of Nat Turner* and the works of William Styron.

To facilitate use of the casebook for the controlled-research paper, the original pagination of the articles and reviews is indicated by numbers in brackets. The bracketed number before the virgule (/) indicates the end of the original page; the number after it signals the beginning of a new page. Bracketed numbers are not used in the Swanson and Malkoff pieces, which have never appeared in print before, or in the frequently reprinted "original" confessions of Nat Turner.

CONTENTS

1. BACKGROUND

The Original Confessions of Nat Turner

THOMAS R. GRAY (reporter)

DISTRICT OF COLUMBIA, TO WIT:

Be it remembered, That on this tenth day of November, Anno Domini, eighteen hundred and thirty-one, Thomas R. Gray of the said District, deposited in this office the title of a book, which is in the words as following:

"The Confessions of Nat Turner, the leader of the late insurrection in Southampton, Virginia, as fully and voluntarily made to Thomas R. Gray, in the prison where he was confined, and acknowledged by him to be such when read before the Court of Southampton; with the certificate, under seal, of the Court convened at Jerusalem, November 5, 1831, for his trial. Also, an authentic account of the whole insurrection, and with lists of the whites who were murdered, and of the negroes brought before the Court of Southampton, and there sentenced, &. the right whereof he claims as proprietor, in conformity with an Act of Congress, entitled "An act to amend the several acts respecting Copy Rights."

EDMUND J. LEE, Clerk of the District. In testimony that the above is a true copy, from the record of the District Court for the District of Columbia, I, Edmund J. Lee, the Clerk thereof, have hereunto set my hand and affixed the seal of my office, this 10th day of November, 1831.

[Seal.]

EDMUND J. LEE, C. D. C.

TO THE PUBLIC

The late insurrection in Southampton has greatly excited the public mind, and led to a thousand idle, exaggerated and mischievous reports. It is the first instance in our history of an open rebellion of the slaves, and attended with such atrocious circumstances of cruelty and destruction, as could not fail to leave a deep impression, not only upon the minds of the community where this fearful tragedy was wrought, but throughout every portion of our country, in which this population

1

is to be found. Public curiosity has been on the stretch to understand the origin and progress of this dreadful conspiracy, and the motives which influence its diabolical actors. The insurgent slaves had all been destroyed, or apprehended, tried and executed, (with the exception of the leader,) without revealing any thing at all satisfactory, as to the motives which governed them, or the means by which they expected to accomplish their object. Every thing connected with the sad affair was wrapt in mystery, until Nat Turner, the leader of this ferocious band, whose name has resounded throughout our widely extended empire, was captured. This "great Bandit" was taken by a single individual, in a cave near the residence of his late owner, on Sunday, the thirtieth of October, without attempting to make the slightest resistance, and on the following day safely lodged in the jail of the County. His captor was Benjamin Phipps, armed with a shot gun well charged. Nat's only weapon was a small light sword which he immediately surrendered, and begged that his life might be spared. Since his confinement, by permission of the Jailor, I have had ready access to him, and finding that he was willing to make a full and free confession of the origin, progress and consummation of the insurrectory movements of the slaves of which he was the contriver and head; I determined for the gratification of public curiosity to commit his statements to writing, and publish them, with little or no variation, from his own words. That this is a faithful record of his confessions, the annexed certificate of the County Court of Southampton, will attest. They certainly bear one stamp of truth and sincerity. He makes no attempt (as all the other insurgents who were examined did,) to exculpate himself, but frankly acknowledges his full participation in all the guilt of the transaction.
He was not only the contriver of the conspiracy, but gave the first blow towards its execution.

It will thus appear, that whilst every thing upon the surface of society wore a calm and peaceful aspect; whilst not one note of preparation was heard to warn the devoted inhabitants of woe and death, a gloomy fanatic was revolving in the recesses of his own dark, bewildered, and overwrought mind, schemes of indiscriminate massacre to the whites. Schemes too fearfully executed as far as his fiendish band proceeded in their desolating march. No cry for mercy penetrated their flinty bosoms. No acts of remembered kindness made the least impression upon these remorseless murderers. Men, women and children, from hoary age to helpless infancy were involved in the same cruel fate. Never did a band of savages do their work of death more unsparingly. Apprehension for their own personal safety seems to have been the only principle of restraint in the whole course of their bloody proceedings. And it is not the least remarkable feature in this horrid transaction, that a band actuated by such hellish purposes, should have resisted so feebly, when met by the whites in arms. Desperation alone, one would think, might have led to greater efforts.

More than twenty of them attacked Dr. Blunt's house on Tuesday morning, a little before day-break, defended by two men and three boys. They fled precipitately at the first fire; and their future plans of mischief, were entirely disconcerted and broken up. Escaping thence, each individual sought his own safety either in concealment, or by returning home, with the hope that his participation might escape detection, and all were shot down in the course of a few days, or captured and brought to trial and punishment. Nat has survived all his followers, and the gallows will speedily close his career. His own account of the conspiracy is submitted to the public, without comment. It reads an awful, and it is hoped, a useful lesson, as to the operations of a mind like his, endeavoring to grapple with things beyond its reach. How it first became bewildered and confounded, and finally corrupted and led to the conception and perpetration of the most atrocious and heart-rending deeds. It is calculated also to demonstrate the policy of our laws in restraint of this class of our population, and to induce all those entrusted with their execution, as well as our citizens generally, to see that they are strictly and rigidly enforced. Each particular community should look to its own safety, whilst the general guardians of the laws, keep a watchful eye over all. If Nat's statements can be relied on, the insurrection in this county was entirely local, and his designs confided but to a few, and these in his immediate vicinity. It was not instigated by motives of revenge or sudden anger, but the results of long deliberation, and a settled purpose of mind. The offspring of gloomy fanaticism, acting upon materials but too well prepared for such impressions. It will be long remembered in the annals of our country, and many a mother as she presses her infant darling to her bosom, will shudder at the recollection of Nat Turner, and his band of ferocious miscreants.

Believing the following narrative, by removing doubts and conjectures from the public mind which otherwise must have remained, would give general satisfaction, it is respectfully submitted to the public by their ob't serv't,

T. R. GRAY

Jerusalem, Southampton, Va. Nov. 5, 1831.

We the undersigned, members of the Court convened at Jerusalem, on Saturday, the 5th day of Nov. 1831, for the trial of Nat, *alias* Nat Turner, a negro slave, late the property of Putnam Moore, deceased, do hereby certify, that the confessions of Nat, to Thomas R. Gray, was read to him in our presence, and that Nat acknowledged the same to be full, free, and voluntary; and that furthermore, when called upon by the presiding Magistrate of the Court, to state if he had any thing to say, why sentence of death should not be passed upon him, replied he had nothing further than he had communicated to Mr.

Gray. Given under our hands and seals at Jerusalem, this 5th day of November, 1831.

JEREMIAH COBB,	[Seal.]
THOMAS PRETLOW,	[Seal.]
JAMES W. PARKER,	[Seal.]
CARR BOWERS,	[Seal.]
SAMUEL B. HINES,	[Seal.]
ORRIS A. BROWNE,	[Seal.]

STATE OF VIRGINIA, SOUTHAMPTON COUNTY, TO WIT:

I, James Rochelle, Clerk of the County Court of Southampton in the State of Virginia, do hereby certify, that Jeremiah Cobb, Thomas Pretlow, James W. Parker, Carr Bowers, Samuel B. Hines, and Orris A. Browne, esqr's are acting Justices of the Peace, in and for the County aforesaid, and were members of the Court which convened at Jerusalem, on Saturday the 5th day of November, 1831, for the trial of Nat *alias* Nat Turner, a negro slave, late the property of Putnam Moore, deceased, who was tried and convicted, as an insurgent in the late insurrection in the county of Southampton aforesaid, and that full faith and credit are due, and ought to be given to their acts as Justices of the peace aforesaid.

In testimony whereof, I have hereunto set my hand and caused the seal of the Court aforesaid, [Seal.]   to be affixed this 5th day of November, 1831

JAMES ROCHELLE, C. S. C. C.

CONFESSION

Agreeable to his own appointment, on the evening he was committed to prison, with permission of the jailer, I visited Nat on Tuesday the 1st November, when, without being questioned at all, he commenced his narrative in the following words:—

SIR,—You have asked me to give a history of the motives which induced me to undertake the late insurrection, as you call it—To do so I must go back to the days of my infancy, and even before I was born. I was thirty-one years of age the 2nd of October last, and born the property of Benj. Turner, of this county. In my childhood a circumstance occurred which made an indelible impression on my mind, and laid the ground work of that enthusiasm, which has terminated so fatally to many, both white and black, and for which I am about to atone at the gallows. It is here necessary to relate this circumstance— trifling as it may seem, it was the commencement of that belief which has grown with time, and even now, sir, in this dungeon, helpless and forsaken as I am, I cannot divest myself of. Being at play with other children, when three or four years old, I was telling them something, which my mother overhearing, said it had happened before I was born—I stuck to my story, however, and related somethings which went, in her opinion, to confirm it—others being called on were greatly astonished, knowing that these things had happened, and caused them to say in my hearing, I surely would be a prophet, as the Lord had shewn me things that had happened before my birth. And my father and mother strengthened me in this my first impression, saying in my presence, I was intended for some great purpose, which they had always thought from certain marks on my head and breast—[a parcel of excrescences which I believe are not at all uncommon, particularly among negroes, as I have seen several with the same. In this case he has either cut them off or they have nearly disappeared]—My grandmother, who was very religious, and to whom I was much attached—my master, who belonged to the church, and other religious persons who visited the house, and whom I often saw at prayers, noticing the singularity of my manners, I suppose, and my uncommon intelligence for a child, remarked I had too much sense to be raised, and if I was, I would never be of any service to any one as a slave—To a mind like mine, restless, inquisitive and observant of every thing that was passing, it is easy to suppose that religion was the subject to which it would be directed, and although this subject principally occupied my thoughts—there was nothing that I saw or heard of to which my attention was not directed—The manner in which I learned to read and write, not only had great influence on my own mind, as I acquired it with the most perfect ease, so much so, that I have no recollection whatever of learning the alphabet—but to the astonishment of the family, one day, when a book was shewn to me to keep me from crying, I began spelling the names of different objects—this was a source of wonder to all in the neighborhood, particularly the blacks—and this learning was constantly improved at all opportunities—when I got large enough to go to work, while employed, I was reflecting on many things that would present themselves to my imagination, and whenever an opportunity occurred of looking at a book, when the school children were getting their lessons, I would find many things that the fertility of my own imagination had depicted to me before; all my time, not devoted to my master's service, was spent either in prayer, or in making experiments in casting different things in moulds made of earth, in attempting to make paper, gun-powder, and many other experiments, that although I could not perfect, yet convinced me of its practicability if I had the means.* I was not addicted to stealing in my youth, nor have ever been—Yet such was the confidence of the negroes in the neighborhood, even at this early period of my life, in my superior judgment, that they would often carry me with them when

---

* When questioned as to the manner of manufacturing those different articles, he was found well informed on the subject.

they were going on any roguery, to plan for them. Growing up among them, with this confidence in my superior judgment, and when this, in their opinions, was perfected by Divine inspiration, from the circumstances already alluded to in my infancy, and which belief was ever afterwards zealously inculcated by the austerity of my life and manners, which became the subject of remark by white and black.—Having soon discovered to be great, I must appear so, and therefore studiously avoided mixing in society, and wrapped myself in mystery, devoting my time to fasting and prayer—By this time, having arrived to man's estate, and hearing the scriptures commented on at meetings, I was struck with that particular passage which says: "Seek ye the kingdom of Heaven and all things shall be added unto you." I reflected much on this passage, and prayed daily for light on this subject—As I was praying one day at my plough, the spirit spoke to me, saying "Seek ye the kingdom of Heaven and all things shall be added unto you." *Question*—what do you mean by the Spirit. *Ans*. The Spirit that spoke to the prophets in former days—and I was greatly astonished, and for two years prayed continually, whenever my duty would permit—and then again I had the same relevation, which fully confirmed me in the impression that I was ordained for some great purpose in the hands of the Almighty. Several years rolled round, in which many events occurred to strengthen me in this my belief. At this time I reverted in my mind to the remarks made of me in my childhood, and the things that had been shewn me—and as it had been said of me in my childhood by those by whom I had been taught to pray, both white and black, and in whom I had the greatest confidence, that I had too much sense to be raised, and if I was, I would never be of any use to any one as a slave. Now finding I had arrived to man's estate, and was a slave, and these revelations being made known to me, I began to direct my attention to this great object, to fulfil the purpose for which, by this time, I felt assured I was intended. Knowing the influence I had obtained over the minds of my fellow servants, (not by the means of conjuring and such like tricks—for to them I always spoke of such things with contempt) but by the communion of the Spirit whose revelations I often communicated to them, and they believed and said my wisdom came from God. I now began to prepare them for my purpose, by telling them something was about to happen that would terminate in fulfilling the great promise that had been made to me— About this time I was placed under an overseer, from whom I ran away—and after remaining in the woods thirty days, I returned, to the astonishment of the negroes on the plantation, who thought I had made my escape to some other part of the country, as my father had done before. But the reason of my return was, that the Spirit appeared to me and said I had my wishes directed to the things of this world, and not to the kingdom of Heaven, and that I should return to the service of my earthly master—"For he who knoweth his Master's will, and doeth it not, shall be beaten with many stripes, and thus have I chastened you." And the negroes found fault, and murmured against me, saying that if they had my sense they would not serve any master in the world. And about this time I had a vision—and I saw white spirits and black spirits engaged in battle, and the sun was darkened—the thunder rolled in the Heavens, and blood flowed in streams—and I heard a voice saying, "Such is your luck, such you are called to see, and let it come rough or smooth, you must surely bare it." I now withdrew myself as much as my situation would permit, from the intercourse of my fellow servants, for the avowed purpose of serving the Spirit more fully—and it appeared to me, and reminded me of the things it had already shown me, and that it would then reveal to me the knowledge of the elements, the revolution of the planets, the operation of tides, and changes of the seasons. After this revelation in the year of 1825, and the knowledge of the elements being made known to me, I sought more than ever to obtain true holiness before the great day of judgment should appear, and then I began to receive the true knowledge of faith. And from the first steps of righteousness until the last, was I made perfect; and the Holy Ghost was with me, and said, "Behold me as I stand in the Heavens"—and I looked and saw the forms of men in different attitudes—and there were lights in the sky to which the children of darkness gave other names than what they really were—for they were the lights of the Savior's hands, stretched forth from east to west, even as they were extended on the cross on Calvary for the redemption of sinners. And I wondered greatly at these miracles, and prayed to be informed of a certainty of the meaning thereof—and shortly afterwards, while laboring in the field, I discovered drops of blood on the corn as though it were dew from heaven—and I communicated it to many, both white and black, in the neighborhood—and I then found on the leaves in the woods hiero-glyphic characters, and numbers, with the forms of men in different attitudes, portrayed in blood, and representing the figures I had seen before in the heavens. And now the Holy Ghost had revealed itself to me, and made plain the miracles it had shown me—For as the blood of Christ had been shed on this earth, and had ascended to heaven for the salvation of sinners, and was now returning to earth again in the form of dew—and as the leaves on the trees bore the impression of the figures I had seen in the heavens, it was plain to me that the Savior was about to lay down the yoke he had borne for the sins of men, and the great day of judgment was at hand. About this time I told these things to a white man, (Etheldred T. Brantley) on whom it had a wonderful effect—and he ceased from his wickedness, and was at-tacked immediately with a cutaneous eruption, and blood oozed from the pores of his skin, and after praying and fasting nine days, he was healed, and the Spirit appeared to me again, and said, as the Savior had been baptised so should we be also—and when the white people would not let us be baptised by the church, we went down into the water together, in the sight of many who reviled us, and were baptised by the Spirit—After this I rejoiced greatly, and gave thanks to God. And on the 12th of May, 1828, I heard a loud noise in the heavens, and the Spirit instantly appeared to me and said the Serpent was loosened, and Christ had laid down the yoke he had borne for the sins of men, and that I should take it on and fight against the Serpent, for the time was fast approaching when the first should be last and the last should be first. *Ques.* Do you not find yourself mistaken now? *Ans.* Was not Christ crucified? And by signs in the heavens that it would make known to me when I should commence the great work—and until the first sign appeared, I should conceal it from the knowledge of men— And on the appearance of the sign, (the eclipse of the sun last February) I should arise and prepare myself, and slay my enemies with their own weapons. And immediately on the sign appearing in the heavens, the seal was removed from my lips, and I communicated the great work laid out for me to do, to four in whom I had the greatest confidence, (Henry, Hark, Nelson, and Sam)—It was intended by us to have begun the work of death on the 4th of July last—Many were the plans formed and rejected by us, and it affected my mind to such a degree, that I fell sick, and the time passed without our coming to any determination how to commence—Still forming new schemes and rejecting them, when the sign appeared again, which determined me not to wait longer.

Since the commencement of 1830, I had been living with Mr. Joseph Travis, who was to me a kind master, and placed the greatest confidence in me; in fact, I had no cause to complain of his treatment to me. On Saturday evening, the 20th of August, it was agreed between Henry, Hark and myself, to prepare a dinner the next day for the men we expected, and then to concert a plan, as we had not yet determined on any. Hark, on the following morning, brought a pig, and Henry brandy, and being joined by Sam, Nelson, Will and Jack, they prepared in the woods a dinner, where, about three o'clock, I joined them.

Q. Why were you so backward in joining them.

A. The same reason that had caused me not to mix with them for years before.

I saluted them on coming up, and asked Will how came he there, he answered, his life was worth no more than others, and his liberty as dear to him. I asked him if he thought to obtain it? He said he would, or lose his life. This was enough to put him in full confidence. Jack, I knew, was only a tool in the hands of Hark, it was quickly agreed we should commence at home (Mr. J. Travis') on that night, and until we had armed and equipped ourselves, and gathered sufficient force, neither age nor sex was to be spared, (which was invariably adhered to). We remained at the feast, until about two hours in the night, when we went to the house and found Austin; they all went to the cider press and drank, except myself. On returning to the house, Hark went to the door with an axe, for the purpose of breaking it open, as we knew we were strong enough to murder the family, if they were awaked by the noise; but reflecting that it might create an alarm in the neighborhood, we determined to enter the house secretly, and murder them whilst sleeping. Hark got a ladder and set it against the chimney, on which I ascended, and hoisting a window, entered and came down stairs, unbarred the door, and removed the guns from their places. It was then observed that I must spill the first blood. On which, armed with a hatchet, and accompanied by Will, I entered my master's chamber, it being dark, I could not give a death blow, the hatchet glanced from his head, he sprang from the bed and called his wife, it was his last word, Will laid him dead, with a blow of his axe, and Mrs. Travis shared the same fate, as she lay in bed. The murder of this family, five in number, was the work of a moment, not one of them awoke; there was a little infant sleeping in a cradle, that was forgotten, until we had left the house and gone some distance, when Henry and Will returned and killed it; we got here, four guns that would shoot, and several old muskets, with a pound or two of powder. We remained some time at the barn, where we paraded; I formed them in a line as soldiers, and after carrying them through all the manoeuvres I was master of marched them off to Mr. Salathul Francis', about six hundred yards distant. Sam and Will went to the door and knocked. Mr. Francis asked who was there, Sam replied it was him, and he had a letter for him, on which he got up and came to the door; they immediately seized him, and dragging him out a little from the door, he was dispatched by repeated blows on the head; there was no other white person in the family. We started from there for Mrs. Reese's, maintaining the most perfect silence on our march, where finding the door unlocked, we entered, and murdered Mrs. Reese in her bed, while sleeping; her son awoke, but it was only to sleep the sleep of death, he had only time to say who is that, and he was no more. From Mrs. Reese's we went to Mrs. Turner's, a mile distant, which we reached about sunrise, on Monday morning. Henry, Austin, and Sam, went to the still, where, finding Mr. Peebles, Austin shot him, and the rest of us went to the house; as we approached, the family discovered us, and shut the door. Vain hope! Will, with one stroke of his axe, opened it, and we entered and found Mrs. Turner and Mrs. Newsome in the middle of a room, almost frightened to death. Will immediately killed Mrs. Turner, with one blow of his axe. I took Mrs. Newsome by the hand, and with the sword I had when I was apprehended, I struck her several blows over the head, but not being able to kill her, as the sword was dull. Will turning around and discovering it, despatched her also. A general destruction of property and search for money and ammunition, always succeeded the murders. By this time my company amounted to fifteen, and nine men mounted, who started for Mrs. Whitehead's, (the other six were to go through a by way to Mr. Bryant's, and rejoin us at Mrs. Whitehead's,) as we approached the house we discovered Mr. Richard Whitehead standing in the cotton patch, near the lane fence; we called him over into the lane, and Will, the executioner, was near at hand, with his fatal axe, to send him to an untimely grave. As we pushed on to the house, I discovered some one run round the garden, and thinking it was some of the white family, I pursued them, but finding it was a servant girl belonging to the house, I returned to commence the work of death, but they whom I left, had not been idle; all the family were already murdered, but Mrs. Whitehead and her daughter Margaret. As I came round to the door I saw Will pulling Mrs. Whitehead out of the house, and at the step he nearly severed her head from her body, with his broad axe. Miss Margaret, when I discovered her, had concealed herself in the corner, formed by the projection of cellar cap from the house; on my approach she fled, but was soon overtaken, and after repeated blows with a sword, I killed her by a blow on the head, with a fence rail. By this time, the six who had gone by Mr. Bryant's, rejoined us, and informed me they had done the work of death assigned them. We again divided, part going to Mr. Richard Porter's, and from thence to Nathaniel Francis', the others to Mr. Howell Harris', and Mr. T. Doyles. On my reaching Mr. Porter's, he had escaped with his family. I understood there, that the alarm had already spread, and I immediately returned to bring up those sent to Mr. Doyles, and Mr. Howell Harris'; the party I left going on to Mr. Francis', having told them I would join them in that neighborhood. I met these sent to Mr. Doyles' and Mr. Harris' returning, having met Mr. Doyles on the road and killed him; and learning from some who joined them, that Mr. Harris was from home, I immediately pursued the course taken by the party gone on before; but knowing they would complete the work of death and pillage, at Mr. Francis' before I could get there, I went to Mr. Peter Edwards', expecting to find them there, but they had been here also. I then went to Mr. John T. Barrow's, they had been here and murdered him. I pursued on their track to Capt. Newit Harris', where I found the greater part mounted, and ready to start; the men now amounting to about forty, shouted and hurraed as I rode up, some were in the yard, loading their guns, others drinking. They said Captain Harris and his family had escaped, the property in the house they destroyed, robbing him of money and other valuables. I ordered them to mount and march instantly, this was about nine or ten o'clock, Monday morning. I proceeded to Mr. Levi Waller's, two or three miles distant. I took my station in the rear, and as it was my object to carry terror and devastation wherever we went, I placed fifteen or twenty of the best armed and most relied on, in front, who generally approached the houses as fast as their horses could run; this was for two purposes, to prevent escape and strike terror to the inhabitants—on this account I never got to the houses, after leaving Mrs. Whitehead's, until the murders were committed, except in one case. I sometimes got in sight in time to see the work of death completed, viewed the mangled bodies as they lay, in silent satisfaction, and immediately started in quest of other victims—Having murdered Mrs. Waller and ten children, we started for Mr. William Williams'—having killed him and two little boys that were there; while engaged in this, Mrs. Williams fled and got some distance from the house, but she was pursued, overtaken, and compelled to get up behind one of the company, who brought her back, and after showing her the mangled body of her lifeless husband, she was told to get down and lay by his side, where she was shot dead. I then started for Mr. Jacob Williams, where the family were murdered—Here he found a young man named Drury, who had come on business with Mr. Williams—he was pursued, overtaken and shot. Mrs. Vaughan was the next place we visited—and after murdering the family here, I determined on starting for Jerusalem—Our number amounted now to fifty or sixty, all mounted and armed with guns, axes, swords and clubs—On reaching Mr. James W. Parker's gate, immediately on the road leading to Jerusalem, and about three miles distant, it was proposed to me to call there, but I objected, as I knew he was gone to Jerusalem, and my object was to reach there as soon as possible; but some of the men having relations at Mr. Parker's it was agreed that they might call and get his people. I remained at the gate on the road, with seven or eight; the others going across the field to the house, about half a mile off. After waiting some time for them, I became impatient, and started to the house for them, and on our return we were met by a party of white men, who had pursued our blood-stained track, and who had fired on those at the gate, and dispersed them, which I knew nothing of, not having been at that time rejoined by any of them—Immediately on discovering the whites, I ordered my men to halt and form, as they appeared to be alarmed—The white men, eighteen in number, approached us in about one hundred yards, when one of them fired, (this was against the positive orders of Captain Alexander P. Peete, who commanded, and who had directed the men to reserve their fire until within thirty paces)—And I discovered about half of them retreating, I then ordered my men to fire and rush on them; the few remaining stood their ground until we approached within fifty yards, when they fired and retreated. We pursued and overtook some of them who we thought we left dead; (they were not killed) after pursuing them about two hundred yards, and rising a little hill, I discovered they were met by another party, and had halted, and were reloading their guns, (this was a small party from Jerusalem who knew the negroes were in the field, and had just tied their horses to await their return to the road, knowing that Mr. Parker and family were in Jerusalem, but knew nothing of the party that had gone in with Captain Peete; on hearing the firing they immediately rushed to the spot and arrived just in time to arrest the progress of these barbarous villains, and save the lives of their friends and fellow citizens). Thinking that those who retreated first, and the party who fired on us at fifty or sixty yards distant, had all fallen back to meet others with ammunition. As I saw them reloading their guns, and more coming up than I saw at first, and several of my bravest men being wounded, the others became panick struck and squandered over the field; the white men pursued and fired on us several times. Hark had his horse shot under him, and I caught another for him as it was running by me; five or six of my men were wounded, but none left on the field; finding myself defeated here I instantly determined to go through a private way, and cross the Nottoway river at the Cypress Bridge, three miles below Jerusalem, and attack that place in the rear, as I expected they would look for me on the other road, and I had a great desire to get there to procure arms and ammunition. After going a short distance in this private way, accompanied by about twenty men, I overtook two or three who told me the others were dispersed in every direction. After trying in vain to collect a sufficient force to proceed to Jerusalem, I determined to return, as I was sure they would make back to their old neighborhood, where they would rejoin me, make new recruits, and come down again. On my way back, I called at Mrs. Thomas's, Mrs. Spencer's, and several other places, the white families having fled, we found no more victims to gratify our thirst for blood, we stopped at Maj. Ridley's quarter for the night, and being joined by four of his men, with the recruits made since my defeat, we mustered now about forty strong. After placing out sentinels, I laid down to sleep, but was quickly roused by a great racket; starting up, I found some mounted, and others in great confusion; one of the sentinels having given the alarm that we were about to be attacked, I ordered some to ride round and reconnoitre, and on their return the others being more alarmed, not knowing who they were, fled in different ways, so that I was reduced to about twenty again; with this I determined to attempt to recruit, and proceed on to rally in the neighborhood, I had left. Dr. Blunt's was the nearest house, which we reached just before day; on riding up the yard, Hark fired a gun. We expected Dr. Blunt and his family were at Maj. Ridley's, as I knew there was a company of men there; the gun was fired to ascertain if any of the family were at home; we were immediately fired upon and retreated, leaving several of my men. I do not know what became of them, as I never saw them afterwards. Pursuing our course back and coming in sight of Captain Harris', where we had been the day before, we discovered a party of white men at the house, on which all deserted me but two, (Jacob and Nat), we concealed ourselves in the woods until near night, when I sent them in search of Henry, Sam, Nelson, and Hark, and directed them to rally all they could, at the place we had had our dinner the Sunday before, where they would find me, and I accordingly returned there as soon as it was dark and remained until Wednesday evening, when discovering white men riding around the place as though they were looking for some one, and none of my men joining me, I concluded Jacob and Nat had been taken, and compelled to betray me. On this I gave up all hope for the present; and on Thursday night after having supplied myself with provisions from Mr. Travis's, I scratched a hole under a pile of fence rails in a field, where I concealed myself for six weeks, never leaving my hiding place but for a few minutes in the dead of night to get water which was very near; thinking by this time I could venture out, I began to go about in the night and eavesdrop the houses in the neighborhood; pursuing this course for about a fortnight and gathering little or no intelligence, afraid of speaking to any human being, and returning every morning to my cave before the dawn of day. I know not how long I might have led this life, if accident had not betrayed me, a dog in the neighborhood passing by my hiding place one night while I was out, was attracted by some meat I had in my cave, and crawled in and stole it, and was coming out just as I returned. A few nights after, two negroes having started to go hunting with the same dog, and passed that way, the dog came again to the place, and having just gone out to walk about, discovered me and barked, on which thinking myself discovered, I spoke to them to beg concealment. On making myself known they fled from me. Knowing then they would betray me, I immediately left my hiding place, and was pursued almost incessantly until I was taken a fortnight afterwards by Mr. Benjamin Phipps, in a little hole I had dug out with my sword, for the purpose of concealment, under the top of a fallen tree. On Mr. Phipps' discovering the place of my concealment, he cocked his gun and aimed at me. I requested him not to shoot and I would give up, upon which he demanded my sword. I delivered it to him, and he brought me to prison. During the time I was pursued, I had many hair breadth escapes, which your time will not permit you to relate. I am here loaded with chains, and willing to suffer the fate that awaits me.

I here proceeded to make some inquiries of him, after assuring him of the certain death that awaited him, and that concealment would only bring destruction on the innocent as well as guilty, of his own color, if he knew of any extensive or concerted plan. His answer was, I do not. When I questioned him as to the insurrection in North Carolina happening about the same time, he denied any knowledge of it; and when I looked him in the face as though I would search his inmost thoughts, he replied, "I see sir, you doubt my word; but can you not think the same ideas, and strange appearances about this time in the heavens might prompt others, as well as myself, to this undertaking." I now had much conversation with and asked him many questions, having forborne to do so previously, except in the cases noted in parenthesis; but during his statement, I had, unnoticed by him, taken notes as to some particular circumstances, and having the advantage of his statement before me in writing, on the evening of the third day that I had been with him, I began a cross examination, and found his statement corroborated by every circumstance coming within my own knowledge or the confessions of others who had been either killed or executed, and whom he had not seen nor had any knowledge since 22d of August last, he expressed himself fully satisfied as to the impracticability of his attempt. It has been said he was ignorant and cowardly, and that his object was to murder and rob for the purpose of obtaining money to make his escape. It is notorious, that he was never known to have a dollar in his life; to swear an oath, or drink a drop of spirits. As to his ignorance, he certainly never had the advantages of education, but he can read and write, (it was taught him by his parents,) and for natural intelligence and quickness of apprehension, is surpassed by few men I have ever seen. As to his being a coward, his reason as given for not resisting Mr. Phipps, shews the decision of his character. When he saw Mr. Phipps present his gun, he said he knew it was impossible for him to escape as the woods were full of men; he therefore thought it was better to surrender, and trust to fortune for his escape. He is a complete fanatic, or plays his part most admirably. On other subjects he possesses an uncommon share of intelligence, with a mind capable of attaining any thing; but warped and perverted by the influence of early impressions. He is below the ordinary stature, though strong and active, having the true negro face, every feature of which is strongly marked. I shall not attempt to describe the effect of his narrative, as told and commented on by himself, in the condemned hole of the prison. The calm, deliberate composure with which he spoke of his late deeds and intentions, the expression of his fiend-like face when excited by enthusiasm, still bearing the stains of the blood of helpless innocence about him; clothed with rags and covered with chains; yet daring to raise his manacled hands to heaven, with a spirit soaring above the attributes of man; I looked on him and my blood curdled in my veins.

I will not shock the feelings of humanity, nor wound afresh the bosoms of the disconsolate sufferers in this unparalleled and inhuman massacre, by detailing the deeds of their fiend-like barbarity. There were two or three who were in the power of these wretches, had they known it, and who escaped in the most providential manner. There were two whom they thought they left dead on the field at Mr. Parker's, but who were only stunned by the blows of their guns, as they did not take time to re-load when they charged on them. The escape of a little girl who went to school at Mr. Waller's, and where the children were collecting for that purpose, excited general sympathy. As their teacher had not arrived, they were at play in the yard, and seeing the negroes approach, she ran up on a dirt chimney, (such as are common to log houses,) and remained there unnoticed during the massacre of the eleven that were killed at this place. She remained on her hiding place till just before the arrival of a party, who were in pursuit of the murderers, when she came down and fled to a swamp, where, a mere child as she was, with the horrors of the late scene before her, she lay concealed until the next day, when seeing a party go up to the house, she came up, and on being asked how she escaped, replied with the utmost simplicity, "The Lord helped her." She was taken up behind a gentleman of the party, and returned to the arms of her weeping mother. Miss Whitehead concealed herself between the bed and the mat that supported it, while they murdered her sister in the same room, without discovering her. She was afterwards carried off, and concealed for protection by a slave of the family, who gave evidence against several of them on their trial. Mrs. Nathaniel Francis, while concealed in a closet heard their blows, and the shrieks of the victims of these ruthless savages; they then entered the closet, where she was concealed, and went out without discovering her. While in this hiding place, she heard two of her women in a quarrel about the division of her clothes. Mr. John T. Baron, discovering them approaching his house, told his wife to make her escape, and scorning to fly, fell fighting on his own threshold. After firing his rifle, he discharged his gun at them, and then broke it over the villain who first approached him, but he was overpowered, and slain. His bravery, however, saved from the hands of these monsters, his lovely and amiable wife, who will long lament a husband so deserving of her love. As directed by him, she attempted to escape through the garden, when she was caught and held by one of her servant girls, but another coming to her rescue, she fled to the woods, and concealed herself. Few indeed, were those who escaped their work of death. But fortunate for society, the hand of retributive justice has overtaken them; and not one that was known to be concerned has escaped.

THE COMMONWEALTH VS. NAT TURNER

Charged with making insurrection, and plotting to take away the lives of divers free white persons, &c. on the 22nd of August, 1831.

The court composed of ———, having met for the trial of Nat Turner, the prisoner was brought in and arraigned, and upon his arraignment pleaded *Not guilty;* saying to his counsel, that he did not feel so.

On the part of the Commonwealth, Levi Waller was introduced, who being sworn, deposed as follows: (*agreeably to Nat's own Confession.*) Col. Trezvant* was then introduced, who being sworn,

* The committing Magistrate.

narrated Nat's Confession to him, as follows: (*his Confession as given to Mr. Gray.*) The prisoner introduced no evidence, and the case was submitted without argument to the court, who having found him guilty, Jeremiah Cobb, Esq. Chairman, pronounced the sentence of the court, in the following words: "Nat Turner! Stand up. Have you any thing to say why sentence of death should not be pronounced against you?

Ans. I have not. I have made a full confession to Mr. Gray, and I have nothing more to say.

Attend then to the sentence of the Court. You have been arraigned and tried before this court, and convicted of one of the highest crimes in our criminal code. You have been convicted of plotting in cold blood, the indiscriminate destruction of men, of helpless women, and of infant children. The evidence before us leaves not a shadow of doubt, but that your hands were often imbrued in the blood of the innocent; and your own confession tells us that they were stained with the blood of a master; in your own language, "too indulgent." Could I stop here, your crime would be sufficiently aggravated. But the original contriver of a plan, deep and deadly, one that never can be effected, you managed so far to put it into execution, as to deprive us of many of our most valuable citizens; and this was done when they were asleep, and defenseless; under circumstances shocking to humanity. And while upon this part of the subject, I cannot but call your attention to the poor misguided wretches who have gone before you. They are not few in number—they were your bosom associates; and the blood of all cries aloud, and calls upon you, as the author of their misfortune. Yes! You forced them unprepared, from Time to Eternity. Borne down by this load of guilt, your only justification is, that you were led away by fanaticism. If this be true, from my soul I pity you; and while you have my sympathies, I am, nevertheless called upon to pass the sentence of the court. The time between this and your execution, will necessarily be very short; and your only hope must be in another world. The judgment of the court is, that you be taken hence to the jail from whence you came, thence to the place of execution, and on Friday next, between the hours of 10 A.M. and 2 P.M. be hung by the neck until you are dead! dead! dead! and may the Lord have mercy upon your soul.

A LIST OF PERSONS MURDERED IN THE INSURRECTION, ON THE
21ST AND 22ND OF AUGUST, 1831.

Joseph Travers and wife and three children, Mrs. Elizabeth Turner, Hartwell Prebles, Sarah Newsome, Mrs. P. Reese and son William, Trajan Doyle, Henry Bryant and wife and child, and wife's mother, Mrs. Catharine Whitehead, son Richard and four daughters and grand-child, Salathiel Francis, Nathaniel Francis' overseer and two children, John T. Barrow, George Vaughan, Mrs. Levi Waller and ten children, William Williams, wife and two boys, Mrs. Caswell Worrell and child, Mrs. Rebecca Vaughan, Ann Eliza Vaughan, and son Arthur, Mrs. John K. Williams and child, Mrs. Jacob Williams and three children, and Edwin Drury—amounting to fifty-five.

A LIST OF NEGROES BROUGHT BEFORE THE COURT OF SOUTHAMPTON, WITH THEIR OWNERS' NAMES, AND SENTENCE.

Daniel,	Richard Porter,	Convicted.
Moses,	J. T. Barrow,	Do.
Tom,	Caty Whitehead,	Discharged.
Jack and Andrew,	Caty Whitehead	Con. and transported.
Jacob,	Geo. H. Charlton,	Disch'd without trial.
Isaac,	Ditto,	Convi. and transported.
Jack,	Everett Bryant,	Discharged.
Nathan,	Benj. Blunt's estate,	Convicted.
Nathan, Tom, and Davy, (boys,)	Nathaniel Francis,	Con. and transported.
Davy,	Elizabeth Turner,	Convicted.
Curtis,	Thomas Ridley,	Do.
Stephen,	Do.	Do.
Hardy and Isham,	Benjamin Edwards,	Convicted and transp'd.
Sam,	Nathaniel Francis,	Convicted.
Hark,	Joseph Travis' estate.	Do.
Moses, (a boy,)	Do.	Do. and transported.
Davy,	Levi Waller,	Convicted.
Nelson,	Jacob Williams,	Do.
Nat,	Edm'd Turner's estate	Do.
Dred,	Wm. Reese's estate	Do.
Arnold, Artist, (free)	Nathaniel Francis,	Do.
Sam,		Discharged.
Ferry and Archer,	J. W. Parker,	Acquitted.
Jim,	J. W. Parker,	Disch'd. without trial.
Bob,	William Vaughan,	Acquitted.
Davy,	Temperance Parker,	Do.
Daniel,	Joseph Parker,	
Thomas Haithcock, (free,)	Solomon D. Parker	Disch'd. without trial. Sent on for further trial.
Joe,	John C. Turner,	Convicted.
Lucy,	John T. Barrow,	Do.
Matt,	Thomas Ridley,	Acquitted.
Jim,	Richard Porter,	Do.
Exum Artes, (free,)		Sent on for further trial.
Joe,	Richard P. Briggs,	Disch'd without trial.
Bury Newsome, (free,)		Sent on for further trial.
Stephen,	James Bell,	Acquitted.
Jim and Isaac,	Samuel Champion,	Convicted and trans'd.
Preston,	Hannah Williamson	Acquitted.
Frank,	Solomon D. Parker	Convi'd and transp'd.
Jack and Shadrach,	Nathaniel Simmons	Acquitted.
Nelson,	Benj. Blunt's estate,	Do.
Sam,	Peter Edwards,	Convicted.
Archer,	Arthur G. Reese,	Acquitted.
Isham Turner, (free,)		Sent on for further trial.
Nat Turner,	Putnam Moore, dec'd.	Convicted.

This Quiet Dust

WILLIAM STYRON

> *You mought be rich as cream*
> *And drive you coach and four-horse team,*
> *But you can't keep de world from moverin' round*
> *Nor Nat Turner from gainin' ground.*
>
> *And your name it mought be Caesar sure*
> *And got you cannon can shoot a mile or more,*
> *But you can't keep de world from moverin' round*
> *Nor Nat Turner from gainin' ground.*
>
> —Old-time Negro Song

MY NATIVE STATE OF VIRGINIA IS, OF COURSE, MORE THAN ORDINARILY conscious of its past, even for the South. When I was learning my lessons in the mid-1930s at a grammar school on the banks of the James River, one of the required texts was a history of Virginia—a book I can recall far more vividly than any history of the United States or of Europe I studied at a later time. It was in this work that I first encountered the name Nat Turner. The reference to Nat was brief; as a matter of fact, I do not think it unlikely that it was the very brevity of the allusion—amounting almost to a quality of haste—which captured my attention and stung my curiosity. I can no longer quote the passage exactly, but I remember that it went something like this: "In 1831, a fanatical Negro slave named Nat Turner led a terrible insurrection in Southampton County, murdering many white people. The insurrection was immediately put down, and for their cruel deeds Nat Turner and most of the other Negroes involved in the rebellion were hanged." Give or take a few harsh adjectives, this was all the information on Nat Turner supplied by that forgotten historian, who hustled on to matters of greater consequence.

I must have first read this passage when I was ten or eleven years old. At that time my home was not far from Southampton County, where the rebellion took place, in a section of the Virginia Tidewater which is generally considered part of the Black Belt because of the predominance of Negroes in the population. (When I speak of the South and Southerners here, I speak of *this* South, where Deep South attitudes prevail; it would include parts of Maryland and East Texas.) My boyhood experience was the typically ambivalent one of most native Southerners, for whom the Negro is simultaneously taken for granted and as an object of unending concern. On the one hand, Negroes are simply a part of the landscape, an unexceptional feature of the local scenery, yet as central to its character as the pinewoods and sawmills and mule [135/136] teams and sleepy river estuaries that give such color and tone to the Southern geography. Unnoticed by white people, the Negroes blend with the land and somehow melt and fade into it, so that only when one reflects upon their possible absence, some magical disappearance, does one realize how unimaginable this absence would be: it would be easier to visualize a South without trees, without *any* people, without life at all. Thus at the same time, ignored by white people, Negroes impinge upon their collective sub- conscious to such a degree that it may be rightly said that they become the focus of an incessant preoccupation, somewhat like a monstrous, recurring dream populated by identical faces wearing expressions of inquietude and vague reproach. "Southern whites cannot walk, talk, sing, conceive of laws or justice, think of sex, love, the family, or freedom without responding to the presence of Negroes." The words are those of Ralph Ellison, and, of course, he is right.

Yet there are many Souths, and the experience of each Southerner is modified by the subtlest conditions of self and family and environ- ment and God knows what else, and I have wondered if it has ever properly been taken into account how various this response to the presence of the Negroes can be. I cannot tell how typical my own awareness of Negroes was, for instance, as I grew up near my birth- place—a small seaside city about equally divided between black and white. My feelings seem to have been confused and blurred, tinged with sentimentality, colored by a great deal of folklore, and wobbling always between a patronizing affection, fostered by my elders, and downright hostility. Most importantly, my feelings were completely uninformed by that intimate knowledge of black people which South- erners claim as their special patent; indeed, they were based upon an almost total ignorance.

For one thing, from the standpoint of attitudes toward race, my upbringing was hardly unusual: it derived from the simple conviction that Negroes were in every respect inferior to white people and should be made to stay in their proper order in the scheme of things. At the same time, by certain Southern standards my family was enlightened: although my mother taught me firmly that the use of "lady" instead of "woman" in referring to a Negro female was quite improper, she writhed at the sight of the extremes of Negro poverty, and would certainly have thrashed me had she ever heard me use the word "nigger." Yet outside the confines of family, in the lower-middle-class school world I inhabited every day, this was a word I commonly used.

School segregation, which was an ordinary fact of life for me, is devastatingly effective in accomplishing something that it was only peripherally designed to do: it prevents the awareness even of the existence of another race. Thus, whatever hostility I bore toward the Negroes was based almost entirely upon hearsay.

And so the word "nigger," which like all my schoolmates I uttered so freely and so often, had even then an idle and listless ring. How could that dull epithet carry meaning and conviction when it was applied to a people so diligently isolated from us that they barely existed except as shadows which came daily to labor in the kitchen, to haul away garbage, to rake up leaves? An unremarked paradox of Southern life is that its racial animosity is really grounded not upon friction and propinquity, but upon an almost complete lack of contact. Surrounded by a sea of Negroes, I cannot recall more than once—and then briefly, when I was five or six—ever having played with a Negro child, or ever having spoken to a Negro, except in trifling talk with the cook, or in some forlorn and crippled conversation with a dotty old grandfather angling for hardshell crabs on a lonesome Sunday afternoon many years ago. Nor was I by any means uniquely sheltered. Whatever knowledge I gained in my youth about Negroes, I gained from a distance, as if I had been watching actors in an all-black puppet show.

Such an experience has made me distrust any easy generalizations about the South, whether they are made by white sociologists or Negro playwrights, Southern politicians or Northern editors. I have come to understand at least as much about the Negro after having lived in the North. One of the most egregious of the Southern myths—one in this case propagated solely by Southerners—is that of the Southern white's boast that he "knows" the Negro. Certainly in many rural areas of the South the cultural climate has been such as to allow a mutual understanding, and even a kind of intimacy, to spring up between the races, at least in some individual instances. But my own boyhood surroundings, which were semi-urban (I suppose suburban is the best description, though the green little village on the city's outskirts where I grew up was a far cry from Levittown), and which have become the youthful environment for vast numbers of Southerners, tended almost totally to preclude any contact between black and white, especially when that contact was so sedulously proscribed by law. [136/137]

Yet if white Southerners cannot "know" the Negro, it is for this very reason that the entire sexual myth needs to be reexamined. Surely a certain amount of sexual tension between the races does continue to exist, and the Southern white man's fear of sexual aggression on the part of the Negro male is still too evident to be ignored. But the nature of the growth of the urban, modern South has been such as to impose ever more effective walls between the races. While it cannot be denied that slavery times produced an enormous amount of interbreeding (with all of its totalitarianism, this was a free-for-all atmosphere far less self-conscious about carnal mingling than the Jim Crow era which began in the 1890s), and while even now there must logically take place occasional sexual contacts between the races—especially in rural areas where a degree of casual familiarity has always obtained—the monolithic nature of segregation has raised such an effective barrier between whites and Negroes that it is impossible not to believe that theories involving a perpetual sexual "tension" have been badly inflated. Nor is it possible to feel that a desire to taste forbidden fruit has ever really caused this barrier to be breached. From the standpoint of the Negro, there is indifference or uncomplicated fear; from that of the white—segregation, the law, and, finally, indifference, too. When I was growing up, the older boys might crack wan jokes about visiting the Negro whorehouse street (patronized entirely, I later discovered, by Negroes plus a few Scandinavian sailors), but to my knowledge none of them ever really went there. Like Negroes in general, Negro girls were to white men phantoms, shadows. To assume that anything more than a rare and sporadic intimacy on any level has existed in the modern South between whites and Negroes is simply to deny, with a truly willful contempt for logic, the monstrous effectiveness of that apartheid which has been the Southern way of life for almost three-quarters of a century.

I have lingered on this matter only to try to underline a truth about Southern life which has been too often taken for granted, and which has therefore been overlooked or misinterpreted. Most Southern white people *cannot* know or touch black people and this is because of the deadly intimidation of a universal law. Certainly one feels the presence of this gulf even in the work of a writer as supremely knowledgeable about the South as William Faulkner, who confessed a hesitancy about attempting to "think Negro," and whose Negro characters, as marvelously portrayed as most of them are, seem nevertheless to be meticulously *observed* rather than *lived*. Thus in *The Sound and the Fury*, Faulkner's magnificent Dilsey comes richly alive, yet in retrospect one feels this is a result of countless mornings, hours, days Faulkner had spent watching and listening to old Negro servants, and not because Dilsey herself is a being created from a sense of withinness: at the last moment Faulkner draws back, and it is no mere happenstance that Dilsey, alone among the four central figures from whose points of view the story is told, is seen from the outside rather than from that intensely "inner" vantage point, the interior monologue.

Innumerable white Southerners have grown up as free of knowledge of the Negro character and soul as a person whose background is rural Wisconsin or Maine. Yet, of course, there is a difference, and it is a profound one, defining the white Southerner's attitudes and causing him to be, for better or for worse, whatever it is he is to be. For the

Negro is *there*. And he is there in a way he never is in the North, no matter how great his numbers. In the South he is a perpetual and immutable part of history itself, a piece of the vast fabric so integral and necessary that without him the fabric dissolves; his voice, his black or brown face passing on a city street, the sound of his cry rising from a wagonload of flowers, his numberless procession down dusty country roads, the neat white church he has built in some pine grove with its air of grace and benison and tranquillity, his silhouette behind a mule team far off in some spring field, the wail of his blues blaring from some jukebox in a backwoods roadhouse, the sad wet faces of nurse-maids and cooks waiting in the evening at city bus stops in pouring rain—the Negro is always *there*. [137/138]

No wonder then, as Ellison says, the white Southerner can do virtually nothing without responding to the presence of Negroes. No wonder the white man so often grows cranky, fanciful, freakish, loony, violent: how else respond to a paradox which requires, with the full majesty of law behind it, that he deny the very reality of a people whose multitude approaches and often exceeds his own; that he disclaim the existence of those whose human presence has marked every acre of the land, every hamlet and crossroad and city and town, and whose humanity, however inflexibly denied, is daily evidenced to him like a heartbeat in loyalty and wickedness, madness and hilarity and mayhem and pride and love? The Negro may feel that it is too late to be known, and that the desire to know him reeks of outrageous condescension. But to break down the old law, to come to *know* the Negro, has become the moral imperative of every white Southerner.

II

I suspect that my search for Nat Turner, my own private attempt as a novelist to re-create and bring alive that dim and prodigious black man, has been at least a partial fulfillment of this mandate, although the problem has long since resolved itself into an artistic one—which is as it should be. In the late 1940s, having finished college in North Carolina and come to New York, I found myself again haunted by that name I had first seen in the Virginia history textbook. I had learned something more of Southern history since then, and I had become fascinated by the subject of Negro slavery. One of the most striking aspects of the institution is the fact that in the 250 years of its existence in America, it was singularly free of organized uprisings, plots, and rebellions. (It is curious that as recently as the late 1940s, scholarly insights were lagging, and I could only have suspected then what has since been made convincing by such historians as Frank Tannenbaum and Stanley Elkins: that American Negro slavery, unique in its psychological oppressiveness—the worst the world has ever known—was simply so despotic and emasculating as to render organized revolt next to impossible.) There were three exceptions: a conspiracy by the slave Gabriel Prosser and his followers near Richmond in the year 1800, the plot betrayed, the conspirators hanged; a similar conspiracy in 1822, in Charleston, South Carolina, led by a free Negro named Denmark Vesey, who also was betrayed before he could carry out his plans, and who was executed along with other members of the plot.

The last exception, of course, was Nat Turner, and he alone in the entire annals of American slavery—alone among all those "many thousand gone"—achieved a kind of triumph.

Even today, many otherwise well-informed people have never heard the name Nat Turner, and there are several plausible reasons for such an ignorance. One of these, of course, is that the study of our history—and not alone in the South—has been tendentious in the extreme, and has often avoided even an allusion to a figure like Nat, who inconveniently disturbs our notion of a slave system which, though morally wrong, was conducted with such charity and restraint that any organized act of insurrectory and murderous violence would be unthinkable. But a general ignorance about Nat Turner is even more understandable in view of the fact that so little is left of the actual record. Southampton County, which even now is off the beaten track, was at that period the remotest backwater imaginable. The relativity of time allows us elastic definitions: 1831 was yesterday. Yet the year 1831, in the Presidency of Andrew Jackson, lay in the very dawn of our modern history, three years before a railroad ever touched the soil of Virginia, a full fifteen years before the use of the telegraph. The rebellion itself was of such a cataclysmic nature as practically to guarantee confusion of the news, distortion, wild rumors, lies, and, finally, great areas of darkness and suppression; all of these have contributed to Nat's obscurity.

As for the contemporary documents themselves, only one survives: the *Confessions of Nat Turner*, a brief pamphlet of some five thousand words, transcribed from Nat's lips as he awaited trial, by a somewhat enigmatic lawyer named Thomas Gray, who published the *Confessions* in Baltimore and then vanished from sight. There are several discrepancies in Gray's transcript but it was taken down in haste, and in all major respects it seems completely honest and reliable. Those few newspaper accounts of the time, from Richmond and Norfolk, are sketchy, remote, filled with conjecture, and are thus virtually worthless. The existing county court records of Southampton remain brief and unilluminating, dull lists, a dry catalogue of names in fading ink: the white people slain, the Negroes tried and transported south, or acquitted, or convicted and hanged.

Roughly seventy years after the rebellion (in 1900, which by coincidence was the year Virginia formally adopted its first Jim Crow laws), the single scholarly book ever to be written on the [138/139] affair was published—*The Southampton Insurrection*, by a Johns Hopkins Ph.D.

candidate named William S. Drewry, who was an unreconstructed
Virginian of decidedly proslavery leanings and a man so quaintly committed to the *ancien régime* that, in the midst of a description of the
ghastliest part of the uprising, he was able to reflect that "slavery in
Virginia was not such to arouse rebellion, but was an institution which
nourished the strongest affection and piety in slave and owner, as well
as moral qualities worthy of any age of civilization." For Drewry, Nat
Turner was some sort of inexplicable aberration, like a man from Mars.
Drewry was close enough to the event in time, however, to be able to
interview quite a few of the survivors, and since he also possessed a
bloodthirsty relish for detail, it was possible for him to reconstruct the
chronology of the insurrection with what appears to be considerable
accuracy. Drewry's book (it is of course long out of print) and Nat's
Confessions remain the only significant sources about the insurrection.
Of Nat himself, his background and early years, very little can be
known. This is not disadvantageous to a novelist, since it allows him to
speculate—with a freedom not accorded the historian—upon all the
intermingled miseries, ambitions, frustrations, hopes, rages, and desires which caused this extraordinary black man to rise up out of those
early mists of our history and strike down his oppressors with a fury of
retribution unequaled before or since.

He was born in 1800, which would have made him at the time of
the insurrection thirty-one years old—exactly the age of so many great
revolutionaries at the decisive moment of their insurgency: Martin
Luther,* Robespierre, Danton, Fidel Castro. Thomas Gray, in a footnote to the *Confessions,* describes him as having the "true Negro face"
(an offhand way of forestalling an assumption that he might have
possessed any white blood), and he adds that "for natural intelligence
and quickness of apprehension he is surpassed by few men I have ever
seen"—a lofty tribute indeed at that inflammatory instant, with ante-
bellum racism at its most hysteric pitch. Although little is known for
certain of Nat's childhood and youth, there can be no doubt that he
was very precocious and that he learned not only to read and write
with ease—an illustrious achievement in itself, when learning to read
and write was forbidden to Negroes by law—but at an early age
acquired a knowledge of astronomy, and later on experimented in
making paper and gunpowder. (The resemblance here to the knowledge of the ancient Chinese is almost too odd to be true, but I can find
no reason to doubt it.)

* See Erik Erikson's *Young Man Luther* for a brilliant study of the development of the revolutionary impulse in a young man, and the relationship of this
impulse to the father-figure. Although it is best to be wary of any heavy psychoanalytical emphasis, one cannot help believing that Nat Turner's relationship with
his father, like Luther's, was tormented and complicated, especially since this
person could not have been his real father, who ran away when Nat was an infant,
but the white man who owned and raised him.

The early decades of the nineteenth century were years of declining prosperity for the Virginia Tidewater, largely because of the ruination of the land through greedy cultivation of tobacco—a crop which had gradually disappeared from the region, causing the breakup of many of the big old plantations and the development of subsistence farming on small holdings. It was in these surroundings—a flat pastoral land of modest farms and even more modest homesteads, where it was rare to find a white man prosperous enough to own more than half a dozen Negroes, and where two or three slaves to a family was the general rule—that Nat was born and brought up, and in these surroundings he prepared himself for the apocalyptic role he was to play in history. Because of the failing economic conditions, it was not remarkable that Nat was purchased and sold several times by various owners (in a sense, he was fortunate in not having been sold off to the deadly cotton and rice plantations of South Carolina and Georgia, which was the lot of many Virginia Negroes of the period); and although we do not know much about any of these masters, the evidence does not appear to be that Nat was ill-treated, and in fact one of these owners (Samuel Turner, brother of the man whose property Nat was born) developed so strong a paternal feeling for the boy and such regard for Nat's abilities, that he took the fateful step of encouraging him in the beginnings of an education.

The atmosphere of the time and place was fundamentalist and devout to a passionate degree, and at some time during his twenties Nat, who had always been a godly person—"never owning a dollar, never uttering an oath, never drinking intoxicating liquors, and never committing a theft"—became a Baptist preacher. Compared to the Deep South, Virginia slave life was not so rigorous; Nat must have been given considerable latitude, and found many opportunities to preach and exhort the Negroes. His gifts for preaching, for prophecy, and his own magnetism seem to [139/140] have been so extraordinary that he grew into a rather celebrated figure among the Negroes of the county, his influence even extending to the whites, one of whom—a poor, half-cracked, but respectable overseer named Brantley—he converted to the faith and baptized in a mill pond in the sight of a multitude of the curious, both black and white. (After this no one would have anything to do with Brantley, and he left the county in disgrace.)

At about this time Nat began to withdraw into himself, fasting and praying, spending long hours in the woods or in the swamp, where he communed with the Spirit and where there came over him, urgently now, intimations that he was being prepared for some great purpose. His fanaticism grew in intensity, and during these lonely vigils in the forest he began to see apparitions:

I saw white spirits and black spirits engaged in battle, and the sun was darkened; the thunder rolled in the heavens and blood flowed in streams

. . . I wondered greatly at these miracles, and prayed to be informed of a certainty of the meaning thereof; and shortly afterwards, while laboring in the fields, I discovered drops of blood on the corn as though it were dew from heaven. For as the blood of Christ had been shed on this earth, and had ascended to heaven for the salvation of sinners, it was now returning to earth again in the form of dew . . . On the twelfth day of May, 1828, I heard a loud noise in the heavens, and the Spirit instantly appeared to me and said the Serpent was loosened, and Christ had laid down the yoke he had borne for the sins of men, and that I should take it on and fight against the Serpent, for the time was fast approaching when the first should be last and the last should be first . . .

Like all revolutions, that of Nat Turner underwent many worrisome hesitations, false starts, procrastinations, delays (with appropriate irony, Independence Day, 1830, had been one of the original dates selected, but Nat fell sick and the moment was put off again); finally, however, on the night of Sunday, August 21, 1831, Nat, together with five other Negroes in whom he had placed his confidence and trust, assembled in the woods near the home of his owner of the time, a carriage maker named Joseph Travis, and commenced to carry out a plan of total annihilation. The penultimate goal was the capture of the county seat, then called Jerusalem (a connotation certainly not lost on Nat, who, with the words of the prophets roaring in his ears, must have felt like Gideon himself before the extermination of the Midianites); there were guns and ammunition in Jerusalem, and with these captured it was then Nat's purpose to sweep thirty miles eastward, gathering black recruits on the way until the Great Dismal Swamp was reached—a snake-filled and gloomy fastness in which Nat believed, with probable justification, only Negroes could survive, and no white man's army could penetrate. The immediate objective, however, was the destruction of every white man, woman, and child on the ten-mile route to Jerusalem; no one was to be spared; tender infancy and feeble old age alike were to perish by the axe and the sword. The command, of course, was that of God Almighty, through the voice of his prophet Ezekiel: "*Son of Man, prophesy and say, Thus saith the Lord; Say, a sword, a sword is sharpened, and also furbished: it is sharpened to make a sore slaughter . . . Slay utterly old and young, both maids and little children, and women . . .*" It was a scheme so wild and daring that it could only have been the product of the most wretched desperation and frustrate misery of soul; and of course it was doomed to catastrophe not only for whites but for Negroes—and for black men in ways which from the vantage point of history now seem almost unthinkable.

They did their job rapidly and with merciless and methodical determination. Beginning at the home of Travis—where five people, including a six-month-old infant, were slain in their beds—they marched from house to house on an eastward route, pillaging, murdering, sparing no one. Lacking guns—at least to begin with—they employed axes, hatchets, and swords as their tools of destruction, and swift decapitation was their usual method of dispatch. (It is interesting that the Negroes did not resort to torture, nor were they ever accused of rape. Nat's attitude toward sex was Christian and high-minded, and he had said: "We will not do to their women what they have done to ours.")

On through the first day they marched, across the hot August fields, gaining guns and ammunition, horses, and a number of willing recruits. That the insurrection was not purely racial, but perhaps obscurely pre-Marxist, may be seen in the fact that a number of dwellings belonging to poor white people were pointedly passed by. At midday on Monday their force had more than tripled, to the amount of nineteen, and nearly thirty white people lay dead. By this time, the alarm had been sounded throughout the country, and while the momentum of the insurgent band was considerable, many of the whites had fled in panic to the woods, and some of the farmers had begun to resist, setting up barricades from which they could fire back at Nat's forces. Furthermore, [140/141] quite a few of the rebels had broken into the brandy cellars of the houses they had attacked and had gotten roaring drunk—an eventuality Nat had feared and had warned against. Nevertheless, the Negroes—augmented now by forty more volunteers—pressed on toward Jerusalem, continuing the attack into the next night and all through the following day, when at last obstinate resistance by the aroused whites and the appearance of a mounted force of militia troops (also, it must be suspected, continued attrition by the apple brandy) caused the rebels to be dispersed, only a mile or so from Jerusalem.

Almost every one of the Negroes was rounded up and brought to trial—a legalistic nicety characteristic of a time in which it was necessary for one to determine whether *his* slave, property, after all, worth eight or nine hundred dollars, was really guilty and deserving of the gallows. Nat disappeared immediately after the insurrection, and hid in the woods for over two months, when near-starvation and the onset of autumnal cold drove him from his cave and forced him to surrender to a lone farmer with a shotgun. Then he too was brought to trial in Jerusalem—early in November 1831—for fomenting a rebellion in which sixty white people had perished.

The immediate consequences of the insurrection were exceedingly grim. The killing of so many white people was in itself an act of futility. It has never been determined with any accuracy how many black people, not connected with the rebellion, were slain at the hands of rampaging bands of white men who swarmed all over Southampton in the week following the uprising, seeking reprisal and vengeance. A contemporary estimate by a Richmond newspaper, which deplored this retaliation, put the number at close to two hundred Negroes, many of them free, and many of them tortured in ways unimaginably horrible. But even more important was the effect that Nat Turner's insurrection had upon the institution of slavery at large. News of the revolt spread among Southern whites with great speed: the impossible, the unspeakable had at last taken place after 200 years of the ministrations of sweet old mammies and softly murmured Yassuhs and docile compliance—and a shock wave of anguish and terror ran through the entire South. If such a nightmarish calamity happened there, would it not happen *here?*—here in Tennessee, in Augusta, in Vicksburg, in these bayous of Louisiana? Had Nat lived to see the consequences of his rebellion, surely it would have been for him the cruelest irony that his bold and desperate bid for liberty had caused only the most tyrannical new controls to be imposed upon Negroes everywhere—the establishment of patrols, further restrictions upon movement, education, assembly, and the beginning of other severe and crippling restraints which persisted throughout the slaveholding states until the Civil War. Virginia had been edging close to emancipation, and it seems reasonable to believe that the example of Nat's rebellion, stampeding many moderates in the legislature into a conviction that the Negroes could not be safely freed, was a decisive factor in the ultimate victory of the proslavery forces. Had Virginia, with its enormous prestige among the states, emancipated its slaves, the effect upon our history would be awesome to contemplate.

Nat brought cold, paralyzing fear to the South, a fear that never departed. If white men had sown the wind with chattel slavery, in Nat Turner they had reaped the whirlwind for white and black alike.

Nat was executed, along with sixteen other Negroes who had figured large in the insurrection. Most of the others were transported south, to the steaming fields of rice and cotton. On November 11, 1831, Nat was hanged from a live oak tree in the town square of Jerusalem. He went to his death with great dignity and courage. "The bodies of those executed," wrote Drewry, "with one exception, were buried in a decent and becoming manner. That of Nat Turner was delivered to the doctors, who skinned it and made grease of the flesh."

III

Not long ago, in the spring of the year, when I was visiting my family in Virginia, I decided to go down for the day to Southampton County, which is a drive of an hour and a half by car from the town where I was born and raised. Nat Turner was of course the reason for this trip, although I had nothing particular or urgent in mind. What research it was possible to do on the event I had long since done. The Southampton court records, I had already been reliably informed, would prove unrewarding. It was not a question, then, of digging out more facts, but simply a matter of wanting to savor the mood and atmosphere of a landscape I had not seen for quite a few years, since the times when as a boy I used to pass through Southampton on the way to my father's family home in North Carolina. I thought also that there might be a chance of visiting some of the historic sites connected with the [141/142] insurrection, and perhaps even of retracing part of the route of the uprising through the help of one of those handsomely produced guidebooks for which the Historical Commission of Virginia is famous—guides indispensable for a trip to such Old Dominion shrines as Jamestown and Appomattox and Monticello. I became even more eager to go when one of my in-laws put me in touch by telephone with a cousin of his. This man, whom I shall call Dan Seward, lived near Franklin, the main town of Southampton, and he assured me in those broad cheery Southern tones which are like a warm embrace—and which, after long years in the chill North, are to me always so familiar, reminiscent, and therefore so unsettling, sweet, and curiously painful—that he would like nothing better than to aid me in my exploration in whatever way he could.

Dan Seward is a farmer, and prosperous grower of peanuts in a prosperous agricultural region where the peanut is the unquestioned monarch. A combination of sandy loam soil and a long growing season has made Southampton ideal for the cultivation of peanuts; over 30,000 acres are planted annually, and the crop is processed and marketed in Franklin—a thriving little town of 7,000 people—or in Suffolk and Portsmouth, where it is rendered into Planters cooking oil and stock feed and Skippy peanut butter. There are other money-making crops—corn and soybeans and cotton. The county is at the northernmost edge of the cotton belt, and thirty years ago cotton was a major source of income. Cotton has declined in importance but the average yield per acre is still among the highest in the South, and the single gin left in the county in the little village of Drewryville processes each year several thousand bales which are trucked to market down in North Carolina. Lumbering is also very profitable, owing mainly to an abundance of the loblolly pines valuable in the production of kraft wood pulp; and the Union Bag—Camp Paper Company's plant on the Blackwater river in Franklin is a huge enterprise employing over 1,600 people. But it is peanuts—the harvested vines in autumn piled up mile after mile in dumpy brown stacks like hay—which have brought money to Southampton, and a sheen of prosperity that can be seen in the freshly painted farmhouses along the monotonously flat state highway which leads into Franklin, and the new-model Dodges and Buicks parked slantwise against the curb of some crossroads hamlet, and the gaudy, eye-catching signs that advise the wisdom of a bank savings account for all those surplus funds.

The county has very much the look of the New South about it, with its airport and its shiny new motels, its insistent billboards advertising space for industrial sites, the sprinkling of housing developments with television antennas gleaming from every rooftop, its supermarkets and shopping centers and its flavor of go-getting commercialism. This is the New South, where agriculture still prevails but has joined in a vigorous union with industry, so that even the peanut when it goes to market is ground up in some rumbling engine of commerce and becomes metamorphosed into wood stain or soap or cattle feed. The Negroes, too, have partaken of this abundance—some of it, at least—for they own television sets also, and if not new-model Buicks (the Southern white man's strictures against Negro ostentation remain intimidating), then decent late-model used Fords; while in the streets of Franklin the Negro women shopping seemed on the day of my visit very proud and well-dressed compared to the shabby stooped figures I recalled from the Depression years when I was a boy. It would certainly appear that Negroes deserve some of this abundance, if only because they make up so large a part of the work force. Since Nat Turner's day the balance of population in Southampton—almost 60 per cent Negro—has hardly altered by a hair.

"I don't know anywhere that a Negro is treated better than around here," Mr. Seward was saying to the three of us, on the spring morning I visited him with my wife and my father. "You take your average person from up North, he just doesn't *know* the Negro like we do. Now for instance I have a Negro who's worked for me for years, name of Ernest. He knows if he breaks his arm—like he did a while ago, fell off a tractor—he knows he can come to me and I'll see that he's taken care of, hospital expenses and all, and I'll take care of him and his family while he's unable to work, right on down the line. I don't ask him to pay back a cent, either, that's for sure. We have a wonderful relationship, that Negro and myself. By God, I'd die for that Negro and he knows it, and he'd do the same for me. But Ernest doesn't want to sit down at my table, here in this house, and have supper with me—and he wouldn't want me in *his* house. And Ernest's got kids like I do, and he doesn't want them to go to school with my Bobby, any more than Bobby wants to go to school with *his* kids. It works both ways. People up North don't seem to be able to understand a simple fact like that."

Mr. Seward was a solidly fleshed, somewhat rangy, big-shouldered man in his early forties [142/144] with an open, cheerful manner which surely did nothing to betray the friendliness with which he had spoken on the telephone. He had greeted us—total strangers, really—with an animation and uncomplicated good will that would have shamed an Eskimo; and for a moment I realized that, after years amid the granite outcroppings of New England, I had forgotten that this *was* the passionate, generous, outgoing nature of the South, no artificial display but a social gesture as natural as breathing.

Mr. Seward had just finished rebuilding his farmhouse on the outskirts of town, and he had shown us around with a pride I found understandable: there was a sparkling electric kitchen worthy of an advertisement in *Life* magazine, some handsome modern furniture, and several downstairs rooms paneled beautifully in the prodigal and lustrous hardwood of the region. It was altogether a fine, tasteful house, resembling more one of the prettier medium-priced homes in the Long Island suburbs than the house one might contemplate for a Tidewater farmer. Upstairs, we had inspected his son Bobby's room, a kid's room with books like *Pinocchio* and *The Black Arrow* and *The Swiss Family Robinson,* and here there was a huge paper banner spread across one entire wall with the crayon inscription: *"Two . . . four . . . six . . . eight! We Don't Want to Integrate!"* It was a sign which so overwhelmingly dominated the room that it could not help provoking comment, and it was this that eventually had led to Mr. Seward's reflections about *knowing* Negroes.

There might have been something vaguely defensive in his remarks but not a trace of hostility. His tone was matter-of-fact and good-natured, and he pronounced the word Negro as *nigra,* which most Southerners do with utter naturalness while intending no disrespect whatsoever, in fact quite the opposite—the mean epithet, of course, is *nigger.* I had the feeling that Mr. Seward had begun amiably to regard us as sympathetic but ill-informed outsiders, non-Southern, despite his knowledge of my Tidewater background and my father's own accent, which is thick as grits. Moreover, the fact that I had admitted to having lived in the North for fifteen years caused me, I fear, to appear alien in his eyes, *déraciné,* especially when my acculturation to Northern ways has made me adopt the long "e" and say Negro. The racial misery, at any rate, is within inches of driving us mad: how can I explain that, with all my silent disagreement with Mr. Seward's paternalism, I knew that when he said, "By God, I'd die for that Negro," he meant it?

Perhaps I should not have been surprised that Mr. Seward seemed to know very little about Nat Turner. When we got around to the subject, it developed that he had always thought that the insurrection occurred way back in the eighteenth century. Affably, he described seeing in his boyhood the "Hanging Tree," the live oak from which Nat had been executed in Courtland (Jerusalem had undergone this change of name after the Civil War), and which had died and been cut down some thirty years ago; as for any other landmarks, he regretted that he did not know of a single one. No, so far as he knew, there just wasn't anything.

For me, it was the beginning of disappointments which grew with every hour. Had I *really* been so ingenuous as to believe that I would unearth some shrine, some home preserved after the manner of Colonial Williamsburg, a relic of the insurrection at whose portal I would discover a lady in billowing satin and crinoline, who for fifty cents would shepherd me about the rooms with a gentle drawl indicating the spot where a good mistress fell at the hands of the murderous darky? The native Virginian, despite himself, is cursed with a suffocating sense of history, and I do not think it impossible that I actually suspected some such monument. Nevertheless, confident that there would be something to look at, I took heart when Mr. Seward suggested that after lunch we all drive over to Courtland, ten miles to the west. He had already spoken to a friend of his, the Sheriff of the county, who knew all the obscure byways and odd corners of Southampton, mainly because of his endless search for illegal stills; if there was a solitary person alive who might be able to locate some landmark, or could help retrace part of Nat Turner's march, it was the Sheriff. This gave me hope. For I had brought along Drewry's book and its map which showed the general route of the uprising, marking the houses by name. In the sixty years since Drewry, there would have been many changes in the landscape. But with this map oriented against the Sheriff's detailed county map, I should easily be able to pick up the trail and thus experience, however briefly, a sense of the light and shadow that played over that scene of slaughter and retribution a hundred and thirty-four years ago.

Yet it was as if Nat Turner had never existed, and as the day lengthened and afternoon wore on, and as we searched Nat's part of the county—five of us now, riding in the Sheriff's car with its huge star emblazoned on the doors, and its [144/145] radio blatting out hoarse intermittent messages, and its riot gun protectively nuzzling the backs of our necks over the edge of the rear seat—I had the sensation from time to time that this Negro, who had so long occupied my thoughts, who indeed had so obsessed my imagination that he had acquired larger spirit and flesh than most of the living people I encountered day in and day out, had been merely a crazy figment of my mind, a phantom no more real than some half-recollected image from a fairy tale. For here in the back country, this horizontal land of woods and meadows where he had roamed, only a few people had heard of Nat Turner, and of those who had—among the people we stopped to make inquiries of, both white and black, along dusty country roads, at farms, at filling stations, at crossroad stores—most of them confused him, I think, with something spectral, mythic, a black Paul Bunyan who had perpetrated mysterious and nameless deeds in millennia past. They were neither facetious nor evasive, simply unaware. Others confounded him with the Civil War—a Negro general. One young Negro field hand, lounging at an Esso station, figured he was a white man. A white man, heavy-lidded and paunchy, slow-witted, an idler at a rickety store, thought him an illustrious racehorse of bygone days.

The Sheriff, a smallish, soft-speaking ruminative man, with the whisper of a smile frozen on his face as if he were perpetually enjoying a good joke, knew full well who Nat Turner was, and I could tell he relished our frustrating charade. He was a shrewd person, quick and

sharp with countrified wisdom, and he soon became quite as fascinated as I with the idea of tracking down some relic of the uprising
(although he said that Drewry's map was hopelessly out of date, the
roads of that time now abandoned to the fields and woods, the homes
burnt down or gone to ruin); the country people's ignorance he found
irresistible and I think it tickled him to perplex their foolish heads,
white or black, with the same old leading question: "You heard about
old Nat Turner, ain't you?" But few of them had heard, even though I
was sure that many had plowed the same fields that Nat had crossed,
lived on land that he had passed by; and as for dwellings still standing
which might have been connected with the rebellion, not one of these
back-country people could offer the faintest hint or clue. As effectively
as a monstrous and unbearable dream, Nat had been erased from
memory.

It was late afternoon when, with a sense of deep fatigue and
frustration, I suggested to Mr. Seward and the Sheriff that maybe we
had better go back to Courtland and call it a day. They were agreeable—relieved, I felt, to be freed of this tedious and fruitless search—
and as we headed east down a straight unpaved road, the conversation
became desultory, general. We spoke of the North. The Sheriff was
interested to learn that I often traveled to New York. He went there
occasionally himself, he said; indeed, he had been there only the
month before—"to pick up a nigger," a fugitive from custody who had
been awaiting trial for killing his wife. New York was a fine place to
spend the night, said the Sheriff, but he wouldn't want to live there.

As he spoke, I had been gazing out of the window, and now
suddenly something caught my eye—something familiar, a brief flickering passage of a distant outline, a silhouette against the sun-splashed
woods—and I asked the Sheriff to stop the car. He did, and as we
backed up slowly through a cloud of dust, I recognized a house standing perhaps a quarter of a mile off the road, from this distance only a
lopsided oblong sheltered by an enormous oak, but the whole tableau
—the house and the glorious hovering tree and the stretch of woods
beyond—so familiar to me that it might have been some home I
passed every day. And of course now as recognition came flooding
back, I knew whose house it was. For in *The Southampton Insurrection*, the indefatigable Drewry had included many photographs—
amateurish, doubtless taken by himself, and suffering from the fuzzy
offset reproduction of 1900. But they were clear enough to provide an
unmistakable guide to the dwellings in question, and now as I again
consulted the book I could see that this house—the monumental oak
above it grown scant inches it seemed in sixty years—was the one
referred to by Drewry as having belonged to Mrs. Catherine Whitehead. From this distance, in the soft clear light of a spring afternoon, it
seemed most tranquil, but few houses have come to know such a
multitude of violent deaths. There in the late afternoon of Monday,

August 22, Nat Turner and his band had appeared, and they set upon
and killed "Mrs. Catherine Whitehead, son Richard, and four daughters, and grandchild."

The approach to the house was by a rutted lane long ago abandoned and overgrown with lush weeds which made a soft, crushed,
rasping sound as we rolled over them. Dogwood, white and pink, grew
on either side of the lane, quite wild and wanton in lovely pastel
splashes. Not far from the house a pole fence interrupted our way; the
Sheriff stopped the car and we got out and stood there for a moment,
looking at the [145/146] place. It was quiet and still—so quiet that
the sudden chant of a mockingbird in the woods was almost frightening—and we realized then that no one lived in the house. Scoured by
weather, paintless, worn down to the wintry gray of bone and with all
the old mortar gone from between the timbers, it stood alone and
desolate above its blasted, sagging front porch, the ancient door ajar
like an open wound. Although never a manor house, it had once been a
spacious and comfortable country home; now in near-ruin it sagged,
finished, a shell, possessing only the most fragile profile of itself. As we
drew closer still we could see that the entire house, from its upper
story to the cellar, was filled with thousands of shucked ears of corn—
feed for the malevolent-looking little razorback pigs which suddenly
appeared in a tribe at the edge of the house, eying us, grunting. Mr.
Seward sent them scampering with a shied stick and a farmer's sharp
"Whoo!" I looked up at the house, trying to recollect its particular role
in Nat's destiny, and then I remembered.

There was something baffling, secret, irrational about Nat's own
participation in the uprising. He was unable to kill. Time and time
again in his confession one discovers him saying (in an offhand tone;
one must dig for the implications): "I could not give the death blow,
the hatchet glanced from his head," or, "I struck her several blows over
the head, but I was unable to kill her, as the sword was dull . . ." It is
too much to believe, over and over again: the glancing hatchet, the
dull sword. It smacks rather, as in *Hamlet*, of rationalization, ghastly
fear, an access of guilt, a shrinking from violence, and fatal irresolu-
tion. Alone here at this house, turned now into a huge corncrib around
which pigs rooted and snorted in the silence of a spring afternoon,
here alone was Nat finally able—or was he forced?—to commit a
murder, and this upon a girl of eighteen named Margaret Whitehead,
described by Drewry in terms perhaps not so romantic or farfetched
after all, as "the belle of the county." The scene is apocalyptic—afternoon bedlam in wild harsh sunlight and August heat.

I returned to commence the work of death, but those whom I left had
not been idle; all the family were already murdered but Mrs. Whitehead
and her daughter Margaret. As I came round the door I saw Will pulling

Mrs. Whitehead out of the house and at the step he nearly severed her head from her body with his axe. Miss Margaret, when I discovered her, had concealed herself in the corner formed by the projection of the cellar cap from the house; on my approach she fled into the field but was soon overtaken and after repeated blows with a sword, I killed her by a blow on the head with a fence rail.

It is Nat's only murder. Why, from this point on, does the momentum of the uprising diminish, the drive and tension sag? Why, from this moment in the *Confessions,* does one sense in Nat something dispirited, listless, as if all life and juice had been drained from him, so that never again through the course of the rebellion is he even on the scene when a murder is committed? What happened to Nat in this place? Did he discover his humanity here, or did he lose it?

I lifted myself up into the house, clambering through a doorway without steps, pushing myself over the crumbling sill. The house had a faint yeasty fragrance, like flat beer. Dust from the mountains of corn lay everywhere in the deserted rooms, years and decades of dust, dust an inch thick in some places, lying in a fine gray powder like sooty fallen snow. Off in some room amid the piles of corn I could hear a delicate scrabbling and a plaintive squeaking of mice. Again it was very still, the shadow of the prodigious old oak casting a dark pattern of leaves, checkered with bright sunlight, aslant through the gaping door. As in those chilling lines of Emily Dickinson, even this lustrous and golden day seemed to find its only resonance in the memory, and perhaps a premonition, of death.

> This quiet Dust was Gentlemen and Ladies,
> And Lads and Girls;
> Was laughter and ability and sighing,
> And frocks and curls.

Outside, the Sheriff was calling in on his car radio, his voice blurred and indistinct; then the return call from the county seat, loud, a dozen incomprehensible words in an uproar of static. Suddenly it was quiet again, the only sound my father's soft voice as he chatted with Mr. Seward.

I leaned against the rotting frame of the door, gazing out past the great tree and into that far meadow where Nat had brought down and slain Miss Margaret Whitehead. For an instant, in the silence, I thought I could hear a mad rustle of taffeta, and rushing feet, and a shrill girlish piping of terror; then that day and this day seemed to meet and melt together, becoming almost one, and for a long moment indistinguishable. [146]

A Shared Ordeal: Interview
with William Styron

GEORGE PLIMPTON

Would you say something about the chronological history of the book?
I've had the idea of writing about Nat Turner ever since the late forties, when I read Nat's original "Confessions," a brief transcript taken down while he was awaiting trial, by a lawyer named Thomas Gray. It was the book I wanted to write when I started out writing—and yet something inside me was hesitant and reluctant. I think I realized that I had a tremendous theme—one that I simply wasn't able to cope with at the time. Furthermore, I was overly smitten by the violent aspects of the revolt, the bloodiness, the massacre itself, which appealed to me as a kind of melodrama. At one point, I remember describing it to Hiram Haydn, my editor then at Random House, with full bloodcurdling delight, and when I told him it was the next book I wanted to write (I had just finished "Lie Down in Darkness") he said to me, "I don't think you have a real understanding of the thing." He thought that the "gothic" part of my nature was too predominant just then to allow me to write a good book about the revolt and its implications. He was right. I don't mean to say that he dictated the choice, but I sensed that he was right.
What finally jogged you into beginning?
The project stayed with me through all those years though I was unable to cope with the writing of it. I kept up with the subject, constantly reading books on slavery, simply because it fascinated me. Then along about 1962, a couple of years after "Set This House on Fire" was published, I was up on Martha's Vineyard and I had just read for the first time Camus' "The Stranger." It is a brilliant book, the best of Camus, and it impressed me enormously: there was something about the poignancy of the condemned man sitting in his jail cell on the day of his execution—the existential predicament of the man—that hit me. And so did the use of the first person, the book being told through the eye of the condemned. The effect of all this was so strong that I suddenly realized that my Nat Turner could be done the same

way: that, like Camus, I would center the novel around a man facing his own death in a jail cell, which of course was true of Turner and how his life ended. And so there, suddenly provided, was the architecture of the book, its framework, along with the idea of telling the story in the first person.

Did it ever give you pause that by writing in the first person you would be telling the story as a Negro?

It was a challenge, of course, since I don't think anything of the sort has been done by a white American writer—to assume the *persona* of a Negro and make it convincing.

What made you feel that you could try what no one else had?

Rank intuition. I doubt that the feelings of the dispossessed, whatever their color, are all that different. If you can sympathize with the dispossessed, you can certainly take on the lineaments of the Negro. To assume that one can't would raise a most dangerous esthetic point, such as to deny Jimmy Baldwin's right to write from the point of view of white people, as he has done, or to suggest that the races are so far apart that even "Othello" cannot be considered valid art.

Did you make any concession in the style of the book to the times of Nat Turner?

The language of the book is in my own literary style, 20th-century *literary* style, which after all is not too different from 19th-century *literary* style. One can read Matthew Arnold and, to be sure, there's a difference, but it's not all that much. So when I set out to write the book, I didn't strive to write like a 19th-century preacher. I tried to write as spontaneously as I could in the form and language I would have written a contemporary novel, at every point, of course, trying to avoid obvious anachronisms like slang phrases and figures of speech which are peculiarly 20th-century. It was a risk, call it arrogance.

What about the accuracy of the 19th-century Negro dialects?

There's enough on record to show that Negroes in the early part of the 19th century spoke very much as rural Negroes in the South speak today. It is a distinct dialect and I believe that with some modifications it has remained frozen for several hundred years. Fanny Kemble, Frederick Law Olmsted and other chroniclers of the era set down Negro speech and it sounds very much like the rhythms of the speech I heard as a boy when I grew up in the Virginia Tidewater. It's with the urban class that the language evolves. As soon as you learn to spell and write, the language becomes educated American English, whatever one might call it, and the dialect disappears. I'm not speaking, of course, of the "hip" sub-language that rises in the city.

Can you say something about your research?

What there is to know about Nat Turner can be learned in a single day's reading. But there is a whole canon of slavery literature. It begins in this century with Ulrich B. Phillips, a Georgia-born historian who tends to sympathize with slavery, [2/3] his position being that slavery was a relatively benign institution. He was not exactly an apologist, but then the plight of the historiography of slavery is that positions of polarity are always taken—Southern apologists who offer the captious argument that slavery, after all, was a great blessing compared to the lot of the working man in the stews of Leeds, Lancashire, Sheffield; and then you have the Northern neo-abolitionists who state that slavery was so abominably oppressive that nothing decent existed within the framework of the institution at all.

How would you state your own position?

One must assume that slavery was an abomination and a horror. But among other things, I simply wanted to tell in the book the truth about what it was to be a slave of a certain sort in the early years of the last century—to portray the horror but at the same time not to shirk what must have been after all the tolerable aspects of the situation.

In this slave society what personal characteristics enabled Nat Turner to conduct his revolt?

His impulses were, historically speaking, those of the traditional revolutionary—that is to say puritanical, repressive and sublimated. Such impulses seem an authentic part of the revolutionary drive: Luther, Castro, Danton, Mao—all of them are basically puritanical. They are trying to find a release and they find it, partially, in revolt. I mean it's amazing that Martin Luther, for example, was an ascetic, a monk, and it wasn't until after his revolution that he got married suddenly and had a large family. It's not only involved in the impulse, but also in practicality. All revolutionary movements have a puritanical side; if you allow loose conduct to get the upper hand, you don't have much of a revolt. Castro, for instance, at least by report, headed a revolutionary movement that was obsessively puritanical: no fooling around in the camps up in those hills. Nat Turner was no exception. In the book he never has a sexual experience directly with a woman. He has an adolescent homosexual experience, quite innocent. Beyond that, Turner lived a sexual life of fantasy, fantasies of women, mainly white women, which in turn led to imagined revelations, and then finally to what Turner supposed were revelations from the Divine Spirit. Of course, I can't prove that this is Nat's psychological history, but I think something like it was part of his psychic makeup.

How much of a socio-political thinker was Nat Turner?

I'm sure Nat Turner was aware in a rudimentary way of the social horrors he was struggling against, but the wellsprings of his revolt were largely religious. His actual dream was two-pronged in a sense— one apocalyptic, that he was divinely ordained to destroy all the white people he could lay his hands on because they were evil; the other, the practical one, that he would capture the armory in the county seat, Jerusalem, and outfitted with weapons march the thirty miles or so to the Dismal Swamp, where he would set up an empire, an enclave, and live there out of sight of the detested white people.

Not unlike Elijah Muhammad's plan for a separate state for Negroes.

Except, of course, that Nat Turner and his crowd [3/30] would have fled and lived as fugitives. Yet it was not all that unpractical a plan. Runaway slaves did live successfully in the swamps of the South. Nat Turner must have had a plan of refuge when he headed out on his revolt. It would have been quixotic of him if he hadn't *something* planned. He was not stupid, after all.

Is there any mention of his plan in the original "Confessions"?

Gray, the lawyer who took down the "Confessions," avoids asking him; or if he did, he never records it. I suspect Gray didn't want to have the outline of the plot generally known. It was one of those things which, if it got around and seeped down to other Negroes, might have caused them to try the same thing again.

The failure of Turner's revolt was due in large part to the lack of support from fellow Negroes, wasn't it? And indeed because many opposed him and fought against him?

It must have been the bitterest part of his ultimate feeling about what he had done, though it's nowhere mentioned in the actual confession. It's *hinted* at, and I think if you read between the lines you can feel that regret. It is historically true that while Nat had a number of very stanch and valiant cohorts, and a bunch of good killers, they did not comprise nearly the number he thought would join him.

What were the after-effects of Turner's rebellion?

For one thing, terrible reprisals: several hundred Negroes were killed by rampaging whites. Then, too, it seems unmistakable that the revolt caused the first actual laws to be passed in the Virginia Legislature prohibiting Negro education, assembly without white supervision, the establishment of patrols, and so forth—all comprising the so-called Black Laws. Before, it had been a passive consensus among white people that it wasn't a good idea to let Negroes learn to read and write; afterward, the restrictions and repressions became both legal and severe, not only in Virginia but throughout the South. Most ironic of all, of course, is the fact that Virginia had been edging toward emancipation, with fierce debates raging in the Legislature. It seems likely that Nat Turner's revolt closed down the issue of emancipation once and for all. Can you imagine the enormous effect on our history if Virginia—then one of the most prestigious of states—freed her slaves? It might have forestalled the Civil War.

Can you describe the process involved in turning characters mentioned in the original "Confessions" into the fictional characters of your book?

The description of the revolt adheres very closely to the original "Confessions" and also to the details outlined in William S. Drewry's book on the revolt, "The Southampton Insurrection," which came along 70 years later. Every character in the book has a prototype. For example, Gray, the lawyer who took down the "Confessions": I don't

know if he was the way I described him. After all I had to create him
out of whole cloth because there is no sense of his personality in either
the "Confessions" or the trial records. So he is a product of my
imagination. I remember specifically that when I started the book with
Nat sitting in the cell on the day of his trial, suddenly Gray entered
and I could see him: I envisioned him as a portly, very condescending
Southern type of his time—that is to say, a racist, a man with an equal
combination of meanness and vindictiveness, and yet I think he had
human warmth, a kind of humanity.

*What about Will, the killer? Were you thinking in any way of the
contemporary militants?*

Will is mentioned in the original "Confessions." He was the slave
of a man named Nathaniel Francis. It turns out that three of Francis's
slaves participated in the revolt, which would suggest that Francis was
a pretty mean son of a bitch. If you had a thoroughly cruel master—
and they did exist—it made you all the more liable to want to participate in the revolt, even to the extent of Will's madness. He just loved
to swing that axe. He was very adept at decapitation and other
niceties.

*Why do you think that Nat, in antithesis to Will, had so much
difficulty bringing himself to kill?*

It's intriguing that Nat was only able to kill the one person he
did—Margaret Whitehead. Throughout his original confession he
states over and over that, for accidental reasons of one sort or another,
he couldn't kill. Will had to do it. But it doesn't hold water that "the
sword was dull," as he often says: I'm convinced that he was suddenly
overtaken by his own humanity. It is partially why the revolt fails.

*Why was it the one girl—Margaret Whitehead—who is indicated
as not only having great admiration for Nat, but even a passion for
him?*

I was trying to suggest that—insofar as the phrase signifies anything—she was a white Southern liberal, meaning [30/32] that she
deeply sympathized with the plight of the Negro, which was not at all
unusual for certain young ladies of the time, oddly enough. True, she
might have had a buried passion for Nat because he was so much
smarter than the white people she was associating with. Nat's feelings
for her were just as I described them in the book: he was smitten by
her, this paragon of the unobtainable, in some obscure and perilous
way so that the killing of her was not only a matter of working out his
frustration but possessing her soul and body as well.

*What about the character Samuel Turner, Nat's first master, who,
if unwittingly, started Nat on the route to the revolt? Who was his
prototype?*

Nothing is known about Nat's first real master; I had to invent his
character. But the prototype of this person would be Gen. John Hart-

well Cocke, a man I admire very much. He was a Virginia landowner and would have been a contemporary of Nat. Cocke was a man of magnificent bearing and decency who was tormented over slavery. He inherited over a hundred slaves which made him a large slaveowner in terms of his era. But he found it impossible to free them, because he didn't have the means to educate them, which was the moral require- ment among decent white men as necessary to the process of freeing a slave. The only possible way was to educate him as Nat Turner's master did in my book, and try to send him to a place like Richmond in the employ of a liberal-minded person and let him work for several years as an apprentice to find his bearings in the town and then give him his emancipation. That was a common procedure. There were freedmen in the cities of the upper South who lived reasonably good lives. It was a terrible dilemma for people like Cocke—in a constant frenzy over slavery—to be faced with the self-righteous proclamations from New England referring to all Southerners as fiends and monsters.

Do you suppose such idealists as Cocke and Thomas Jefferson ever privately wondered if education would lead to such acts as Turner's rebellion?

I rather doubt it. However, in Turner's case, history went trag- ically awry because he was not given his freedom—at least that is my assumption. The two keys to Nat Turner and his revolt are that, first, education gave him a sense of his own worth as a human being—given it by a master who was truly solicitous of his welfare. Second, the promise of freedom which had been [32/34] proffered, was suddenly snatched away from him. If there is a historical parallel to be made between Nat Turner and what is happening to Negroes *en masse* today it is surely that of the disparity between the promise and the fulfillment. Basic psychology dictates that when you are offered the sweetest of promises and you experience only total frustration of it, you're driven round the bend. America is, and always has been, a great tease.

In Turner's time, the two in-institutions which sold the Negro down the river were the legal system and the church. Either, or both, could have at one time exerted their influence for the better. But they didn't, and it was perhaps the cruelest sell-out of all time.

The church abandoned the Negro in the 19th century and took up Hugh Hefner in the 20th. Churchmen in America have always been followers instead of leaders.

The parallel between contemporary times and Turner's anguish is compelling . . .

I began the book and was concerned with the subject back in the forties, long before the civil-rights struggle was truly joined. The central meaning of the book is not consciously contemporary, though I would be the first to admit that the parallels are unavoidable. If there is a focus to Nat Turner's vision, it is surely that of the Bible. One must remember that he is a religious fanatic. And the book, as you can tell, is a sort of religious parable and a story of exculpation. The last words of the book are the last words of the Bible, the last words of the Book of Revelation. I mean without revelation, the book doesn't make sense. It should be apparent that the book expresses the idea of Old Testament savagery and revenge redeemed by New Testament charity and brotherhood—affirmation. It's in there somewhere, *hoped* for, lurking in the terrible story. [34]

Into the Mind of Nat Turner

RAYMOND A. SOKOLOV

"US GOTTA KILL ALL DEM WHITE SONSABITCHES. AIN'T DAT WHAT DE LAWD done told you? Ain't dat right, Nat?"
It was as if by those words we were committed. *Us gotta kill . . .* I talked on, detailing my plans . . . Later I asked questions, and found that none of my followers shrank from the idea of killing; I made it plain that murder was an essential act for their own freedom and they welcomed this truth with the solid acceptance of men who, as I have shown, had nothing on earth to lose.

That's not Rap Brown talking about a black-power meeting in 1967. The scene is the tidewater country of southern Virginia in 1831, and the man so coolly hell-bent after Whitey is Nat Turner, an educated black preacher who led the only carefully planned and effective slave revolt in American history. Turner's band of 75 Negroes rampaged through Southampton County, slaughtered 55 white men, women and children and then quickly vanished from memory. It would all have remained a fleeting and bloody footnote in the history textbooks if novelist William Styron, himself a tidewater man, hadn't been obsessed with Nat Turner and what made him kill.

Styron brooded for twenty years about the insurrection. He combed the skimpy records and slowly thought himself into the mind of Nat Turner. Finally, the psychic integration worked so well that Styron took a step as unique in American letters as the revolt is in its history. To write "The Confessions of Nat Turner," Styron became Nat and told Nat's story as if he were Nat, in one long astonishing recreation of the way it must have felt to be a slave in 1831. After 136

Raymond A. Sokolov, "Into the Mind of Nat Turner," *Newsweek* (October 16, 1967). Copyright *Newsweek, Inc.*, October 1967. Reprinted by permission.

years in limbo, Nat lives, and Styron's book has put the man whom Edmund Wilson called the "black John Brown" back into the conscience and consciousness of white America.

Three years ago when Styron was still in the brooding stage, the New American Library bought the paperback rights to "Nat" for $100,000. Last month Harper's Magazine printed a 50,000-word excerpt from the novel and paid more to Styron ($7,500) than to any other author in its 117-year history. The Book-of-the-Month Club also set a house record for a novel by forking out $150,000. Then Random House began cranking the presses for the 428-page hardcover edition. Well before "The Confessions" was published officially this week at $6.95, 200,000 copies had been run off, and bookstores had already ordered 55,000. With all of this food for his soul to digest, Styron hasn't got around yet to selling "Nat" to the movies, but prospects couldn't be rosier.

Far rosier, in any case, than they must have seemed in the late '40s when he first began digging into the sparse traces that Nat Turner's bloody moment had left in official history. Only one document survives: a 5,000-word pamphlet called "The Confessions of Nat Turner," which was dictated by Nat to Thomas Gray, "a somewhat enigmatic lawyer," and published in Baltimore in 1831. Harriet Beecher Stowe drew on the pamphlet for her interminable sermon of a novel, "Dred," in 1856. And a pro-slavery Ph.D. candidate at Johns Hopkins named William S. Drewry produced a full-length, heavily biased study in 1900 called "The Southampton Insurrection," which gathers together what was left of Nat 70 years after the fact. It wasn't much: "The bodies of those executed, with one exception, were buried in a decent and becoming manner. That of Nat Turner was delivered to the doctors, who skinned it and made grease of the flesh. Mr. R. S. Barham's father owned a money purse made of his hide. His skeleton was for many years in the possession of Dr. Massenberg, but has since been misplaced."

By 1967, the people of Southampton County have misplaced, destroyed or forgotten nearly every physical trace of the rebellion. Aside from a curt historical marker on a quiet backwoods highway, the rest is moldering legend, more Faulknerian than Faulkner. Old-timers point out the site of the sycamore tree where Nat was hung in the county seat of Jerusalem, now called Courtland. As children, they would knock on it and ask, "Nat, wha'd you do it fo'?" But the sycamore has disappeared along with Nat's sword (once kept in the top of a piano by a local family). A few houses attacked by the rebels still stand, but no one has bothered to find out for certain whom they belonged to or to preserve them against decay. At Cross Keys, a gutted old manse on Nat's route is now a nocturnal love nest where couples have scrawled their names on the walls. What neighbors claim was the old Travis house where Nat lived is now ironically the home of a

Negro family. And the jail nearby where Nat is supposed to have
stayed briefly after his capture was condemned not long ago by the
State Department of Highways as a traffic hazard and razed.

Apart from a few contemporary newspaper references and the dry
court records, the historian has nothing more to work with. "Any C+
history student," says Styron, "can master the official sources in several
days." From there on out, the imagination is the only possible source.
"If there were ever a free hand for a novelist, this was it," observes
Southern historian C. Vann Woodward.

It was a golden opportunity beset with one tremendous obstacle—
Nat himself. Not even Herman Melville's supremely powerful tale of a
slave rebellion, "Benito Cereno," is told from the Negro viewpoint. But
Styron has gambled everything on doing just that, writing the autobiography Nat had no time for, "a [65/66] speech from beyond the
grave to an intelligent reader of his own time."

And so Styron's "Confessions" begins with Nat in jail after the
insurrection, freezing and hungry, listening to Thomas Gray read back
his confession, calmly awaiting the inevitable verdict. Gray explains to
Nat that as a slave he is property, chattel—not "inanimate chattel" like
a wagon or a mule, but "animate chattel" that can be tried for a felony.
Thus at the very beginning, with dramatic coolness, Styron shakes the
skeleton in America's closet. Gray's calm lawyer's words are, thinks
Nat:

the quintessence of white folks' talk I had heard incessantly all my life and
which I could only compare to talk in one of my nightmares, totally implausible yet somehow wholly and fearfully real, where owls in the woods
are quoting price lists like a storekeeper, or a wild hog comes prancing on its
hind legs out of a summer cornfield, intoning verses from Deuteronomy.

Did anyone who ever lived speak so well, one wonders, but what
Styron has done is to give Nat the visionary words that would reflect
his mind. When Nat actually speaks, he's careful not to startle Gray
with his eloquence: "I'd feel like I could say a whole lot more to you,
Mr. Gray, if you'd get them to take off these here manacles." To fellow
slaves he has yet a different voice. Still in jail, Nat recalls a lecture he
gave to Hark, a fellow slave who became his right-hand man in the
revolt. Angry at Hark's Stepin Fetchit routine, Nat scolds him: "I don't
mean you got to risk a beatin'. I don't mean you got to be uppity and
smart. But they is some kind of limit."

These early pages move slowly. There is so much scene-setting
and then the trial to get through, unavoidable machinery but a bit to
the side of the book's true pulse, which is Nat. When he returns to jail
after the trial, the real "Confessions" begins. Nat begins with himself at
12 being taught, contrary to the law, to read. Under the well-meant
tutelage of his master Samuel Turner, Nat grows up a petted "house

nigger," priggish, ashamed of his field-hand brothers, hating his own condition and the whites who put him in it, scorning Negro women and taut with repressed passion for "a young white woman now, some slippery-tongued brown-headed missy with a sugar-sweet incandescent belly who as I entered her cried out with pain and joy and enveloped me convulsively with milky-white legs and arms."

So at 30 Nat explodes from a lifetime bottled up with the fierce rhetoric of the Old Testament. Convinced by a vision that the time has come, he gathers his handpicked lieutenants in the woods and exhorts them to slaughter. But at the moment of truth, Nat himself "could not give a deathblow" to Joseph Travis. During three days of continual murder, Nat himself kills only once. His victim: young Margaret Whitehead, the naïve schoolgirl who had unknowingly aroused him with her friendship.

Ultimately the revolt fails as the rebels, many befuddled with applejack, meet the militia and a force of loyal, armed slaves. Nat hides out in a cave for two months until he is captured without a fight by one man. The novel ends with Nat on his way to the hanging sycamore dreaming of Margaret Whitehead: "She arches against me, cries out, and the twain—black and white—are one."

Underlying the basic story of revolt is a steady, rock-ribbed thrum of Biblical language. Styron intends "a kind of religious allegory . . . with Old Testament savagery and rage finding its ultimate answer at the end of the book in New Testament grace and redemption." And even though Styron devotes much energy to filling in "the abysmal ignorance of Americans as to what slavery was . . . how slaves existed physically, what they ate and what they wore," he insists that Nat was not a proto-Marxist but a religious fanatic.

Like every salient feature of Nat, the religious fervor comes through as language, a white-hot dialect of the spirit. The revolt fails, but the voice, which modulates through every possible key of Negro and human sensibility from the highest flights of meditation to the battered syntax of gut-deep rage, speaks across great barriers of time and race. This voice was Styron's big gamble. If it had failed, the book would have been a disaster, a melodrama clotted with pretension. But it works. Pure literary convention hooked up to a great ear, it works. The rest follows naturally. One believes in Nat, in his tortured sexuality and in the value of his desperate, hopeless revolt. Styron lifts us up and puts us down in the Virginia tidewater, 1831, and makes us think as a brilliant slave, we are convinced, must have thought. But all the while, the twentieth century is still there on the other side of the book jacket with its own shackled Negroes waging a revolt every bit as desperate.

The desire to make connections between Nat and Rap and hundreds yet unknown—between then and now—is dangerous but inescapable. However, Styron does feel that violent revolution is most likely to occur when oppression eases. "Virginia in 1831 was split down the middle," says Styron. "The East wanted to retain slavery, and the West was desperately trying to get rid of it. There were endless debates in the legislature—practically 50-50. But Nat Turner's revolt caused such a panic that it shut down the debate once and for all." Styron believes that, through tragic irony, Nat was one of the causes of the Civil War. "I think there was a good possibility that Virginia might have freed its slaves, and I think the whole upper South would have followed its lead. By 1860 the whole complexion of America would have been different—there would perhaps have been an enclave of Deep [66/67] South slave states that could have been pressured out of slavery."

Styron is extremely reluctant to draw any parallels about "backlash" between Nat Turner's revolt and the current ghetto riots. "I want the book to exist on its own terms as an American tragedy," he says. "And I certainly don't mean to indiscriminately glorify the figure of the Negro rebel against society today. You can see Nat Turner as an archetypal American tragic hero, but this doesn't make Rap Brown an archetypal American hero, nor does it make what he is preaching capable of anything but disaster. I think violence on a purely psychic level can be a cathartic in the best sense of the word—it can satisfy the Negro's longing to assert his identity. But I don't think that's enough in 1967."

The book is certain to be a storm center. "Bill's going to catch it from black and white," predicts author James Baldwin, a longtime friend. Almost an elder statesman of black militancy by now, Baldwin finds no effrontery in this Southern white author's affecting a Negro voice. "It'll be called effrontery," he predicts, "but it isn't that. It's a very courageous book that attempts to fuse the two points of view, the master's and the slave's. In that sense the book is hopeful. It's important for the black reader to see what Bill is trying to do and to recognize its validity."

Baldwin read the novel in galley proofs at the end of an eighteen-month stint in Turkey, during the Detroit riots. From that perspective, Nat Turner seemed full of timely import: "The bill is in," says Baldwin to white America. "You are all like Massa Samuel Turners pretending not to sell us out. But we've always known you'd shoot us. You've created a population with nothing to lose."

Do those words sound strangely like Nat Turner's description of his rebel band? It may be no coincidence, since Styron admits that knowing Baldwin, who stayed at his home for five months in the early '60s writing "Another Country," made it possible for him to create Nat: "I think Jimmy—this is the confessions of William Styron now—I think that Jimmy broke down the last shred of whatever final hangup of Southern prejudice I might have had which was trying to tell me that a Negro was never really intelligent—a black Negro, not a, you know, white Negro, but a black, black homely Negro. Perhaps it was his diamond-bright intelligence which allowed me to say, 'When I plunge into Nat Turner, it will be with no holds barred, and he will respond with as much intelligence as I can bring to his voice.'"

Baldwin grinned hugely when he heard this. "Yes, I think there's some of me in Nat Turner," he agreed. "If I were an actor, I could play the part."

Naturally, neither man means that Baldwin *is* Turner. But the long talks they had together every evening when Baldwin came down from his desk for dinner seem to have acted as a catalyst between Styron and the Turner known from history. The two writers talked about their lives night after night and often sang together. "After all," chuckles Baldwin, "we have the same songs." They are also at one in their view that race is not a Negro problem but a trap for black and white together. "This is a troubling book," Baldwin observes. "Styron is probing something very dangerous, deep and painful in the national psyche. I hope it starts a tremendous fight, so that people will learn what they really think about each other."

"Styron is a man who has always concerned himself with the question of blacks and whites," remembers Prof. William Blackburn of Duke University. In 1943 a runty, 18-year-old Marine V-12 officer candidate walked into Blackburn's creative-writing class holding a short story with the unpromising title, "Where the Spirit Is." As a diffident afterthought, the young author had written in parentheses on the title page: "Dubiously submitted." Blackburn read it and had no doubt at all the boy had something. Soon after, the same slovenly but gung-ho marine handed in a tale about the brutal hanging of a Negro in a Southern town. Blackburn had it published in an anthology of Duke student writing, and William Styron's career was launched.

Until that moment, only Nostradamus could have picked him as a future novelist. Born June 11, 1925, in Newport News, Va., Styron grew up with the New South in "middle, middle, middle-class" surroundings. His father, William C. Styron Sr., worked as an engineer at the shipyards in Newport News. "Bill was a smart little kid," beams the elder Styron, now a spry 78. "I'm not boasting. At 5 he read the word 'Hercules' off a barber chair, and in his first year at school he could spell words like formaldehyde." This infatuation with words wasn't just accident. Styron family albums are dotted with fine prose dating as far back as 1786. And so when Norman Mailer's father asked Styron Sr. some years ago how Bill came by his literary talent, the proud old tidewater man replied: "He grew up with cultivated people."

Styron also grew up at the last time when it was possible to experience something of the Old South. His grandmother told him stories about slaves she once had owned, "how she loved them and knitted socks for them." Their descendants were everywhere and nowhere during Billy's Depression youth. "I don't think I had any meaningful contacts with Negroes then," he says, "but I have a sense of being constantly surrounded by Negroes, having Negroes who bathed me, rubbed me with soap, but never making contact. They were another presence, and on the other hand they were part of me."

For Styron the Negroes were a saving "opposite" in the Virginia that he calls "Byrdland—the absolute heartland of a deadened, unenlightened culture. I mean, well, the image to me of perfect vacuity is a horse show in Virginia, with sort of stupefyingly blond people with pipestem legs, all looking at horses. And I was fated to be born there, of an absolutely impeccable WASP background."

Styron turned peccable when his mother died. He was 13, broken up by the death, and started "going wild in that little village." Father Styron sent him to board at Christchurch, an Episcopal school for boys, where he organized the Christchurch Bachelors' Society and created its "infamous easy method of writing love letters." In his class yearbook, "Sty" was named "biggest griper."

Styron went on to Davidson College in North Carolina. By 1947 he had seen active duty as a Marine lieutenant (though he was commissioned too late to take part in actual combat), graduated from Duke University and settled in New York City determined to write.

For a while, Styron tried his hand at [67/68] publishing in the trade-book division of McGraw-Hill, then called Whittlesey House. The job lasted four months. Styron refused to wear a hat, infuriated his conservative boss by reading The New York Post and capped his assault on the firm's sobriety by dropping large balloons out of his office window. One day a gust of wind carried one of them back in through his boss's open window. Fired, he fell back on checks from home.

Professor Blackburn sent him to Hiram Haydn's writing class at the New School for Social Research. Styron already wanted to write about Nat Turner, but Haydn persuaded him to wait and try something else first. The something else became "Lie Down in Darkness," a novel set mainly in Newport News that bears down Faulkner-style on a fractured family torn apart by alcohol and insanity. "At one of the first classes," recalls Haydn, himself a novelist and for a long period Styron's editor, "I read aloud the first fifteen or twenty pages of Bill's work. The reading was followed by the kind of hush you get in church."

But it took Styron three years to finish his novel. To this day, his work routine has remained the same, slow as a glacier and just as irreversible. A legendary night person, Styron rises after noon, sits down with an Eagle No. 2 pencil and a pad of yellow legal-size paper, and thinks. The words, when they come, stay there, and a day's total rarely exceeds three pages. "Revision doesn't enter into the writing of his books," says Bob Loomis, his editor at Random House and a friend from Duke. "He can't write chapter two if chapter one isn't right."

As a result of this geological pace, Styron at 42 has only written three novels and one novella. He turned in the manuscript of "Lie Down in Darkness" just before leaving for Marine retraining. The Korean War was on and he had been recalled. By this time Styron had lost his old esprit de corps and was on his way to the dove position he takes on the Vietnam war today. Most of all he wanted to keep on writing, and that was impossible if a North Korean shot him. A long-forgotten eye defect came to the rescue and got him a discharge just in time for the publication of his novel. The book sold well and won him a Prix de Rome. Highly complex, a concertina of flashbacks, "Lie Down in Darkness" also won him wide critical praise and an audience that was to grow steadily.

With the money from it he went to Europe and began writing "The Long March," a novella based on a murderous forced march he had gone through at Camp Lejeune during the second Marine stint. At the same time he hooked up with the expatriate crowd around The Paris Review. They were very Harvard-Yale—George Plimpton, Peter Matthiessen, Donald Hall—but they took to Styron, helped him burn his stomach out with cheap brandy and asked him to write the credo for the first issue of their dynamic little magazine.

Somehow he pulled himself out of Paris and went to Rome, where in 1953 he met and quickly married Rose Burgunder, one of Baltimore's greatest gifts to American letters and the daughter of a wealthy department-store magnate. Next year they returned to Manhattan where he started another novel, while James Jones and Norman Mailer became virtual boarders in his apartment. Thomas Guinzburg, a Paris Review crony now president of Viking Press, remembers that "the three of them were always Indian wrestling. I've always felt they missed the normal college experience."

To this hearty mayhem, Rose Styron played den mother, quartermaster, chef and nightwatchman. "She's my Jewish mama," smiles Styron. "She's very beautiful, and I would have married her anyway—but she happens to be Jewish. And not many boys from Virginia do that."

In 1954 the Styrons swore off New York and chose bucolic peace in Roxbury, Conn. Over a thirteen-year period [68/69] punctuated with occasional returns to Europe and summers on Martha's Vineyard, the Styrons have produced four children and two long novels. Behind the scenes, James Terry, Styron's devoted Negro caretaker, and his wife see that everything keeps on running smoothly.

Otherwise the scene is much the same. Still working the same strange hours, Styron eked out "Set This House on Fire" over a five-year period. A bulky account of American degeneracy abroad, based on his own saturnalian grand tour, it was thumped by the critics as wordy and rambling. Some of the adverse reaction undoubtedly had to do with the book's negative stance toward America. For Styron, the bad notices only meant it was time to start writing again. Knocking back healthy tumblers of Virginia Gentleman bourbon before dinner, French vintage wine during dinner and Scotch afterward, he pushed on into the project he had always wanted to do—Nat Turner.

As the years rolled by, the myriad friends who pack the white frame Styron home began to think he would never finish. Sometimes Bill would stay at work in the colonial barn across the way and leave Rose to take care of the guests. But most often he was there in the living room dispensing bottled cheer and epigrams to neighbors like Arthur Miller and Alexander Calder and friends as diverse as playwright Lillian Hellman and Kennedy Clansman Richard Goodwin.

The Styrons were guests at the White House during John Kennedy's time and still see Bobby Kennedy at the Vineyard. But Styron's views on the war keep him out of today's official Washington. Though he contributed a phrase to President Johnson's 1964 civil-rights speech ("our unending search for justice"), he hangs LBJ's letter of thanks in the bathroom and declares he would refuse an invitation to the White House.

But Styron is a writer, not an activist. For an artist, history, no matter how extreme its events, is incomplete without the act of imagination that releases the deepest imports of its energies. "All of a sudden," says Styron, "I realized that all my work is predicated on revolt in one way or another. And of course there's something about Nat Turner that's the ultimate fulfillment of all this. It's a strange revelation."

In January, when Styron wrote the last word of "The Confessions of Nat Turner," it was very late but he couldn't sleep. "I heard Mozart playing on the phonograph all night," recalls Rose, "and the next morning we kept the children home from school to celebrate."

It was over. Four years of waiting, a mountain of yellow legal pads and a thousand Eagle pencils. End product—the book of the year, and, more than that, one of those novels that is an act of revelation to a whole society. As James Baldwin puts it: "He has begun the common history—*ours*."[69]

Slavery in the First Person:
Interview with William Styron

R. W. B. LEWIS AND C. VANN WOODWARD

Woodward: This novel of yours, Mr. Styron, deals with a historical event that recalls to my mind a comparable event of a later period. Of all the rebels in the history of slavery, John Brown and Nat Turner certainly stand out above all others, but there is a remarkable difference in the historical and literary attention that has been paid to these men. Much was known about John Brown and the place where he lived, so we have 40 or so biographies of him. Yet we have little, in fact extremely little, comparatively speaking, about Nat Turner.

Styron: I think the major reason so little is known about Turner compared to John Brown is the simple fact that Nat Turner's insurrection occurred at a time when communication facilities in this country were primitive. It came before the invention of the telegraph, before the railroads had invaded that part of Virginia. Had this revolt occurred in 1841 or 1842 instead of 1831, the situation might have been entirely different.

Lewis: Did the rebellion become nationally known? [33/34]

Styron: It did become nationally known, especially in the South. It caused a wave of terror in the South, as a matter of fact. But it was an isolated incident; about a year later I think it was forgotten all over the country.

Woodward: The Turner rebellion was a far more bloody affair than the Harper's Ferry incident.

Lewis: Including the Negroes killed out of revenge. I take it that a huge number was killed.

Styron: Yes, there were reprisals. It is not known exactly how many innocent Negroes were slain after the revolt. It was somewhere between 120 and 200, a vast number certainly.

Woodward: Then, too, I would say that Nat Turner's rebellion was far more of a threat to slavery than John Brown's raid, which never really had a chance. Nat Turner's was a terribly frightening thing to a slave society, with good reason.

R. W. B. Lewis and C. Vann Woodward, "Slavery in the First Person," *Yale Alumni Magazine* (November 1967). © 1967 Yale Alumni Publications, Inc. Reprinted by permission.

Styron: Yes, there is no doubt that the rebellion caused absolute panic. I saw one account from an upcountry Virginia resident describing the absolute frenzy that had taken possession of that part of Virginia, which was far removed from Southampton County where the revolt occurred. A hundred miles away people were just packing up, looking over their shoulders.

Woodward: Another thing: there were no whites involved in Turner's rebellion and he did not know people of consequence. John Brown had a lot of writer friends, and prominent and literate people were involved in the conspiracy and they left a number of accounts.

Styron: By the time of John Brown's raid, communications were also more sophisticated. You had newspaper coverage of a very heavy order; you had telegraph reports of the raids going to Washington every half-hour and that sort of thing.

Lewis: So in working with Nat Turner, his actual confession in jail is your only basic document, isn't it?

Styron: That's the single document that means anything. There are some newspaper reports from the *Richmond Enquirer*, but one feels that the accuracy is always in question. People seemed to be bewildered by the revolt itself, so the newspaper accounts seem sketchy and unauthenticated.

Woodward: A question arises here of accuracy and the fictional treatment of historical events. I have read this novel carefully, twice in fact, and for me this work is not inconsistent with anything historians know about this event or about the period. It does not pretend to be history, but it seems to me to be a valid and authentic use of history for the purposes of fiction and to be faithful in its respect for the period, the time, the place.

Styron: I am grateful that you do feel that way because I realize that in a book like this there is a basic responsibility involved. It is a tightrope walk in a sense. You want to use the art of fiction to its ultimate degree as far as you can, and at the same time you want to be faithful to the time and place.

Lewis: You said in your author's note that this was not intended to be an historical novel, but rather a "meditation on history." That is, I take it, a meditation on the mysterious processes of history in general. [34/35]

Styron: I intended that statement to do two things. One, to literally take the curse of the phrase "historical novel" off the book. Also it is a meditation on history in the sense that I hoped to encompass a meditative quality as I wrote.

Lewis: As a matter of fact, I wanted to ask about the meditational quality. Although the actual rebellion is the climax, I suppose, of the story, the way in which the rebellion turned out is known by about page 40. By this point we know pretty much who was killed, we know that Nat only killed one person, we know how his owner was killed, and we know how several other people were killed. So there are no facts held back at this point, which means, I take it, that you did not want to center so much on the melodrama, but on Nat brooding about the entire adventure while waiting to be hanged. Is that right?

Styron: Yes. I feel it would have been much too easy to write this story as a melodrama, and I think had I written it 15 or 20 years ago, when I first conceived the notion of writing it, it would have had a melo-dramatic overlay. Obviously, the bloodshed and violence had to figure in to some degree and it did in the end; it would have been shirking my responsibility not to describe it. On the other hand, that was not the sole reason I had for writing the book. I wanted also to explore in some kind of depth this whole area of American life and history, to take on the lineaments as well as I could of a slave and, using that persona, walk myself through a time and a place in a manner of self-discovery. I was learning all along as I wrote about Nat what it must have been to be a slave.

Woodward: The boldest decision you made, in my mind, was to tell this story as Nat Turner himself. It was especially bold when you consider that while historians know what it was like to own slaves, they can tell you very little about how it was to be a slave. And this, it seems to me, is what you are trying to do, without being a slave yourself, and without being a Negro yourself.

Styron: There was a wonderful combination of lucky shots there for me. Obviously I was fascinated, as other people are, with the time, but to have taken on the garb of just any old slave would not to me have been a very interesting adventure. When one considers the total anonymity of slavery, one can see what an important factor it was for me to try to turn myself into a unique slave, that is, one of the few slaves in history who achieved identity.

Lewis: I am interested also in this process of meditation, of self-inquiry, on the part of Nat Turner which you participate in. The very structure of the book fascinates me in this regard. It reminds me of what Joseph Heller said about Faulkner's *Absalom, Absalom!* with which I think this book has something in common. He said it had "a haunting structure," and I think this book does too since it begins and always returns to the jail, to Nat at this moment, meditating on the development of his plan, on his hatred, and also on the failure of the rebellion. He is meditating a failure, isn't he?

Styron: He is. This is part of his strength. And I think it is quite clear that his anguish over his failure to have achieved anything in the rebellion is more or less connected to his failure to make contact with God, who, of course, ordered his life and with whom he carried on a very close relationship.

Lewis: The religious element is very strong throughout, as well as the biblical element.

Styron: Well, it had to be. I believe that Nat had a very strong sense of society betrayal, but far more predominant in his personality was a deep abiding sense of religious fanaticism, his motivation coming straight out of the Old Testament.

Woodward: On the one hand, Nat Turner conforms to a Christ kind of figure: the age, the trade as a carpenter, the trip to Jerusalem, the martyrdom are all parallel. But you did not, and to my mind [35/36] rightly, make much of this. Instead you clearly indicate that Nat identifies with such Old Testament figures as Joshua and Gideon.

Styron: Yes, he was an avenging Old Testament angel in a sense. As I wrote the book, the parallels that you mention became quite clear to me. But I intentionally avoided the mention of Christ as much as I could throughout the book. He is almost never mentioned. Because if the book does have a sense of redemptive quality, it is only at the very end that it comes. This, of course, can be interpreted in several ways, but nonetheless I did see Nat as a man profoundly motivated by the empathy he feels with the old prophets—Ezekiel, Jeremiah, Isaiah, et cetera.

Lewis: To some extent, I take it, the Book of Revelations, too. There is a good deal of apocalyptic imagery, isn't there?

Styron: Yes, certainly. It is my own invention, of course, but I think it would have appealed to Nat's mind—this kind of crazy, entangled mind—because I think that the author of the Book of Revelations was a man similarly tormented, perhaps even insane.

Lewis: This is evidenced by the totality of the mission: to exterminate all the white people in the county and perhaps everywhere eventually.

Styron: I think he did intend to kill everybody on the way. There is a book that I might mention here, the only other reference book, by a man named William S. Drewry, called *The Southampton Insurrection,* which was published 70 years after the event, in 1900. Drewry has all sorts of interesting theories; they are theories, however, and one takes them with a grain of salt. He theorized that once Nat captured Jerusalem he might then have lessened the totality of his fury and become somewhat more sophisticated in his approach to warfare. My own theory was that a man so gifted and so intelligent as Nat would have realized that this scorched earth policy, this total destruction, total annihilation, would have been the only effective way to seize a prize and to gain momentum. Especially when you, as a slave, were so ill-equipped, total death, total murder, would have been the only logical course.

Woodward: He saw quite clearly what you have described, I think, and steeled himself to the act with adamant hatred. But when he came down to it, as you picture him, he could not go through with it. I mean he killed only one person, and that one very late in the game.

Styron: That is right. I do not know if this was true. This was naturally part of my insight as a novelist rather than anything having to do with facts of the matter. The original confessions of Nat are sketchy and one has to read between the lines constantly. I do feel, though, that he was unable to kill. In his confessions he constantly says that the sword glanced off someone's head or the sword was too dull to kill. This seems to me to be patently an evasion of some sort. He does eventually kill this single person, an eighteen-year-old girl named Margaret Whitehead, and I had to plunge into some sort of psychological state in order to achieve the kind of insight I did, which I hope has some accuracy.

Lewis: It is a fact that the girl was the only person he killed?

Styron: It is a fact. The Whiteheads, it is clear from Drewry's book, lived very close to the farm where Nat was a slave. They were among the more prosperous and better educated people in that region. All these things began to take on a certain architecture in my mind and it occurred to me that since Nat killed no one else, and he killed this girl who was a beautiful girl and who was considered one of the belles of the county, then the psychological truth behind the matter is that Nat did not hate her: he loved her, or at least had a passion for her . . . [36/37]

Lewis: He desired her.

Styron: He desired her. He wanted her. She represented to him all sorts of unattainable things. I believe this must have been true in history. I cannot prove it, but if there is any psychological truth in this insight, it lies partially in the fact that often one wishes to destroy the thing that one most earnestly desires.

Lewis: To go back for a moment to Nat's youth and childhood, it seems clear that his final motivation was definitely a result of his upbringing. A sense of social betrayal and psychological betrayal is always balancing the religious impulse. At about age 20, Nat first has a sense of being owned; he says he is half-deranged at the thought of being owned, especially owned twice. He was a mature, rather educated, intelligent person who had, in relative terms, a rather pleasant life until his sudden realization of being a chattel. Is that part of his motivation?

Styron: I think that is a large part of it. I tried to portray the fact that under certain conditions slavery could be at least a tolerable way of life. I was never trying to argue, naturally, anything in favor of slavery; I went from the assumption that it was an abomination. But given certain aspects of decency on the part of a solicitous master, and given an intelligent and impressionable young Negro like Nat, I think life was and could have been a tolerable thing, even more than tolerable. Yet, such was the insecurity that one lived in during slave times, I think Nat snapped into a kind of obsessive fanaticism when he was sold at the age of 21. He suffered a trauma he could not recover from, simply because the event was so cataclysmic, so total and so enduring that he could not find the hope that a non-slave might have found at a similar time in his life.

Lewis: And he was uniquely prepared not only to have this dreadful trauma, but to see the abomination of the experience in a way other slaves never could.

Styron: Yes, because by this time his intellect had flowered to the extent where he was able to view the sale of his own body to a nonentity like the Reverend Eppes as a monstrous abstraction, as an intellectual thing as well as a terrible personal cataclysm.

Woodward: I am interested in Nat's attitude toward his former master, Samuel Turner, whom he loved, adored, worshipped. When he realizes his betrayal he has this blinding flash of hate which is directed at Turner. Yet there seems to be an ambiguity here because Turner was not to blame, he really was honest in his promises to Nat and he was not responsible for the betrayal itself.

Styron: He wasn't responsible. But insofar as Nat responded to the act, I visualized him as perhaps in the Freudian sense going back to the father symbol as something he was deeply attached to. If that person was connected, even inadvertently, with betrayal, I had the feeling that rightly or wrongly Nat's rage would direct itself toward this father symbol. I do not mean to overpsychoanalyze Nat, but I felt that this was the way Nat, as I lived his life, felt.

Lewis: It was a very moving and terrible moment when he discovers he has been hijacked by the Reverend Eppes. But I suppose he had to make this violent and perhaps thoroughly irrational rejection of Turner before he could ever entertain his great plan.

Styron: The way I visualize Nat's relationship to all the various paternal figures, the ultimate moment in his sense of betrayal comes when he is sold by the Reverend Eppes to Moore, the illiterate farmer. By this time all of his paternal symbols have vanished and this causes him to snap, and this is the moment when he allows the ultimate paternal symbol, that is God, to embrace him. From then on this fanaticism is predominant in his life. [37/38]

Lewis: At this point I think we ought to mention a certain reaction to the novel that I am sure will come up; that is, its contemporaneity, the extent to which it can be turned into a parable on the present race situation.

Woodward: Already, in a review of the book I prepared for a journal, the editor suggested titling it "Black Power 1831."

Lewis: That's what is going to happen, I'm sure.

Woodward: Living in the environment of the present mood of Negro rebellion and knowing many of its participants well, I am sure the author had some of this in mind as he wrote. However much of this consciousness he put into the novel was not, as I read it, obtrusive. I think each reader will have his own reaction.

Styron: I feel compelled to point out, perhaps self-consciously, that I conceived of this story, was fascinated by Nat Turner, long before the civil rights movement became an overwhelming aspect of our lives.

Obviously there are parallels; I would be the first to admit them. But for me to have twisted anything in the book to heighten the relationship of the events in the book to the events of today would have been some sort of betrayal of my own vision of Nat and his story.

Woodward: I am very glad you refrained.

Lewis: The book puts the reader in mind, of course, of the uprisings, of the riots, of the cry of black power, of the way in which the black power groups splinter, of the varieties of motive, of the instant white reaction that we must have tougher, more stringent and repressive laws. But I would assume that one of the meanings of the phrase "a meditation on history" is that while never alluding to the present situation and the so-called Negro revolution, the novel probes to the sources of the kind of thing we are undergoing now and in that sense deals with a generality of history, and I think that is one of the book's great distinctions.

Styron: I am glad you feel that because a book like this runs a danger, and I am afraid it has already begun, of being heralded as a kind of paradigm of events that are now going on. There is no reason to draw strict parallels from Nat Turner in order to explicate current events; I would be appalled if some person tried to do this in a dogged and deterministic fashion. I did not intend that in the slightest.

Woodward: The kind of general correspondence to current events which you are explaining is evident, I think, in Nat's feeling that some whites had victimized him by their friendliness and benevolence and good will.

Styron: Well, when Negroes, today as in Nat Turner's case, get a taste of freedom, are teased with it before it is jerked away or seems unattainable, there is an overwhelming sense of powerlessness. And perhaps at that point, under certain conditions, revolt becomes something of a psychic imperative. In that sense, there are general parallels.

Lewis: To return to Nat, and to his singular qualities, I was particularly struck by his meditation which begins the third part of the novel on the relative rarity of pure hatred, of what he calls calm and intelligent hatred.

Styron: I think that the Negro of antebellum years in the South, who was without any contact with white people, was [38/39] literally so far down the psychological ladder that he could hardly hate in the way Nat is describing. For one thing, I do not think the intelligence of the average Negro who lived in a shack on the edge of a big tobacco or cotton plantation had come to full flower. He had been reduced to the level of an animal and quite consciously so. This sophisticated hatred, to me, must have arisen among Negroes who had been in contact with white people, especially those who had gained some education like Nat Turner.

Lewis: I take it that calm, intelligent hatred would be a quality of someone who had been on the whole better treated. Not hate in a frenzied wild way, like Will, who came to his hate sheerly through years of savage mistreatment.

Styron: No, no, I am talking about the more sophisticated kind of hate that Nat had.

Woodward: Toward the end, Nat Turner's environment was certainly not one of intolerable oppression. As you picture him, he is relatively fortunate as a slave, and his last master is a congenial type.

Styron: Yes. Historically, one of the actual facts that we know about the insurrection is that his last master, Travis, the man whom they brutally murdered, was a lenient, kind, tolerant man. But this meant nothing to Nat by that time. This was the worst sort of thing. The better treatment he had as he advanced up the so-called ladder as a slave, the more respect he received from white people, the more he had a desire to cut their throats.

Lewis: One last thing about Nat's actual performance during the rebellion. You said earlier that you felt a person of his intelligence and with his capacity for planning would pursue a scorched earth policy. In fact, though, Nat was not even able to lead in the slaughter. Is there an inevitable contradiction here, namely, that the kind of person who had the capacity to organize a rebellion would also have a sensibility which forbade him from carrying it through?

Styron: Yes, I think it is quite apparent that he was a man who had very little taste for blood. Again I am improvising on the actual record, but it is quite clear to me that when Nat was faced with the actuality of the blood and the exposed intestines . . .

Lewis: He vomited.

Styron: Yes, he got sick. This is a perfectly good human reaction and I am sure that historically this is what helped undermine the rebellion. It was a failure of his own leadership.

Lewis: He says at the end, doesn't he, that he would do it all over again, except he would spare Margaret Whitehead? In other words, he would not kill anyone another time.

Styron: I guess so, if you want to look at that little paradox that way. It certainly meant that Nat, by the time of his own death, had come to a guarded understanding of the quality of Christian redemption, whether he accepted it or not.

Lewis: Well, it is a unique combination of circumstances and qualities, and I think it is a unique novel.

Woodward: I quite agree. I would myself think it was the most profound treatment we have had of slavery in our literature. And the only one that tells the story from the slave's point of view. [39]

2. REVIEWS

The Slave Who Became a Man

WILFRID SHEED

NAT TURNER MAY HAVE BEEN THE FIRST OF THE GREAT NEGRO PREACHER-reformers, a line that has fanned out since in such different directions as Martin Luther King, Adam Clayton Powell and James Baldwin, the boy-preacher turned, or half-turned, novelist. In an oppressive situation, ministers and men of the Book have a natural edge in literacy and self-confidence: and even a slave like Turner was able to accumulate enough white-man's self-sufficiency, plus white-man's cartography and logistics, to lead the only facsimile of a revolt the slaves were ever able to mount.

William Styron has undertaken to reconstruct Nat Turner, using the public record as skeleton and fleshing him out with motives and whatnot. The result, in view of current events, can hardly be read as an exercise in pure esthetics. The author mumbles something in his introduction about "perhaps the reader will wish to draw a moral . . . but," etc., thus saving his book for art, but there is no "perhaps . . . but" about it. A novel on this subject has to be part politics, ours and his, at the moment.

Of course we are going to ransack it for parallels. And of course, under whatever light camouflage, the parallels are going to be there, for the author gets his ideas from the same place we do, from the air around us. And how better to learn about Turner's motives than from living man with the same (apparent) motives? Thus, Styron uses history quite properly to put his own experience into fancy dress and see how it looks. No historical novel has ever done more.

Turner's rebellion took place in the long hot summer of 1831, in the state of Virginia. (Farther south, in the unfoliated cotton fields, there was less privacy to conspire in.) When it was over, 59 white people were dead; the insurgents were all rounded up and either hanged or shown a clemency worse than death; and the preacher himself, now safely in irons, was induced to write a confession which Mr. Styron has managed to merge quite smoothly into his novel.

The first of many such lessons for the white community; but they seem to have learned even less than usual from this one. The owners were baffled to find their Negroes acting together, which ran counter to the sub-scientific cant of the period. They were baffled twice over to find how much those tiny brains (read Dr. Pepper's monograph on the Negro skull) could hate. On the other hand, the slaves had acted with less than West Point precision. Some of them hit the cider-presses, and some on the fat-cat plantations had even fired on their brothers. So by the end, the clichés had rallied and were back in the saddle.

But in truth, Turner had done an extraordinary job. He could not, in his rather cramped circumstances, have had personal contact with more than a [1/2] handful of his troops. He picked them up one by one, zealots and slobs alike, as he burned his way from farm to farm, and tried to weld them instantaneously into an army. At that, he very nearly succeeded: he was within half a mile of the armory at Jerusalem, Va., his nicely titled goal, when his luck ran out.

At his sanctimonious trial another familiar argument introduced itself. The white folks began to talk backlash—we tried being nice to these baboons and look where it got us—and no doubt they were able to follow through on it and no doubt an era of repression was Turner's immediate legacy. At the same time, he gave the Negroes a legend which has not yet lost its potency. Turner was, for instance, a big influence on Marcus Garvey, the daddy of the Black Nationalist movement. Garvey's disciples included Malcolm X's father. And so on, through how many bloodlines, to today's Negro leaders.

The Turner revolt, as Styron tells it in this novel, was a revolution of rising expectations. His version of Nat grows up spoiled, comparatively, by a kind master who promises him eventual freedom. This mirage cuts Nat temporarily adrift from his own people and renders him something of a prig—not necessarily a handicap in a leader. Later, when the freedom bubble bursts messily and he is handed down through a homosexual parson to a medium-brutal redneck farmer, and finally up again, too late, to a decent master, his arrogance will endure, as both a comfort to himself and an inspiration to others.

Simultaneous with this quirky character training goes an even quirkier, self-inflicted theological training. The Good Book which the owners have fed to their darkies in selected spoonfuls turns out, in larger doses, to be equivalent to a keg of nitroglycerine. All the violence and underdog determination that the masters skip over blandly in their own Scripture readings nests deep in Nat Turner. For this is his whole education, his whole intellectual universe. Joshua, David, vengeance. If you can't get Mao-Tse-tung on Revolution, the Old Testament is not bad for your one book.

To complete the package, Turner has natural spiritual gifts, sharpened to brilliance by fasting and strenuous chastity. His preaching, as Styron records it, is hard and urgent. The preacher was the natural leader for Negroes—not because of their ignorance and superstition (these were as likely to work against him), but because he could do the work of years in minutes. With one spellbinding performance he could weld his audience, give them some point of concentration and the energy to pursue it. Unfortunately, as the failure of Turner's rising shows, the hypnosis is likely to wear off at the wrong moment: preacher-intoxication is not enough for a whole campaign.

In fact, it even wears off Turner himself: before Armageddon commences, he decides he will have to break training and get himself a wife. Then, when battle is joined, the two sides of the Good Book split inside him, Vengeance against Love, and he cannot lift his sword. He believes in killing with all his heart, but as he tries to do it God leaves him, and does not return until, minutes before his own hanging, Turner has a vision of reconciliation.

The message seems to be that the Negro has every right to kill the white man, but cannot escape pollution in the process. The ending is covertly sentimental, one of those chins-up sad endings, and part of its effectiveness will be determined, as I say, by your view of the race question and the other and smaller part by whether the novel has worked with you as a novel.

And here we run into difficulties. There is no doubt that Turner is still worth writing and speculating about; but whether he can be successfully written about fictionally is another question. The historical novel is traditionally so clumsy a method of investigation that the reader usually winds up doubting whether the characters ever existed at all, in any form. And Styron has only exaggerated the difficulties by telling his story in the first person.

First of all, there is the old diction problem—in this case, finding a language for an early 19th-century slave and sticking to it. This involves writing a whole book in mimicry of a speech one has never actually heard. The best you can hope for is a language technically correct but thin and colorless as convent school French: with all the idioms woodenly in place, but with none of the juice and flavor of a man at home in his own language. Since we are looking into the mind and motives of the narrator, it does not help to get our answers in Berlitz.

This part of his problem Styron has done very well with indeed. Nat's speech is not just a pedantic reconstruction, but a plausible, timeless blend of Southern-Biblical: a little stiff, but not by 19th-century standards (anything looser would rouse suspicions of another sort), and generally serviceable. One grows frustrated at times watching the author squeeze his own excellent prose into this whalebone of rhetoric: but he gets off some fine phrases, and the writing in fact carries one over a good deal of wasteland.

The diction problem turns up in a more acute form when it comes [2/3] to Turner's own consciousness. We are in effect being asked to spend a short lifetime in the head of one skillfully animated museum piece. What does Turner think about all this time? Not the things we would think about, of course: the author has been careful to expunge the 20th century. But equipping his hero with a complete 1831 sensibility is something else. Styron is on safe ground while he is sticking to a certain *type* of thought—just as a mimicker of movie stars is safe if he sticks to certain key phrases—but the result of this can only be monotony beyond the call of monomania. A long book told from one point of view is always a risk: here the risk is prohibitive.

To enrich the cramped psyche of his narrator, Styron has simply inserted endless chunks of his own nature writing—some of the best nature writing going, but largely irrelevant to the narrative and to Nat's focus at the particular moment. Important dramatic scenes are interrupted time and again for the sake of long weather and crop reports, almost as if the author's own attention had wandered. Worse, the weather is always just right for the scene: sultry for tension, cold for failure, etc. We even have clouds passing over the sun on cue.

These and other Victorian devices lend an artificiality to the whole enterprise. The tone is often closer to late-Victorian than early-Victorian. "For many years it had been my habit. . . ." "Thus my duties, compared to what I had been used to, were light and fairly free of strain." It reminds one of the novels that begin "When I was a boy at the turn of the century." And how about this for honest muttonchop indignation? "It was plain now that the sight of the dying child had caused even his adamantine heart to be smitten by guilt." Or for elegance of feeling, what about this tribute to a lady's hand? "That soothing many-fingered delicacy." One hears the voice of W. C. Fields fading away on that line; and then, as Turner refers (more than once) to "the days before my execution" we pick up Stephen Leacock. "I died, I buried myself. Would that all who write sea stories would do likewise."

I am not suggesting that the novel is full of false laughs: Styron's taste is much too good for that. But the question arises, can a pastiche of this kind, however skillful, serve as a vehicle for genuine feeling? The answer, in terms of fiction, of the "felt-life," surely has to be "no." There are so many techniques for insuring immediacy and complicity that Styron is forced to deny himself. Instead, he must make do with that old pack-drill of declarative sentences, slowly marching past. "*I felt a blinding pain . . . for days I lay in a fever . . . I felt my cheeks burning,*" all the earnest devices of the Victorian novelist telling you what to feel and how strongly to feel it.

The only scenes that break loose from this rhetorical straitjacket for long are scenes of straight dialogue. (The monologues are characteristically tiresome.) Otherwise, a simple brief narration of Nat Turner's trials would be far more moving than this windy, florid elaboration of them. Unfortunately, the padding and the stentorian descriptions and the majestic theme make the novel look "important," instead of simply ingenious, and this kind of thing can cause trouble for authors. This is the novel Styron always wanted to write, and we should now be glad he's gotten it over with, and can get on with the ones he doesn't want to write. Four-hundred-page imitations can be left to less talented novelists.

But if the book fails by default, as a novel, it does succeed in many places as a kind of historical tone poem. Styron's version of the old South is not the usual derivative, Daddy's-plantation stuff but a place freshly imagined stone by stone. Some sense is conveyed of the many varieties of slave experience, and the many kinds of Negro it produced. The Amos 'n' Andy dialogue sounds note-perfect, and so does Nat Turner's contempt for it. The servant's need to play the buffoon (traditional to all cultures, but treated as unique in each one) required for corrective a dour, humorless scold like Turner. When he tells them to lay aside their banjos, he is striking the first blow against the Natural Rhythm Theory.

But, to return to our beginnings, did Turner strike the blow, or was it Styron himself? Is this book really, as Styron says, a meditation on history, or a meditation on the daily papers? The answer comes in two parts. Styron has nothing new to say about Negro motives—outside of a few period visions and voices, Turner's reasons for revolting are just what you would expect. But he does have something to say about the physical situation of slavery, the way that America looked and sounded and smelled from underneath: the only position the American Negro has known to this day. There may be something to be said for documenting this year by year, the 1820's and then the 1830's and after that the 1840's, until the size of the atrocity is recorded and dimly understood. If so, Styron has performed a signal, non-literary service in writing this book.

Now, I hope he will get back to work. [3]

Nat Turner:
A "Meditation on History"

MELVIN J. FRIEDMAN

WILLIAM STYRON HAS UNTIL NOW BEEN A VICTIM OF BAD TIMING. *Lie Down in Darkness* (1951) was pushed to the background by two of the best-selling serious novels of recent times, *Catcher in the Rye* and *From Here to Eternity*—both published the same year. Styron's Peyton

Melvin J. Friedman, *"The Confessions of Nat Turner:* The Convergence of 'Nonfiction Novel' and 'Meditation on History,' " *Journal of Popular Culture* (Fall 1967). Reprinted by permission.

Loftis was clearly no match for Salinger's Holden Caulfield despite the dramatic details leading to her suicide; nor was the backdrop of the Hiroshima bomb, crowding in on Peyton's monologue, enough to offset the appeal of events leading to Pearl Harbor depicted in *From Here to Eternity*. Reviewers, led by Malcolm Cowley in *The New Republic*, did not help Styron's case by pointing out Faulknerian echoes in *Lie Down in Darkness*.

Styron published his novella *The Long March* two years later in *Discovery No. 1*. This was three years before the famous Parris Island Marine incident of 1956. Again Styron's timing was unfortunate. (Random House partly saved the situation by bringing out *The Long March* as a Modern Library paperback in 1956.)

Set This House on Fire (1960) was regarded as too cineramic by a generation of critics who were beginning to despair of anything approaching the extravagance and overblown qualities of Hollywood.[1] Ironically enough, the most articulate and convincing spokesman for *Set This House on Fire* was the French novelist and critic, Michel Butor. In a brilliant preface he wrote for the French translation of Styron's novel (*La Proie des Flammes*) he explained much about the book which had eluded Styron's American reviewers. By implication Butor was almost welcoming Styron to the ranks of the *nouveau roman* (of which he is a most prominent member) and offering him a kind of adopted literary homeland—the one Faulkner received [166/167] from André Malraux, Jean-Paul Sartre, and Valery Larbaud in the '30's.

Styron has had this uncanny ability, then, to enter and reenter, with each successive book, through the back door of American literature. His acceptance as a major contemporary novelist—which he clearly is—has been slow and grudging. Anthony Burgess' *The Novel Now: A Guide to Contemporary Fiction* (W. W. Norton, 1967) gives Styron three sentences. This is symptomatic. If a practicing novelist like Burgess, who is so firmly committed to the virtues of an allusive style and the metaphoric possibilities of language, can dismiss Styron so perfunctorily in a book scrupulously limited to the recent novel, what can one expect from the less discriminating literary public? A few distinguished critics, like Malcolm Cowley, Maxwell Geismar, Frederick Hoffman, and Louis Rubin, have all along been convinced of Styron's worth, but he has never been the favorite of the Establishment that Saul Bellow, for example, has been; nor has he enjoyed the bittersweet popularity of a Salinger or a Mailer.

The situation may now have changed. *The Confessions of Nat Turner*, the account of a Negro slave revolt in southeastern Virginia in 1831, appeared the October following the "hottest" summer of racial

---

[1] See especially Richard Foster's "An Orgy of Commerce: William Styron's *Set This House on Fire*," *Critique: Studies in Modern Fiction*, III (Summer 1960), pp. 59–70.

disturbances the country has had. In a series of interviews accompanying publication of his most recent novel, Styron maintained that he had the idea for the book in mind for twenty years; it was in no way a commercial response to the racial unrest of the moment. Indeed Styron was already speaking of his novel-in-progress in the July 1963 *Esquire* ("Two Writers Talk It Over"). He discussed it in even more substantial detail in the April 1965 *Harper's* ("This Quiet Dust"). Timing was finally working in Styron's favor as he finished *The Confessions of Nat Turner* early in 1967—in time for the October 9 publication date. His fourth book is certain to have the commercial success denied his first three. The prepublication appearance of the entire second part (45,000 words) in the September 1967 *Harper's* and the briefer excerpt, complete with photographs, in the October 13, 1967 *Life* are sure indications that Styron has finally "arrived" in the way Bellow "arrived" with *Herzog* or Truman Capote with *In Cold Blood*.

The comparison with *In Cold Blood* is very much to the point. Capote caused a critical stir by announcing that he had written the first "nonfiction novel," a new genre he uncovered to describe the brutal and virtually unmotivated murder of a prosperous family in western Kansas. While Capote did not have Styron's advantage of growing up near the events of his book and having the raw material on hand, ready to be released at the propitious moment, he was to compensate in part by spending long periods of time in and around Holcomb, Kansas, observing and notetaking. (His methods of research and composition were unusual enough to attract considerable attention in their own right.) *In Cold Blood* was even more gaudily advertised than *The Confessions of Nat Turner:* its publication as a book was preceded by a four-part serialization in *The New Yorker; Life* filled seventeen pages with photos and its usual "in depth" coverage; *Time* and *Newsweek* gave it elaborate critical and biographical consideration; almost every [167/168] book review organ in the country acknowledged its literary credentials by assigning to it the most talented of their stable of reviewers.

The great difference up to now in the reception of the two books is that Styron, at this writing (only a handful of reviews have appeared), has fared rather well at the hands of the reviewers while Capote received severe critical tongue-lashings from Stanley Kauffmann in *The New Republic,* William Phillips in *Commentary,* and Sol Yurick in *The Nation.* (One can hope that Styron will be spared the kind of attack which Capote received from Kenneth Tynan in the London *Observer;* it is hard to forget a sentence like: "It seems to me that the blood in which his book is written is as cold as any in recent literature.")

Styron has called *The Confessions of Nat Turner* "a meditation on history" (in his "Author's Note" preceding the novel). He might have used, with some appropriateness, Capote's coinage "nonfiction novel."

Styron has as scrupulously consulted his sources as Capote did before him; except that he had to depend largely on a twenty-page pamphlet written 135 years before his book while Capote was able to consult directly with the participants in the action he described. The result is that Capote's chief concern was liberating his book from the fugitiveness of reportage while Styron's was controlling the flights of his own fancy and imagination. Thus Capote clings to the word "novel" and all its imaginative associations while Styron latches on to the respectably solid word "history."

In the years leading up to *Nat Turner* Styron did a certain amount of journalistic writing, almost as if he were undergoing a necessary apprenticeship to writing his book. Much of this was connected with the Negro problem. He wrote two articles for *Esquire* in February and November, 1962 on the Benjamin Reid case. He championed the cause of an illiterate Negro who was condemned to the death sentence in the Connecticut State Prison at Wethersfield. Styron turned out to be more than just a "Southerner of good will who lives in the North" (his own expression); he proved to be a humanitarian who used his rhetorical gifts to save a human life—a Negro life on this occasion.

Styron wrote three book reviews for *The New York Review of Books*, in 1963 and 1964, on the role of the Negro. The book closest to the novel he was then beginning to write was Herbert Aptheker's *American Negro Slave Revolts;* Styron's review of it seriously challenges Aptheker's position on "slave rebelliousness":

But one does not have to be a white supremacist to note that Aptheker fails almost completely in his attempt to prove the universality of slave rebelliousness. Save for two enthusiastic but localized conspiracies—that of Gabriel in Richmond in 1800, and that of Vesey in Charleston in 1822, both of which were nipped in the bud—there was only one [168/169] sustained, effective revolt in the entire annals of slavery: the cataclysmic uprising of Nat Turner in Virginia in 1831.[2]

Styron begins another of these reviews on a fondly nostalgic note:

I can recall with clarity from childhood my North Carolina grandmother's reminiscences of her slaves. To be sure, she was an old lady well into her eighties at the time, and had been a young girl growing up during the Civil War when she owned human property. Nonetheless, that past is linked to our present by a space of time which is startlingly brief.

He soon deserts his tone of nostalgia in favor of a more sobering rhetoric: ". . . the ante-bellum Black Laws of Virginia, which even now read like the code of regulations from an inconceivably vast and much longer enduring Nazi concentration camp."[3]

[2] "Overcome," *The New York Review of Books*, September 26, 1963, p. 19.
[3] "New Editions," *The New York Review of Books*, Special Issue, 1963, p. 43.

The surest anticipation of *The Confessions of Nat Turner* is the essay Styron wrote for the special issue of *Harper's* (April 1965) concerned with "The South Today." Styron not only speaks in this essay, "This Quiet Dust," of Nat Turner and of his plans for his novel-in-progress, but makes a statement which should always haunt critics of his work and of Faulkner's:

Most Southern white people *cannot* know or touch black people and this is because of the deadly intimidation of a universal law. Certainly one feels the presence of this gulf even in the work of a writer as supremely knowledgeable about the South as William Faulkner, who confessed a hesitancy about attempting to "think Negro," and whose Negro characters, as marvelously portrayed as most of them are, seem nevertheless to be meticulously *observed* rather than *lived*. (p. 137)

Philip Rahv quoted this passage in the best review I have seen to date of *The Confessions of Nat Turner* (*New York Review of Books*, October 26, 1967). Rahv, unlike several of the other early reviewers, seems content that Styron has turned over the narration to a quasi-educated Negro slave and has bestowed on him the mature power of Styron's own rhetoric. He is not at all offended by the first-person which controls the point of view of the novel. The ambiguity of the Styron-Nat Turner narrative relationship seems to work for Rahv, who admits, "This is a first-rate novel, the best that William Styron has written and the best by an American writer that has appeared in some years." (p. 6)

Other reviewers have proved more cautious in their response. Wilfrid [169/170] Sheed raises the question of pastiche—which has been raised before in connection with Styron's work[4]—and ends by feeling that if the book fails as a novel it might succeed "as a kind of historical tone poem." (*New York Times Book Review*, October 8, 1967, p. 3) The historian C. Vann Woodward, reviewing it in *The New Republic* (October 7, 1967), seemed to experience another kind of uneasiness—perhaps the kind historians feel when confronted with a literary text.[5]

In the end, the principal objections to *The Confessions of Nat Turner* will probably be that it is written in the first-person (usually regarded, and wrongly, as hopelessly old-fashioned) and in the words of an ante-bellum Negro. We find out from the excellent long piece in

[4] See J. D. Scott, "New Novels," *New Statesman and Nation*, April 19, 1952, p. 473. See also my "William Styron: An Interim Appraisal," *The English Journal*, L (March 1961), pp. 151–153.

[5] *The Nation* had the inspired idea of commissioning two reviews of *The Confessions of Nat Turner*, one by a literary scholar, Shaun O'Connell, and the other by a historian, Herbert Aptheker. O'Connell is mainly interested in its virtues as a novel while Aptheker concentrates on historical "accuracy" and fidelity. See *The Nation*, October 16, 1967.

Newsweek (October 16, 1967) that James Baldwin's stay with the Styrons for five months in the early '60's and his close association with them since had something to do with Styron's positing the point of view with a Negro, Nat Turner. But we should not forget that Styron's own idiom is grafted on to Nat's in much the way, as Philip Rahv has told us, that "Faulkner bypassed in *As I Lay Dying* Darl's native speech in favor of his own." One can go back as far as *Madame Bovary* to find certain of the same effects. Even though Flaubert's novel is clearly not first-person,[6] we are limited through much of it to Emma Bovary's point of view—but always to Flaubert's language and syntax. Henry James was also uncompromising in retaining his own elaborate syntax and richly suggestive language even though he frequently turned over the point of view to characters whose mentalities were scarcely capable of manipulating these verbal effects.

But more to the point than either Flaubert or James is Marcel Proust. In *Remembrance of Things Past* he has written a Flaubert-James type novel but in the first-person. This first-person is among the most complex we have in the history of the novel. (One critic recently pointed to nine distinct uses of the "I" in Proust's book.)[7] Styron might have learned something from Proust in his own elaborately ambiguous narrative technique in *The Confessions of Nat Turner*. The style does not differ appreciably from either *Lie Down in Darkness* or *Set This House on Fire*, especially in the richly metaphoric descriptions of landscape. It is the change from the third to the first person which would unsettle most of Styron's readers. Yet Styron has given fair warning of what he would do in his 1967 novel by experimenting frequently with changes in person and point of view in his earlier full-length fiction. Thus he gave us three pages of second-person discourse ("If you are particularly alert at that unconscionable hour you notice his voice . . .") at the beginning of *Lie Down in Darkness* as well as a fifty-page monologue towards the end. We got long excerpts from Cass Kinsolving's "confessions" in *Set This House on Fire* as well as Peter Leverett's "background" first-person. What seems to have happened is that Styron decided to settle on the first-person in his latest novel—not the first person of the 18th century *journal intime*, but a much more complex one.

[6] The novel does begin, however, in the first person plural and maintains this narrative focus through the first three pages: "We were in study-hall when the headmaster entered, followed by a new boy not yet in school uniform and by the handyman carrying a large desk." It is no secret that Styron was much taken by *Madame Bovary*: ". . . *Madame Bovary* is one of the few novels that moves me in every way, not only in its style, but in its total communicability, like the effect of good poetry." (*Writers at Work: The Paris Review Interviews*, ed. Malcolm Cowley, New York: Viking, 1960, p. 274.)

[7] See Bruce Morrissette's excellent "The Evolution of Narrative Viewpoint in Robbe-Grillet," *Novel: A Forum on Fiction*, I (Fall 1967), p. 24.

What Louis Rubin has written recently about Proust applies splendidly [170/171] to *The Confessions of Nat Turner:*

[*Remembrance of Things Past*] is a novel which is not only told in the first person, but in which the first person narrator writes directly about himself when younger. Here, one might say, there is more than a merely apprehended personality telling us the story; the authorial personality is a definite individual, a character. . . .

Not only that, but the narrator as well as the younger "I" about whom he writes evolves before our eyes during the course of the novel.[8]

Styron's novel, in the main part, is supposed to record Nat Turner's confessions as told to a lawyer, Thomas R. Gray, while he awaited execution. It wanders across diverse periods of time, in good Proustian fashion, while the successive "I's" which constitute Nat Turner come to life in their own special blocks of narrative. We see Nat always in what amounts to a Bergsonian state of becoming. We seem to be caught up in a kind of *durée,* in the very flux of time as Nat "evolves before our eyes." *The Confessions of Nat Turner* must certainly be grouped among those works which Wyndham Lewis classifies as "time-books" (see *Time and Western Man*)—of which Proust's *Remembrance of Things Past* is a charter member.

There is something else ominously Proustian about the book. The element of sex has the same ambiguous quality as the element of narration. While there is clearly nothing to match the famous opening pages of Proust's *Cities of the Plain* or the later goings-on between Charlus and Morel, Styron does describe with some vividness the homosexual relationship between Nat Turner and another young Negro, Willis:

I reached up to wipe away the blood from his lips, pulling him near with the feel of his shoulders slippery beneath my hand, and then we somehow fell on each other, very close, soft and comfortable in a sprawl like babies; beneath my exploring fingers his hot skin throbbed and pulsed like the throat of a pigeon, and I heard him sigh in a faraway voice, and then for a long moment as if set free into another land we did with our hands together what, before, I had done alone. Never had I known that human flesh could be so sweet.[9]

This passage lacks the delicacy of Proust; it suffers from too much sensuality and is perhaps too cliché-ridden. It could just as easily be a description of heterosexual love—which is never the case with Proust.

---

[8] Louis D. Rubin, Jr., *The Teller in the Tale* (Seattle: University of Washington Press, 1967), pp. 108–109.

[9] *The Confessions of Nat Turner* (New York: Random House, 1967), p. 204. All references will be to this edition.

The suggestion of ambiguity is, however, artistically sound. The sexual interests of Nat are meant to be vague, confused, and unclear. His later love for the white girl Margaret Whitehead, who Gallicly punctuates every [171/172] third sentence with *au fond*, is less real than the attachment for Willis, mainly because it remains unexpressed and unconsummated. Yet it shares with it a delicate ambiguity. We seem to have reached with Nat Turner (what Henry Miller in *The Cosmological Eye* pointed to in Proust) "that plane of depolarized love wherein the sexes fuse." The kinds of love he experiences are further confused by his religious, prophetic zeal, nurtured particularly on *Ezekiel*. Thus little distinction is made between Nat's sexual relations with Willis and his baptism of him:

I grasped the back of his head and shoved him under, pressed him down beneath the foaming murky waters. It was the instant of my first baptism, and the swift brief exaltation I felt brought a sudden flood of tears to my eyes. After a second or two I brought him up in a cloud of bubbles, and as he stood there dripping and puffing like a kettle but with a smile as sweet as beatitude itself on his shining face, I addressed myself to the blue firmament. (p. 206)

There is not a great deal of difference, certainly not in the texture, between this passage and the earlier one concerned with the homosexual experience.

There is some reason for believing, then, that Proust had something to do with the shaping of *The Confessions of Nat Turner*. There is no doubt that Camus also lent a helping hand. This brings us back to the matter of Styron's use of the first-person. Styron told George Plimpton in a *New York Times Book Review* interview (October 8, 1967):

Then along about 1962, a couple of years after "Set This House on Fire" was published, I was up on Martha's Vineyard and I had just read for the first time Camus' "The Stranger." It is a brilliant book, the best of Camus, and it impressed me enormously: there was something about the poignancy of the condemned man sitting in his jail cell on the day of his execution—the existential predicament of the man—that hit me. And so did the use of the first person, the book being told through the eye of the condemned. The effect of all this was so strong that I suddenly realized that my Nat Turner could be done the same way: that, like Camus, I would center the novel around a man facing his own death in a jail cell, which of course was true of Turner and how his life ended. And so there, suddenly provided, was the architecture of the book, its framework, along with the idea of telling the story in the first person. (p. 2) [172/173]

One recalls that the first-person of *The Stranger* is geared to a very low key. The " 'I' appears as a pronoun of surfaces only," as Bruce Morrissette has observed. This is clearly not the case with Styron. The lushness of the opening description of *The Confessions of Nat Turner* somehow overwhelms the first-person and sacrifices it, at least temporarily, to the pronoun "one" ("one must try to visualize," etc.); the "I" does not appear in Nat's discourse until the sixth sentence. This is quite different from the ironically underplayed beginning of *The Stranger:* "Mother died today. Or, maybe, yesterday; I can't be sure."

We should recall at this point Styron's description of his novel as a "meditation on history." "Meditation" is the important word here. Camus also wrote a meditation, but his is a meditation on self rather than on history. I am thinking of his later book *The Fall* which is also written in the first-person. It is a work of great moral and philosophical urgency; it avoids the easy and painless surfaces of *The Stranger*. The "I" in this book has a complexity and ambiguity which recalls Proust's first-person. Jean-Baptiste Clamence, Camus' "underground" narrator of *The Fall,* has something in common with Nat Turner; they both go through Cartesian-type purgations and their confessions might easily be placed side by side with Descartes' *Discourse on Method*. (It should be recalled that this last work was also written in the first-person and that its author was famous for another work known under its shortened title, *Meditations*.)

The Fall, then, seems to be more to the point than *The Stranger*. Yet the manipulation of the first-person, with its elaborate syntax and metaphorical turnings, in *Remembrance of Things Past* strikes me as closer to *Nat Turner* than either of Camus' books. In any case, there is much evidence that the first-person is an honorable narrative mode in the 20th century and that Styron is not being old-fashioned in using it. Styron indeed shows astounding versatility with his use of Nat Turner's "I." It would be difficult to find nine different modes of the "I" as with Proust, but there are certainly at least three. Nat has three "languages": the one of his thoughts; the one of his conversation with most white men (Samuel Turner, his enlightened early master, is an exception); and the one of his conversation with fellow slaves. The first, on the surface, is uniquely present in Nat's "meditation." The second and third fill the majority of his conversation. Yet the second and third melt imperceptibly into the first so that the elaborate Ciceronian periods, which characterize Styron's own style, are softened by the colloquial manner of the dialogue. Much of the first-person confessional is actually a blending of the three—with the sophisticated mode of Nat's thoughts being dominant. Styron compromises more with the vernacular than Proust was willing to do. His "I" has a certain kind of elasticity which Proust's doesn't.

What I have been trying to say is that despite the caution expressed by several early reviewers there is no reason to doubt the value of the point of view and narrative mode used in *The Confessions of Nat Turner*. Proust served his apprenticeship by writing *Jean*

Santeuil in the third [173/174] person. He saved the first person for the work of his maturity, *Remembrance of Things Past*. The lesson might be applied to Styron who says that he waited twenty years before he finally "released" *The Confessions of Nat Turner*. In the meantime he wrote two books mainly in third person and experimented with the first person, in a somewhat modified way, in *Set This House on Fire*. It may be that he too was waiting for the maturity necessary to use the first person in the uncompromising way he did in *The Confessions of Nat Turner*.

I suspect that commentators on the novel will finally applaud Styron's decision to turn over his book to Nat's long meditation. These "antimemoirs"[10] are intriguing, then, not only because they offer a convenient historical backdrop for the recent events in Watts, Newark, Detroit, and Milwaukee. [174]

[10] I borrow this word from the title of André Malraux's most recent book, the tone of which might suggest something about Nat Turner's confessions—although Malraux insists in his preface that his work is without confessional elements. For an interesting discussion of Malraux's *Antimémoires* and its reception in France see "Letter from Paris," *The New Yorker*, November 11, 1967, pp. 188–194.

William Styron and Human Bondage

LOUIS D. RUBIN, JR.

I

"If this is true, from my soul I pity you . . ."
—Judge Cobb, sentencing Nat Turner.

This time Styron was off to a good start. "A wonderfully evocative portrait of a gifted, proud, long-suppressed human being . . ."— Alfred Kazin in *Book World*. "The most profound fictional treatment of slavery in our literature . . ."—C. Vann Woodward in *The New Republic*. "One of those novels that is an act of revelation to a whole society . . ."—Raymond A. Sokolov in *Newsweek*. "A first-rate novel, [1/2] the best that William Styron has written and the best by an American writer that has appeared in some years . . ."—Philip Rahv in the *New York Review of Books*. There were a few dissents, to be

Louis D. Rubin, Jr., "William Styron and Human Bondage: *The Confessions of Nat Turner*," *The Hollins Critic* (December 1967). Reprinted by permission.

sure, but it was clear that *The Confessions of Nat Turner* was making its way from the outset.

In that respect it was in startling contrast to *Set This House On Fire*, which when it appeared in 1960 was jumped upon by almost everybody. That novel had the misfortune to be the long-awaited second novel by a man whose first book was a tremendous success. In the nine years that followed *Lie Down in Darkness* (a novella, *The Long March*, didn't really count), the critics grew tired of waiting. Almost everyone had predicted great things for William Styron, and the longer it took for him to produce a second big book, the more exasperated everyone became. So that when Styron finally managed to complete his second novel, its publication was almost certain to be anti-climactic. In addition, *Set This House On Fire* was very long, it was filled with much soul-torment, and there was no neat tragic pattern such as characterized Styron's first novel. Thus when *Set This House On Fire* finally appeared, all the journalistic reviews began scolding at once. Supposedly the new book was windblown, self-indulgent, sentimental, bathetic, over-written, and so on—the chorus of castigation rose to an impressive decibel volume. Only a corporal's guard of reviewers dared to disagree, to insist that while *Set This House On Fire* wasn't a flawless novel, it was nevertheless a very impressive accomplishment, a moving work of fiction, in every way worthy of if not superior to *Lie Down in Darkness*, so that its author need in no way feel that he had failed to live up to his notices.

During the seven years between *Set This House On Fire* and Styron's new novel, however, critical opinion has pretty much come around to the viewpoint that Styron's second book was a quite respectable performance. Once the reviewers in the critical quarterlies, who are notably unswayed by journalistic reviews, began writing about the book, the initial verdict was reversed. Critical essays and chapters of books appeared which treated *Set This House On Fire* as a work which, though flawed in parts, contains some of the better writing of our time. For example, a good critic, Frederick J. Hoffman, has this to say about *Set This House On Fire* in his recent book *The Art of Southern Fiction:* "Styron's most recent novel sets the imagination agoing, in the expectation of an American literature of existentialism . . . But it is perhaps [2/3] best not to name it that, for fear of weighing it down with labels and classifications. The important fact is that Styron has used his talents mightily and to a good effect in this novel."

Set This House On Fire is the story of Cass Kinsolving, an artist unable to paint. A World War II veteran, married and living in Europe, he must undergo a terrifying stay in the lower depths before he can win his way back to sanity and creativity. The leading characters, very unlike most Southern fictional folk, engage in long, probing psychological analyses of their inner souls. There are no Negroes (though there is a memory of them), no First Families going to seed, no church services, no blood-guilt of generations, no oversexed Southern matrons. It is thoroughly, completely modern, even cosmopolitan. Cass Kinsolving is a man in bondage; in Paris, Rome and Sambuco he lives in an alcoholic daze, tortured by his inability to paint, drinking, wandering about, pitying himself, doing everything except confronting his talent. He had sought to find a form for his art outside of himself; he could not put up with his creative limitations, and he looked to the society and people surrounding him for what could only be found within himself: the remorseless requirement of discovering how to love and be loved, and so to create. Only through violence and tragedy could he win his way through to self-respect, and attain an equilibrium with the world that enables him to function effectively.

All very odd and strange, this sort of thing: Styron wasn't supposed to write that kind of a novel. What also perplexed many reviewers was that this process and this outcome were not presented ironically or obliquely; there wasn't the self-conscious distrust of high rhetoric and ultimate judgment that characterizes much "existential" fiction today. The language was unabashedly resounding and rhetorical. And because it was the kind of book it was, the form of the story was restless, groping, searching, and not at all neat and tidy.

The difficulties inherent in any attempt to use the high style to deal with contemporary life are of course obvious. Our sense of irony is too strong to permit it to function without severe qualification. Faulkner, for all his greatness, could never successfully handle an intelligent modern man learning how to cope with contemporary urban society: his Gavin Stevens is among his less convincing characterizations. Robert Penn Warren managed it in *All The King's Men,* but to do so he had to filter the rhetoric through a wisecracking, hard-boiled-type narrator who could protect his more sounding declarations from irony by getting there first himself. Few other contemporaries even dare to try it; they fear, and with reason, that they will come out of it talking like the later prose of Carl Sandburg.

Styron's attempt, in *Set This House On Fire,* was not completely successful either. There is a shift of character focus in the novel, to the effect that part of the true explanation for Cass Kinsolving's plight lies not in his own past experience but in that of his friend Peter Leverett. This isn't ultimately fatal; such is Styron's artistry that we accord Kinsolving the right to feel and think as he does, in defiance of the strict logic of plot. The main thing is that *Set This House On Fire* works; one way or another, it adds up. There are moments when Cass's believability seems to be in jeopardy, but each time Styron comes through.

Styron, Hoffman remarks, "moved away [in *Set This House On Fire*] from the special moral dimensions of the Southerner looking at portraits of colonels, or addressing himself to the landscape of his

youth, or to the special qualities of feudal [3/4] vengeance or pride
. . . he has assumed a larger risk, moved into a more competitive
field, entered a tradition of psychological and moral analysis that has
been occupied by Kierkegaard, Mann, Sartre, and Camus before him."
So concluded many another critic after reading Set This House On
Fire, though usually without Hoffman's ability to perceive that in so
doing, Styron had written an excellent novel. Yet the implication,
voiced by numerous other critics as well, that in Set This House On
Fire Styron had ceased to be a "Southern writer," in the way that
Faulkner, Warren, Wolfe, Welty, Lytle, and so forth had been Southern writers, was unwarranted, I think. For the so-called "Southern
quality" in modern American fiction is not at bottom a matter of subject matter or theme, so much as of attitude: it is a way of looking at
the nature of human experience, and it includes the assumption that to
maintain order and stability the individual must be part of a social
community, yet that the ultimate authority that underlies his conduct is
not social but moral. It is, in short, a religious attitude, though most
often it does not involve the dogmas of revealed religion. This attitude,
not the presence of the particular institutions and events that cus-
tomarily embody the attitude, is what has enabled the work of the
better Southern novelists to seem so "meaningful" in our time. It is
precisely this attitude, too, that has made possible and believable the
use of the full, unstinted high rhetorical mode that so marks much of
the work of Faulkner, Warren, Wolfe, and others. We will not buy
rhetoric unless we believe in the absolutes that justify it, and the
Southern writers do believe in them. In many ways Styron's second
novel represents a kind of examination into the soundness of such a
view, ending in a confirmation. Cass Kinsolving's emotions and ideals
are examined and tested in the furnace experience of Paris and
Sambuco, and are finally pronounced sound. Whereupon Cass may
come home.

He comes back, however, not to the community in which he grew
up, but to another place, where he is ready to install himself—another
Southern community, but one without historical and social links with
his own past. It had been necessary for him to leave the scene of his
past behind him, to travel to another continent and there ratify the
individual and social worth of those attitudes and ideals, indepen-
dently of their institutions and for himself, in order to make them his,
and not merely something automatically bequeathed to him.

Thus for Styron, Set This House On Fire represented a clearing
away as it were of the debris of the Southern fictional texture—all the
accustomed artifacts of setting, history, community that have for
several generations provided the experience out of which Southern
fiction has been created. But the underlying attitude toward the nature
of human experience in time remains, and far from representing any
kind of abdication of what has come to be recognized as the Southern

literary mode, *Set This House On Fire* is an extension, perhaps the only possible extension, of that mode into a new day and a different kind of experience.

Toward the close of the novel Cass Kinsolving hears his family stirring about the house in the morning light, and thinks as follows: "I didn't know what it was but there they were sort of strutting face to face and soundlessly clapping their hands together, like Papageno and Papagena, or something even more sweet, paradisiac, as if they were children not really of this earth but of some other, delectable morning before time and history." As if there could be any possible doubt of the literary mode out of which that style of rhetoric comes! [4/5]

II

"It might offend Negroes that I as a white man have presumed to intrude on the consciousness of a Negro."—
William Styron, Interview in *Book World.*

Which brings us, seven years later, to *The Confessions of Nat Turner.* This time the scene is again the South—the Commonwealth of Virginia, scarcely more than an hour's ride by automobile from the very city in which Peyton Loftis, Peter Leverett, and William Styron were born and grew up. Furthermore, *The Confessions of Nat Turner* is an historical novel, based squarely on the single most complex and pervasive theme of all Southern history, the presence and role of the Negro. The central character and narrator is a preacher, whose thoughts and deeds are based on Biblical admonition and whose language is charged with Scriptural rhetoric. So that Styron would seem to have come full circle—starting out with Peyton Loftis from Port Warwick in Tidewater Virginia, then north to New York City; then eastward across the ocean to Paris and Italy with Cass Kinsolving, and at length back home to the South. Now it is Tidewater Virginia once more, the year is 1831, and there is the selfsame Black Shadow that has darkened the pages of Southern literature from the romances of William Gilmore Simms on through to Mark Twain, George Washington Cable and Thomas Nelson Page, and more recently William Faulkner, Robert Penn Warren, and every other Southern writer of the Twentieth Century so far.

But there is a difference. The story is told both *by* and *about* a Negro. Styron has sought to put himself into the mind and heart of a slave preacher who in August of 1831 led a bloody insurrection in Southampton County, Virginia. No Southern writer has ever really done this sort of thing before with much success. The faithful Negro retainers who relate in such ornate dialect Thomas Nelson Page's idylls of Virginia plantation life Befo' De War were stereotypes, designed to exhibit the graciousness and romance of ante-bellum society. Joel

Chandler Harris's Uncle Remus was also a delightful old darky, but he knew his place, and his creator was careful most of the time to keep to the surface of things. Even Faulkner, who Ralph Ellison [5/6] says has written more accurately and truly about the Negro than any other writer living or dead, black or white, shows us not the Negro so much as the white man learning to see the Negro—learning to see him more sharply and honestly than ever before.

Styron goes further. He is satisfied with nothing else than to try to *become* Nat Turner. Now it seems to me that, from the standpoint of the developing cultural history of the South, this very attempt is important of itself. In the years after 1865, writers such as Page and Harris created Negro narrators to tell their stories under the naive belief that this was a comparatively easy thing to do, since their notion of what it was like to be a Negro was itself something quite simple. Their Negro was the "Old Time Darky," faithful, true, obedient, whose every thought and allegiance was for Massa (sometimes spelled Marster, sometimes Mars', occasionally Maussa). A Thomas Nelson Page was confident that he understood the Negro; it never occurred to him that he might not. The great Southern novelists of the 1920s, 1930s and 1940s—Faulkner, Warren, Wolfe, the others—made no such easy assumptions; rather, they focussed upon the difficulty, the impossibility even, of the white man knowing what Negroes really thought and felt. This recognition that the complaisant pastoral figure that a Thomas Nelson Page could so naively accept as a "true" representation of the Negro was in fact a vast oversimplification, symbolized a long step forward in the white South's willingness to accord the Negro full human status. Now comes a fine novel by a leading Southern writer of the post-World War II generation, essaying to portray the innermost thoughts of a Negro, and doing so without very much self-consciousness. One cannot help but see this as emblematic of an important social breakthrough. For the point about Styron's characterization of Nat Turner is that Nat's existence as a Negro is not seen as making him in any recognizable way importantly "different" from what a white man might be in similar circumstances. Nat Turner comes eventually to hate all white men; but this emotion is not portrayed as an inherent racial characteristic. Rather, it is a response, a desperate and tragic one, to the social inhumanity of human slavery. A Negro as seen by William Styron is in no important or essential way different from a white man. Social conditions, not heredity and biology, set him apart. The walls of separateness are man-made.

Nobody, of course, knows "who" the real Nat Turner was. Except for a twenty-page "confession" dictated to a white lawyer and read before the trial court as evidence, there is little to go on. Not much additional information is to be found in the only book written about the Nat Turner Insurrection, William Sidney Drewry's *The Southampton Insurrection*, published in 1900 by a long-since defunct publishing house dedicated to defending the Confederate Heritage and racial segregation.

That Styron's Nat Turner is surely not the "real" Nat Turner is indisputable—in the sense that every human being is a unique personality, so that nobody could possibly reconstruct anything resembling the real Nat Turner without abundant evidence. In any event, *The Confessions of Nat Turner*, as the Southern historian C. Vann Woodward says, is "not inconsistent with anything historians know" and is "informed by a respect for history, a sure feeling for the period, and a deep and precise sense of place and time." This seems to me likewise indisputable.

Yet at least one other Southern historian, and a good one, has told me that he felt that Styron had committed a grievous historical mistake, in that he makes Nat Turner, a slave preacher on a Southside Virginia plantation thirty years before the [6/7] Civil War, think and talk exactly like a modern Black Power advocate; Styron's Nat Turner, he believes, sounds not like a slave, but like Stokely Carmichael. This is a severe criticism. Though I think it is not true, I confess that there are certain moments in Styron's novel in which one gets something of this feeling. Nat's reiterated insistence on the need of all Negroes to strike the Happy Darky pose when dealing with whites—"I replied in tones ingratiating, ministerial—the accommodating comic nigger"— tends to make the reader uncomfortably aware on such occasions of the author laboring to present the "Negro point of view." Doubtless Virginia slaves learned to do exactly what Nat says, but Nat's self-conscious theorizing about it would seem somewhat anachronistic. Similarly there are several passages in which Nat and other slaves talk at some length about the "smell" of white people—we glimpse the author waxing ironic about certain off-echoed white shibboleths. (Cf. Thomas Jefferson, in the *Notes on the State of Virginia:* "They secrete less by the kidneys, and more by the glands of the body, which gives them a very strong and disagreeable odor"—as if there were bathrooms available for the slaves at Monticello!)

But these instances are relatively few, and are unimportant. So also the argument that by making Nat Turner into a much more intellectual and reflective person, possessing a much more complex vocabulary than the real-life Nat Turner could probably have had, Styron violates the historicity of the situation. This seems to me to overlook the fact that Nat Turner could never have been a "representative" Negro slave of the 1830's. A "representative" slave could not possibly have led the Nat Turner Insurrection. Furthermore, it is not required or fitting that Styron's Nat Turner be "representative," "typical"; on the contrary, he *must be* an exaggeration. [7/8] His thoughts, his emotions, his language must be plausible only to the extent that the reader must feel a slave preacher in Southside Virginia in the year 1831, given the admitted uniqueness of Nat Turner's situation, *could* conceivably have thought and felt and spoken as he does. Besides, what is really involved here is the reader-writer relationship; for after all, is not the reader already engaged, by the mere fact of reading the book, in an "illogical" activity, inasmuch as he is being asked to imagine that what he is reading is the thoughts and words of a long-dead Negro preacher about whom almost nothing whatever is known? To echo Doctor Johnson, surely he that imagines this may imagine more. What matters is that Negro slaves (and Negro freedmen) *did* have to play roles in order to deal with the whites, and Nat's awareness of the role differs from that of most Negro slaves only in that it is made conscious and articulate. The truth is that Styron's Nat Turner is nothing more and nothing less than a tragic protagonist, and we ask representativeness and typicality of such a character no more than we ask that Sophocles show representative and typical Greeks of ancient Thebes in the *Oedipus Rex.*

III

"To a mind like mine, restless, inquisitive and observant, there was nothing that I saw or heard to which my attention was not directed."—Nat Turner, "Confession" (1831)

The Confessions of Nat Turner is told in the first person present. The language purports to be that of Nat, but not as spoken to anyone. Nat is thinking, "explaining" himself—to the reader, to "posterity," to himself. Though in point of strict logic this is quite impossible, it is an acceptable literary convention, much as the Shakespearean soliloquy is a literary convention.

The use of Nat as narrator affords Styron several advantages for telling his story. First of all, since Nat is a preacher, and deeply immersed in the language and style of the King James Version, we will accept from him a high rhetorical style which we might otherwise not permit, especially from a Negro slave in ante-bellum Virginia. More importantly, we soon become aware that when Nat actually talks, whether to whites or Negroes, his language is much more idiomatic and colloquial. The reader's awareness of the difference in language and voice, of the contrast between the manner in which Nat thinks or remembers and the way that he talks, is essential to the form and meaning of the novel. For not only must Nat, despite his learning, continue to play the role of humble, barely-literate slave before his betters, but the very fact of his intelligence and learning serves to isolate him all the more. The whites, no matter how sympathetic (and some *are* quite sympathetic), must by reason of time and place inevitably view Nat as an inferior, a freak—a slave, less than human, a bond-servant, one who surprisingly can read and write, but is still an inferior creature.

This of course is the true horror of slavery for Nat. He *is* considered less than a Man, and open, human contact with the whites is utterly forbidden him. The result is loneliness and rage. He comes to *hate* the whites because they have placed him and kept him in this position, and his rage is most keen at those times when he is being most patronized. For those whites who are kindest to him—in particular the girl Margaret Whitehead—inevitably do most to reinforce his consciousness of his inferior status, since they believe they are *not* patronizing him while still expecting him to remain safely in his place. In her romantic, naive way Margaret Whitehead [8/9] means only the best for Nat, and genuinely likes and admires him, yet she fails utterly to comprehend the nature of Nat's position and cannot for a moment grasp what torture is involved for Nat. In part her good intentions are only an aspect of her sentimentality; in being "frank," she condescends. Yet she *does* mean well; she does, in her own way, even love Nat, and before he dies Nat comes to realize that.

The contrast between what Nat thinks and can think, and what he must say and appear to be to whites whether of good intentions or bad, enforces the sense of isolation and loneliness that characterizes Nat's life. With the slaves, he does not have to pretend in the same way; in their company he can be himself as he cannot with white people. But his fellow bondsmen, being without his literacy and intelligence, cannot communicate with him either, especially after he has conceived his plan for a revolt and must bend every effort to manipulate and direct them toward his ends. Not even Hark, his closest friend and his chief lieutenant in the Insurrection he organizes, can understand or imagine what Nat is thinking or feeling. Thus Nat Turner as depicted by Styron is cut off from whites and blacks alike, and the violence of his protest is his Insurrection.

There is still another advantage in Styron's use of Nat as narrator. In the very contrast between the complex, subtle diction of Nat's thoughts, and the verbally crude language he must use to express himself aloud, there evolves a tension which grows more and more acute as the narrative develops and as Nat increasingly comes to comprehend the nature of his enforced isolation. The gulf between Nat's private self and his role in time and place builds up toward a point at which language itself will no longer suffice to provide order. There must then be the explosion of action, whereby language and deed are unified through violence—and the tragedy is accomplished.

Why did Nat Turner stage his Insurrection? This, after all, is the question that Styron sets out to answer by writing his novel. Because slavery was evil, and for a slave capable of a high degree of thought and feeling, intolerable—yes. Because Nat in particular had been promised his freedom by his first owner, only to be betrayed into renewed and hopeless bondage—yes. These are the topical answers. But because [9/10] William Styron is the fine novelist that he is, they are not the full or even the most important answer.

Nat Turner, a human being, rebels because he is deprived by his society of the right to love and be loved. I do not mean by this merely that Nat rebels because he is denied sexual fulfillment, though he is (save for one youthful homosexual experience Styron's Nat Turner is an ascetic, thereby providing psychological grounding for his messianic religious visions). The question is larger than that. Nat cannot love—physically or spiritually. The world he inhabits is such that at best he can expect from whites only pity, and at worst outright hatred, while from his fellow slaves he can expect only inarticulate admiration at best, and at worst envy and contempt. Thus he cannot *give* himself to anyone. No one wants him for what he is. For everyone, white and black, friend and foe, he must play a role. For his first owner, who educated him, he is a noble experiment, an object of benevolence, a salve to the slave-holding conscience. For Margaret Whitehead he is a sympathetic auditor to whom she can pour out her girlish fancies and exhibit her broad-mindedness. For his last owner he is a clever, valuable mechanic, a source of financial profit. For his fellow slaves he is a Leader, one who can plan and organize their revenge. Even to his fellow conspirator Hark, who does indeed love and admire him, he cannot be fully himself, for Hark's imagination and intelligence are too limited to enable him to share Nat's innermost thoughts. Denied, therefore, the right to give himself, to love, Nat can only hate, and the result is destruction.

What good, the interrogating lawyer asks Nat, did his Insurrection accomplish? The lawyer answers his own question:

"Here's what it got you, Reverend, if you'll pardon the crudity. It got you a pissy-assed record of total futility, the likes of which are hard to equal. Threescore white people slain in random butchery, yet the white people firmly holdin' the reins. Seventeen niggers hung, including you and old Hark there, nevermore to see the light of day. A dozen or more other nigger boys shipped out of an amiable way of life to Alabama, where you can bet your bottom dollar that in five years the whole pack of 'em will be dead of work and fever . . ."

"One hundred and thirty-one innocent niggers both slave and free cut down by the mob that roamed Southampton for a solid week, searching vengeance," the lawyer continues. And finally, the Nat Turner Insurrection will mean much more harshly repressive laws for the slaves:

". . . when the Legislature convenes in December they're goin' to pass laws that make the ones *extant* look like rules for a Sunday School picnic. They goin' to lock up the niggers in a black cellar and throw away the key." He paused, and I could sense him leaning close to me. "*Abolition*," he said in a voice like a whisper. "Reverend, single-handed you done more with your Christianity to assure the defeat of abolition than all the meddlin' and pryin' Quakers that ever set foot in Virginia put together. I reckon you didn't figure on that either?"

"No," I said, looking into his eyes, "if that be true. No."

There was and is no Happy Ending for the Nat Turner Insurrection. Styron knew this, and his novel shows it. It did not bring Negro slavery one whit closer to an end; if anything it retarded progress. The harsh Black Codes enacted throughout most of the South in the decades before the Civil War were due at least in part to the fear of servile revolt that the Nat Turner Insurrection had triggered. [10/11]

IV

"This attempt to separate truth from fiction has been exceedingly difficult, owing to the numerous misrepresentations and exaggerations which have grown up about the subject."—Drewry, *The Southampton Insurrection.*

In staging his Insurrection, Nat Turner believed that he was doing the Lord's bidding, as it had been revealed to him in a series of supernatural visions. Styron was careful to give these moments of revelation a solid psychological basis: they come always after Nat has gone without food for several days, and is weak and feverish. Yet *The Confessions of Nat Turner* is not primarily a psychological study. The limits of Nat's personality are not defined by the science of abnormal psychology. He represents, and is, the strong man in bondage, a human caught in a situation not originally of his making but ultimately requiring his total commitment. Faced with evil, Nat cannot hide from it, but his appalling attempt to right matters only brings defeat and greater suffering. In other words, it is a tragic situation, and the resolution of it is Tragedy.

The specific events of Nat Turner's life which impelled him toward the Southampton Insurrection are unknown. As novelist, Styron had therefore to give him a history, and it was the task of his creative imagination to make the personal history contain the meaning forced upon the subject by history. Thus Styron represents Nat during his youth as having been favored and set apart by his owner, and imbued with much hope and optimism. When instead of being freed he is sold into renewed bondage, Nat's sense of personal rage and helplessness forces him to take account of the wretched lot of his less-gifted fellow slaves, for whom he had once felt contempt and disdain. It is at this stage in his life that the conviction of religious mission comes upon him (in which respect Styron departs from the 1831 "Confession," for Nat Turner says there that from his childhood onward he had felt himself "intended for some great purpose"). Nat then begins mapping out his plan to lead an insurrection. The growth of the spirit of rebellion in Nat is charted by Styron with calculated deliberateness; the calm, carefully chosen language with which Nat tells his story only serves to intensify the sense of impending crisis and explosion.

In *The Southampton Insurrection* Drewry repeatedly expresses astonishment over the fact that Nat Turner himself had been treated with kindness by his owner, and had stated as much in his "Confession." Drewry insists that not only Nat but almost all the slaves in antebellum Virginia were kindly treated. This is proved, he declares, by the fact that so few slaves joined Turner. Most remained loyal to their owners, and some distinguished themselves by their bravery in defending their white families against the insurgents. Thus the only explanation Drewry can suggest for the Insurrection is that Abolitionist propaganda had inflamed the mind of Nat Turner, already crazed by a fanatical belief in his supernaturally prophetic destiny.

The true explanation, as is obvious, is that it was precisely *because* Nat Turner himself was treated well and had so distinguished himself in education and intelligence that he was prompted to lead his revolt; as Styron shows, his superior attainments and status only made more clear to him the hopelessness of servile bondage. Thus nothing could so madden Nat as the occasional expression of pity on the part of a white man or woman. In one of the finest episodes in the novel, Styron depicts Nat's sensations upon seeing a Northern-born wife of a planter break down and [11/12] weep at the sight of a particularly wretched and abject Negro. This unusual passage cannot be satisfactorily excerpted; suffice it to say that it is a masterful portrayal of complex emotions of hate, lust, love and shame contending within a man's heart. "I was filled with somber feelings that I was unable to banish," Nat remarks afterward, "deeply troubled that it was not a white person's abuse or scorn or even indifference which could ignite in me this murderous hatred but his pity, maybe even his tenderest moment of charity."

The point is that in this and numerous other instances, *The Confessions of Nat Turner* is a very *wise* book. Styron's understanding of his material is most impressive. When one thinks about it, the possibilities for melodrama and easy pathos inherent in the subject matter of this novel are very broad. What a less gifted novelist might have produced, one shudders to think. Styron, for example, barely mentions the period of ten weeks that actually elapsed between the suppression of the Insurrection and the capture of Nat Turner, during which Nat himself hid out in the woods and fields. Another novelist might have attempted to make this episode the occasion for a long, pseudo-philosophical meditation by Nat on the meaning of what has happened. But Styron lets Nat's thoughts about what he has done arise in the actual retelling of the story—in, that is, his confession—so that by the time the actual Insurrection itself takes place, what it means has been convincingly anticipated and prepared for us. The events of the Insurrection, therefore, bloody as they are, are not merely horrible; they are the motivated, terribly meaningful violence climaxing an intolerable situation.

One could make many other observations about William Styron's new novel. Most of them have already been made or will soon be; publication of the novel is obviously one of the more noteworthy literary events of recent years. Its importance lies simply in the fact that a dedicated and talented American novelist has written a book dealing with one of the most fateful and pressing concerns of our country's history, one that is by no means fully resolved. The topical relevance of this book is obvious—so much so that one need not comment on it.

This observation should be made, however: at a time when many influential critics have been saying that the day of the novel is done, Styron has produced a first-rate work of fiction while working very much within the traditional novel form. By bringing his intelligence and imagination to bear upon an important and deeply human situation, he has reinvigorated the form, and shown that it is still quite alive. He has thus given the lie to all those tired critics who have been going about lamenting the death of the novel, and proclaiming the superior merits of this or that substitute. It is time, therefore, that we cease bewailing the passing of the demigods of an earlier generation, and recognize the fact that with such writers as William Styron, Saul Bellow, and John Barth regularly producing prose fiction for us, we have no occasion for complaint. A novel as good as Styron's can hold its own in any company. [12]

Nat's Confessions

IRVING MALIN

THE OFFICIAL DOCUMENT WHICH OPENS THESE CONFESSIONS STATES THAT although the "late insurrection in Southampton has greatly excited the public mind," there need not be great fear: Nat Turner and his savage followers have been captured. T. R. Gray, the white lawyer, suggests, nevertheless, that from now on (i.e. November 5, 1831) slaveowners should rigidly enforce their laws and not permit another black fanatic to rise again. Although this public announcement is superficially calm and authoritative, it contains an underlying note of anxiety—the legal language barely hides the concern of Gray and the whites he represents.

Then Styron plunges us into the consciousness of Nat Turner. He describes a visionary scene of a promontory, a boat, and a white building:

Irving Malin, "Nat's Confessions," *Denver Quarterly* (Winter 1968). Reprinted by permission.

Now as I drift near the cape I raise my eyes to the promontory facing out upon the sea. There again I see what I know I will see, as always. In the sunlight the building stands white—stark white and serene against a blue and cloudless sky. It is square and formed of marble, like a temple, and is simply designed, possessing no columns or windows but rather, in place of them, recesses whose purpose I cannot imagine, flowing in a series of arches around its two visible sides.

The contrast between Nat's mysterious, peaceful vision and Gray's document is obvious. It represents the gulf between private insight (note the emphasis on "I see") and public cloudiness, between the real life of the mind and the lies of social intercourse. But it does more. It introduces images which recur throughout Nat's confessions: the temple, the voyage, and the light.

At first we feel that this introductory vision is a bit forced and artificial. Nat's words seem unnatural and "poetic," especially when he delights in piling adjective upon adjective. But as we *learn* to see through his eyes, we realize that we needlessly jumped to conclusions. [92/93] Our bias—how could *a slave* see such things?—inhibited us; we relinquish our ingrained prejudice and submit to his various "voices, dreams and recollections." We know Nat not as typical slave but as quirkly individual.

Why should he confess? Why does he feel no remorse for his rebellious deeds? What made him commit murder? Such questions are answered as Styron moves from Nat's present confinement to monstrous events of the past. Again he sacrifices simple chronology—the novel moves in apparently eternal and ahistorical time. Images recur; events reverberate; the unconsciousness takes command. (This is not to imply that Styron is overly Freudian—all the events we read about are never completely explained; the human spirit remains mysterious.)

Nat is an exile. Not only is he separated from his many white owners—from Turner, Travis, Moore, and the Reverend Eppes—he is also separated from his fellow Negroes because he can endure visions of ultimate freedom. There are several powerful passages which capture his exile from his black brothers: "For even now as a child I am contemptuous and aloof, filled with disdain for the black riffraff which dwells beyond the close perimeter of the big house—the faceless and nameless toilers who at daybreak vanish into the depths of the mill or into the fields beyond the woods, returning like shadows at sundown to occupy their cabins like so many chickens gone to weary roost." But as Nat ironically notes, he cannot really separate himself from these "faceless" others. He needs them for his rebellion. *They are all caught by color.* The more we study his ambivalence towards both races, the more we sense his heroic ability to give up such dualities and to fight violently for "wholeness."

Although Nat could find some degree of wholeness by means of sexual intercourse—his homosexual embrace of Willis is his only clear, joyous attempt—he is less interested in physical gratification than religious ecstasy. He resembles other prophets and revolutionaries—see, for example, *Young Man Luther*—who somehow transcend or transform their sexual longings until they marry divinity.

If there is any sense of wholeness in these confessions, it arises when Nat urges his followers to identify with the Hebrews. He thinks of himself as a prophet; he regards slavery as "Egyptian" bondage; he uses the biblical campaigns of Joshua to map his own ill-fated strategy. Thus he muses about taking Jerusalem (the Southern town as well as the biblical holy land): "Although Joshua's initial concept had been a planned ambush—luring the people out—it was through a [93/94] somewhat similar maneuver of capturing an empty town that he defeated the cities of Ai and Bethel—and this led after all to the ultimate downfall of Gideon and the Children of Israel's inheritance of the land of Canaan." He must carry out propitious, timeless designs.

But Nat's role as prophet-leader is in continual conflict with his repressed sexuality. He wants to destroy the "Egyptian" slave-masters; but he also wants to *rape* them. This great conflict is expressed when he kills Margaret, the soft, religious girl. Afraid to acknowledge that he loves her sexually and spiritually—that, indeed, he identifies more with her than with such murderous Negroes as Will or Sam—he must deface her. She is, ironically enough, the only white he ever murders. But Styron does not stop with this cruel and strangely sympathetic irony. He demonstrates that when Nat goes to his death, he finally "marries" Margaret: *"Yet I would have spared one. I would have spared her that showed me Him whose presence I had not fathomed or maybe never ever known."* This marriage is the source of Nat's almost-miraculous redemption; it enables him to acknowledge "Lord Jesus" once again. Perhaps he becomes "whole" conveniently here because Styron forces him to move from fragmentation to completion (in the way the confessions themselves move). The completed cycle, although "bright and fair," unsettles us: we respond as we do to the false resolutions of *Light in August*—a novel oddly similar to this one—by hoping that they are true but knowing that they are probably idle lies.

Styron allows his narrator to speak distinctively. Although we do not believe initially that Nat can employ such words as "murmuration," "ineffable," and "estuary," we submit gradually to his language. We realize that his heightened, "unnatural" words mirror his religious consciousness as he looks at himself in the cosmic drama. By employing an "alien" language for his narrator, Styron manages to achieve an odd majesty that introduces and symbolizes the "other" world in which Nat really dwells.

Because we become so used to this fantastic language, we are shocked when Nat must confine himself to slave clichés in order to communicate with the whites (and the blacks). After musing about the "fading echo of plunging hoofbeats and roosters crowing far off in the fields beyond Jerusalem," he says aloud to one jailkeeper: "Marse Kitchen . . . I'm hungry. Please. I wonder if you could fetch me a little bite to eat. Kindly please, young mastah." The contrast between the "fading echo" and the "little bite to eat" captures the two worlds (of spirit and body) Nat must bridge every day. [94/95]

Language is the center of Nat's consciousness. It is through words that he can lead his followers, convincing them of their noble mission. It is through words that he can understand the slave condition. It is through words that he can reach the Lord. In a crucial passage he tells us "So near to the white people, I absorb their language daily. I am a tireless eavesdropper, and their talk and comment, even their style of laughter, vibrates endlessly in my imagination." But he "absorbs" language most fully when he reads the Bible and *The Life and Death of Mr. Badman;* and the fact that he is a "man of the book" shapes the course of his life and death. As he waits to die, Nat naturally asks for the Bible from T. R. Gray so that he can again immerse himself in the flow of spiritual language and forget to address young "mastahs." It is fitting, therefore, that he intones passages from Revelation at the end; truth, we are made to believe, can be revealed—as well as hidden—by words.

There are recurring symbols to reinforce Nat's symbolist imagination; these help to endow reality with luminous meaning. I have already mentioned the temple, the voyage, and the light. Nat dreams of a white temple because he is obsessed by the idea of a "great, good place" in which he can be at ease with the Lord. He continually stresses *interiors:* the Turner library where he first discovers Bunyan's works; the shrine in the woods to which he retreats; the prison which confines him; the sanctuary of the Lord; the recesses of his own mind. Each place is somehow mythic. Here he is alone in the Turner great hall:

Dismantled of everything that could be moved—of crystal chandeliers and grandfather's clock, carpets and piano and sideboard and chairs—the cavernous room echoed with a tomblike roar to my sudden sneeze. The reverberation smashed from wall to wall with the sound of waterfalls, cataracts, then became silent.

The passage perfectly captures the magical sense of place and destiny. We can even say that the "tomb"-quality symbolizes the Southern cemetery which has buried slaves (and, unwittingly, slaveowners) for generations.

It is not surprising that Nat is concerned with the voyage. He wanders (as do the Hebrews) from place to place, seeking the one in which he can live forever. Throughout these confessions he stresses useless movement: slaves are traded from county to county; Hark [95/96] runs away into the woods, hoping to get North, but goes in circles; Hark is made to climb ladders he fears; all gestures are violent and erratic. While in jail Nat studies the random movements of a fly and wonders whether he resembles it: "Who could say that flies were not instead God's supreme outcasts, buzzing eternally between heaven and oblivion in a pure agony of mindless twitching, forced by instinct to dine off sweat and slime and offal, their very brainlessness an everlasting torment?" He wants, unlike the fly, to move steadily to the temple of *his choice.*

But here the light assumes great symbolic importance. Nat recognizes that the slaveowners have endowed light and dark with special qualities. Although he regards himself as enlightened and pure-in-heart, his masters study only his physical blackness and call it Satanic. The entire region, we can say, has falsely substituted symbol for reality so that it cannot see the true nature of things. It is surely ironic that Nat wants to achieve the white temple when he has been destroyed by whites. Going to his death, he hopes for the fair morning star of Jesus to lift him (and all men) out of his symbolically colored condition.

I have dwelt upon the three symbols at such length that I may have given the wrong impression. Nat's confessions do not take place only "in the country of the mind." They are rooted in the Southern soil. Such "elemental" things as horses, flies, mules, and sweet potatoes are married to abstractions of freedom and responsibility. It is this completely rendered marriage which finally accounts for the power of such passages as the following:

Others played mumbletypeg with rusty stolen jackknives, or simply drowsed in the sunlight, waking now and then to exchange their sorry belongings: a straw hat bartered for a homemade jew's harp, a lucky hairball from a cow's belly for a bag of pilfered snuff. I looked at them briefly, then returned to Job's racking, imponderable vision. But I found it difficult to concentrate, for although I had recovered somewhat from my fever I could not dislodge the sensation that I had somehow been utterly changed and now dwelt at a distance from myself, in a new world apart.

Nat vividly pictures the "sorry belongings" *and* the "new world apart." He sees them both clearly, trying desperately to reconcile them. He finally does when he dies. But his creator, Styron, manages to achieve the same reconciliation on every page of these remarkably unified and powerful confessions.[96]

A Note on the History

HERBERT APTHEKER

I HAVE BEEN ASKED TO COMMENT UPON WILLIAM STYRON'S NEW NOVEL from the viewpoint of a historian and to do so within very brief limits. The assumption behind this request is, I take it, that a historical novel should bear some resemblance to reality and that, indeed, through the creative act it may perhaps deepen the grasp of that reality; assumed, also, is the idea that each generation's historical novels tell at least as much about that generation as about the past they depict. At any rate, these are assumptions that I do hold.

The discrepancies between the realities of the Turner rebellion and Mr. Styron's rendition thereof are numerous, often quite serious, and form, I believe, a pattern amounting to consequential distortion— a distortion widespread in the United States at the present time.

The discrepancies stem both from omission and from either false or quite dubious affirmations. One of the very well-established facts concerning the slave, Nat Turner, is that he fled from his owner in the mid-1820s, stayed away about one month and then, moved by religious qualms, returned to the service of his earthly master. We know, too, that upon his return he was berated for this act by many of his fellow slaves—they "murmured against me," as he said. No hint of this is in the novel and this part of the actual *Confessions* is omitted from the fairly extensive quotations used within the book. Especially important here—and elsewhere in the *Confessions*, but not in the novel—is the evidence of the impact upon Turner of the anti-slavery feelings present among his peers.

Perhaps the most dramatic moment in the actual *Confessions* comes when Turner's court-appointed interrogator demands to know from him whether or not he sees now—in jail and in chains—that he was mistaken in what he had undertaken, especially since he is soon to be executed. The interrogator himself reports Turner's reply: "Was not Christ crucified?" This direct, simple and great flash is not in the novel.

Where Styron does quote from the *Confessions*, he is mainly accurate; where he is not, his omissions are instructive. He has Turner

Herbert Aptheker, "A Note on the History," *The Nation* (October 16, 1967). Reprinted by permission.

saying that "my mother strengthened me" in a belief in his special capacities; the actual *Confessions* has Turner saying "my *father and* mother"; the italicized words are omitted. A little further along, Styron quotes Turner as saying that "my mother" and others offered the opinion that with his marked "sense" he would develop into a difficult slave; but actually in the *Confessions* at this point, Turner said "my *grand*mother." At still another point, Styron has Turner say, "I never laid eyes on my grandmother"; Turner, however, not only "laid eyes" on her but remembered her rather well and specifically says that he "was much attached" to her.

In fact, while American slavery certainly dealt awful blows to the family structure of the slaves, it never fully destroyed it—in large part because of the women's ingenuity and resistance; and a rather unusual feature of Turner's life—well documented—is that he remembered both his father and his mother and a grandmother, too. The father— also a slave—fled and made good his escape (this fact is in the novel), but he did not do so before having left a clear mark on the memory and the consciousness of his son. All this may be in conflict with the so-called Moynihan thesis, but that is the fault of the thesis—not of Nat Turner! Indeed Turner tells us that his parents taught him how to read—though he adds that he has no memory of just how early this occurred. This may be contrasted with Styron's long and repeated references to the "experimental" benevolence of a master who under-took Turner's education.

There is repeated reference in the novel to the Great Dismal Swamp, lying in the southern part of Southampton County—locale of the revolt—and extending into North Carolina. Styron has Turner reject this as a possible refuge for the discontented slaves, insisting that to reach it and to survive therein was not possible. The historical fact is that the swamp *was* the refuge, for generations, of fugitive slaves, many of whom not only made it but survived in it, carved out a community life, resisted capture, and used it as a base from which to launch punitive expeditions against plantations. Indeed, many con-temporaries thought—when the Turner uprising became known—that it was in fact another such assault.

The Turner rebellion cannot be understood unless it is seen as the culminating blow of a particular period of [375/376] rising slave unrest. This was never absent in the South for long; it appeared and reappeared in waves and the Turner cataclysm was the highlight of one such wave which commenced about 1827 and played itself out in 1832. In the *Confessions* indeed, the interrogator specifically asked Turner about this and whether his outbreak was part of other such efforts just past and perhaps impending. Turner said no to this but added in a perfectly straightforward way that since he had been moved to rebel, others similarly situated might also similarly be moved.

An important feature of this marked unrest just before the Turner outbreak was that it resulted in the reinforcement of the already massive machinery of control—a machinery never mentioned in the novel but fundamental to an understanding of slave militancy and protest. Not only were new repressive laws passed—just *before* the outbreak—but additional police measures were taken at the specific requests of Southern state governors, including the Governor of Virginia. Furthermore, this reached the highest levels of government, so that at the orders of the Secretary of War, federal forts were reinforced in the spring of 1831 both in Louisiana and in Virginia—and Turner and his men rose up in August.

None of this fits a pattern which weaves through the novel—and has been stated by its author elsewhere quite explicitly—that the system of slavery had "dehumanized the slave and divested him of honor, moral responsibility and manhood," and that "the character (not characterization) of 'Sambo' . . . did in fact exist."* Certainly in the novel the bulk of the slaves are made into "Sambos" and I am afraid this *is* characterization; that it is not character is demonstrated by the actual record of the Negro people in the United States both during and after slavery.

Space permits only three more specific comments. The character of Will who plays so vital a part in this novel has no resemblance to anything history shows of the Will who participated in the Turner uprising. While Styron makes him a mad monster finally engaging in a power play with Turner, in the *Confessions* one meets Will through Turner's mouth only when—just before the launching of the attack— he found Will as a newcomer among the conspirators. Turner says only that he greeted Will and then asked him how he came to be there, and that Will replied that freedom was as valuable to him as to any man and that he meant to try for his; this, says Turner, was enough to put him in my confidence and Will joins the fray and loses his life. All this is to be contrasted with the lustful, sadistic, crazy figment that appears and reappears with filth in his mouth and blood on his hands through page after page of the book.

The novel emphasizes in many ways that Turner was able to recruit only about seventy or seventy-five men, while the county held over 7,000 slaves of whom many hundreds might physically have been expected to join. But the records of history—unlike the novel—do not show efforts at recruitment other than the original handful of six. It is these six who commence the uprising, in one parish of the county; and in a day and a half of desperate struggle actually are joined by perhaps seventy more. All things considered—including the system of control, the stakes involved, the apparent lack of prior preparation—

---

* These are Styron's words in his review of my *American Negro Slave Revolts*, in the *New York Review of Books*, September 26, 1963.

this argues for discontent so deep that scores would actually risk their lives in order to express it. The repeated references in the novel to masters arming loyal black slaves to resist the rebels are made up out of whole cloth; there is no evidence of this whatsoever and to believe it or offer it shows an utter misapprehension of the nature of American slavery.

Finally, one of the themes of the novel is the uniqueness of this event. Of course, each event is unique, but the idea here repeatedly offered is that the Turner uprising was "the only one sustained, effective revolt" in the history of United States slavery. This is not true. The actual fruition in uprising, in armed attack, occurred frequently in the United States on the part of slaves, from 1691 in Virginia to 1864 in Mississippi; this apart from uprisings in coffles and aboard domestic slave-trading vessels; the massive participation of runaway slaves in the Seminole Wars; and the persistent phenomenon of maroons everywhere in the slave region.

This novel reflects the author's belief that the views of slavery in the United States associated with the names of Frank Tannenbaum and Stanley Elkins—which, *in substance*, are those of U. B. Phillips, the classical apologist for plantation slavery—are valid. The data do not support such views, however; and whether "Sambo" is seen as the creation of racism or the creation of a latter-day socio-psychological environmentalism, the fact is that "Sambo" is a caricature and not a reality.

Nat Turner, however, *was* real; perhaps a novelist will yet come along to do justice to him, as, about thirty years ago, Arna Bontemps did justice to another great slave rebel, Gabriel, slave of Prosser, also of Virginia, in his book *Black Thunder*. [376]

The Failure of William Styron

ERNEST KAISER

THE PROBLEM OF CREATING NEGRO CHARACTERS IN HISTORICAL FICTION (within the veil and in slavery) is very difficult even for Negro writers. Margaret Walker's novel *Jubilee* (1967) written after talking with people who knew the early characters and steeping herself in the family history and Arna Bontemps's novel *Black Thunder* (1935, 1964)

Ernest Kaiser, "The Failure of William Styron," in *William Styron's Nat Turner: Ten Black Writers Respond,* edited by J. H. Clarke. Reprinted by permission of the author.

about Gabriel's Virginia slave insurrection of 1800 are just two examples of this. Du Bois in parts of *The Souls of Black Folk* and James Weldon Johnson's poem "O Black and Unknown Bards" succeed in evoking the slaves' emotional reaction to slavery. Historical fiction about Negroes that has real characters and is true to history is almost impossible even for the most understanding white writers in the racist, separatist United States.

There have been, nevertheless, a few novels dealing with Negro slave uprisings and unrest: Harriet Beecher Stowe's *Dred* (1856), G. P. R. James's *The Old Dominion* (1856), Mary Johnston's *Prisoners of Hope* (1899), Pauline C. Bouve's *The Shadows Before* (1899), A. Bontemps's *Black Thunder* (1935, 1964), Frances Gaither's *The Red Cock Crows* (1944) and Daniel Panger's *Ol' Prophet Nat* (1967). There are also the plays *Nat Turner* by Paul Peters (published in Edwin Seaver's *Cross Section*, 1944) and *Harpers Ferry: A Play about John Brown* (1967) by Barrie Stavis that have been [50/51] produced in our time. In addition to these works, there were Herbert Aptheker's *American Negro Slave Revolts* (1943) and his 1937 master's thesis at Columbia University (published as *Nat Turner's Slave Rebellion* in 1966) plus a long bibliography in each book. Lately we have had F. Roy Johnson's *The Nat Turner Slave Insurrection* (1966) and John Lofton's *Insurrection in South Carolina: The Turbulent World of Denmark Vesey* (1964). So this was the considerable body of writing available to William Styron when he, in the late 1940's, began to look for material on Nat Turner. Now Finkelstein, in his book *Existentialism and Alienation in American Literature* (1965), calls Styron a disciple of Faulkner and an existentialist whose fiction is technically good but more subjective and narrower in focus than Faulkner's and thus of less significance. Mike Newberry's review of Styron's third novel *Set This House on Fire* (1960) (the other two are *Lie Down in Darkness* [1951] and *The Long March* [1953]) in *Mainstream* (Sept. 1960) calls him a writer of overwhelming ability who is extremely pessimistic and without a moral point of view in this novel. John Howard Lawson, in an essay "Styron: Darkness and Fire in the Modern Novel" (*Mainstream*, Oct. 1960), disagrees somewhat with Newberry. He calls Styron a brilliant and sensitive writer who has moved from the Freudian, psychoanalytic frame of reference of his first novel to the existentialism of the third. Comparing his compassion to Chekhov's in the first novel and his social understanding to that of Thomas Wolfe's last novel *You Can't Go Home Again* in the third, Lawson says that Styron is angry at the evil of the social environment which destroys people but also feels that the trouble is mystical and hidden in the soul. This conflict, he says, creates faults in his writing. Styron, Lawson continues, must face the fact that he is abetting in his writing the corruption of life and art which he passionately opposes and is thus another promising American talent deteriorating like

Mailer, James Jones, and others. I would add that *Set This House on Fire* is obviously a very [51/52] heavily autobiographical novel like the novels of Thomas Wolfe. Lawson comments that this third book has anti-Italian, anti-Semitic, and anti-Negro stereotypes. Cass (Styron), the central character in the novel, speaks of his nightmares being tied up with Negroes. His guilt, says Lawson, is specifically related to his feeling as a white southerner that he has participated in shameful treatment of Negroes.

But when Styron comes to write his fourth novel *The Confessions of Nat Turner* (1967) which has haunted him since 1948, his talent really deteriorates and goes downhill as Lawson had noted earlier. His social view, instead of developing, has remained where it was in his third novel or even gone backward. He has read all of the works on Nat Turner and slave rebellions and rejected them. Herbert Aptheker points out in a footnote to his article-review of Styron's *The Confessions* ("Styron-Turner and Nat Turner: Myth and Truth," *Political Affairs*, Oct. 1967) that Styron borrowed a few years ago the manuscript of his master's thesis written in 1936 and published as *Nat Turner's Slave Rebellion* in 1966. It was kept several months and then returned. In a review of Aptheker's *American Negro Slave Revolts* and Stanley M. Elkins's *Slavery*, Styron attacks Aptheker's book, retitles and reduces it to *Signs of Slave Unrest* and the U.S. slaves' organized rebellion to very little. But he praises highly the Elkins book describing the dehumanized, Sambo slave (*New York Review of Books*, Sept. 26, 1963).

In his article "This Quiet Dust" (*Harper's*, Apr. 1965) which was reprinted in the book *Best Magazine Articles 1966*, Styron says that he distrusts any easy generalizations about the South by white sociologists, Negro playwrights, southern politicians, and northern editors since his own "knowledge" of Negroes as a southern youth was gained at a distance through folklore and hearsay. (Why Negro playwrights, who are on the other side of the racial fence, should be thrown in is beyond me.) Then he proceeds to project his [52/53] own generalization that although Ralph Ellison is right about the constant preoccupation of southern whites with Negroes, perpetual sexual tension between Negroes and whites in the South is greatly exaggerated, so effective have been the segregation laws from the 1890's to the present. And this assertion is based solely on his own experiences. But the sociologists, playwrights, and editors (never mind the southern politicians) have better information than mere personal experience on which to base their generalizations. The corollary of Styron's idea of little interracial sex in the South is the mythology that white women are put on pedestals by white men in the South. Harry Golden, a northern liberal now living in the South, believes this along with Styron. He restates the myth in his book *Mr. Kennedy and the Negroes* (1964). Styron admits that there was enormous interracial sex during slavery. (The southerner Ross Lockridge Jr.'s mammoth historical novel *Raintree County* [1948] has the white wife become insane when the white slaver moves his Negro woman into the same house with her.) The article "The Plight of Southern White Women" (*Ebony*, Nov. 1957) says that southern women, told that they were nice ladies by the men, were kept home off juries, away from high-paying jobs and voting booths—out of competition. Also that white women were enslaved along with the Negroes in the South and that the freedom of these two groups has always run closely parallel; that white women were used as a shield behind which white men committed cowardly acts of violence against Negroes; and that southern white women hate playing the roles of Scarlett O'Haras.

Styron's writing of *The Confessions*, he says further in "This Quiet Dust," is an attempt to *know* the Negro. And yet, he rejects here, as he has elsewhere, Aptheker's documented books on American Negro slave revolts when he states baldly that in 250 years of slavery, there were no uprisings, plots or rebellions except those led by Gabriel Prosser in Virginia in 1800, Denmark Vesey in South Carolina in [53/54] 1822 and Nat Turner in Virginia in 1831. He again accepts wholeheartedly the fraudulent and untenable thesis of Frank Tannenbaum and Stanley M. Elkins (see my refutation in an essay in *Freedomways*, Fall 1967) that American slavery was so oppressive, despotic and emasculating psychologically that revolt was impossible and Negroes could only be Sambos.

The problems of Negro-white relations in the South that come up in Styron's essay reveal the level of his understanding of the Negro problem: he doubts that there are sexual relations to any degree between the races in the segregated South; he explains the question of Nat Turner's intelligence, precocity, and apprehension; he states boldly that Americans believe that the slave system, though morally wrong, was conducted with such charity and restraint that insurrection and murder were unthinkable; he has a constant preoccupation with "knowing" Negroes; and he seems to relish the horrible details of the whites' bestiality toward Negroes. Examples of bestial descriptions in his article are his unnecessary, gruesome explanation that the doctors skinned Nat Turner's dead body, after he was hanged along with 17 other Negroes, and made grease of his flesh; and the lurid details in his novel of the killings of whites by Negroes.

Styron, after having read Aptheker's master's thesis on Nat Turner, puts all the ideas that Aptheker refuted in his essay. Styron says that the greedy cultivation of tobacco caused the economic depression in Tidewater Virginia before 1831; Aptheker says that the fall in the price of cotton caused the disaster. Styron largely accepts W. S. Drewry's book *The Southampton Insurrection* (1900); Aptheker rejects it as untruthful; Styron says that stringent codes for policing slaves followed the revolt; Aptheker says that many of these stringent codes preceded Nat's revolt. Styron says that Virginia was edging close to emancipation; Aptheker's book says that there never was in the South a flourishing emancipation movement. Nat Turner's rebellion, in which many whites were killed, says Styron further in this essay, was an act of futility. [54/55] It caused about 200 Negroes to be tortured and killed and obviously should never have taken place at all. Aptheker shows that Nat Turner's revolt was the culminating blow of a period of rising slave unrest which began about 1827 and played itself out in 1832; it brought historic social forces to a head. The revolt blew off the lid which the slavocracy had clamped down upon the press and the rostrums of debate and lecture. From then on until the Civil War, continues Aptheker, there was a confrontation of Abolitionists and slavocrats, of North and South. Styron also says that today in southeast Virginia Negroes are living amiably with white paternalism which includes restricting Negroes from owning new-model Buicks or their children from going to school with whites. This is a total lie. I am a native of that part of Virginia and have scores of relatives there who not only carry on large-scale, mechanized farming and own and drive big automobiles if they are able to; they also are activists in the NAACP chapters there, and there have been court suits all over the area in the past several years which have resulted in some desegregation of the public schools in that area. Styron should look at the quarterly *Race Relations Law Reporter* (published at Vanderbilt University School of Law, Nashville, Tenn.) for the last eight years and see the scores of Virginia desegregation cases there.

It is clear from this essay's whole approach to and attitude toward Negroes that Styron has no equipment either factually or psychologically to write a novel about Nat Turner or any other Negro for that matter. His essay is a 20- or 30-year throwback to the racism and paternalism of the 1930's and 1940's. In the author's note in *The Confessions,* Styron says Nat Turner's rebellion was the only effective, sustained revolt in the annals of American Negro slavery. That makes Aptheker's 409-page doctoral dissertation at Columbia University, published as the book *American Negro Slave Revolts* in 1943 and twice since, just a pack of lies! Styron says further in his review of Aptheker's *American Negro Slave* [55/56] *Revolts* mentioned above that the view of the slave as in revolt against slavery is a part of the white man's fantasy. On the contrary, his view of the slaves as Sambos is but a common variety of southern racist fantasy based on ignorance and buttressed by Tannenbaum and Elkins's false thesis while the revolt thesis is based on solid historical research by Aptheker and many others, Negro and white.

He also says further in his note that his novel is not so much an historical novel as it is a meditation on history. It is a meditation all right and that of an unreconstructed southern racist.

He says in his essay that the novel has a psychoanalytical empha-

sis upon Nat's so-called tormented relationship with his father following psychoanalyst Erik Erikson's book *Young Man Luther*. Aptheker's
article-review of *The Confessions* shows that while Styron quotes from
Turner's *Confessions*, he also twists certain facts to suit his Freudian
thesis in the novel. In many other cases, says Aptheker, he falsifies the
known facts of Nat Turner's history, and Styron admits in the author's
note that he has allowed himself the utmost freedom of imagination in
reconstructing Turner's early life and the motivations for the revolt.
The unspeakable arrogance of this young southern writer daring to set
down his own personal view of Nat's life as from inside Nat Turner in
slavery! Instead of trying to get the true feeling of the Negroes of the
period as Howard Fast did in *Freedom Road* (to say nothing of
Margaret Walker's and Arna Bontemps's hard historical work in *Jubilee* and *Black Thunder* respectively), Styron, who doesn't really know
the Negroes living in Virginia today, deigns to speak personally for the
slaves.

As Lawson has pointed out, Styron's early novels had only anti-
Negro stereotypes. But *The Confessions* is infinitely worse. All of the
Negro stereotypes are here: the filthy, racist language of American
whites: nigger, nigger, nigger on almost every page, black toadeater,
darky, pickininny, ginger-colored Negro with thick lips. He puts in over
and over the [56/57] Negro's black color: the white woman's fingers
upon the Negro's black arm. Aptheker's article-review also gives many
other examples of Styron's despicable, racist descriptions of Negroes.
The language of *The Confessions* equals in its vile racist filth that
found in J. C. Furnas's *Goodbye to Uncle Tom* (1956) which I pil-
loried in *Freedomways*, Spring 1961. Other stereotypes in the novel are
the servile, cringing slave, the slave who loves his slave-master, the
slave craving a white woman and the main stereotype which the whole
book points up: the slave who confesses the details of the plot or revolt
against slavery for freedom to a white man when caught like a child
who has done something wrong against his parents. The ignorant
Styron even has the temerity to attempt to explain how much hatred
Negroes have for the white man and why. His ignorance and arrogance know no bounds. Like every white southerner, Styron has to
know the Negro, as he says in "This Quiet Dust," although he really
knows nothing and wants to find out nothing of Negro life and history.

This novel is a witches' brew of Freudian psychology, Elkins's
"Sambo" thesis on slavery and Styron's vile racist imagination that
makes especially Will and Nat Turner animals or monsters. Styron has
to rationalize the oppression of Negroes in one way or another. Elkins
says that the American slave system was so oppressive that Negroes
had to be Sambos and Freud says that there were dark, ineradicable,
primitive drives or instincts in Turner that made him a beast. Aptheker
says in his article-review that the fictional image of the Dunning school
of history was *The Clansman, Gone with the Wind* of the U. B.

Phillips school, and William Styron's *The Confessions of Nat Turner* of the Elkins school. Having rejected the Negro people's history, Styron cannot see Turner as the hero he was and as the Negro people see him; as a slave who led a heroic rebellion against the dehumanization of chattel slavery. This novel makes Styron look like a Rip Van Winkle who has slept through the Negro [57/58] people's twelve-year freedom struggle of the 1950's and 1960's.

But just as Michael Harrington, Jason Epstein, Norman Podhoretz and other reviewers seized upon Elkins's *Slavery* as a rationale of the Negro slave as a "Sambo" personality thus relieving themselves of the great guilt of American Negro chattel slavery; so, as Aptheker has pointed out in his article-review, reviewers of Styron's *The Confessions* have seized upon this book as pointing up the current Negro ghetto uprising as led by mad Negroes, as futile, stupid rebellions which should be put down ruthlessly. Critics Elizabeth Hardwick and Norman Podhoretz have written about the decline of book reviewing in the U.S. into advertising blurbs. Historian Christopher Lasch, in *The New Radicalism in America* (1965), says that journalism has degenerated into public relations, advertising and propaganda. An outstanding literary critic, Stanley Edgar Hyman, in *Standards: A Chronicle of Books for Our Time* (1966), talks about truth as unfashionable in literary journalism. Harry Golden, in an essay in the "What I Have Learned" series (*Saturday Review*, June 17, 1967) states that "journalists are writers who have no education and disdain looking up words in dictionaries or subjects in encyclopedias, relying on their memories." Certainly the decline of book reviewing and the ignorance of journalists are sharply pointed up by the near unanimity of high brow, middle brow, low brow, liberal and conservative reviewers in praising Styron's novel. But they all, with no research behind the novel or historical knowledge of the South in the 1820's and 1830's, seem to be basically approving of the novel's thesis rather than really reviewing the historical novel which they were not equipped to do. As Thomas Lask says in a review of Kenneth Tynan's *Tynan Right and Left* (*New York Times*, Dec. 12, 1967), under the cover of esthetics these reviewers are condemning what they hate in politics or approving what they like.

Newsweek (Oct. 16, 1967) in a cover story called *The* [58/59] *Confessions* an act of revelation to a whole society. Wilfrid Sheed, the book review editor of *Commonweal*, in a front page review in *The New York Times Book Review* (Oct. 8, 1967), called the novel artificial but knowing no history he could only accept Styron's view of history; Eliot Fremont-Smith, in a two-part review in the *New York Times* (Oct. 3–4, 1967), also knowing nothing of Negro history, goes all out. He calls the book a triumph, a rare book that shows us our American past, our present, ourselves, compelling, convincing, a rich and powerful novel. The *New Republic's* reviewer was C. Vann Woodward, a historian who has already swallowed Elkins's thesis whole and uncritically in "The Anti-Slavery Myth" (*American Scholar,* Spring 1962). In the Oct. 7, 1967, issue, Woodward repeats the lie that Nat's rebellion was the only slave rebellion of consequence in the largest slave society in the nineteenth century world as well as the Elkins thesis that Negro slaves were servile Sambos. Accepting and repeating all of Styron's slave stereotypes, he says that the novel shows a respect for history and has a sure feeling for Nat's period. Woodward calls the novel the most profound fictional treatment of slavery in our literature enbracing all the subtleties and ambivalences of race in the South.

In *The Nation* (Oct. 16, 1967), the reviewer Shaun O'Connell, a young English teacher at the University of Massachusetts, is completely overwhelmed by Styron's novel. Obviously knowing nothing of Negro history, O'Connell accepts all of Styron's false psychological twistings and all of his invented "facts" about Turner's life as valid and sensible. He thinks that Styron, a twentieth century southerner, has really gotten inside a nineteenth century Negro slave and portrayed him accurately. He says that Styron has improved his craft and modulated his style; that *The Confessions* is the best of his novels. He also calls Styron's "This Quiet Dust" an important essay. And all of this is called fiction criticism by *The Nation* editor's note. *The Nation* does carry in [59/60] the same Oct. 16th issue "A Note on the History" by Herbert Aptheker which says more briefly what Aptheker spells out in his *Political Affairs* (Oct. 1967) article-review on the novel. And that is plenty as we have seen above. We will only say here that Aptheker again nails the lie repeated by the historian Woodward and Styron that the Nat Turner revolt was the only sustained U.S. Negro slave revolt, armed attack or uprising. He says that there were slave uprisings from 1691 in Virginia to 1864 in Mississippi. He also points out that Styron lyingly makes a monster of Will who in reality was not like that at all.

Other reviewers, with no knowledge, just accepted the novel as accurate. *The National Observer* (Oct. 9, 1967) headed the review "Fiction Vivifies the Facts of a Tidewater Tale." Poppy Cannon White, in a review of the book in her column in the Negro newspaper *New York Amsterdam News* (Nov. 25, 1967) says that *The Confessions* seems persuasive, historically accurate, and is a remarkable document. She says that the hero of the novel looks, sounds, and feels like truth, but she finds Turner portrayed as a madman hard to take. The book wallows in violence, she says, but she thinks of the violence as she thinks of Truman Capote's nonfiction, violent novel about multiple murder *In Cold Blood* (1965): these are books, she says, about tortured minds and dark recesses of the spirit. Mrs. White disagrees about Nat Turner's revolt being the only one; she says that there were hundreds of revolts. In a later column (Dec. 9, 1967) devoted to *The Confessions,* she says that she received a lot of mail about her previous column reviewing the novel; that some letters agreed and some disagreed with her statement that Nat's revolt wasn't the only sustained revolt in American slavery. Mrs. White then contrasts *The Confessions* and other slave novels with another new novel, Harold Courlander's *The African,* a book, she says, concerned with a man, with real people who have a past and a culture. *Time* magazine called the book a new peak in the literature of the South. *Harper's* called it a masterpiece of storytelling. The [60/61] historian Arthur Schlesinger, Jr., called the book in *Vogue* the finest American novel published in many years. Philip Rahv, in *New York Review of Books,* called it a first-rate novel . . . the best by an American writer that has appeared in some years. Edmund Fuller in the *Wall Street Journal* said that Styron without doubt is the foremost writer of his generation in American fiction. *Commentary* magazine said it is a superb novel with immense understanding. The *Los Angeles Times* called it one of the great novels by an American author in this century.

One of the mostly southern liberals working for the Southern Regional Council reviewed the novel in *New South* (Fall 1967), the Council's magazine. He found the novel richly deserving of its critical acclaim since it is an important work of fiction dealing successfully with race and the whole historical setting of slavery, one of the more important themes in American life. The reviewer defends the novel against the two critical reviews of the novel that he had seen: (1) the mild criticism of Wilfrid Sheed in *The New York Times Book Review* who doubts the ability of a twentieth century white southerner like Styron to speak from the consciousness of a nineteenth century black slave and also finds technical faults in the novel; (2) H. Aptheker's charges in *The Nation* that the novel has all the rationalizations of slavery plus the slave stereotypes. The *New South* reviewer again drags out the Elkins thesis and compares the Negro slaves to the Jews in the Nazi concentration camps. But this has been refuted. (See my essay in *Freedomways,* Fall 1967). He also sidesteps Aptheker's charge of historical inaccuracy; says the novel's main achievement is its showing of the horror and cruelty of slavery. He agrees with other reviewers when they seized upon this novel and used it as an argument against today's riots. They also say that Nat's revolt prevented Virginia from solving its slavery problem. He thinks that the real moral issue today as in history is not the violence but the cause for violence.

Even James Baldwin, Styron's friend, chimes in by saying [61/62] Styron has begun the common history—ours. And the veteran biographical and historical novelist Irving Stone, deploring the decline of what he calls the "great school of historical novelists" (*New York Times,* Jan. 19, 1968), says that *The Confessions* is the one recent historical novel that impressed him. Robert Coles, a Harvard psychiatrist, the author of the book *Children of Crisis* (1967) and the latest self-styled white "authority" on Negroes, finds Styron's psychological and historical explanations of Nat Turner completely satisfying and valid in his long, six-page review in *Partisan Review* (Winter 1968). Another high-brow magazine *Dissent* (Jan.–Feb. 1968), in its review by James MacPherson, is also favorable and uncritical in its approach to Styron's novel. The historian Martin Duberman, in a very long, uncritical, glowing review in the *Village Voice* (Dec. 14, 1967), swallows Styron's novel hook, line and sinker. Agreeing with Styron that the Elkins "Sambo" thesis is the most valid explanation of American slavery, Duberman thinks that the novel is very accurate history as well.

There were some dissenting reviews. Herbert Aptheker, an authority on Negro history and especially slave revolts, in addition to the short piece in *The Nation*, wrote a devastatingly critical article-review in *Political Affairs* (Oct. 1967) which we have mentioned several times. Richard Greenleaf's review of the novel in *The Worker* (Oct. 8, 1967) called it anti-Negro and a libel on Nat Turner. Another *New York Amsterdam News* columnist Gertrude Wilson wrote on Oct. 21, 1967, that Styron had done a good job in *The Confessions* and that she hoped that her column readers would read the novel; also that the novel showed that white people could understand what it is like to be black. Later she had second thoughts. In her Dec. 30, 1967, column titled "Styron's Folly," she asked: why is the book such a success among whites? She concludes that the book is so popular with whites because it proves that if Negroes retaliate against injustice by violence, they will be quelled by violence. The book also gives, she says, the blessing of history for continued violence against Negroes. Mrs. Wilson also found in Howard H. Meyer's recent biography of Thomas W. Higginson that Nat had a slave wife (with a different master from his) whom he couldn't protect at all in slavery. (There is a brief account of Nat's wife in Samuel Warner's [62/63] *The Authentic and Impartial Narrative of the Tragical Scene of the Twenty-Second of August, 1831* [1831] as well as an article on Nat Turner's family and descendants in the *Negro History Bulletin* [Mar. 1955].) She concludes that Styron's stereotyped picture of Nat as a celibate, as one of repressed lusts who is violently aroused by a sweet young white girl, is a lie. This book is history twisted, she says, to fit the sexual fantasies of our own times.

As anyone who has read the Negro critic Albert Murray's essay "Something Different, Something More" (in Herbert Hill's *Anger and Beyond,* 1966) knows, he denounces social fiction by Negro writers which attacks our system and society and takes refuge in the art-as-mostly-technique approach to creative writing. So Murray, familiar with Styron's considerable technique in his first three novels, hoped that Styron, a so-called reconstructed southerner, would bring his fourth novel off even though he had picked a difficult subject for a white American novelist. But Murray is compelled to put *The Confessions* down and he does this in a brilliant essay-review (*The New*

Leader, Dec. 4, 1967). He says that Styron failed to identify intimately with Nat Turner; that his Turner is one whom many white people will accept at a safe distance but not the hero with whom Negroes identify. Accusing Styron of building a weak Turner character according to the Elkins Sambo thesis and Freudian castration (he also calls this pro-slavery image Marxist, which it isn't), he says that Styron has added a neo-Reichean hypothesis about the correlation between sex repression and revolutionary leadership; between Negro freedom from slavery and sexual desire for a white woman. Styron, he says, never realized that the Negro conception of Nat Turner as an epic hero, a special, dedicated breed of man who had given his last full measure of devotion to liberation and dignity was already geared to the dynamics of rituals and myth and hence to literature. Criticizing Styron for ignoring the many slave revolts, Murray accuses Elkins of making slavery overwhelming for Negroes but letting such a monstrous system have little effect on the whites who operated it. Murray uses Kenneth Stampp's *The Peculiar Institution* (1956) to [63/64] document the great impact of the Nat Turner and other slave revolts on the slavocracy. When Styron has Nat Turner say that Negroes were bragging in brass when they said that they would kill whites, Murray replies that Negroes fought in the Revolutionary War, the War of 1812 and very bravely a little later against their Confederate slave masters in the Civil War. Describing the characters Nat Turner in *The Confessions* and the female Peyton in *Lie Down in Darkness* as having a lot of Styron's own personality in them, Murray says that if white writers want to think Negro and create Negro characters, they must be able to sing the spirituals and/or swing the blues, or, in other words, know the rugged facts and the psychological subtleties and nuances of Negro life.

Loyle Hairston did a fine critical essay-review of the novel for *Freedomways* (Winter 1968). Cecil M. Brown, a perceptive Negro critic, also did a brilliant, analytical job on Styron in his long review in *Negro Digest* (February 1968). And there are two long critical reviews of *The Confessions* by the Negro psychologist Lloyd T. Delany and the sociologist Gerald M. Platt in the new magazine *Psychology Today* (January 1968). Platt accepts some of the false "facts" in Styron's novel and Delany calls the book a valiant and honest attempt to view the horrible institution of slavery. But Delany also calls the book Styron's confessions which are historically inaccurate, stereotyped and racist. Both Delany and Platt say that the novel presents the revolt in a vacuum with no historical context; but most important, they both show clearly and in great detail that the novel is psychologically false through and through in terms of human motivation and psychological theory and is morally wrong as well.

This novel is a good example of the absurdity of the separation of art and politics, art and sociology. This separation is nourished and encouraged by all liberal magazines such as *The New Republic, The Nation, Commentary, New York Review of Books, Dissent, Commonweal, The New Leader, The Progressive, The Reporter* and others [64/65]—magazines that fight for progressive social policies and measures but take a stand-pat, art-for-art's-sake approach to fiction, plays, cinema, music and painting. Styron has lived through twelve years of the Negro social revolution and struggle in the U.S., but this upheaval has not touched him as a novelist. He wrote *The Confessions* just as he would have written it in 1948. His writing is impervious to Negro social change and struggle and to the facts of Negro history. His book is a throwback to the racist writing of the 1930's and 1940's. The decline in the writing of Styron, Ellison and many other American novelists is directly traceable to this tragic American separation of art and politics, art and sociology—as John Howard Lawson pointed out in his essay on Styron (*Mainstream*, Oct. 1960).

Sidney Finkelstein calls truthful fiction (in his book *Existentialism and Alienation* and in a review of two of Philip Stevenson's novels [*Political Affairs*, Oct. 1962]) those novels and short stories that take up the central problem of American life: that is, the conflict between the democratic principles on which the nation was founded and the forces of violence against the working people—a conflict which has been continuous throughout American history. Novelists like Stevenson, Albert Maltz, and Phillip Bonosky are attempting to help humanize U.S. human relations and extend democracy to the dispossessed even if this interferes with property and profits. This struggle, says Finkelstein further, for a more rational, realistic and truthful view of life, which includes the fight for Negro equality and rights, is a struggle for humanization of nature and social relations against alienation. The artists who depict this many-sided struggle of alienated human beings moving toward more humanization are a force in the humanization of reality. But, as Finkelstein points out, when the writers themselves are alienated and psychologically sick, as in Styron's case, their view of society and of other human beings is colored by their subjective, Freudian views of their own problems and the effect of their art is further alienation rather than humanization. [65]

Nat Turner Revisited

RICHARD GILMAN

PUBLISHING HISTORY HAS TO BE MADE BEFORE LITERARY HISTORY CAN
begin, but one doesn't necessarily follow on the other. It would surely
have been better for William Styron, as an artist, had he been less well
known, less professionally involved in great publishing expectations,
when *The Confessions of Nat Turner* made its appearance among
us. Had he been freer from the institutional condition of so many
well-known American writers, free from their imposed fate as at least
nominal trustees of literary values which have almost no public literary
uses, only ideological, psychic and commercial ones, he might have had
the detachment to see his book more nearly for what it is and his possibilities as a novelist might thereby have been better served. For Styron
is a talented writer, but one whose ambitions have always exceeded his
gifts; and the great acclaim for *Nat Turner*, which is a less than noteworthy literary accomplishment, can only do him injury, I think.

That acclaim can do injury is no new theme in American cultural
history. But as personality continues to diminish the area of impersonal
values, in art as well as politics, we need to go on reminding ourselves
of it. We need, too, to go on reminding ourselves of how culture is
becoming more and more a question of power, not of values, or rather
of how power, regarded as the supreme value, has made culture increasingly a pragmatic affair. The relevance of this to *Nat Turner*, is
that the book was immediately swept up into areas of power and
influence wholly outside its existence as literature, and, even more
crucially, before such existence could even be brought into question.

The book had a life laid out for it in advance. It was expected to
be "big," a "major achievement," an inspiriting national document, a
quasi-religious *act*. And it has been fought over in those terms. It is all
part, I think, of the curious overvaluation of literature in an age which
for the most part dislikes literature and makes less and less effort to
find out what it is. Styron is an unwitting accomplice in this double
game. Though one can be certain he didn't set out coldly and with
calculation to write a "great" book that would traduce literature, he

Richard Gilman, "Nat Turner Revisited," *The New Republic* (April 27,
1968). Reprinted by permission of The New Republic. © 1968 Harrison-Blaine
of New Jersey, Inc.

was in a fine position to do it. His whole career has indicated that he is the kind of writer for whom largeness of "subject" is a guarantor of literary achievement, and for whom the taking of literary risk—sans imposing subject, sans reliance on the tradition, sans extraliterary alliances—the dangerous effort to fashion new instrumentalities of consciousness, has never played a measurable role.

His books have therefore been "big," but he has never advanced the art of fiction or even vigorously helped sustain it, while never, it also has to be said, corrupting it either. But I think that with a "subject" such as Nat Turner, an imaginative occasion or proposal of that kind, you either advance fictional art or set it back. It wasn't the same in this case for Styron as with *Lie Down in Darkness,* a novel which did little more than perpetuate a convention—that of doomed, neurotic Southern passion—though it did it rather well; if you are going to try to imagine yourself into an alien phenomenon, into a new tradition, so to speak, then you are going to have to find new *literary* means. You aren't going to get away, from the judgment of literature at least (Styron is of course more than in the clear before other, less rigorous tribunals), on the plea of having done something socially significant.

This "important" act has been, it's clear, the validation for white readers (the book has also, of course, a handful of Negro admirers) not so much of any particular attitude toward Negroes but of our *seriousness* towards them, of the fact, rather, that we can be serious about them, can use our skills and imaginative prowess to try to understand what it might be like to be black, to live under slavery, to be *the other.* And if Styron had succeeded in this attempt at understanding, this miraculous transposition, then the opposition to the book on the ground of its historical inaccuracy—the heart of the widespread Negro protest against it—would seem to have little standing. But I don't think Styron has succeeded, which is why although I sympathize with the Negro protest and believe most of it more than understandable, I think it wrongly directed, aimed at a symptom rather than a cause.

For *Nat Turner* seems to me a mediocre novel, not a beautiful or even well-written work of fiction which happens to contain historical inaccuracies or perversions of [23/24] historical truth. And it is just the wide acceptance by Negro critics of the book of the prevailing white literary opinion, the judgment that *Nat Turner* is triumphant precisely as literature (for Negroes a corollary judgment follows: that literature can be a devilish weapon) that so seriously undermines the efficacy if not the justice of their protest.

For if the book is a literary triumph, then its conquest is all that matters; nobody not directly affected by them is going to care very much about historical inaccuracies, since isn't art always its own justification and what in any case can we really know about history except by way of efforts like Styron's? A literary triumph, power, the juggernaut of success; and something more: the remaining prestige of literature, a prestige that has almost nothing to do any longer with intrinsic virtue or efficacy but is like the emanation from a titular monarch in a nostalgic parliamentary democracy. All this, and the opaque, mysterious outlines of history dissolve so that the past comes into line with what some of us want to feel now.

That is to say, the prestige of literature has been used to get around history's obduracy, its refusal to allow its *facts* to constitute meaning; but the imagination, which only respects facts as grist, remains insouciant. In this way the historical Nat Turner can be used by whites, as the protagonist of a new drama, which may or may not be patronizing to Negroes or subversive of their truth but is in any case comforting to us. At the same time, because literature's prestige is felt by Negroes, too, it becomes the instigation for a violent effort to repudiate Styron's newly shaped myth and put another in its place: that of Nat Turner's nobility, grandeur, his representative existence as spearhead of Negro consciousness, as exemplar of clear, clean, un-deviating urgency towards liberation. It is as though another novel, by someone with Styron's reputed skill of course, in which Nat Turner is portrayed heroically, self-confidently, in line with present-day Negro ideas about what they themselves are, or should be, is what is pain-fully craved.

But we cannot tree history through literature and bring it down to go on any leash; we can't know *the* truth about Nat Turner through the imagination, but only such imaginative truths as Nat Turner, as any historical personage, might perhaps inspire. It is a mark of that overvaluation of literature coupled with a distrust of what it can really do which I mentioned before, that we go on believing in the power of fiction (or any kind of imaginative writing) to wrest secrets and intimate meanings from history. The irony of the debate over the novel's historical truth is that it cannot either be validated or dis-credited that way. For the point (which has to be made again and again in this age of utilitarian sensibility) is that literature, as litera-ture, has nothing to do with history, other than being able to draw upon it as it is free to draw upon anything.

The novel, for example, is the record of the imagination in prose forms, not a series of reflections or enhancements or interpretations of what has actually, physically, morally or even psychically happened in the world, or even what has been thought about that. If anything, literature, like all art, is the account of what history has failed to produce on its own, so that men have to step in to make good the deficiency. From this point of view Styron is entirely justified in his claim that he has not sought to reproduce history but to "meditate" on it, such meditation being part of the process of making good its deficiencies through art. History, as that which has existed outside the imagination, the sum of all that has actually happened (art happens virtually), demands of men that they find other ways besides literature by which to get at its "real" or intrinsic truths.

We would be in a much better position to experience *Nat Turner* instead of using it for one or another kind of corroboration if we understood that in meditating on history Styron has sought to use it and not simply recapitulate it, to find a springboard in it for his true novelist's work, which is to create something that history has thus far not contained. It is, in fact, anything but extreme to say that insofar as he was trying to do a novelist's work he had no essential interest in history at all, no interest, at any rate, that can begin to account [24/25] for the work or for the kind of energies that went into it.

Startling as it may sound, I think that Styron compromised and fatally injured his book by choosing a Negro for his protagonist. The one critic who, to my knowledge, has seen that the novel is not centrally about Negro reality at all is my colleague Stanley Kauffmann, whose extremely perceptive essay in the current *Hudson Review* points out how *Nat Turner* is in no real sense "historical" fiction of the kind we are familiar with (such fiction, if it works as literature, has, I might add, no more connection with history than the wish to use it as pretext) but fiction with a tragic and religious impulse and ambition, and how in failing to realize its ambitions it ends in almost full literary failure.

It may not be any comfort to those Negroes for whom the book is a willed and outrageous perversion of their past and Styron a conscious racist, but that fact that his unrealized ambitions were of the kind described by Kauffmann means that we are freer to address ourselves to his project in literature where, as I've said, the book must rest or fall.

The novel's main themes or impulses, as they can be distinguished from its narrative line, have to do with an opposition between Old and New Testament values and moralities—"savagery and revenge" *vs* "charity and brotherhood," as Styron has himself described it, as well as with a conflict between an intense desire for spiritual purity and absolute service of the Lord and a sensuality irreligious and even blasphemous in its implications, and, still more centrally, one between ardent faith and thorough-going doubt.

What is hoped for, what a novel on such themes might conceivably attain, is an imaginative act of resolution wherein these contrarieties might be transcended, or, more satisfyingly, be held in a tension which is itself new vision. And the astonishing thing is how few critics and readers have been able to see that Styron has failed to bring anything like this off. For his contrarieties never clash, his opposing thematic forces never engage one another. At every moment when a religious drama might take shape the novelist energy is shifted to a mere narrative of events, a "story" whose own constituents, whatever their original existence as facts, are the stuff of melodrama.

As Kauffmann writes, "The central defect of the book is that Styron has written a novel about a religious agonist without fulfilling—in any way he might have chosen—the religious agony."

That the book hasn't been seen as a failed religious drama is due of course—unless we are to postulate mass incompetence, epidemic illiteracy on the part of critics and readers—to the fact that people have strenuously wanted to see it as something else. They have wanted to see it, whites and Negroes alike, as a novel about a black man, about slavery and rebellion against slavery, and they have wanted to see this kind of novel, for reasons I've touched on, as constituting a document, a manifesto, a statement backed by the prestige of literature, with immediate social and political consequences. To wish to see any work of imaginative literature this way is to make it highly unlikely that what the imagination has actually done is going to be seen or recognized.

I said before that I think Styron's choice of a Negro for his protagonist was fatal to his deeper purpose. The point is that for this purpose the protagonist did not have to be a Negro and his being one in fact introduces all sorts of distractions and irrelevancies into the book. For there is nothing in Turner's Negroness that accounts for his religious fanaticism or even provides it with a basis, unless that might be the clichéd notion that oppressed and enslaved people might naturally turn to God. And there is a great deal in Styron's character being Negro that works against any successful imaginative appropriation of what being Negro is.

Thus when Nat thinks, after listening to the indictment of his actions by his atheist lawyer Gray, "Maybe he is right . . . maybe all was for nothing, maybe worse than nothing, and all I've done was evil in the sight of God. Maybe he is right and God is dead and gone, which is why I can no longer reach Him"—we are in the presence of ideas and implications which are, to say the least, more suggestive of contemporary, *white*, death-of-God theological [25/26] controversies than of anything having to do with being Negro or with slavery *circa* 1830.

Again, what has being Negro have to do with the following reflection of Nat's: ". . . think what an obstacle would be set in my path toward spiritual perfection if I should ever have any commerce with a *woman!* Difficult as it might become, I must bend every effort toward purity of mind and body so as to unloose my thoughts in the direction of theological studies and Christian preaching." One might say, but no, what are you thinking, surely a Negro might have that kind of hang-up, might find sex and religious vocation at odds. Of course, but Styron isn't supposed to be writing about such a Negro, one who *could be anything*, but about Nat Turner, a slave, a man whose only reality in our imagination is as a slave and the leader of a slave revolt. And here the perversion of history—there is no shred of evidence that

Turner had any such problems or was even troubled by sexual desire; he was in fact married, which Styron ignores—can be seen as the result of aesthetic confusion and not as wilful calumny.

The misleading dilemmas, misleading because they aren't the dilemmas that being a Negro or a slave might conceivably pose, but the dilemmas proper to a certain kind of religious fanaticism; the misleading psychology, misleading because, again, Styron hasn't made a reading of Negro or slave mentality but only of a religious fanatic who happens to be Negro; the misleading tensions, misleading because they are never pertinent to the principal narrative and never embodied in relevant actions—all this exhibits the fatal internal contradictions that bring *Nat Turner* to its knees as fiction.

But there is internal evidence of a more significant kind. In the very quality of the writing, its fundamental tones, prescriptions, choices and aspirations, the book continuously reveals its failure as literature of a high order, or rather, its existence in all but a few moments as literature of a false order.

To begin with, there is the matter of the book's kinds of speech. Kauffmann has pointed out how the dominant tone of elevated, biblically-oriented utterance is mostly unconvincing, smacking of authorship, how Nat's internal speech, his thoughts, clashes with his matter-of-fact dialogue, and how there is something egregiously false about the sudden appearance, in a context of heavily formal and lofty speech, of such modern colloquialisms as "Hot damn . . . don't shit me . . . I fix yo' preacher ass . . . I knock you to yo' fuckin' black knees."

But beyond this there is a whole range of simply inadequate or inferior writing. There are the clichés of Negro thinking or of thinking about Negroes:

"A Negro's most cherished possession is the drab, neutral cloak of anonymity he can manage to gather around himself, allowing him to merge faceless and nameless with the common swarm. . . ."

"Though it is a painful fact that most Negroes are hopelessly docile, many of them are filled with fury, and the unctuous coating of flattery which surrounds and encases that fury is but a form of self-preservation."

There are the clichés or banalities of thinking or feeling in general:

"Prayer again hovered at the margin of my consciousness, prowling there restlessly like some great grey cat yearning for entry into my mind."

"All I could feel was despair, despair so sickening that I thought it might drive me mad, except that it somehow lay deeper than madness."

"I sink away into some strange dream filled with inchoate promise and a voiceless, hovering joy."

And finally, most decisively I think, there are the clichés of *novel-writing*, the inherited procedures and ritualistic activities which Styron cannot rid himself of, though to jettison them—especially with such a subject—might have made it possible for the book to have been something new and alive to the imagination. Kauffmann refers [26/28] to them as "padding," and though they can be seen that way I think they are something more damaging, something at the heart of Styron's failure and not at its periphery. They have to do with transitions, integumentary passages and even more with descriptions, physical setting and atmosphere—all the elements which a novelist of a conventional kind thinks indispensable but which literally *tell us nothing*.

The verisimilitude for which Styron has been so much praised, his apparent rendering of the very sights, sounds and smells of Virginia in the early 19th century, seems to me a supererogatory and even inimical work to his main imaginative purpose. And at this point it scarcely matters whether we want to regard that as the writing of a tragic spiritual drama or as an attempt to know what being Negro is like.

For this whole physical construction, this thick detail, this "sensitivity" to nature and lyric evocation of place, is all irrelevant to Nat Turner as a fictional creation, has nothing to do with his conflicts or hopes or fears, with his position within the field of fictional energies.

Above all it has nothing to do with the moral or existential meanings which presumably Styron is pursuing: landscape, weather, sounds, all exist for their own sakes, as in a travel book whose author has no interest in anything but letting us know what it feels like to be somewhere. But Styron has set out to let us know what it feels like to be *someone*, and what are we to do, Negro or white, slave or free, with all these evocations which tell us only that we are somewhere (and somewhere not even in the present) and don't even inform us of what we feel about it:

"Above the river and the swamp beyond, a white rack of cloud hovered, covering the heavens, impermeable, its surface crawling with blackened streaks of mist like tattered shawls."

"Far off the mill groaned, a muffled watery rushing and mumbling. The light here was diaphanous, the air warm and drowsy, astir with darting buggy shapes and the chattering of birds."

The book is filled with this sort of thing, which isn't even interesting in its own right. That a cloud is like a tattered shawl, that the light is diaphanous, that, in another passage, a bobcat's scream is "like the sound of claws scraped . . . across the bare face of the heavens"— what do these things do for fictional reality? What they do, the reason they're there, is to attempt to convince us, by their mere presence, of the novel's authenticity, of its being grounded in something real. But fictional reality is established, never more so than at present when the apparatus of verisimilitude has been seen to be, in Nathalie Sarraute's phrase, "useless trappings," only by what is pertinent to the effort to bring into existence a new imaginative fact. To create a landscape and a weather for Nat Turner, without bringing him into any new relationship with them, is merely to write, to be an author, to engage in novelistic practises that have no relevance.

On one or two occasions Styron's writing does become relevant, moves to establish a new imaginative fact, and in doing this achieves temporarily the thing for which the whole book has been praised. Passages such as the following do indeed establish the condition of knowing what it might be like to have been a Negro slave:

"The white faces, viewed for the first time so closely—especially those of the females, only lightly touched by sun and weather—have the sheen and consistency of sour dough or the soft underbellies of mushrooms; their blue eyes glint boldly, startling as ice, and I regard each yawning pore, each freckle, with the awe of total discovery."

". . . her voice, gentle and indulgent as it descends from the rare white prodigious atmosphere above me . . ."

They indicate what Styron is capable of, but they are extremely rare; I've quoted half the ones I was able to find. With a persistency that is a function of his aesthetic confusion Styron shuts off these kinds of fictional investigations before they can go far enough [28/32] to lead him into a new kind of novel and returns to the conventional procedures and styles of vision with which he is most comfortable.

Some years ago Richard Wright wrote of Gertrude Stein's *Melanctha* that it was "the first long serious literary treatment of Negro life in the United States," and that it was her "struggling words" that "made the speech of the [Negro] people around me vivid." Wright went on to describe how he "gathered a group of semi-literate Negro stockyard workers" in order to test the novel's authenticity and how they "understood every word," and sat there "enthralled."

That Negroes today aren't enthralled by *Nat Turner* isn't necessarily a fatal judgment on it. The point, however, is that anyone who continues to be enthralled by Gertrude Stein's book will understand that she was able to imagine herself into a Negro character because, in the first place, she didn't set that as her aim, and in the second place because she was able to find new literary means to establish her intentions. *Melanctha* contains almost no descriptions, no novelistic integuments, no "atmosphere" and no evocations of anything beyond itself. Besides this, it is an extremely "small" book, a quiet effort of "struggling words," the furthest thing from a *statement*. It remains a novel that demonstrates as *Nat Turner* also does in its exemplary failure, how the imagination can only serve history, which is to say, us, by doing its own very different, compensatory and atoning work. [32]

Historical Fictions

MARTIN DUBERMAN

THIS IS A DEPRESSING VOLUME—FOR THOSE WHO BELIEVE THE PAST CAN and should be protected from the propagandists, for those with the lingering hope that the races in America can be reconciled, for those who have regarded the blacks as a saving remnant that might help our country become something better than what it has been.

The book is a commentary—perhaps "assault" would be the more appropriate word—by 10 black writers on William Styron's novel, "The Confessions of Nat Turner." There are legitimate complaints, historical and literary, to be made against Styron's book, and as presented by two of the ten essayists, Vincent Harding and Mike Thelwell, those complaints are cogently, even poignantly, set forth. Harding and Thelwell recognize that Styron, as a novelist, is entitled to certain prerogatives of invention and fantasy, but they point out that he has not been content to advertise his work as "fiction"; in the preface to the novel (and in a number of public comments and debates since its publication) Styron has insisted that he "rarely departed from the *known* facts about Nat Turner and the revolt of which he was the leader."

By inviting critics to treat his book as a work of history as well as one of fiction, Styron has increased his vulnerability to attack. Even had he not, the attack would have come, for as Thelwell points out, the acclaim given the novel by white critics and the terms in which that acclaim has been formulated (e.g., Styron reveals "the agonizing essence of Negro slavery") has turned the book into a cultural phenomenon about which extraliterary questions become inescapable.

My own feelings about Styron's book are that, although seriously flawed as a novel, it is, at the same time, superlative history. By this, I do not mean that Styron cannot be faulted for the occasional omission or distortion of detail (an inescapable by-product of *any* work of history, no matter how rigorous and scrupulous the historian), but that the "Confessions" provides the most subtle, multifaceted view of antebellum Virginia, its institution of slavery and the effects of that institution on both slaves and masters, available in any single volume.

Martin Duberman, "Historical Fictions," *The New York Times* (August 11, 1968). © 1968 by The New York Times Company. Reprinted by permission.

This opinion is furiously rebutted by the 10 black writers in this collection. Three sets of "distortions in the Confessions" particularly outrage them. The first has to do with Turner's family background. By failing to credit the role played in Nat's upbringing by a black grandmother and father, and by de-emphasizing the influence of his mother, Styron has, it is charged, written a kind of early-day adjunct to the Moynihan Report, whereby the instability of black family life carries the inevitable corollary that the "significant others" in Nat's life had to be whites.

The second set of distortions concerns Nat Turner's sex life. Styron, it is said, has dropped Nat's black slave wife from history, has focused his desires instead on a young white girl and, by throwing a homosexual episode into the package, has ended by creating a Nat Turner who is all at once impotent, queer, sexually repressed, and full of secret lusts for white flesh.

The third indictment against Styron centers on his description of the revolt itself and the part Nat Turner played in it. Nat's vacillation at the moment of crisis, his refusal or inability to kill any white other than the young girl who had been the focus of his repressed desires, the inanity of his few black allies and the indifference or hostility of the other slaves, create the impression, Styron's critics argue, that Nat was a coward, a fool, an incompetent, or all three, and imply, moreover, that blacks are at all times incapable of engineering their own liberation.

These are the most detailed of the indictments made against Styron, but they by no means exhaust the grievances listed by the 10 authors. Among the additional, more general charges made by individual essayists, is that Styron has exaggerated the benevolent aspects of slavery, that he has portrayed all or most Negroes in slavery as "Sambos," that he has minimized the powerful resistance blacks made to bondage, that he has misunderstood the black temper, the psychology of uprisings, the very nature of American society.

Some of the essayists insist that Styron's distortions are deliberate, the conscious design of (in Ernest Kaiser's phrase) a "vile racist imagination." Two or three of the writers are willing to entertain the notion that Styron may not have intentionally maligned the character and historical significance of Nat Turner (Alvin F. Poussaint, the Boston psychiatrist, even detects in many parts of the novel, the author's "strong empathy" for Nat), though they feel that his stereotypic liberal views have prevented him, despite good [1/26] intentions, from understanding the black psyche and the black experience.

In drawing their charges, the essayists imply that in regard to all these matters—Nat Turner's personality, the institution of slavery, the psychology of insurrection, etc.—the historical evidence establishes clear patterns that run counter to those presented by Styron. They are certain, for example, that the "real" Nat Turner was, in the words of

John Henrik Clarke, "a virile, commanding, courageous figure." It is as unthinkable to them that Turner could have been irresolute in battle or ambivalent about committing murder, as it is that he could have hankered after a white woman or not "dearly loved" his black wife.

According to their countermodel, Nat Turner was one of the world's great military geniuses and one of its most resolute white haters. (Poussaint chides Styron for suggesting that Turner could have believed in "the basic humanity of some slave-holders.") This would make Nat Turner, among other things, a dedicated killer and racist—qualities which I doubt most of the essayists would ordinarily single out for praise. In any case, they see Turner not as a human being, but as an epic force, a figure immune to the usual range of error, compassion and desire.

If this is what blacks mean by "rediscovering" black history and finding historical figures with whom black youths can identify, then the prospects are grim, for in the case of Turner at least, the figure they present for emulation is frighteningly one-dimensional, even pathological. It is a question, moreover, whether the new emphasis on black heroes really will demythologize our past (as is claimed and needed), or whether it will replace one set of myths with another. To give just one other example: We have heard much of late of Crispus Attucks, who, we are being told, was a runaway Negro slave killed in the "Boston Massacre"—the first blood to be shed in the American struggle for independence. The fact is we don't know whether Attucks was a Negro, a mulatto, an Indian, or even a runaway, and no one, of course, can assign the moment or the vein from which the "first blood" for independence spurted forth.

Blacks are entitled to their version of Turner, Attucks and others, but let them not pretend that those versions are incontestably validated by the historical evidence. As regards Turner, for example, the historical documentation is so skimpy and contradictory that only by embroidering or ignoring it (the very sins for which they denounce Styron) can the black writers in this collection establish their predetermined and dogmatic "lessons." The chief—indeed with the exception of a few scattered references in contemporary accounts—the only source on Nat Turner is the 20-odd-page "confessions" taken down when he was in jail by a white racist lawyer named Thomas Gray.

The full text of these original confessions is printed as an appendix to this volume, as if to suggest that it carries some kind of unarguable certification for the views of the essayists. It does present some "facts," like Turner's family lineage, which contradict Styron's version—but even on this level, the black essayists should have been the first to remind us (as they do in so many other contexts) that Turner's confessions were filtered through the eyes and words of a white man and are therefore automatically suspect.

Since, to the contrary, most of the essayists seem to believe that the original confessions are Absolute Truth and that every account which deviates from them partakes of malignant intent, it is surprising they did not chastise Styron more severely for underplaying the one character trait of Turner's that emerges most clearly from those confessions—that he was a religious fanatic of terrifying, perhaps psychotic, proportions.

For matters incidental to Turner's own career—and especially for the view that rebellions like his were not rare (as Styron states) but rather frequent occurrences—the essayists rely heavily on Herbert Aptheker's "American Negro Slave Revolts." But they do not mention that most historians consider Aptheker's evidence suspect, based as it often is on inference and rumor (nor that historians are equally leery of the "oral tradition" which some of the writers are reduced to citing).

The essayists wish to believe that the "craving for freedom" was to be found in every Negro breast, and that therefore there is no "big mystery," as John Oliver Killens puts it, about the causes of Nat Turner's rebellion. But since there were millions of slaves and very few revolutionaries, the phenomenon of Nat Turner does need further explanation—as does the failure of the vast majority of Negroes to rebel. Evidence of Negro apathy or acquiescence will not disappear by the mere reiteration that it never existed. Denmark [26/28] Vesey's Charleston insurrection in 1822—to give but one example—is known to have been betrayed by black informers.

By insisting that all slaves "craved freedom," the essayists force themselves into a bizarre view of the institution of slavery. For slavery could not have been as barbaric as they otherwise insist if it inculcated self-love and masculine assertion in the slaves, rather than the self-hate and loss of identity more usually taken to be its products.

Only when slavery is viewed as an essentially benign institution (the position associated with the scholarship of Ulrich B. Phillips and bitterly denounced by the essayists), can it follow that it left no deep personality scars on its victims. But the weight of historical evidence and opinion suggests that American slavery was harsh enough to produce serious character disorders in many slaves. If this be "slander," then I suppose we shall now have to brand Bruno Bettelheim an anti-Semite for pointing out that prisoners in the concentration camps tended to identify with their S.S. guards and to become infantalized.

What makes Styron a better historian than any of his critics is that he will not bury unpleasant evidence or minimize the complexities of past experience in order to serve some presumed contemporary need. It seems to me grotesque to say, as some of these writers do, that because Styron portrays an occasional master as kindly, he therefore believes slavery was benevolent; Styron recognizes that some slaves had kind masters *and* that slavery was abominable. It seems to me absurd to claim that Styron "dehumanizes every black person in the book" because he portrays some Negroes as Sambos and endows others with conflicts and uncertainties (traits which I hitherto took to be among the telltale signs of humanity); Styron recognizes that slavery produced Uncle Toms *and* rebels.

Finally, I think it is obscene to say that Styron is "an unreconstructed Southern rebel" and that his purposes in writing the "Confessions" were to confirm white racists in their view that Negroes are ingrates and incompetents and to defuse black militancy by suggesting that all rebellions are acts of futility. Styron's chief crime, it appears, is his refusal to reduce any man to caricature, whether as Hero or Oppressor. His chief disability—that is, to those who wish to exploit rather than to understand the past—is his insistence on holding contradictory views in tension, on embracing paradox.

After several hundred years of white myth-making and polemic, it looks as if we're now in for some innings by the blacks. One hoped it was going to be different this time around. But that, I suppose, was one of the more recent myths: that blacks in this country could somehow transcend the destructive racism that permeates our culture, that they, unlike the whites, might somehow avoid distorting the past as a way of inciting one half of mankind to hate the other. [28]

3. THE WORLDS OF WILLIAM STYRON

The Long Dark Road

WILLIAM STYRON

DEWEY LASSITER WALKED ALONG THE ROAD SLOWLY, THE DUST RISING in little vaporous clouds around his bare feet. He stopped at intervals to roll up the wet ends of his overalls, which slipped down to his ankles every few steps. In the distance, not more than half a mile across the broad, flat Delta country, he could see the lights of the store glowing faintly. Dewey increased his pace, still pausing occasionally to adjust his pants leg.

It was getting darker now, the boy thought to himself. He'd better be getting home, or he'd catch it plenty from his mother.

"Maw's gonna whup me," he thought aloud. He was surprised at the sound of his voice.

"Maw's gonna whup me," he said again, louder. From a heavily clumped pine grove off to the right beyond the cotton he heard the echo, "—whup me!" He laughed. [266/267]

He shouted, "Maw's gonna whup me!" and the echo came back as before—"gonna whup me!" Then he was silent. He had better hurry, he thought, or he really would catch it.

From somewhere there came the harsh, long call of a bluejay. The boy walked on.

Lassiter's General Merchandise was typical of the many small country stores which one sees in the South. Its clapboard front, begrimed with the dust of many storms, was partly shielded by a flimsy roof, which was supported by two splintered and blackened posts. Between the posts were two old-style gas pumps and a pump for kerosene. And beside the door was a battered bench, hollowed through use and stained gray with time, above which was the fly-specked window and the chipped lettering: "A. J. Lassiter, Gen'l M'd'se."

The bench was the focal point for all local social activity. Worn into its grain, impressed into its gray and solid planking, were the imprints of many an overalled rump, and in its splintered fibre were the memories of numberless afternoons devoted to talking and spitting and thinking.

A.J. himself was an immense, ruddy-faced man of about forty with flaming red hair. He had a coarse and broad face, full of robust good humor; and his monstrous, balloon-like body, which seemed to overflow his shirt and pants with a fleshy and Gargantuan enormousness, gave him an appearance of stout and amiable heartiness. But A.J.'s most startling characteristic was his laugh.

It was no ordinary laugh. It was something akin to an explosion. When A.J. was amused, his massive face would seem to widen perceptibly, and his mouth would break out [267/268] into an enormous grin. For a brief moment there would be a suspenseful silence; then it would begin. From somewhere in the depths of his voluminous bulk would emanate a sort of wheezing groan which built up gradually until his whole ruddy face and the entire immensity of his frame was convulsed by latent tremblings and rumblings. And then, his head thrown back, mouth agape, and face constricted with mirth, he would eructate in an ear-splitting paroxysm of exuberant, uninhibited laughter. And minutes would pass before he had, with countless wheezes and renewed outbursts of jollity, regained his composure.

A.J. had a family. His wife Mamie had borne him two sons and a daughter. The girl, Louesta, was now nineteen and studying to be a nurse in Memphis. The boys were Roy, who was twenty, and Dewey, who was just going on fifteen.

Roy worked in a garage in Clarksdale, twenty miles up the river. A.J. had wanted him to stay home and help on the farm, but Roy had told the old man he would rather "get out on his own." Roy was big and heavy like his father, and rather stupid. His new-found independence in Clarksdale consisted mainly of fierce gin bouts with his friends and parties on the weekends with the whores in Memphis, and more gin.

Dewey opened the screen door and went into the store. It was eight o'clock. He could tell by the big clock with the Agrico sign on it. It said eight fifteen, but always ran a little fast. No one was in but the old man, who was cutting some cheese in the back.

"Hi, Paw," he said. [268/269]

A.J. looked up. "Hello, son," he said, smiling his broad smile. "C'mon back."

The boy went back to the big square wooden table. It had always sort of excited him, that huge heavy piece of wood with its countless cleaver marks and its warm mixed smell of strong cheese and raw, bloody meat. It was a savage sort of feeling that the block aroused in him, a feeling faintly bringing to mind pictures of blood, gore, and guts, like the sacrificial altar of the Aztecs he had seen in a history book. But it reminded him, too, of good food, of thick steaks, tender chops, and of Sunday dinners.

The old man was cutting through a big waxed block of yellow cheese, cutting it in long, easy strokes so that uniformly shaped wedges fell at the edge of the knife.

"Where you been to, Dewey?" he asked.

"Been fishin' down to the branch."

"Ketch anything?"

"Naw, dad-dratted catfish pulled my line in. Los' my bait an' my hook, an' I slipped in too."

A.J. looked up and saw the boy's wet overalls. He chuckled. "That'll learn you. Cain't ketch no catfish with pork rind. Holts on too hard. Gotta use 'hoppers or red worms." He laughed silently, his great body heaving. "Fell in! That'll learn you. Who'd you go with?"

"Lynwood Huckins."

"Why, that's George Huckins's young'un, ain't it?"

"Yep."

"Did he tell you 'bout his paw ketchin' that nigger?"

"Yep."

"Reckon he's mighty proud."

"Yep, Lynwood said they're goin' to lynch that nigger."

"Now, son, don't say that." His father's face had lost [269/270] its usual smile. "That nigger's gonna git a fair and square trial."

"Where's Maw?" the boy asked.

"She's up to the house. She's waitin' supper on you now. You better git up there or she'll whup you." He laughed. "You don't want to get whupped."

And he thought about his mother, how she hardly ever said anything when she was mad like that, except to say, "Fetch me a cane, Dewey." But then, it never hurt very much, and besides, the old man had told her that he thought Dewey was getting too old to be whipped. The old man was like that—easy-going—wouldn't even cuss a nigger. Anyhow, it wasn't how it hurt his tail; but it hurt his feelings more. She was getting easier on him now. Maybe he *was* getting old.

"Yer brother Roy called up," A.J. said. "Said he'd be here around nine o'clock."

The son of a bitch, Dewey thought, the son of a bitch. The boy had nothing but hate and loathing for his brother, and he'd admit it to anyone. His own flesh and blood, but he detested the very sight of him. And he'd be here tonight, his fat, pasty yellow face, and his bleary eyes, his smelly breath and dirty nails, and he'd talk about himself.

And he'd be mean and nasty, and probably drunk, and he'd cuss

Dewey and make him miserable like he'd been doing ever since he could remember. His own flesh and blood.

And the old man was just crazy about him. It was "Roy this" and "Roy that" and "He's goin' to be a success in this gosh-dern world, mark me!" And all the time the son of a bitch was in Clarksdale drinking and laying out in the gutter all the time, and he'd come back to the store about [270/271] once a month, and all you'd hear was talk about how drunk he was last Saturday in Memphis and how much tail he got that night. Then he'd make Dewey run up to the boot-leggers at Injun Mound and get him some whiskey and wouldn't give him anything except maybe a dime. The son of a bitch.

His mother hadn't whipped him, so Dewey felt relieved after supper. It was dark when he went back down to the store, which was connected with the house by a narrow path some eighty yards through the cotton field. From the back of the store he could see Nate Smith's battered old Ford under the dusty glare of the lights, and he knew that Nate and the old man would be out front on the bench talking.

He heard them as he rounded the corner of the store.

". . . and if'n I had my way, A.J., I'd take that black bastard and rope 'im to the highest tree in Mississippi!"

Dewey sat down on the strip of concrete near the pump and across from the two men. He listened, feeling the sand cool and brittle between his toes.

"Well, I wouldn't be saying anything as rash as that, Nate." His father's voice was low and steady and rich. "As I sees it," he said, with a trace of a smile playing around the corners of his wide mouth, "as I sees it, the State is the decidin' thing in all such matters of justice. When the prosecutor and the judge is elected by the people, the people is supposed to back up their decisions, and as I sees it, after they says their decisions, the people should let well enough alone."

But Nate was vehement in his convictions, "I know, I know, but goddamit—" His face was dead set, earnest. "All right, let's look at it like this. Suppose you was ol' man [271/272] Hooker. He was crippled up, almost helpless, A.J.; you know that yourself. All right. You're sleepin' over your store one night peaceful-like. Suddenly you wake up and hear somethin' creepin' around. You're helpless now, A.J., and you're all alone. You holler, 'Who's there?' and then you see somethin' like an ape over your bed, and he's stranglin' you with his big, black, common nigger hands! Why, goddamit, A.J., John Hooker didn't have no more strength than a baby. How can you sit there—" He stopped, breathing hard, and his lean, wrinkled face was a mixed study of anger and overworked imagination.

A.J. was calm and reassuring. He placed his fat hands on Nate's knee comfortingly.

"I know, I know," he said softly; "calm yourself now, Nate; there ain't no use gittin' so riled. The way it looks to me is that nigger is safe behind the bars up to Injun Mound, and there ain't nothin' me and you can do but let justice go its way and—"

"Yes, but goddamit, he was a nigger, a black, common, dirty son of a bitch of a nigger, and—"

"Sure, sure, it was a pretty terrible thing to do, I'll admit, even for a white man, let alone a nigger; but there just ain't one thing we can do. Let's just forget about it an' have a drink."

He looked at Dewey, and the boy knew what to do. Dewey went into the store and got three coca-colas out of the drink case and brought them out and gave one to the old man and one to Nate. Then he went over and sat down again on the concrete steps.

He took a swallow of the coca-cola, and it tasted good. And then he suddenly became aware of something. It was something he could not place exactly; but there was a [272/273] certain feeling that made him uneasy. It was not a feeling that something was wrong; but he was conscious of the fact that there should be something there that wasn't. Something vital in the atmosphere was missing. He couldn't place it.

The air was hot and sultry, and he could smell the loamy, heavy odor of the Delta soil. He heard the steady drone of the flies and there was still the distant piping song of the frogs. A grasshopper spanked up against the screen and clung there momentarily, then buzzed away. From across the field he could hear the sudden, haunting, echoed call of a whippoorwill. A car passed on the road.

They were all there. But something was the matter.

"Yes, A.J.," he heard Nate say in his halting, cracked voice, "I ain't as spry as I used to be. Ol' Doc Barham up in Memphis says its dia-bee-tees. Cain't travel much. Like to come up here and talk with the boys, though."

The boys, the boys. That was it. Where were they? Monroe Davis and Charley Cutchin and Dexter Capps and all the rest. It wasn't right. Something was missing.

And then the horrible thought struck him, smote him with the jolt of a two-ton tractor. It was a lynching party. That's what Lynwood Huckins had said, had said that all those friends of his old man and old Huck himself were going up to Injun Mound and break that jail and get that nigger out of there and string him up; it was a secret. It was a secret. They were going to take him and string him up.

And then a strange feeling of unutterable terror came over the boy. He was afraid, but he could not comprehend his fear. He was conscious of strange, benumbing reality, knowing that somewhere not far away something inhuman [273/274] and terrible and brutal was happening. It was fierce, unbelievable, untrue. But the incredible thing was there; and time passed slowly as he sat there, dazed, listening blankly to the drone of the two men's voices and the steady thrumming of the flies and the slow, interminable ticking of the clock.

Then suddenly he heard the faint sound of a car horn far down the road. It shocked him suddenly and hard. For the sound, as slight and noiseless as it really was, like the soft rustling of a mouse in the moldering antiquity of a forgotten attic, was to him as enormous and as frightening as the report of a cannon.

And now, above the sound of a horn, which was blowing continuously, he could hear the staccato clacking of a cut-out on a high-powered engine. It was Roy. Dewey looked at the clock. Nine thirty.

The car, wheeling and lurching off the dusty road, came to a jarring halt in front of the store. The men, who until then had been obviously lost in the meanderings of their conversation, looked up in gaped-mouth astonishment at the car. Then the old man recognized his son and got up heavily and rose to greet him.

"Ho, Roy. Where you been?"

The youth did not answer his father, but leaned a drunken, leering face out of the window and began to laugh. It was startling to Dewey, and there was something hideous and obscene in the laughter. It was a ghastly and fiendish travesty on the laughter of his father, which, coming now with no apparent cause or reason and lacking any of the good-natured robustness of his father's laugh, seemed to echo a sound of loathesome and sickening bastardy in its foul coarseness. [274/275]

Then he stopped suddenly and turned his drowned eyes on the startled people.

"They're bringin' that nigger up here."

The old man stared at his son, and then, as if the full but yet incomprehensible horror had dawned upon him, he leaped to the window.

"What you talkin' about, Roy? What nigger?" His words were almost savage, but they were the words of a man who has just been stricken by some nameless fear and, instead of planning escape, attempts to cover his terror with disbelief.

"What's the matter with you?" he cried, his huge body trembling with each gasping breath. "What nigger you talkin' about?"

"You know what nigger I'm talkin' 'bout," Roy said drunkenly. "They done sprung that nigger from jail. Dexter Capps and Charley Cutchin and a big bunch of them. They're bringin' him up here!" And then, with a sodden leer, he said, slowly and thickly, "They're goin' to burn him."

The old man stood there clutching the side of the door so that the backs of his hands were white. His voice was a whisper as he spoke to Roy.

"It ain't goin' to happen. So help me God! It ain't goin' to happen."

Just then Nate, who had been listening intently to all that had taken place, gave a sudden yell. "Listen! Listen! They're comin'!"

And they turned their eyes to the south, down the dark road.

Dewey could see, not far away, a white glare of headlights; and he heard the jumbled noise of many cars, going fast, as they sped in a whirl of dust down the road. [275/276]

The cars, drawn up in caravan fashion and numbering perhaps ten, stopped on the opposite side of the road. Each one was packed with five or six farmers. The men got out of the cars and walked over in front of the store and stood there, muttering in little angry groups and smoking and spitting and waiting.

Dewey heard his father talking. "What you all come out here for? I don't want any . . ."

"Look, A.J.," it was Jim Bickford's voice. "We had to bring him out here to git away from town. Anyhow," he said meaningfully, "there's kerosene out here."

"But hang it all, Jim, I don't want . . ."

Then Dewey heard his brother. "Here comes the truck! Here comes the truck! Hot damn!" He had staggered out of the car and was standing in the middle of the road, reeling and shouting and laughing like an idiot.

The son of a bitch, Dewey thought, the son of a bitch.

The truck, a huge hay wagon with slatted sides, stopped noisily in front of the store. The crowd of men gathered around it.

"Bring the bastard out of there!" someone shouted.

"Get that rope!"

Two men moved toward the store.

The old man lumbered over to the door. "Stop it now," he panted. "It's wrong!" His huge face was contorted and red. "Stop it—"

The men brushed him aside. "Git out of the way, A.J.," they said.

The two beefy farmers who had been in the truck got out. Between them, almost slumped to the ground, was the nigger. He was thin and short, so small that he looked like a dwarf beside his captors. Dewey could not see his [276/277] face, but he could hear him. He was moaning. It was like nothing the boy had ever heard. It was something like the thin, piteous cry of a dog that has been caught in a steel trap; and yet it was something like the stricken wail of a woman, something mournful, terrible, and lost.

The two farmers pushed their way through the crowd, dragging the nigger between them. "This'll be all right," one of them said.

They pushed the nigger down on the steps, and he slumped lifelessly against the screen door, sweating, his eyes closed, still moaning.

Then Charley Cutchin stepped up beside the nigger and, grasping his collar, jerked him up. Charley was a tall and skinny man, thin almost to the point of emaciation. He wore steel-rimmed glasses and his eyes were bloodshot.

"Listen, nigger, you know what we're goin' to do?"

The nigger opened his eyes and looked at the cadaverous figure swaying before him. The white-shirted men had crowded around the door and were gathered there in a sweating mass beneath the lights, muttering and shuffling nervously.

"I tell you what we're goin' to do," he said, in a low voice; "we're goin' to hang you by your goddam black nigger neck. And then," he whispered, pointing to the gas pump, "we're goin' to burn you."

The nigger slumped back against the door, his hands in front of his face. And then he began to speak for the first time. He was sobbing now; the words came hoarsely.

"Don' burn me, suh; don' burn me."

Roy pushed through the crowd and lurched toward Charley.

"Let's get started, Cutchin; the police might be comin'." [277/278]

"Yeah," said Charley, "let's get started."

The men moved back again toward the road, and six of the farmers grabbed the nigger. The nigger had now collapsed, and he shuddered as they dragged him over beneath the rafters. Roy, who had been holding the rope, threw the looped end around the nigger's neck and jerked it roughly. A little grazed, bloody patch showed where the fiber of the rope had scraped the skin.

Charley grasped Roy's arm.

"Take it easy, goddamit; we don't want to do it too soon!" He turned to Jim Bickford. "Get the truck."

Dewey saw them bring the truck up and back it up to within a few feet of the nigger, who had now fainted away completely and was being held up by Charley. A young boy had climbed a ladder and was tying the free end of the rope to a rafter which supported the roof.

And Dewey saw the crowd of men, perspiring, red-faced, and silent, who now stood as a mass, motionless, at the edge of the road. Hardly a word was spoken. They watched and remained silent. Dewey could hear only the steady thrum of the night flies, and the low muttering of the little group of men who stood around the nigger, intent, nervous, quiet. The old man was sitting on the bench alone with his head in his hands, rocking back and forth, and saying: "Oh, Jesus, oh, my sweet Jesus."

Charley, with Nate and Bickford, picked up the nigger, the rope still tied around his neck, and put him in the back of the truck. There was a dull thump as they dropped him in a lifeless heap on the planking.

Jim kicked him, kicked him hard, so that he sprawled out on the floor of the truck.

"Wake up, nigger," he said. [278/279]

But the nigger would not move.

Roy shouted to the three men on the truck. "Throw some kerosene on the son of a bitch. That'll fix him!"

Someone handed a can of kerosene to Charley. Charley unscrewed the top and threw the contents into the nigger's face. The kerosene soaked into his clothes and dripped down on the floor of the truck. The nigger woke up and began to scream, awfully, hoarsely, and like a woman. The kerosene glistened on his black face.

"Don' burn me!" he screamed, "Oh Lord, don' burn me!"

Charley knocked him down with the kerosene can. The nigger, stunned, lay on the floor, sobbing and moaning.

Someone shouted from the road. "Let's get it over with, Cutchin!"

Dewey saw the three men jump down from the truck. Roy reeled into the driver's seat and started the motor. There was a tremendous roar, and a blue burst of flame exploded from the exhaust. Over all there was the heavy odor of kerosene, and the terrible moaning of the black figure in the back of the truck. The nigger got up and began to hold on to the slatted sides of the truck. He was screaming again, screaming in a high-pitched wail that echoed above the sound of the motor into the stillness of the night.

"Let 'er go, Roy," Charley shouted.

Dewey saw the truck lurch forward. There was a grinding of rubber against the gravel. The nigger's hands were torn loose from the palings as the rope drew tight around his neck and stifled his screams. He skidded sideways across the floor of the truck as the machine tore from beneath him. There was a heavy jolt, and a crack of [279/280] loosening timbers. The body swung gently beneath the rafters.

Dewey was running, running across the cotton fields, and he could feel the clumps of earth between his toes and there was a smell of kerosene still in his nostrils . . . running, running, running. . . .

Running. And the great forest loomed far and away. For there was somewhere the smell of kerosene and sweat and burning flesh. Far and away. And beyond the fields of cotton there was a great forest. Far and away, Dewey, far and away. The tears stung his eyes, his eyes, Dewey, far and away. And running through the fields where the brambles are and the sound of a lark, Dewey, far and away. And running from death and burning niggers and Roy Roy Roy son of a bitch sooo-o-o far and away. The old man's laugh sitting with head in hands and the smell of kerosene, Dewey, Dewey, Dewey, Dewey, it is me, me me, Dewey, me doan' burn *me* suh like a woman. Late late in the evening and the hounds are calling; somewhere the river flows far and away. Oh my Jesus my sweet Jesus and murmuring voices far and away.

In the distance a train whistle blew, wailing up through the valley. All was quiet. [280]

William Styron:
The Metaphysical Hurt

FREDERICK J. HOFFMAN

WHILE WILLIAM STYRON HAS QUITE CORRECTLY REFUSED TO BE CALLED a "Southern writer," in an interview for the *Paris Review* he did admit that the South supplies "wonderful material."

Take, for instance, the conflict between the ordered Protestant tradition, the fundamentalism based on the Old Testament, and the twentieth century— movies, cars, television. The poetic juxtapositions you find in this conflict—a crazy colored preacher howling those tremendously moving verses from Isaiah 40, while riding around in a maroon Packard. It's wonderful stuff and comparatively new, too, which is perhaps why the renaissance of Southern writing coincided with these last few decades of the machine age.[1]

It is futile to stir up the old clichés about "decadence," "Southern tradition," the "Southern model," etc.[2] Styron has better and larger fish to fry. He is, above all, concerned with a basic and timeless issue, though it surely has its place in twentieth-century literature.

It is, in brief, the problem of believing, the desperate necessity for having the "courage to be." Almost all of his fiction poses violence against the human power to endure it and to "take hold of himself" in spite of it. The pathos of his creatures, when it is not directly the result

[1] Interview conducted by Peter Matthiessen and George Plimpton, for *Paris Review*, reprinted in *Writers at Work*, edited by Malcolm Cowley (New York: Viking, 1958), 273.

[2] For what it is worth, I give a partial list of the speculations on Styron's "Southernness": John Aldridge, in the *New York Times Book Review*, September 5, 1951, p. 5; Malcolm Cowley, "The Faulkner Pattern," *New Republic*, 125 (October 8, 1951), 19–20 (both of these strongly emphasize the Southern tradition); Elizabeth Janeway, in *New Leader*, 35 (January 21, 1952), 25 (she cries "Nonsense" to the idea that *Lie Down in Darkness* is a story, fable, what have you, of decadence in a Southern family); and Harvey Swados, "First Novel," *Nation*, 273 (November, 1951), 453 (who criticizes Styron for "investing his corrupt family with significances").

of organizational absurdity,[3] comes from a psychological failure, a "confusion," a situation in which the character, trying to meet an awkward human situation, makes it worse and (almost invariably) retreats clumsily or despairingly from it. [144/145]

Writing to the *Paris Review* (of which he has been an Advisory Editor) for its first issue, on the ever-present questions of "the times" (*are* they worthy, or *do* they promise good literature, etc.), Styron said:

I still maintain that the times get precisely the literature that they deserve, and that if the writing is gloomy the gloom is not so much inherent in the literature as in the times. . . . The writer will be dead before anyone can judge him—but he *must* go on writing, reflecting disorder, defeat, despair, should that be all he sees at the moment, but ever searching for the elusive love, joy and hope—qualities which, as in the act of life itself, are best when they have to be struggled for, and are not commonly come by with much ease, either by a critic's formula or by a critic's yearning. . . .[4]

There is nothing very complicated about this. It is a fairly simple set of human explorations. In a way, it is a twentieth-century restatement of Baudelaire's "Le Gouffre." Only here, in Styron's fiction, it takes on a far less subjective, isolative character. Lack of belief causes great cracks in the human landscape: and men look, desperate and afraid, across them at each other. Most of what they do has the character of trying to heal the wound, close the gap, but by means of ordinary secular devices. Alcohol has an important role in the lives of Styron's characters, but it is not a way of closing the fissure; it temporarily makes things *appear* improved, but it may ultimately lead to disaster. It is simply not a surrogate of God, though God's absence is surely responsible for the increase of its use.

I do not mean to suggest that Styron inhabits or has created a simple-minded world. It is perhaps the most difficult feat of all, this one of asserting not only the pre-eminence of values (love, joy, and hope[5]) but of creating meaningful situations in which men and women struggle to gain them, or even to understand them. The "modernness" of Styron's world, then, is not related to nihilism, but to humiliation, and to struggle: the ghastly struggle just to *assert* one's humanness, to get over the barriers to understanding, to clear one's

---

[3] As in *The Long March* (New York: Random House, 1956).

[4] The *Paris Review*, 1 (Spring, 1953), 13.

[5] They, and other matters emphasized by Styron, point to William Faulkner's Nobel Award Speech in 1950. Styron was, of course, powerfully influenced by Faulkner, but has managed, I think, to bring the influence under control. He once said to David Dempsey, about *Lie Down in Darkness:* "Faulkner's [influence] was the hardest to shake off. The early parts of my novel were so imbued with his style that I had to go back and rewrite them completely. . . ." *New York Times Book Review,* September 9, 1951, p. 27.

personality of [145/146] obsessions. Another way of putting it is that the Styron hero is trying for a clear view and a steady hand, like the hand of Cass Kinsolving *after* he has freed himself of the imprisonment within despair and within the obsessive indulgences used temporarily to combat it.[6]

ii

Styron's minor prose is largely confined to asserting these essentials, as though the essays and sketches were a clearinghouse, to provide the novels a freer range of observation and action. The brief sketch on the funeral of William Faulkner, in *Life* magazine of July 20, 1962, puts a cap upon the lot; he speaks reverently, not only of his dead hero, but of the very substance and center of Yoknapatawpha County: the famous square in downtown Oxford, the courthouse and jail, the statue of the Confederate soldier.[7] Even a very early short story, "The Long Dark Road," selected by his teacher, William Blackburn, for inclusion in a Duke University anthology, concerns one of those calamitous explosions of human irrationality (in this case, a lynching) which Styron repeatedly described afterward in his two major novels.[8] His essays include one against capital punishment, in which he puzzles over why it is that the poor are condemned so much more often than the rest, and meditates upon "the soul" of the victim, which "will have been already so diminished by our own humanity" by the time it is "taken."[9]

The Long March gives an insight into the simplest variant of Styron's moral speculation.[10] If we assume that the human creature deserves (or can rise to) dignity and even nobility, but is often the victim of accident and absurdity, *The Long March* illustrates our assumption with the simplicity of a blackboard demonstration. As the novel opens we see, "in the blaze of a cloudless Carolina summer," in a Marine training camp,

What was left of eight dead boys [which] lay strewn about the landscape, among the poison ivy and the pine needles and loblolly saplings. . . . (p. 3) [146/147]

---

6 *Set This House on Fire* (New York: Random House, 1960). See also his remark, in the interview published in *Writers at Work*: events like Hiroshima, he said, "don't alter one bit a writer's fundamental problems, which are Love, Requited and Unrequited, Insult, et cetera." (p. 281).

7 *Life*, 53 (July 20, 1962), 39–42. Faulkner, of course, used this square repeatedly and gave a "mythical history" of almost every timber and brick, in the long expository passages of *Requiem for a Nun* (1951).

8 In *One and Twenty* (Duke University Press, 1945), pp. 266–80.

9 "The Death-in-Life of Benjamin Reid," *Esquire*, 58 (November, 1962), 142.

10 It is not Styron's first novel, but his second, in time of publication (1953). But it must be considered a minor work.

A propos only of the general absurdity of this military world, the "bone, gut, and dangling tissue" point to a haphazard regime, and even to a mad one; at least, its absurdity is a compound of accidental and humanly willed disasters.

In subsequent events, the Colonel (Templeton) of the Marine troop orders his men on a 36-mile hike, to prove nothing at all except that his men can and should walk the distance. Lieutenant Culver, the novel's hero, is also its center, because he is the only one whose personality is seen in more than one dimension. There is a phrase from Haydn, recalled from a brief peacetime stretch in Washington Square, with a wife, a cat, and a record player, which haunts his mind throughout and is apparently to remind one of a saner world beyond this spectral and weird military enclosure. The Haydn plays a role roughly similar to a recording of Mozart's *Don Giovanni* in *Set This House on Fire*, which Kinsolving uses to "blast" the "ghosts" of his neighbors in Sambuco. In any case, it is one of Styron's frequent insertions from the "cultivated world" which always makes one wonder if they are necessary.

Styron is very sophisticated and erudite; he will break in with a Haydn phrase or a quotation from *Oedipus at Colonus*, to set the unwary on an unnecessary search for a "Waste Land" type of significance.[11] Here, in *The Long March*, the references are of course used with a stark simplicity. The clarity and beauty of the Haydn phrase contrast with the true absurdity of the hot, sticky North Carolina scene. The central victim of its absurdity is Captain Mannix, a friend of Culver's who persists beyond all but his human endurance to fulfill the Colonel's absurd orders.

[His persistence] lent to his face . . . an aspect of deep, almost prayerfully passionate concentration—eyes thrown skyward and lips fluttering feverishly in pain—so that if one did not know he was in agony one might imagine that he was a communicant in rapture, offering up breaths of hot desire to the heavens. . . . (*March*, pp. 113–14) [147/148]

Aside from the evidence this passage offers of Styron's close study of Faulkner's style,[12] it is a statement concerning the world of the absurd. Mannix does not defy its absurdity; he simply goes about to prove that he can meet its terms, and becomes in the end a reduced figure as a result of his efforts. Perhaps, by way of extenuation, it

[11] See Michel Butor's "Préface to *La Proie des flammes*, French translation (by Maurice Coindreau) of *Set This House on Fire* (Paris: Gallimard, 1962), a very interesting series of suggestions concerning the quotation from Sophocles.

[12] The style used in describing Mannix generally reminds one of Faulkner's Labove, of *The Hamlet*. The characteristic attitude of deep, almost obsessive concentration is not unusual in Faulkner's novels. But of course, Faulkner does more than *say* his character is deeply moved; the *style* communicates the madness.

should be said that the terms here are extraordinarily simple. Despite the fact that this world is absurd, there are few problems of communication here. It is not the military world that usually bothers Styron's persons, but the civilian world living in the shadow of a war, a "bomb," and, principally, in a circumstance that permits no easy belief.

iii

It is this combination of appalling and threatening circumstances that makes Lie Down in Darkness[13] so sad a novel. Throughout the interior monologue (pp. 335-86) of young Peyton Loftis, the atom bomb just dropped on Hiroshima appears as a menacing minor overtone. This is not a war novel, however; nor is it a novel devoted to diagnoses of civilians hurt by neurosis-inducing fright or guilt. It is, in fact, a "witness novel," that testifies to a special depth of human suffering and struggle. It is, as such, one of the representative novels of the 1950's and 1960's: the postwar novel of anxiety and manners, to which American Jewish novelists have made so substantial a contribution. There is a point at which the total impact of unhappiness is so great that one has the impression that it is God's will it should be so. But this is not true. The agony is not that of sheer victimization. Superficially, it is set off by a husband and wife who are incompatible and whose sins are visited upon their child.[14] Once again superficially, the novel poses a morality and religion inadequate to the pressure and demands made upon them by the modern world. At any rate, the noises and smells of Port Warwick,[15] Virginia, are sufficiently strong to emphasize the fact that industry has invaded a world accustomed to being governed by a fairly slow, "closed" tradition and manners. [148/149]

I think it is a mistake to assume that Darkness is simply a study of "decadence" or "degeneration," two terms that have been too easily applied to both Styron and Faulkner. They do not explain anything. Far from being what Elizabeth Janeway says they are, "hardly conscious enough to be decadent,"[16] the three Loftises are all too alive to the pressures and conditions that continue to get in the way of their understanding each other. The agony of human error is so great that there is no real center of blame. Helen Loftis may at times be thought of as the root source; and at times her narrow, religiously excused sentiments toward pleasure and SIN (as she capitalizes it) do appear responsible. But Milton Loftis is deeply at fault, in having taken to

13 New York and Indianapolis: Bobbs-Merrill, 1951.
14 There are two children, but the cripple, Maudie, starts few speculations and is surely an awkwardly simple "companion" of Helen Loftis' too narrow and too dry Protestantism.
15 The setting of Darkness, as well as the birthplace of Peter Leverett, narrator of Set This House on Fire. It is probably based upon Newport News, Virginia, a port city where Styron was born in 1925.
16 See the New Leader, 35 (January 21, 1952), p. 25.

drink and adultery too quickly, as though they were nostrums available on the medicine shelf. And, finally, Peyton Loftis, alone in
Manhattan, rejected by her husband whom she has quite openly
"deceived," is both culpable and pitiful. In short, one comes eventually
to the conclusion—as happens often in O'Neill plays—that no one is
either totally guilty or blameless; that there is a "fate," terribly and
pathetically human, that hovers over the novel.

In his not having settled for easy answers, his refusal simply to
settle for "decadence" or "Southern *malaise*" as an explanation of his
Loftises, Styron has struggled toward a great achievement in *Darkness*. Once again, there is a complement of "erudite" references; this
time, however, they are largely effective. The epigraph gives us the cue
for the title, which is from Sir Thomas Browne's *Urn Burial:*

. . . since our longest sun sets at right descencions, and makes but winter
arches, and therefore it cannot be long before we lie down in darkness, and
have our light in ashes. . . .

The last words are repeated at the end of Peyton's monologue, as she
prepares to commit suicide:

. . . Perhaps I shall rise at another time, though I lie down in darkness and
have my light in ashes. . . . (p. 386)[17]

Lie Down in Darkness, as its title directs it to be, is concerned
with human mortality, with the relentless drive [149/150] of the death
wish, which is underscored, of course, by a sense of almost total hopelessness. It is significant that the young Peyton, in the "present scene"
of Port Warwick of 1945, is dead; we see her alive only in the past. In
fact, we are aware of death in her and working in her in several ways:
the coffin itself, of whose contents her father desperately tries to avoid
imagining; before that, the body buried in Potter's Field, on Hart's
Island, and claimed by her distraught husband of a few months and
his friend; before that, death in her body (the womb painfully resists
its function in Peyton's several affairs) as she fearfully walks the
streets of Manhattan, vainly seeking the forgiveness of her husband,
and fighting the cynical view of a mechanical, atomic world. And we
may go back, almost to the beginning of her life, when the seeds of
death are planted, as she reacts to the sheer hopelessness of her
parents' incompatibility and to the almost incestuous tenderness with

[17] This monologue is perhaps one of the most obvious borrowings from
Faulkner, specifically from Part Two of *The Sound and the Fury*, an interior
monologue which leads to a suicide, which must therefore have been communicated to us from death. But Styron offers us his quite original version of the
situation; the resemblance is by no means unflattering to him.

which her father treats her, by way of overcompensating for the coldness and emptiness of his married life.

Darkness is so constructed that we are forever beholding the fact of death; the coffin holding Peyton's "remains," present before us, poses simply the question "Why did she die?" For, as the epigraph offers us no hope of immortality and bids us prepare for our own death, the corpse of an eighteen-year-old girl is an ever-present *memento mori.*

There are many answers to the question, and none. Peyton killed herself, or did her father, in his last view of her, frighten her into a pact with death? As she prepares to leave Port Warwick with her husband (as it is, her last time in her birthplace alive) she speaks desperately and angrily of

". . . Daddy! He's had so much that was good in him, but it was all wasted. He wasn't man enough to stand up and make decisions and all the rest. . . . Aren't things bad enough in the world without having him crawl back to that idiot? . . ." (*Darkness*, p. 317)

The poignancy of these random and angry remarks is not realized until we read the interior monologue preceding [150/151] the suicide. Peyton has finally had to realize that her father is and will be no protection for her, that she must expose herself to life, alone, which means going, naked, to death.

For *Darkness* is, much of the way, a story of ordinary middle-class incompatibility and adultery: "ordinary," because the description of it is mean, tawdry, and without hope. Neither husband nor wife is heroic in any of it, though for a short time he appears in one of those interludes of fidelity and good intentions. It is also, and in close relationship to its other function, a novel which concerns the modern sensibility's frantic compulsions, its all but helpless drive toward self-destruction. When it is over, Milton Loftis, in his fifties and on the way to the funeral of his only remaining child, rushes into the rain away from his wife and his mistress, acknowledging for the first time *le néant* in all of its emptiness:

Loftis pulled Helen about so that she faced him and began to choke her. "God damn you!" he yelled, "If I can't have . . . then you . . . nothing!"
"People!" Carey [the minister] cried. "People! People!" He couldn't move.
"Die, damn you, die!"
. . . .
The last [Carey] saw of him was his retreating back, amid all the wind and rain, as he hustled on, bounding past wreaths and boxwood and over tombstones, toward the highway.
Then Helen steadied herself against Carey, and she pressed her head next to the wall. "Peyton," she said, "Oh, God, Peyton. My child. Nothing! Nothing! Nothing! Nothing!" (*Darkness*, pp. 388–89)

The full impact of this passage can come only after a careful reading of the entire novel. There is truly "Nothing!" left. Milton and Helen Loftis finally face this prospect, Helen ironically in the presence of her minister, whose pitifully futile attempts to bring her the solaces of religion now end in a pathetic figure, quite unable to give her the desperately needed words of God's grace. The [151/152] stresses and strains are all in the present, as are the ironic meanings of the stench, the noise, the burial ground, and the Negro revival.[18] Their importance can be sensed, however, only in the past. Through the history of their marriage, and especially in the attractive upper middle-class residential community overlooking the bay, the move toward the hopeless conclusion is inevitable; but its inevitability doesn't always "show." There are times of comparative peace, when both husband and wife seem willing to give in a little.

Nevertheless, three major conditions hover always on the edge of their lives, and make for the pathos of the final hours: Helen's religion (or, her spiteful and even pitiful uses of it); Milton's drinking, which he uses as an easy escape from acknowledging the pathetic sadness of their fate; and Peyton's self-indulgent dependence upon an all but incestuous relationship with her father. Perhaps Styron is saying: These people do not deserve a better fate. Or he may be saying: they are ineluctably fated to end as they do. But beyond any "naturalistic" or "fatalistic" view of them he sees them as persons engaged in pitifully trying to save themselves, or each other, from a fate they are somehow not able to forestall. As he himself said, to David Dempsey:

I wanted to tell the story of four tragically fated people, one of them [Maudie] the innocent victim of the others. It was important to me that I write about this thing, but I can't tell you why. I didn't conceive it, directly at any rate, as a contemporary statement of any kind. The symbols are there, I suppose, but to me the important thing was the story.[19]

It is, of course, *not* a "contemporary statement," except in the limited sense that industrial ugliness intrudes upon the Loftis world, and the explosion of the Hiroshima bomb sounds menacingly in the distance during Peyton's tragic last day in New York City. The great achievement of *Darkness* is that it is a *universal* situation. There is nothing peculiarly Southern, or even especially [152/153] characteristic of the "U.S.A." in the novel. It is a bit too much the melodrama to

[18] The Negro revival, with "Daddy Faith" presiding and Ella Swan attending with her daughter, La Ruth, is once again an "echo" of Faulkner, this time of Part Four of *The Sound and the Fury*, the celebration of Easter in the Negro church, with the Reverend Shegog, a visiting preacher from Saint Louis, officiating. Styron gains an easy contrast by inserting the evangelical event on the edges of the cemetery, and the effects are not nearly so felicitous as those in Faulkner's novels.
[19] *New York Times Book Review*, September 9, 1951, p. 27.

be called a tragedy. Yet the images of a death hovering over life are sufficiently clearly there, to make the whole comparable to the seventeenth century of *Urn Burial,* and of John Donne's sermons.

In short, *Darkness* poses the metaphysical problem of death in a setting in which there is insufficient accommodation for it. The ambiguities of a love and a happiness that seem always beyond reach, for one reason or another; the further perplexities of a man who loves too much, too earnestly, and too vainly: these are novelistic meditations not unlike the poetic and religious meditations typified by the novel's epigraph.

They say a number of things: for one, that we are all doomed; that our lives are but a preparing for death; most importantly, that we somehow (without overtly wishing to, but nevertheless, as if compulsively) help our own way toward self-destruction. Styron is saying that *any* inducement to neurotic behavior, any psychological self-flagellation, is suicidal. The most tragically compelling question at the novel's end is which of the three is the most doomed: Peyton, whose body has been dug up from Potter's Field; Milton, who walks away from her grave crying out "Nothing!" like a middle-class excommunicated King Lear; or Helen, who turns away from the minister of her faith, to repeat the "Nothing!" several times to a blank wall? They are akin in their being doomed, in their having lived a life that somehow has unavoidably led to their doom, in their willing their doom by not acting (perhaps, by not being able to act) to prevent it.

Styron avoids a total surrender to melodrama in several ways. One of these is style. One of the qualities that distinguish writers of Styron's generation from their predecessors of the 1920's is that, for Styron's contemporaries, style actually *does* function to qualify life. Perhaps this is because, most of the time at least, our younger novelists must somehow always "rescue" their work from naturalism and its nihilist metaphysics. They somehow have to [153/154] improvise their own definitions of evil, their own theological metaphors. So, at crucial points, their characters are moral heroes, or moral clowns, or both.

Saul Bellow's Tommy Wilhelm, weeping desperately at a funeral of someone he has never known alive, at the end of his remarkable story, *Seize the Day* (1956), is an excellent case in point. The fact is that Loftis, no less and no more than his contemporary *personae,* improvises definitions as he invents poses to meet the terrible abysses left in their own society by the abject but somehow comprehensible failure of institutional religion to give protection in extreme crises. These circumstances, it seems to me, make for the kind of tragic failure that we see in this first of Styron's two great novels. Death hovers over the Loftis family from beginning to end; it is through death that we see their lives, as though we too were following the hearse, or waiting for the driver to repair its several mechanical failures, and steadily looking back on the scene of their tragic and impotent lives.

I don't believe that Styron intends the "Daddy Faith" episode at the novel's end to serve the same purpose as does Dilsey's Easter Sunday service in Faulkner's *The Sound and the Fury*. The aesthetic "competence" of Dilsey as a character, and the degree of Faulkner's preparing her for her culminating scene are both more acceptable in terms of the Compson débâcle. Besides, the Compson gallery is much more varied. There is very little to go on, for example, when we try to compare Milton Loftis with Quentin Compson's father. Both drink steadily; each is undoubtedly disillusioned with his marriage; the attitude of each has a strong influence on his children. But these are surface resemblances. Styron has earned the right to his own novel.

iv

Set This House on Fire bears a relationship to *Darkness* as an epic resembles a "tragedy of manners." Neither term quite successfully defines either novel, but there is an extensiveness of scope and scene in *House*, a [154/155] largeness of ambition, that do not seem relevant to *Darkness*. The suggestiveness of the title is similarly involved in seventeenth-century metaphysics. This time, the source is John Donne's sermon "To the Earle of Carlile, and his Company, at Sion." In Styron's use of it, in his ambitious epigraph, it reads partly as follows:

> . . . God, who, when he could not get into me, by standing, by knocking . . . hath applied his judgements, and shaked the house, this body, with agues and palsies, and set this house on fire, with fevers and calentures, and frighted the Master of the house, my soule, with horrors, and heavy apprehensions, and so made an entrance into me. . . .[20]

In identifying both his major novels with seventeenth-century texts, Styron is in a sense also identifying them with the twentieth century: for in their contexts, he sees strong resemblances between the two centuries,[21] at least within the limits of certain basic meditations upon "last things."

---

[20] Epigraph to *House*, n. p. Note that the title of *Darkness*, which must have been a commonplace metaphor of death, is also found here: "then this soule cannot be a smoake, a vapour, nor a bubble, but must lie down in darknesse, as long as the Lord of light is light it selfe . . ."

[21] There have been other speculations: Michel Butor's "Préface" to the French translation says much about Sophocles' play, *Oedipus at Colonus* (see pp. xi, xviii), as does André Bonnichon, in "William Styron et le Second Oedipe," *Etudes*, 315 (October, 1962), 102. This association is of course given encouragement through Styron's having Cass Kinsolving quote from the play (see *House*, pp. 117–18). One American critic links Styron's thought with that of Sören Kierkegaard's *The Sickness unto Death*, and quotes the text to prove it (See "Cass Kinsolving: Kierkegaardian Man of Despair," *Wisconsin Studies in Contemporary Literature*, 3, 1962, 54–66). Another suggests an obscure seventeenth-century document, Henri Estienne's, translated by Richard Carew as *A World of Wonders*

House can of course superficially be seen as a conflict between the country bumpkin and the millionaire, but this theme dissolves into farce if pushed too hard. It is true that Cass Kinsolving is in the power of Mason Flagg; their names are also significantly involved, as is that of Peter Leverett, the narrator of Part One, and the listener of Part Two.[22] There is no doubt that Kinsolving is the hero of the novel, as Flagg is its villain. Both tower over everybody else in the novel, so that the next to final event in Sambuco, Italy (Kinsolving's killing of Flagg by forcing him over the cliff on the approach to a village beyond) is a struggle of giants. The real struggle is not the physical one, but Cass's struggle within himself. Flagg is indispensable to that struggle, of course: as he pushes Cass's weaknesses to the point of ridicule, he also provides the means of release from them.

Cass must be considered the hero of *House;* Peter Leverett says, "It is certainly not myself." (*House*, p. 4) In fact, Leverett is primarily designed to be observer and [155/156] listener; even his hateful lashing out at Mason Flagg appears to be only an "observation," after all. Leverett is almost "computer-machine" American: "I am white, Protestant, Anglo-Saxon, Virginia-bred, just past thirty,[23] tolerable enough looking though possessing no romantic glint or cast, given to orderly habits, more than commonly inquisitive, and strongly sexed— though this is a conceit peculiar to all normal young men." (pp. 4–5) He is set up, first, to be attracted (because of an admiration of his apparent superiority) to Mason Flagg; then, to be repelled by him, as he slowly gathers in "counter" impressions; then, to be overwhelmed by Cass's pathetic status; finally, to be committed irrevocably to Cass's triumph over both Flagg and his own inner weaknesses. Leverett is also designed to communicate all of these facts without drawing attention to himself, despite the fact that he grows morally from step to step of the novel's progress.

Leverett is, in short, a "stamped out" model, a pigmy observing

---

(Jerry A. Bryant in *South Atlantic Quarterly*, 62, 1963, 539–50). John Howard Lawson blames Styron for what he regards as the failure of *House* on his inadequate social perception, his having used Freud to set aside Marx (See *Mainstream*, 13 [October, 1960], 9–18). These interpretations have varying usefulness. The wonder is that there are so many, but it seems more sensible to note that Styron's approach to life is more "universal" than ideological or regional.

[22] Leverett has, inevitably, raised questions of the influence of F. Scott Fitzgerald's Nick Carraway of *The Great Gatsby* (1925). But Leverett is not nearly so well sketched in as Carraway, and Kinsolving is surely no Gatsby. The *idea* of having a narrator, like Conrad's Marlow, question and probe at the same time as he narrates, is of course there; and there is a rough similarity of Part Two to the last section of Faulkner's *Absalom, Absalom!* (1936), where Shreve McCannon and Quentin Compson try together to reconstruct the legend of Thomas Sutpen.

[23] Nick Carraway of *The Great Gatsby* remembers, in the noise of a crucial encounter on a hot July afternoon in 1922 at the Savoy Plaza Hotel, that he has just reached the age of thirty. The fact meant much more to Fitzgerald than it does to Styron.

the struggles of giants. Since he has had no real temptations in his life, he has had to make neither compromises nor progress. Or, if there *is* progress in him, it is not interesting. What *is* of interest is the way Styron maneuvers him in both time and space. Only in Leverett's past is there a Mason Flagg: Cass's involvement with him occurs in the Sambuco "present," and this fact is of some importance to the novel's meaning. The "Thing" against which Cass struggles *didn't* start with Flagg, as he says to Peter; it started far back, in childhood, in youth, in The War, and *in himself*. To call him "villain" is not to say that he was evil. To Cass, he was "just scum." ". . . Beast, bastard, crook, and viper. But the guilt is not his! . . ." (*House*, p. 249)

Part of this strange "absolution" has to do with the *roman policier* aspect of *House:* Flagg did not kill Francesca, though he did rape her and did leave her half-dead; the village half-wit, Saverio, completed the job. But Cass's killing Flagg *did* take place and is of the essence. In killing him, Cass destroyed the nastiness inside him: the meanness which Michel Butor strangely calls "la condition américaine," as he calls the novel an "allégorie" [156/157] of this condition and of "une invitation à la surmonter. . . ."[24] Whether it was "American" or not, Cass did triumph over a "something" within him that had (in affecting his mien) frightened prostitutes in Paris, driven him to thoughts of murder and suicide, and led to prodigious feats of drunkenness, the cost of which, for some weeks, led to a bondage to the arrogant "scum," Mason Flagg.

If anything, the idea of the millionaire's son, with an overly indulgent mother, an abundantly fertile imagination,[25] an extraordinary interest in sex (associated with a tendency toward impotence), is a legitimate one. But this fact does not make *House* "une allégorie de la condition américaine . . ."[26] The story of Mason Flagg is one of inventive nastiness; he is like Fitzgerald's Tom Buchanan, who, having played football at Yale, in middle age "drifted here and there unrestfully wherever people played polo and were rich together."[27] But while Buchanan is almost sullenly rich, Flagg takes advantage of his position almost creatively, certainly with verve and *esprit*. Peter Leverett refers in one place to him in "the dual role of daytime squire and nighttime nihilist." (*House*, p. 158) It is true that the strategies and the energy that go into the creation and the satisfaction of his whims are prodigious.

[24] "Préface," to *La Proie des flammes,* p. xi.

[25] At one point Flagg points out, to Leverett, the difference between third-rate lying "and a jazzy kind of bullshit extravaganza, . . . meant with no malice at all, but only with the intent to edify and entertain." (*House*, p. 172) This remark has to do with his legendary war experiences in Yugoslavia as an agent behind the lines; he had actually been a draft dodger.

[26] Butor, *op. cit.*

[27] New York: Scribner's, 1925, p. 7.

That they lead eventually to Flagg's being the Mephistophelean playboy, the archangel of all anti-christs, is true, and important; because by the time Cass Kinsolving confronts him (despite Cass's disclaimers) he needs a worthy antagonist. For, if we go back, we must remember that the "Thing," this *"quelque chose comme ça"* that was destroying Cass's soul and causing him to destroy his body, had started early and grown huge before he finally projected it upon his enemy and, in a traumatic crisis, expelled it in as noisy a catharsis as has been noted for a long time in American fiction.

The crisis is religious in one sense, though it scarcely has a basis in theological symbolism.

"A man cannot live without a focus," he said [to Leverett in South Carolina]. "Without some kind of faith, if you want [157/158] to call it that. I didn't have any more faith than a tomcat. Nothing. Nothing! . . ." (*House*, p. 54)[28]

In this context, a lack of faith is like a lack of light and air, a secular "dark night of the Soul," of the sort described in the passage of Donne's sermon, used as the novel's epigraph. In Cass's kind of world, God will not "set this house on fire"; the initiative will have to come from Cass himself. And, while the cure seems to be complete, as he tells about it in South Carolina, there is no reason to believe that it might not break out again. It is true, however, that he has "met his match," has expelled his tormentor and killed him. More than that, he has seen the "scum" in himself and killed it; it seems to have disappeared forever over the edge of the cliff near Sambuco.

Part Two of the novel, in which Cass and Leverett "go after" the Sambuco incident together, trying to collaborate on explanations and reasons, carries as its epigraph the last stanza of Theodore Roethke's title poem of the 1953 book, *The Waking*.[29]

> *This shaking keeps me steady. I should know.*
> *What falls away is always. And is near.*
> *I wake to sleep, and take my waking slow.*
> *I learn by going where I have to go.*

These lines should give us a clue to the "peace" Cass has discovered finally. It is an uneasy peace, for "What falls away is always. And is near." Roethke's own experience, as the evidence of the poems gives it, involved a great dependence upon the father-image, a "falling away" from it, an apparent solution in marriage and in the pleasures of sex,

28 This is the same "Nothing!" that afflicted both Milton and Helen Loftis in *Darkness*.
29 New York: Doubleday, 1953, p. 120.

and a crisis of "nothingness."[30] There is no doubt that in both cases the experiencing of *il niente, la nullità,* was traumatic, a major challenge to the heroic self. As the fascist *carabiniere* asks of him,

". . . Have you not pictured to yourself the whole horrible vista of eternity? . . . The absolute blankness, . . . stretching out for ever and ever, the pit of darkness which you are hurling yourself into, the nothingness, the void, the oblivion?" (*House,* pp. 195–96) [158/159]

In one sense at least, the condition is "américaine." Cass has come from the country near Wilmington, North Carolina, on the Cape Fear River; at sixteen or seventeen he had come into the city, in the hope of finding sexual experience, and had lain with Vernelle Satterfield, whom he'd discovered near the 'bus station, selling copies of the Jehovah's Witnesses magazine for five cents apiece.

". . . in her little bedroom—she led me in with great piety and dignity, but that bed really *loomed,* I'll tell you—she had the goddamdest gallery of Jesuses you ever saw. . . . It was like a regular Jesus cult. It would have put some of those Italians back in the Abruzzi to shame." (*House,* p. 263)

The comic scene has its serious overtones. For Cass, a Protestant Southerner, seems always to have identified his failures with his religious backgrounds. More than that, he sees himself as forever in the role of the poor, ignorant American, trying desperately each time to "prove himself," and failing each time. In the weeks in Paris, with his Catholic wife and his Catholic children, he again suffers a (this time, serious) lapse in confidence. "You know," he tells Leverett, "the old Anglo-Saxon hellfire which we just can't ever get rid of." (p. 268) Here, trying to justify himself as a painter, he suffers from what he calls "wild Manichean dreams, dreams that told him that God was not even a lie, but worse, that He was weaker even than the evil He created and allowed to reside in the soul of man, that God Himself was doomed, and the landscape of heaven was not gold and singing but a space of terror which stretched in darkness from horizon to horizon." (pp. 275–76)

There is no doubt that the experience is similar to the Kierkegaardian *Sickness Unto Death.*[31] Cass's "cure" for it consists of wild plunges into excess: drinking, gambling, "the vices" if you will. He is more prodigiously a drunk, with a more Gant-ian appetite than ever Milton Loftis could have had. His experiences of "Nothing!" are grandly climactic, leading into agony dreams, long bouts with the

[30] See my essay, "Theodore Roethke: The Poetic Shape of Death," in *Theodore Roethke: A Tribute,* edited by Arnold Stein (Seattle: University of Washington Press, 1965), pp. 94–114.

[31] See Lewis Lawson, *op. cit.*

[159/160] whisky bottle,[32] gambling, and whoring. He even goes the way of the modern scientific humanist, stealing a hundred capsules of a new medicine, which Flagg had himself "lifted" from the P.X. in Naples, in order to help his friend Michele. (pp. 206–10) But, of course, the act, like others of his life, is scarcely a triumph, and certainly does not lead to a conquest of self.

That conquest must come melodramatically. At least Cass has an antagonist he can recognize; he survives all of the terrors of his *nullità* because of that. Mason Flagg has finally, in *his* excesses, provided Cass with an opportunity to rid himself of his. "Not to believe in some salvation," he says later to Leverett, "to have disbelief rolled over on top of ones head like an un-removable stone yet at times like this . . . to see such splendour and glory writ across the heavens & upon the quiet sand and to see all certitude & sweetness in ones own flesh & seed scampering tireless & timeless on the shore, and then still not believe, is something that sickens me to my heart and center. . . ." (*House*, p. 294)[33]

The story of Cass's illness and of his own curing of it has something of the existentialist impact of Faulkner's *A Fable*.[34] Or, it is a dramatization of Faulkner's key phrases in the Stockholm Address of 1950.[35] The fact is that many great artists of the twentieth century have had visions of this Manichaean struggle: Catholics, Protestants, and Jews have all had some hand in portraying the agony, and some have suggested—or imagined—a cure. *Set This House on Fire* is notable for its having come really to grips with the problem, and left it after a masterpiece of story-telling; this, Faulkner, in all his earnestness, was not able to do in *A Fable*, though he certainly managed elsewhere. Styron's most recent novel sets the imagination agoing, in the expectation of an American literature of existentialism, as Ihab Hassan has said.[36] But it is perhaps best not to name it that, for fear of weighing it down with labels and classification. The important fact is that Styron has used his talents mightily and to a good effect in this novel. The subject of both it and *Darkness* is the "Nothing!" [160/

[32] As Leverett says, seeing him at his worst in Sambuco: "Something held him in torment and in great and desperate need: I never saw anyone I wanted so to get sober" (*House*, p. 201).

[33] Here Styron indulges in one of his uncommon "Agrarian" attacks upon the North: "I should have been brought up north in N.Y. suburbs, Scarsdale or somewhere on that order, where I might never have learned the quality of desire or thirst or yearning & would have ended up on Madison Ave. designing deodorant jars, with no knowledge or comprehension of the freezing solitude of the bereft and prodigal son . . ." (*House*, p. 294).

[34] New York: Random House, 1954.

[35] See *William Faulkner: Three Decades of Criticism*, edited by F. J. Hoffman and Olga W. Vickery (Michigan State University Press, 1960), pp. 347–48.

[36] "The Character of Post-War Fiction in America," *English Journal*, 51 (January, 1962), 7.

161] that both Helen and Milton Loftis cry out as he leaves her and the grave of the girl he has killed by tenderness. It is also Kinsolving's word; but he denies it dramatically, and appears at the end of *House* to have found a way of keeping it from him forever.[37] [161]

[37] A translation of this essay on Styron appeared in *Configuration Critique de William Styron,* edited by Melvin J. Friedman (Paris: M. J. Minard, 1967). There have been some minor revisions for publication in this place.

Encounter with Necessity

IHAB HASSAN

. . . we lie down in darkness, and have our light in ashes.—SIR THOMAS BROWNE, *Urn Burial*

I

William Styron's first novel, *Lie Down in Darkness,* 1951, remains one of the outstanding works of postwar fiction. This is not sly praise. *The Long March,* 1953, and *Set This House on Fire,* 1960, are in no way shoddy, and indeed the latest of Styron's novels is an exceptional work, as ambitious in meaning as his first may be deft in execution. The three books project very different types of heroes though each is preeminently a hero of our time. Captain Mannix, the protagonist of *The Long March,* is an awkward and unwilling rebel, a soft, scarred, bearlike man who defies the authority of his Marine commander. "Born into a generation of conformists, even Mannix . . . was aware that his gestures were not symbolic, but individual, therefore hopeless, maybe even absurd. . . ."[1] *Set This House on Fire* is a torrid, complex story of crime and punishment, the terror of guilt and the horror of freedom. Its hero, Cass Kinsolving, finally chooses being rather than nothingness because for him, "to choose between them was simply to choose being, not for the sake of being, or even for the love of being, much less the desire to be forever—but in the hope of being what I

[1] William Styron, *The Long March* (New York, 1953), pp. 55f.

From Ihab Hassan, "Encounter with Necessity: Three Novels by Styron, Swados, and Mailer," in *Radical Innocence: The Contemporary American Novel* (Princeton University Press, 1961). Reprinted by permission of Princeton University Press.

could be for a time."[2] In all three novels, Styron reveals a brooding imagination, sometimes obsessive, and a dark gift of poetry. The [124/125] legacy of Faulkner is perhaps apparent in his earliest work; but it is a legacy that Styron has learned to put to his own service—one does not feel quite the same way about other talented writers, such as William Humphrey—and it is mainly recognizable in the intensity of the author's relation to a certain kind of material. For though Styron is a Virginian by birth, he has tried to shake loose from the local colorist's view of things without foregoing the advantages the Southern tradition provides. Thus, for instance, does he say of *Lie Down in Darkness:* "Only certain things in the book are particularly Southern. I used leit-motifs—the Negroes, for example—that run throughout the book, but I would like to believe that my people would have behaved the way they did anywhere."[3] Other motifs which we like to identify as Southern occur in his fiction: the Biblical rhetoric of story telling, the conflict between a tradition of religious fundamentalism and modern skepticism, racial contrasts, the industrialization of an agrarian society, etc. But his concern with some of these motifs, particularly the demonic power of guilt, the black oppressiveness of death or decay, the lurid ironies of Protestantism in the South—"a crazy colored preacher howling those tremendously moving verses from Isaiah 40, while riding around in a maroon Packard"—betrays an imagination nearly religious in intensity, a sensibility closer to the baroque tradition of John Donne and Sir Thomas Browne than to the gothic school of Poe and Company.[4]

The epigraph to *Lie Down in Darkness* contains the following statement from Sir Thomas Browne's *Urn Burial:* ". . . since our longest sun sets at right descencions, and makes but winter arches, and therefore it cannot be long before we lie down in darkness, and have our light in ashes." There is no single hero-victim in the novel. Milton Loftis, his wife Helen, and their daughter Peyton are all locked in a domestic tragedy in which love must wear the face of guilt, and the search for childhood innocence must acquaint the seeker with death. All lie down [125/126] in darkness. But there is one character whose light is found in ashes: Peyton.

I pray but my prayer climbs up like a broken wisp of smoke: Oh my Lord, I am dying, is all I know, and *oh my father, oh my darling,* longingly, lonesomely, I fly into your arms! . . . Myself all shattered, this lovely shell? Perhaps I shall rise at another time, though I lie down in darkness and have my light in ashes.[5]

2 William Styron, *Set This House on Fire* (New York, 1960), pp. 500f.
3 Malcolm Cowley, ed., *Writers at Work* (New York, 1959), p. 272.
4 *ibid.*, p. 273.
5 William Styron, *Lie Down in Darkness* (New York, 1957), p. 386.

This is the stream of Peyton's doomed consciousness before she jumps from a washroom to her death. The two passages quoted, one lying at the outset of the novel, the other very near its close, form a kind of frame, a frame of two mirrors reflecting the darkness and the light of a single life, Peyton's, which in turn refracts the fate of all the others. For Peyton's darkness, however "clinical" it may seem—and there is no doubt that it is more dramatic than clinical—must still illumine the universal urge of human beings to clutch some impossible idea of eternal childhood or innocence, must illumine and expiate that urge. "The real point of *Lie Down in Darkness*," Geismar rightly perceives, "is that, dealing with the Electra complex itself, it has not only made it human and domestic but has returned it, so to speak, to its natural home of childhood feeling itself."[6] This is one aspect of a radical innocence to which Peyton, no simple innocent, is a perverse victim.

The drama of Peyton, however, is enacted within at least three circles of meaning: social, domestic, and private. First, there is the South of the tidewaters in Virginia. The scene conveys, from the beginning, a feeling of something recently denatured and agelessly dissolute:

Riding down to Port Warwick from Richmond, the train begins to pick up speed on the outskirts of the city, past the tobacco factories with their ever-present haze of acrid, sweetish dust. . . .

. . . instead, you look out once more at the late summer landscape and the low, sorrowful beauty of tideland streams winding through marshes full of small, darting frightened noises and glistening and dead silent at noon. . . . [126/127]

Halfway between the railroad station and Port Warwick proper . . . the marshland, petering out in disconsolate, solitary clumps of cattails, yields gradually to higher ground. Here, bordering the road, an unsightly growth of weeds takes over, brambles and briars of an uncertain dirty hue. . . . The area adjacent to this stretch of weeds is bleakly municipal in appearance. . . . Here there are great mounds of garbage; a sweet, vegetable odor rises perpetually on the air and one can see—from the distance fairly iridescent—whole swarms of carnivorous flies blackening the garbage and maybe a couple of proprietary rats, propped erect like squirrels, and blinking sluggishly, with mild, infected eyes, at some horror-stricken Northern tourist.[7]

Nature may be deformed by factories and gas tanks squatting on the landscape, but nature also knows its own forms of corruption. In this, nature reflects Southern society—"The ground is bloody and full of guilt where you were born and you must tread a long narrow path towards your destiny," Milton's father says to him before sending him

[6] Maxwell Geismar, *American Moderns* (New York, 1958), p. 243.
[7] *Lie Down in Darkness*, pp. 9, 10, 68.

off to the university.[8] There are scenes—the engagement dance of
Loftis, the wedding party for his daughter, the country club meetings
with Dolly, or the descriptions of the Cartwrights—which reveal the
manners of a society resistant to incursions and still operant. But these
ceremonial scenes should be balanced against the glib wisdom of
Berger, the New York invert who says to Peyton, "It is symptomatic of
that society from which you emanate that it should produce the dis-
solving family: *ah, ah,* patience, my pretty, I know you say symptomatic not of that society, but of *our* society, the machine culture, yet so
archetypal is this South with its cancerous religiosity, its exhausting
need to put manners before morals, to negate all *ethos*—call it a *husk*
of a culture."[9]

Negation becomes gradually more emphatic in the three generations which the novel encompasses: Milton's father with his grandilo-
quent wisdom; the Loftises themselves, and the minister, Carey Carr,
still genteel in their impotence; and Peyton or Berger for whom
cynicism or self-destruction is the [127/128] measure of salvation.
Milton's father says to Loftis, "My son . . . we stand at the back door
of glory. Now in this setting part of time we are only relics of van-
quished grandeur more sweet than God himself might have imagined:
we are the driblet turds of angels, not men but a race of toads, vile
mutations who have lost our lovewords . . ."; and Peyton says to Dick
Cartwright, her contemporary, "Those people back in the Lost Generation. Daddy I guess. . . . They thought they were lost. They were
crazy. They weren't lost. What they were doing was losing us."[10] And
so the progress of negation leads to the historical event which casts a
sinister shadow on the last pages of the novel: the explosion of the
Bomb. For it is just as the war ends that Peyton commits suicide; and
it is as she reaches out for the last time, reaches out in selfish desperation for her husband, Harry, that he retorts, "Do you realize what the
world's come to? Do you realize that the great American commonwealth just snuffed out one hundred thousand innocent lives this
week? There was a time, you know, when I thought for some reason
. . . I could spend my life catering to your needs. . . ."[11] But does
the insanity of the world overshadow Peyton's need or become merely
the ghastly correlative of her disease?

Nor does the novel show religion to be a means of genuine social
or spiritual salvation. The religiosity of Helen is an extension of her
egotism, an inversion of her feminine possessiveness, a token of her
revulsion against instinct and life. The gracious dialogues, so redolent
with self-pity and theatrical despair, she conducts with Carey Carr are
almost the perfect parody of a courtship. Yet Carr, though earnestly

8 *ibid.*, p. 74.
9 *ibid.*, p. 363.
10 *ibid.*, pp. 184, 235.
11 *ibid.*, p. 377.

devoted to his Episcopal church, cannot raise his faith above the level of poetic compassion. He is good as chorus and preceptor, useless as comforter or savior. When in the final scene of Peyton's funeral Milton goes for Helen's throat in a rage, Carr can only stand by terrified and exclaim, "People! People."[12] Carr is indeed more impotent than Daddy Faith, the Negro revivalist whose [128/129] baptismal rites fill the strange epilogue of the book. There is power and frenzy in this scene of Negroes ducked in the waters of life, cleansed and purified; there is also awe and joy and simplicity of faith, qualities that are absent from the lives of white people. Drowning is the controlling image of Peyton's last moments, but it is the element of rebirth for Ella and La Ruth. The white girl does not find the father and lover she so desperately needs, but the black congregation finds both: "You, Daddy! Daddy Faith! You loves us! You, Daddy!"[13] Yet what can the contrast do but sharpen our sense of incongruity? How can the tormenting events of the novel be explained in a scene of primitive religious fervor except ironically? The tragic tensions of civilized life, as Styron knows, are not so easily resolved; nor can we all worship at the altar erected on a raft which Styron thus describes: "On it had been erected a sort of stage, surrounded on four sides by a golden damask curtain; embroidered designs—dragons and crosses and crowns, Masonic emblems, shields, bizarre and unheard-of animals, an amalgam of myth and pagan ritual and Christian symbology—all these glowed against the curtain in green and red phosphorescent fabrics, literally hurting the eyes."[14] The depletion of religious symbols from their meaning parallels the depletion of manners from their content.

Domestic life in *Lie Down in Darkness* is equally corrupt. For this is a story of infidelity, of vengeful love, blocked, hurt, and perverted, of adults who can never escape their childhood. It is a story of a husband unfaithful to his wife, a mistress unfaithful to her husband, a girl unfaithful to the man she marries. It is the story of a woman, Helen, who can love only what she can control—her crippled daughter, Maudie, or the childish part of her husband, Milton; of a man whose sensuality is merely a form of dependence on Dolly, and whose love, for Peyton, can never become sensual; of a girl who frantically needs a husband, Harry, precisely because she loves her father, and who hates the mother who is viciously jealous of her. These [129/130] ambivalences of love are created by a man-child, girl-woman, and mother-neuter—the images of reversion in the novel are legion—who bind the family in a circle of guilt. Something, truly, is rotten in Denmark, as not Hamlet but the mortician, Mr. Casper, reflects, for it is the custodians of death who also hold, it seems, our conscience in

---

12 *ibid.*, p. 388.
13 *ibid.*, p. 397.
14 *ibid.*, p. 392.

custody. Yet the root of corruption may be a kind of innocence, an excess of love which, as Milton understands, always requires forgiveness. Where there is no forgiveness, vengeance takes over—and death. For the living, death is nothingness. It is what Milton feels when his efforts, after Peyton's suicide and Maudie's earlier death, fail to conciliate Helen: "With nothing left! Nothing! Nothing! Nothing!" It is also what Helen feels too late: "Peyton," she said, "Oh God, Peyton. My child. Nothing! Nothing! Nothing! Nothing!"[15] Strangely enough, it is only Dolly, the outsider, the interloper, who is simple or stupid or forgiving enough to escape the final seal of negation.

And of course there is no surcease of terror as we move from the domestic to private experience where all terror begins, where it must end. The hell of love, the hell of purchasing one's happiness with another's pain, the hell, even, of failing to know the love one is supposed to know—these are dramatized in scene after scene. The gist of it all is that no one has a chance: "Oh Christ, have mercy on your Peyton this evening not because she hasn't believed but because she, no one, had a chance to ever."[16] Peyton must be locked in her destiny; locked in an interior monologue, the formal equivalent of her absolute isolation; locked in a nightmare of strutting pigeons and screeching katydids, those birds that haunt Peyton throughout the novel, symbolizing her sexual guilt and her childish yearnings for freedom, and rustling with their wings over her death; locked, again, in a stream of memories from which the sole escape is drowning in the airless void of time, so that at last her flightless birds may ascend, one by one, "through the suffocating night, toward paradise."[17] What paradise? That of a [130/131] stricken mind, a heart dazed by its strange necessities? A paradise of childhood, never lost and yet never to be regained? A fool's or saint's paradise?

Obviously this is not the vision of an ancestral South which Styron described as "a land of prim pastoral fences, virgin lumber, grazing sheep and Anglo-Saxons: these, the last, spoke in slumbrous Elizabethan accents, rose at dawn, went to bed at dusk, and maintained, with Calvinist passion, their traditional intolerance of evil."[18] It is rather a vision of tragic ambiguities and ironic necessities, of human experience spanning the abyss. It is a vision which must create its own distinctive form.

Lie Down in Darkness is a brilliant formal accomplishment. Its focus is narrow in space and diffuse in time. Peyton's hearse is constantly in our view, and the story is quite literally its halting progress, from the Port Warwick railway station, where the remains of Peyton

15 *ibid.*, pp. 388f.
16 *ibid.*, p. 384.
17 *ibid.*, p. 386.
18 *ibid.*, p. 226.

arrive, to the cemetery, where she is laid to rest. The physical fact of death is simple and immitigable. The complexity is temporal, for time, after all, is a function of man's urge to experience and to understand. Time is consciousness—and consciousness in our time has cracked and splintered. Time in the novel, consequently, is cracked, too; the story is revealed in flashbacks, and flashbacks within flashbacks. The fate of the Loftis family cannot be related by following the Aristotelian precepts of plot. The fate of the Loftises is, to be sure, settled before time began and, as Freudians know, time begins when we fall from childhood. This seems in accordance with the Aristotelian notion of a tragic necessity. But the dramatic emphasis of the novel is not on the end; it is rather on the beginning in which middle and end are swallowed. Nor is the logic of necessity clear; it is rather inscrutable as experience itself and demonic as guilt, the ruling principle of the book. Time, therefore, does not become merely the passive medium through which guilt is inherited and expiated. It is an active agent, not erosive in any predictable way—Dolly, Milton, [131/132] Helen, and Peyton come together and fall asunder several times in the course of the novel—but destructive in a mysterious fashion. None of the characters can fully penetrate his situation. Remembrance of things past guarantees no wisdom or control.

Fractured time makes for a fractured consciousness. Each of the seven sections of the novel is dominated by the point of view of one of the characters, though there are shifts within each section too. Together, these points of view constitute an ironic commentary on the limitations of each. Reality is larger than any of the characters can assess, and the novelist himself can assess it only by suspending his judgment in compassion for the helpless isolation of all. Or he can assess it, again, by deliberately creating various levels of narration in the same episode, creating, that is, an ambiguity which must stay unresolved. The crucial incident of Peyton, dressed in tight shorts, nuzzling up to her father is an example. We see the scene itself, as it must have occurred, through the jealous eyes of Helen who narrates the incident to Carey Carr and at the same time indulges her own vicious stream of secret thoughts; and we see it again, almost simultaneously, through the eyes of the novelist looking over Helen's shoulder. The incestuous interchange of feeling or gesture, whatever it was, thus appears in a haze of refracted light; reality is sicklied over with the cast of illusion; for the only power to assess facts may rest with fancy.

Retrospection in time leads to introspection in the stream of an isolated consciousness—thence the charged images welling up from the past, shards and splinters of experiences forgotten, repeated with hopeless urgency. Hence the involuted sentences, pressing and crowding the meaning of a whole life into one tortured, inexorable, poetic fragment:

Helen, Helen, he thought drowsily, *my lost, my lovely, why have I forsaken you?* Visions white as sunlight, perfect as one flower, a gardenia, once re-membered from a dance that never stopped till dawn, they came to him briefly, vanished, and he believed he slipped off for a spell, thinking of Helen dressed like a cat, bearing down [132/133] on him with a knife: only it wasn't a knife, it was something else, a flower or something, and they were in Charlottesville, and there was Peyton too, her lips pressed to his, saying Daddy Daddy Bunny dear, the globe revolving monstrously out of night into day again, turning and turning. . . .[19]

Day merges into night, reality into dream. The counters of dreams are symbols, which seek, in their obscure way, to make the inalienable privacy of the soul public. These Styron uses with tact, though his obvious and awkward handling of Peyton's "birds" may be a greater concession to pathology than he usually permits himself. But the syntax of dreams is that of free associations, and it is these Styron employs to make vital connections between his characters. Thus, for instance, does Peyton begin by thinking of Harry and end, in the same movement of feeling, thinking of Milton:

How many times have I lain down to sin out of vengeance, to say *so he* [Harry] *doesn't love me, then there is one that will,* to sleep then and dream about the birds, and then to wake with one eye open to the sweltering, joy-less dawn and think *my life has known no father, any road to any end may run,* to think of home. I would not pray to a polyp or a jellyfish, nor to Jesus Christ, but only to that part of me that was pure and lost now, when he [Milton] and I used to walk along the beach, toward Hampton, and pick up shells.[20]

This is deft transition. But no transition can establish the real connections in Peyton's life. Her "initiation" to adult recognitions ends in suicide. The pattern of her encounter with experience is finally a closed one, but it is not, for all its external neatness, intelligible. And in a strange way, a way undefinable by any dogma or creed but perhaps simply by the compassion art bestows, her ashes do give forth light. This is what *Lie Down in Darkness,* however overwritten it may be in parts, however elusive its resolution may seem, manages to dramatize for our minds. Stunned and horrified, the reader's mind is purified without recourse to a genuinely tragic catharsis. [133]

[19] *ibid.,* p. 152.
[20] *ibid.,* p. 368.

William Styron's Clown Show

ROY ARTHUR SWANSON

WILLIAM STYRON IS A SELF-CONSCIOUS ROMANTIC WHO IS VALIANTLY
trying to succeed as a lyrical, existentialist tragedian. His models include Faulkner and Joyce; but his productions are in the class of
Thomas Wolfe and James Jones.[1] A following of critics that persists in
obtuseness has elevated him to the status of a major American writer.[2]
A following of undiscriminating readers has put his works on the best
seller lists. His timely attendance upon the Black rebellion in America
has won him greater attention, more literary prizes and the profitable
tag "controversial." He has become a phenomenon; and phenomena
must be remarked.

At this writing, Styron is forty-three, and his major literary credits
in fiction include three novels[3] and a novella.[4] Impressionable readers

---

[1] Styron apparently suffers no aversion to membership in this class. See "Two
Writers Talk It Over" in *Esquire*, LX (July 1963), pp. 57–59: the two writers are
Styron and James Jones. See also "The Shade of Thomas Wolfe," Styron's review
of Andrew Turnbull's biography of Wolfe, in *Harper's Magazine*, vol. 236, no.
1415 (April 1968), pp. 96–104: "I think his influence may have been especially
powerful upon those who, like myself, had been reared as Wolfe had in a small
Southern town or city, and who in addition had suffered a rather mediocre secon-
dary education, with scant reading of any kind. . . . I feel nothing but a kind of
gratitude when I consider how I succumbed to the rough unchanneled force of
Wolfe as one does to the ocean waves."

[2] A notable exception is Richard Foster, whose "An Orgy of Commerce:
William Styron's *Set This House on Fire*" (*Critique* III [Summer 1960], pp. 59–
70) prompted Styron to reply in pique to the editors of *Critique*, saying, as Mr.
Foster indicated to me, something to the effect that Foster ought to be writing for
Confidential magazine. Mr. Foster concludes that "we must be willing to throw a
writer like Mr. Styron back into the hopper of anonymity and make him at last
prove his claim to the amount of attention he has had from us undeserved." I am
in substantial agreement with this conclusion.

[3] *Lie Down in Darkness* (1951), herein abbreviated as *LDD*, with page
references to the first edition (New York: Bobbs-Merrill Co.); *Set This House on
Fire* (1960), herein abbreviated as *SHF*, with page references to the first edition
(New York: Random House); and *The Confessions of Nat Turner* (1967), herein
abbreviated as *CNT*, with page references to the first edition (New York: Random
House).

[4] *The Long March* (1952, 1953), in *Discovery* 1, ed. John Aldridge and Vance
Bourjailly (New York: Pocket Books, 1953), pp. 221–283, herein abbreviated as'

---

may mistake the verve and sweep of the novels for belletristic accomplishment; they may, with Max J. Herzberg and the staff of the Thomas Y. Crowell Company, regard the novella as "a small classic."[5] But close inspection of any of Styron's fictional works reveals much that is shoddy and second-rate; for example:

It had been an evil day, and the rain that streamed against the windows, blurring a distant frieze of gaunt gray pines, had seemed to nag with both remembrance and foreboding—of tropic seas, storm-swept distances and strange coasts. (LM, 11)

This ought to be recognized as tired romantic prose. "To nag with . . . foreboding" has a Gothic sound, but even as lyricism it is unintelligible. Tropic seas, etc., may be remembered and there may be forebodings of these; still, to present rain as the agent of its own remembrance and foreboding is to do disservice to the device of personification. And "a swollen obbligato of demented sounds" (LM, 41) is Gothic nonsense. The phrase, "one ever rapt in some litany of punishment and court-martial" (LM, 30), makes sense despite the Victorian throwback with which it opens and the malfunctional hysteronproteron of its close. "The news had not seemed yet to spread around the command post" (LM, 17) is an example of stylistic, if not grammatical, futility. And to have a character feel "intolerably hot—with a heat" (LM, 102) is hardly to warrant for one's prose the accolade of classic simplicity.

"He felt his heart pounding" (original prose?) "and a cold dread" (presumably he felt this too). "He pulled himself together some" (Tidewater colloquialism?) "and moved down the hall on precarious tiptoe, trying to avoid knocking things over" (LDD, 310). Styron pads his prose with fashionable adjectives: colossal, enormous, strange, vague, sightless, hopeless, inexpressible, palpable, impalpable, wild, agonized, etc. He makes excessive use of the word "some." He affects high-sounding metaphors, e.g., "She sipped the water slowly and then, when the glass was empty, placed it on the window ledge, watching her frosty thumbprints fade and vanish, silver ghosts of snails contracting inward upon some sightless wonderland infinity" (LDD, 146): "inward" is superfluous, and the last three words are really a comedy of the abstruse.

His longest novel, Set This House on Fire, is pocked with Gothic and Thomas Wolfean patches of would-be splendor: "the gray hue

---

LM, with page references to the Vintage Books edition (New York: Random House, 1956). Styron has also published a good number of articles and reviews; these, as well as his pre-1951 short stories, will not be considered in this essay.

  5 The Reader's Encyclopedia of American Literature (New York 1962), p. 1100.

. . . of disaster"; "through the floodgates of his destiny"; "a bloody amazing intaglio"; "a vestige of sudden moonlight"; "I slipped seaward toward Europe with all Manhattan aglitter in my eyes, its cenotaphs and spires exorbitant and heaven-yearning"; "I followed his gaunt and hustling vision, multi-reflected, down the mirrored corridor"; "a low-throated, placid, soft threnody of despair"; "in flight toward the in-accessible sun"; "I was still a mean little cesspool of bitter, pent-up, frustrated, hopeless desires"; "long ago at dusk in some southern encampment where white barracks stretched in shadeless ranks to the far horizon and men marching shouldered rifles in the twilight and, wild, triumphant, a band tarantaraed beneath a grove of pines—oh how long away!"[6]; etc.

Can Styron's loyal readers defend his uninspired reiteration of "carrousel"[7] in Set This House on Fire and "paradigm" in The Confessions of Nat Turner, or his use of "most" as a synonym of "almost," or his tedious catalogues of trees, shrubs, and foods indigenous to Tidewater Virginia or the Carolinas, or his reiteration of the inevitable phrase "in terms of" (e.g., SHF, 315, "in terms of Sambuco"!), or his imagistic gulls (see n. 19) obtrusively hovering in the wake of the Holy Ghost above mists and water, or his dull and deadening clusters of obscenity and profanity, or his overworked image of the dog?

About his dog imagery: apparently it serves as an omen of human mortality[8] and, by extension, the mortality of God.[9] Milton Loftis' intuitions of mortality are configured in this scene:

It was getting colder. He pulled himself up. A dog snarled at his feet and he kicked at it feebly, hating all dogs forever. Surely this was a punishment, but unconsciously, perhaps mercifully so, he somehow made his way back to the house, concerned solely with the matter of not bleeding to death. (LDD, 214)

In The Long March (pp. 7–8) Lieutenant Culver is found to have had "a friendly beagle named Howard whom he took for hikes in Washington Square . . . until . . . 'the day the roof fell in'" (i.e., the day he was recalled to active service and the prospect of combat). In each instance the image of the dog is consonant with memini mori.

[6] Pp. 27, 29, 42, 96, 174, 180–181, 212, 218, 250, 451.
[7] There is also "a fitful carrousel of sleepy sounds" in LM, 62.
[8] Cf. the hounds as malum signum in Don Quixote; Goethe's Mephisto as a black dog; Kafka's Joseph K., the circumstances of whose death in The Trial enjoin the simile of a dog; the fear of dogs suffered by Joyce's Stephen Dedalus; Beckett's Lucky on a leash; the dog that follows and is kicked to death by Pär Lagerkvist's Tobias (a modern version of the dog that follows the resurrected Tobias in The Book of Tobit); Gunter Grass's Hundejahre.
[9] Loss of faith; secularization of deity; the Hound of Heaven reduced to a mere dog. See below, n. 18.

The imagery becomes acutely symbolic in *Set This House on Fire*. Cass Kinsolving is morbidly depressed by a sight of the Fates: "Three women in rags, ageless, their skin stained the color of walnut, labored up the side of the mountain toward Sambuco, carrying on their backs loads of brush and fagots. . . ." Kinsolving muses that "these crooked shapeless things could possess no souls—but from tormented gristle and flesh, as if from animals" (p. 341). Then, having asserted the animal mortality of the flesh denied *animam resurgendam*, Styron introduces a dying animal (a dog that has been run over and crushed by a bus or a truck: "*'Ah Dio!'* someone said. 'Put him out of his misery!'" And: "*'Buon Dio!'* the same voice said again. 'Somebody finish the poor animal!'" (pp. 342–343). The local physician comes by and bludgeons the dog with a stick; failing to kill the dog quickly, he merely increases its misery: he aims badly, and the stick breaks. Later, Kinsolving dreams "of women with burdens, and dogs being beaten, and these somehow all seemed inextricably and mysteriously connected" (p. 344). Still later, he relates to Luigi his dream of a dog run over by a bus in which he (Kinsolving) had been riding and of the dog's metamorphosis into a woman whose mien is that of the fated human; this time the bus driver clubs the animal in repeated, unsuccessful blows:

> "Then—" he said. "Then I looked down through the billowing dust, and this is what I saw. It was not the dog's head he was beating, but the head of the woman, this scrawny peasant woman with the fagots. Somehow she had turned into the dog. Lying there crushed and mangled, with her poor tormented body pressed against the dust, she let out piteous cries, shrieking, 'God! God!' over and over again." (pp. 357–358)

Then Kinsolving speculates upon an ineffectual deity who "had created suffering mortal flesh which refused to die, even in its own extremity. Which suffered all the more because even He in His mighty belated compassion could not deliver His creatures from their living pain" (p. 358). The dog as moribund humanity, and as an obsolescent deity in whom humanity cannot cease to believe or center its need, is an effective symbol, particularly in its analogy of the intractability of man's fate—persisting, as it does, in the face of all his vigorous efforts to change it. Styron's insight is superior to his prose, which has the woman turned into the dog, when actually the dog had turned into the woman, and which attaches to the word "mighty" an ambiguity (does it qualify "belated" or "belated compassion"?) that borders on indeliberate humor.

Styron, in selecting the image of the dog as a symbol of human mortality and divine inefficacy, is neither original nor artistic in his manipulation of that symbol. Unlike his doctor and bus driver, he does manage to beat the dog to death. Our rejoinder to his *memento mori* had best be *cave canem*.

He goes on to have his Nat Turner recollect, "Beyond my maddest imaginings I had never known it possible to feel so removed from God—a separation which had nothing to do with faith or desire, for both of these I still possessed, but with a forsaken solitary apartness . . ." (*CNT*, 10). The last three words constitute another of Styron's abstruse triads: has a more inept kenning of "alienation" ever been devised? In any case, while Nat Turner ponders separation from God, "Hark's breathing [comes] through the wall like the sound of an old dog dying."

To date each of Styron's major fictional works begins in the atmosphere of human mortality. *Lie Down in Darkness* opens upon Peyton Loftis' funeral. *The Long March* begins with a short mortar round's claiming the lives of eight marines in a stateside chow line. *Set This House on Fire* is initiated with a reference to murder and with Peter Leverett's smashing his car into a hapless, half-blind Italian. *The Confessions of Nat Turner* immediately discloses Nat Turner and Hark awaiting execution. Each work then develops the sense of alienation that accompanies hopeless human suffering in a meaningless world deprived of direct spiritual satisfaction.

In Styron's *magnum opus*, *Set This House on Fire* (in this case "*magnum*" has to modify "*opus*" as an adjective of quantity instead of quality), a long, impressive epigraph is followed by a story the real merit of which is vitiated by excessive length, clumsy narrative, putatively clever construction, and a poorly wrought existentialist theme.

The epigraph, from a John Donne letter, sustains Styron's pretensions to familiarity with seventeenth-century English clerical prose: the epigraph to his novel is a passage from Thomas Browne's *Hydriotaphia*. Styron likes to truncate epigraphic clauses and offer them as seemingly hortatory titles: Browne's "we lie down in darkness" is bereft of its subject, and Donne's "God . . . hath . . . set this house on fire" loses its subject and auxiliary verb. The Donne passage may have attracted Styron because of its evocation of the epigraph to *Lie Down in Darkness;* Donne wrote that "this soule . . . must lie in darknesse." As titles, *Lie Down in Darkness* and *Set This House on Fire* become prescriptions to contemporary men, from whose lives the graciously secure light of deity has been removed. We are advised to face up to the horror, darkness and meaninglessness of an existence unrelieved by God and to light our way with the fires of our own suffering.

Styron's Cass Kinsolving is, in his person, a Jeremiad of suffering, whose house (i.e., body) is set on fire by his unsuccessful flight from materialism, a flight fueled by alcohol in a combustion chamber of domestic responsibility. To put it more simply, he is a "lush" for whom his author fails to find real literary dimension.

Kinsolving, a bespectacled Protestant,[10] has an antipathy to Christianity; or at least he has separated himself from the Biblical God. He retains a Kierkegaardian *Angest* (or *Angst*) and by means of it sets his house on fire; the setting on fire is his doing, there being no God now to start the conflagration. He characteristically rejects the *New Testament* myth embodied in his Irish Catholic wife, whose nickname, Poppy, signifies the opiate of religion, just as her Mick[11] name, Pauline (née Shannon), hints at the organization of the Christian religion. But he does not and cannot reject his wife in herself. Kinsolving represents alienated modern man, and his wife represents the abandoned but still much needed mainstay of Christianity or Christian love. This theme of the insufficiency of secular existence is prefigured in *Lie Down in Darkness*. In this novel God is repeatedly invoked in bland interjection (e.g., "Oh, God, it's so wrong!" [p. 160]) and the word "God" is reduced to an expletive. In addition, Peyton's marriage is viewed as one sanctified by a mundane Eucharist, "the champagne its mystical blood, the cake its confectionery flesh" (p. 287: a pathetic affectation of irony). Furthermore, Milton Loftis, whose religious opiate is a transubstantiation not of God's blood but of the Dionysian vine itself, is addressed by Cherry Pye as "Poppy" (pp. 308–309).

The problem defined by *Set This House on Fire* is how to achieve the spiritual and sexual satisfaction enjoyed by the likes of John Donne—and by the likes of the *religiosus medicus* as well—when the religion that served the seventeenth century with respect to such satisfaction has failed to serve the twentieth. Styron's definition of the problem is badly blurred by two failures: (1) his appearing to offer a solution to the problem and (2) his antiheroic characterization of Kinsolving along with his supersaintly portrait of Poppy.

Kinsolving sets his "house" on fire and, fostered by his Poppy-love[12] and uplifted by his learning how to choose, rises from his own ashes[13] and finds fulfillment in Charleston, S.C. His progress to maturity ("ripeness is all," etc.) includes his getting away with murder. His victim, Mason Flagg, is a sado-hedonistic waterfly flaunting the arrogance of wealth. He is erratically brilliant and creatively imaginative but lacking in the staying power that would predispose him to

---

[10] Styron identifies Kinsolving as a "southern methodist" (p. 362) but accords him an affinity with Judaism. Kinsolving admires a Jew, Navy Captain Slotkin, to whom he directs impassioned apostrophes (see n. 18); and he is taken for a "Mr. Applebaum" by a New York art instructor (p. 387). With this affinity he is not unlike a Jew who has lost the Talmudic faith of his fathers and resents his loss as much as he resents their faith.

[11] Poppy (p. 300): "Hush about being a Mick! . . . I'm a Mick, and the children are *half*, and you're just about the biggest bigot I know."

[12] The pun is Styron's. Note the juxtaposition: "So after the war, when I was going to art school in New York, I met Poppy. Love at first sight" (p. 253).

[13] Like his motor-car accident victim, Luciano di Lieto, he emerges "like the Phoenix risen from the ashes of his own affliction" (p. 506): a paltry parallel.

constructive—or destructive but firm—intellectualism. He is a male Hedda Gabler in his desire to control and direct at least one life other than his own; but he lacks Hedda's dignity and complex intelligence. Flagg is a portrait of the individual whose need for security and self-realization is translated into the desire to own a slave who is secure in a genuine talent and manifests a mode of integrity: Kinsolving becomes the slave-designate. This desire, a perverse sublimation, lends itself to condescension, insults, ostentation, conspicuous consumption, torture, and rape. Kinsolving proves to be the wrong slave: his talent is only that of the cartoonist, and he achieves a hitherto nonexistent integrity under the domination of Flagg. He proves, in fact, what Styron's Nat Turner proves, that the compression of human dignity by slavery is a force which transforms that amorphous dignity into a well-defined, solidly molded, and irrefragable counterforce. Kinsolving is Flagg-Gabler's Ejlert Løvborg, the man who finds himself. Misleadingly, Styron, tied to the structure of his novel, has to let Kinsolving-Løvborg survive the fatality of self-realization so as to be in a position to tell his existentialist tale to WASP Peter Leverett, narrator.

The novel's projected existentialism is rather a vapid adaptation of pedestrian jargon as it is needlessly summed up for the ordinary reader in the concluding set-to's between Kinsolving and the police corporal Luigi, a pragmatic Fascist:

I thought of being. I thought of nothingness. I put my head into my hands, and for a moment the sharp horror of *being* seemed so enormous as to make the horror of nothingness less than nothing by its side. . . . (pp. 489–490)

A proclivity toward religious instead of atheistic existentialism is indicated in Luigi's identification of Kinsolving's *Angst:*

"You *sin* in your guilt!" And suddenly I ceased trembling and became calm as if like some small boy on the verge of a tantrum I had been halted, the childish fit arrested by some almighty paternal voice. I sat back again and gazed out at the dark gulf, and the spell of anxiety vanished, as quickly as it had come. (p. 490)

Being, nothingness, horror, guilt, trembling, arrested, dark gulf (= pit or abyss), anxiety: a catalogue of existentialist bywords that was already conventional in 1950, seven years after Sartre published *Being and Nothingness.* "Fear" (panic, terror) and "freedom" (liberty) are not far from the above passage:

It occurred to me in the most desolate and creepy way that by these lies of [Luigi's], all this mad deception, what he had done was to simultaneously allow me to *escape into freedom* and to trap himself. . . . Yet as he told me these things and it dawned upon me the position we were both in, sheer crazy *panic* came over me: it was the *idea of liberty*. . . . And the notion of this awful and imminent *liberty* was as *frightening* to me as that *terror* that must overcome people who *dread* open spaces.[14]

Finally, Luigi delivers the novel's *Existenz* message:

I wept out of my own understanding. And that understanding was that this existence itself is an imprisonment. . . . We are serving our sentences in solitary confinement, unable to speak. All of us. (p. 497)

All of this is college-sophomore Sartre and Camus; and there are anticipations of it in *The Long March*. When Styron published his novella in 1953, he was two years short of thirty, the conventional age of the intellectual climacteric in existentialist literature. Joseph K., Roquentin, Meursault: each is *en l'an de [son] trentiesme aage*. Styron's Nat Turner, like his Peter Leverett, is, by a stroke of good luck as serendipitous as the name "Whitehead" (in *CNT*), "just past thirty." Lieutenant Culver, the novella's Peter Leverett, "was thirty, and seventy-two virtually sleepless hours had left him feeling bushed and defeated. And there was another subtle difference he felt about his advanced age—a new awakening, an *awareness*—and therein lay the reason for his *fears*."[15] There is a similar awakening recorded in the notebook of Cass Kinsolving:

Funny thing this going into town this afternoon on the bus, to get something for my supurating [*sic*] toes how it occurred to me, that in less than a week I'd be turning 30, and how it shocked me—though I suppose the shock of being 30 is the corniest thing in the world. Dans le trentième [*sic*] an de mon age, etc. etc. I kept wondering if it is really true as Ive heard it said, if a man at thirty has not through his own blood & sweat & toil seen the first glimmering light of success & achievement he never will.[16]

The shock is not superlatively corny for Kinsolving or for Styron. The author, by that wearying device of hard-boiled self-belittling, has his spokesman suppose that it is. It doesn't work. It is like Kinsolving's language: his misspellings are in character; but his faulty quotation of Villon betrays Styron's shortcomings. Conversely, Kinsolving does not make gaffes in Italian because Styron's Italian is impressive—and in

[14] P. 492; *italics added*. The atrocious grammar in this passage (e.g., "to simultaneously allow . . . and to trap"!) could be attributed to Styron's characterization of Kinsolving except that atrocities like this appear regularly in Styron's fictional works. "Cass's dreadful style," writes Richard Foster (see n. 2), "is the style of his mind, and as Cass is the ultimate focus of the book's thematic concerns, it is the ultimate style of the book. It is the style, in all of its variations, of an appallingly vulgar, morally and intellectually null, sentimentality."

[15] P. 36; italics added to existentialist terms.

[16] This passage is largely a colloquial restatement of two paragraphs on pp. 27–28 of Camus' *Le mythe de Sisyphe* (Paris: Gallimard, 1942); cf. especially: "Un jour vient pourtant et l'homme constate ou dit qu'il a trente ans."

Set This House on Fire he will not let us forget his competence as he riddles his text with colloquial Italian words and phrases. A good artist can be subtly effective in translating his competence into literary experience; immature artists like Styron cannot elude pedagoguery.

Villon, Kafka, Sartre, and Camus succeed in their renditions of the age-thirty climacteric because they can be indifferent, not to the climacteric, but to the futility of their efforts to change the existence to which the climacteric exposes them. They have no need to make a show of indifference in their own right or in the speeches of their characters. The indifference of Camus' Meursault does not have to be stated, and its gradations toward affinity with universal indifference are quite clear. The self-conscious writer—that is, specifically, the author who writes self-consciously—affects an I-couldn't-care-less attitude and bolsters his affectation with Byronic self-ridicule as a means of disarming his reader. It never works. Styron, like Hemingway, is such a writer; but Hemingway at least had style.

That minority of critics which finds little to praise and admire in Styron's works may consider *The Long March* his best novel because it is his shortest novel. It begins well enough, except for the inevitable "loblolly saplings" jargon of the fading-magnolia-and-rustling-sycamore South and the inevitable clichés: "flicker of recognition," "palpable fury," "plummeted down," "welter of blood," "sweltering summer," and "pulsing ache"; except for the introduction into a short paragraph, which catalogues "weak *stomach*," "*blood* . . . spilled," "*buttocks*," "*head* cold," "litter of *intestine* and shattered blue *bones*," "*belly*," "*fist*," and "*teeth*," of the stylistically ridiculous parallel, "On the one *hand* he himself had been shocked. . . . And on the other *hand* . . . he was too old" (pp. 5–6, *italics added*). It begins well enough because the scene is adequately set *in medias res*. But the challenge to any writer who must account for antecedent events is the flashback transition. Styron cannot avoid entanglement in the pluperfect tense. And, as soon as we read "Lieutenant Culver had been called back to the marines early that spring" (p. 6), we confront an anaphora of "had" which is equivalent to the sign "Aspiring Novelist at Work."

The novella is readable inasmuch as Styron does win our curiosity about the progress and conclusion of the march. The trouble is that a novella-length story is utterly inappropriate to the *experience* of a thirty-six-mile forced march; or maybe it is just that in Styron's hands it is. The march is over before we have had much of a chance to contemplate Culver's plight; the pain and suffering is centered, with a grotesqueness that approaches the comic, in Mannix.

In the antiheroic Captain Mannix, Styron attempts to fashion an everyman to serve as the object of Culver's existentialist awareness. The name "Al Mannix" (All Mankind) is a too cagily disguised "everyman" to be anything but obtrusive—another "Aspiring Novelist at Work" sign. In committing himself to the pointless completion of an absurd march, Mannix suffers his Achilles' heel to be pierced by a crucifixion nail[17] which imposes upon him the affliction denoted by the name "Oedipus." The god-surrogate against which he rebels is Colonel "Old Rocky" Templeton: the temple of Yahweh and the Rock of Ages. Mannix, like antihero Kinsolving, is alienated *Mensch:* "a dark heavy-set Jew from Brooklyn, Culver's age" (pp. 16–17)—another pair of thirtyish coevals appears, as noted above, in *Set This House on Fire.* As an antihero:

it had been [Mannix] . . . who had said, "None of this Hemingway crap for me, Jack"; he was nobody's lousy hero, and he'd get out of this outfit some way. Yet, Culver speculated, who really was a hero anyway, any more? Mannix's disavowal of faith put him automatically out of the hero category, in the classical sense, yet if suffering was part of the hero's role, wasn't Mannix as heroic as any? (p. 43)

Culver, like Peter Leverett, serves as an index-finger sign reading "To the Alienated Man" and pointing at the antihero; he is the cartoon of a character, the more so in that he does not even serve as a first-person narrator. Proto-Kinsolving Mannix, however, has some depth and is Styron's most nearly well-drawn character. He rebels against conformity by conforming intensely. He endures the march to spite the Colonel, "like a chain-gang convict who endures a flogging without the slightest whimper, only to spite the flogger" (p. 72). He speaks in the context of "proud and willful submission, rebellion in reverse" (p. 73). He apparently wants to suffer, insofar as he discovers the nail in his shoe before the march begins and makes no effort to obtain a different pair of shoes. His is the inverse pride of a child who foregoes dessert rather than eat his vegetables and seeks to hurt his parents by his own self-denial. Mannix finds great satisfaction in suffering; and his suffering, passive in itself as suffering always is, wins the name of action. As the story ends, he stands helplessly naked before a Negro maid, who asks, "Do it hurt?" He answers, "Deed it does" (pp. 119–120). "Do" is to "deed" as "hurt" is to "does": bearing pain becomes doing; suffering has been transformed into action. The message is wrought by a pun, a wisp of Joycean[18] small talk, recalling the second epigraph to *Lie Down in Darkness.*[19]

Kinsolving and Mannix are existentialist rebels, and each has his

---

[17] N.B. " 'It's worse than the nail.' He paused. 'Jesus Christ' " (p. 86).

[18] Cf. echoes of Joyce in *SHF:* the juxtaposition of "dog" and "God" (p. 358; *Ulysses,* p. 600); and *"Slotkin old father, old rabbi, what shall I do? Teach me now in my need"* (p. 428; partially reiterated on p. 453; cf. "Old father, old artificer, stand me now and ever in good stead," the concluding line of *A Portrait of the Artist as a Young Man*).

[19] "Carry me along, taddy, like you done through the toy fair" (*Finnegans Wake,* 268.8): "taddy" is a pun on "daddy" (Joyce's "my cold mad father, my cold mad feary father"—*FW* 268.1–2). From this same page, the last in *FW,* "A gull. Gulls" doubtless gave Styron his idea for his gull imagery in *LDD.*

awareness personified in an alter-ego, respectively, Leverett and Culver. Mannix is in a passive revolt; his rebellion is an intensification of passivity, the essence of which is action. The authority to which Kinsolving vengefully submits is the financial stranglehold of Mason Flagg. Kinsolving's passivity cannot transcend itself as action; and Kinsolving must abandon passivity in favor of action. He rises up and strikes down; Mannix rises up to define the *action* of being struck down.

Mannix and Kinsolving complement each other and, taken together, adumbrate Styron's Nat Turner, the intensely passive and destructively active rebel with whom Styron must indeed have been preoccupied throughout his career as a writer. His Nat Turner embodies the futility, absurdity, frustrated dignity, and spiritual need that informs the various characters in his first three major fictional works.

The Confessions of Nat Turner is not Styron's best novel. His best to date will have to be, as intimated above, *The Long March,* with its brevity, however unsuited that brevity may be to the task at hand, with its story line, and with its characterization of Mannix. Nonetheless, *The Confessions of Nat Turner* exhibits his best writing. The anacolutha and stylistic howlers that mar his earlier works are less in evidence. To be sure, his Nat Turner uses the phrase "in terms of," which is generally a post-World-War-II academic catchall; and, in 1831, he feels "the electric passage across [his] cheek of strands of chestnut-colored hair" (p. 373). For all that, the drive and continuity of Styron's quadripartite first-person narrative holds the promise that he may yet master his craft. In this novel, the sycamores, grits and bacon, and "juniper trees and loblolly pine" are not excrescent *suth'n* embellishments. There is no third-person abortion of first-person narrative to match this passage from *The Long March:*

They looked up, startled. Hands hooked as usual—Culver wanted to say "characteristically"—in his belt, he stood serenely above them. (p. 87)

(*Culver* wanted to say? To whom? To the reader, presumably, if "Culver" were "I" in the first draft of the novella.) Nat Turner's educated English, carrying the narrative to the very moment of his execution, is actually the substance of his train of thought; this stream-of-consciousness is much more convincing than the imitations of Faulkner and Joyce in *Lie Down in Darkness.* Against this English the "nigger talk" reflects in well-cadenced refrain the compelling throb of oppressed lives.

Styron's Nat Turner is a Mannix in his intensified playing of the role assigned him by Authority. Mannix plays soldier; Nat Turner plays manually-skilled slave. He cannot fulfill himself in passivity, as Mannix does. His spiritual sensitivity and his profound perception of outrage propel him toward Kinsolving's mode of rebellion.

Mannix and Kinsolving rebel each in the interest of his individual worth:

> Born into a generation of conformists, even Mannix (so Culver sensed) was aware that his gestures were not symbolic, but individual, therefore hopeless, maybe even absurd, and that he was trapped like all of them in a predicament which one personal insurrection could, if anything, only make worse. (*LM*, 55–56)

Kinsolving's gestures are individual, but they include his making Francesca's cause his own, as he nurses her dying father and avenges her rape. They become potentially symbolic.

Nat Turner rebels in the interest of all who share his burden. His impersonal insurrection is unequivocally symbolic. That it also is hopeless and maybe even absurd, that it worsens the predicament, is existentialistically ironic.

If only Styron would not stumble over his own constructs of existentialist irony! He tells a good story: none of his major fictional works is really a failure in this respect. Fortunately or unfortunately, as the case may be, he also wants desperately to have something to say—to give artistic expression to his fumblings and gropings with existentialist paradox and with perturbations relevant to spiritual mystery. As an American novelist he wants to effect a mystic confluence of North and South, Christian and Jew, Black and White, and heterosexual and homosexual.

In one sense, his timing is always off. His imitation of Faulkner in *Lie Down in Darkness* is immature and amateurish. Faulkner offers more than stream-of-consciousness, italicized time shifts, and themes of incest and familial decadence; and Faulkner's passion-play symbolism is not captured by "Jesus Christ" and "God" interjections. At his worst, Faulkner is not responsible for such prose as "Helen dressed like a cat, bearing down on him with a knife: only it wasn't a knife, it was something else" (p. 152). Nor would he include as part of one time sequence, within the space of one page, "But he found himself rather pleased that she was here" and "her presence here made him feel uneasy and discontented" (p. 177). After establishing his propensity for Thomas Wolfean long-windedness and Faulknerian complexity, for neither of which he had properly honed his talents, Styron made an untimely attempt at classic simplicity in his novella. He proved equally unready for this. The existentialist theme of the novella was handled competently enough to produce a few threads of promise. When he tried to weave these into a fabric of Dostoevskian magnitude in *Set This House on Fire*, he betrayed his apprenticeship. It is to his credit that he may have understood this: his autobiographical protagonist, Kinsolving, is a cartoonist trying to be a painter. Then, protracting his superficial existentialism, he combined his antiheroes, Mannix and Kinsolving, and thrust them into the racial arena as the alienated,

Old-Testament-oriented Christian rebel, Nat Turner. Again he was not ready. His Nat Turner should have been, not an onanistic, introspective Hamlet, but a towering black Theseus, whipped by doubts, temptations, human failings and lusts, yet magnified by his mission—not a housebroken, bisexual antihero, but an imperiously mystical epic hero.

In another sense, his timing is always right. The critics were ready for a darling when *Lie Down in Darkness* appeared, and they took the author of this Faulknerian *tour de force* to their hearts. *The Long March*, with its classic look, succeeded as a change of pace; and it and *Set This House on Fire* rode the existentialist vogue. And *The Confessions of Nat Turner* capitalized on the new black insurgency.

Styron's artistic timing is off; his commercial timing is precise. He has come on as a best-seller novelist with a loyal critical following, except for the sudden host of black critics, whose concern for authenticity he has been ill-equipped to share.

With regard to Caucasian book buyers, *The Confessions of Nat Turner* could not have been better timed. It is, dreadful to say, *the* American novel of the 1960s. It is a triumph of sex and violence. It cannot fail to titillate the newly courageous homosexual horde. The white male reader is offered vivid pictures of virginal buttocks and lubricious pudenda in concert with a grand flatus of the Negro stereotype (ostensibly under Styron's liberal attack but open to all the relish of prejudice). The white female reader is given the vicarious pleasure of violent invasion. And, while the black lesbian and fag will find enough prurient paragraphs, the black heterosexual—and all blacks to whom Black is Beautiful—will find only what they have been protesting against: this is sad, because Styron certainly wanted to write a pro-black book. He made the mistake of combining black and white under the heading of "men" instead of cogently differentiating *men* that are black from *men* that are white.

John Oliver Killens has to be right when he says, "The first mistake was for Styron to attempt the novel. It seems to me that the second mistake William Styron made was to pretend to tell the story from the point of view of Turner, and it was a colossal error, one that required tremendous arrogance. And naiveté."[20]

Styron assumes that it is possible for a white man to think like a Negro and, conversely, for a Negro to think like a white man. He further assumes that this kind of thinking is prerequisite to any understanding between the two races and cultures. There is evidence, or at least good argument, that male writers (e.g., James Joyce) and female writers (e.g., Virginia Woolf) can think like members of the opposite sex; theoretically, this transpersonalization can extend to matters of

---

[20] "The Confessions of Willie Styron," in *William Styron's Nat Turner: Ten Black Writers Respond*, ed. John Henrik Clarke (Boston: Beacon Press, 1968), p. 36.

race in certain rare individuals. Styron is clearly not one of them. He, attempting to think like a Negro, tells the story of Nat Turner in the first person and then ridiculously complicates his attempt by having Nat Turner think like a white man. His Nat Turner has to be able to think like a white man in order to hate the white man as a man and not as an object of "the helpless, resigned fury one feels toward indifferent Nature throughout long days of relentless heat or after periods of unceasing rain" (p. 258); and, once able to hate the white person, Styron's Nat Turner is also able to love him—first in the figure of his "owner," Samuel Turner; then in his elaborate fantasies of sexual union with white women; and finally in the exquisite, invitingly flirtatious person of Margaret Whitehead.

The sexual fantasies of Styron's Nat Turner are daydreams of violent union with white women, of violating and raping white women, not of loving or caressing them tenderly. His love, a corollary to his hate, must be violent, for it must be forced upon indifferent whites. And his loving hatred of white women, his being "unhinged by desire and hatred" (p. 372), is symptomatic of his race's need to violate the whites. The virile black shaft that he would plunge into the sheaths of white women, specifically that of Margaret Whitehead, the woman he genuinely loves, is ultimately the black sword or ax that must disembowel or dismember all whites: "*Ah, how I want her,* I thought, and unsheathed my sword" (p. 413).

When he kills Margaret Whitehead, he does so with what is at last a profound indifference. Earlier he had, at Margaret's request, put a wagon-crushed turtle out of whatever pain it felt by smashing its head with a hickory stick. After his sword-thrusts have managed only to wound Margaret Whitehead and cause her great pain, he puts her out of her misery by bashing her head in with a fence rail, killing her as casually as he had killed the turtle.[21] Having learned to hate and love the white man as a man by learning to think as a white man, he learns also the white man's indifference, that most effective dispensation of cold brutality and amorality. He pleads "not guilty" because he doesn't "feel guilty"; his attitude toward the white men, women, and children whom he and his followers have slain matches the callousness of the Irish overseer who had raped his mother.[22] It is by indifference that

[21] Cf. the dog and the old woman in *SHF*, discussed above.

[22] Eugene D. Genovese (*The New York Review of Books*, Sept. 12, 1968), one of Styron's defenders against the response of the ten black writers, says that "there are no instances of rape in Styron's book." He is quite wrong. Black is raped by white, and white is raped by black in the book. Will's murder of Sarah Travis is clearly a rape murder: he is lying between her "thrashing, naked thighs" before and while he chops her to death with his hatchet. Will differs from Nat Turner here in two ways: (1) he has not learned indifference, and (2) his gestures are not symbolic. In the novel, Nat Turner's murder of Margaret Whitehead is a symbolic rape. Styron's Nat Turner must be celibate if his gestures are to be properly symbolic and not individual.

paradox and tragedy are manifested: the indifference of Nature to
Man, the indifference of men to men, and the fatal indifference of Man
to Nature. Styron, however, is devoid of the artist's indifference that is
necessary to the literary expression of indifference. His Nat Turner
learns white indifference in much the same way that he learns to read.
If skin color is merely an accident, like height or weight, it will not
prevent the members of one race from entering the subjective domains
of the other—from, so to speak, learning the other race. If skin color is
an attribute, like talent or strength, then one race can only *learn about*
the other. The existential paradox, in this event, would be that, while
blacks and whites are all men, there is an unbreachable barrier of
attributes between *black men* and *white men*. Blacks and whites can
and must learn to live *with* each other; contrary to the premise of
Styron's novel, they cannot, so long as they *are* black and white, live *as*
each other.

Styron's Nat Turner is just too white. There is a preponderance of
whiteness in the combination of white William Styron as black Nat
Turner as white Nat Turner: black Nat Turner proves to be William
Styron in blackface: the spirit is willing but the flesh is white.

Jean Genet is wise enough to know that intellectual miscegenation
is the matter of a clown show. *The Blacks*, a drama conceived by a
white man, presents black actors in blatantly obvious whiteface. Genet
deals directly with the barriers of attributes. He puts real Negroes on
the stage and, as artist, pares his nails in the wings. Styron smears
whiteface over his blackface and, as actor, manages only to remove his
blackface in the process. He is left with his white face hanging out.

His failure at playing Negro is reminiscent of his failure at playing
woman in *Lie Down in Darkness*. His departure from the circum-
ference of his talents is less extended in his portraits of Mannix and
Kinsolving than it is in his cartoons of Peyton Loftis and Nat Turner.
Still, all of his first four major fictional works collapse under scrutiny
because he is a storyteller trying vainly to be a tragedian: "Tragedy, by
God, that's what we'll give 'em!" Cass (Styron) Kinsolving tells Cripps
(*SHF*, 119); "We'll bring back tragedy to the land of the Pepsi-Cola
and the peanut brittle and the Modess Because. That's what we'll do,
by God!" (pp. 118–119). Tragedy is not the plethora of violence and
frustration that Styron compiles, just as Greek tragedy is not the
stiltedly archaic, translation-English pottage of the Oates-O'Neill *Complete Greek Tragedy*, on which Cass (Styron) Kinsolving so proudly
depends. Cass Kinsolving is a Thomas Wolfean Orestes, not a Greek
Orestes-Cassandra. And Peyton Loftis is Styron as Quentin Compson
III (Benrus clock and all) playing a suicidal Molly Bloom; she is no
Sophoclean or Euripidean Electra. Styron's Faulknerian Greek-tragedy
incest motif (Peyton and her father, Milton Loftis) is as egregiously
overdone as his college-mall existentialism and his Negro-dreams of
white "poontang." The Jewishness of Peyton's husband, Harry Miller,

is as shallow as Mannix's, or as Kinsolving's predisposition to Jewishness, or as Nat Turner's contemplation of the Star of David. Styron does not need to have Peyton tell her husband not to "be so Christlike": Harry Miller achieves no more of this similitude than Mannix or Kinsolving or Nat Turner does.

For all her girdled female beauty and her nymphomania, Peyton Loftis is no more than a man's idea of a woman. She, in her nakedness and following her twelve-story death leap from a woman's toilet room, rises from her ashes as Captain Mannix standing faggily naked and exhausted (drunk up, burnt out) before a Negro maid in a shower room. She rises again to set her house on fire as Cass Kinsolving, while Tony Cecchino receives his due as Mason Flagg. And it is again Peyton-Styron, as Nat Turner, whose nether parts are thrice scorched with a "blazing stick" by Wash (= purgation: the fire that refines) in a ten-hole privy. This is not the stuff of tragedy; it is the self-conscious romanticism of a seedy impresario who, overwhelmed by Joyce and Faulkner, mistakes his clown show for existentialist high tragedy and grand endeavor.

William Styron's *Divine Comedy*

KARL MALKOFF

THE HIGHLY CHARGED ATMOSPHERE IN WHICH *The Confessions of Nat Turner* appeared has at least temporarily displaced the novel from literary history and left it embedded in the sociological present.[1] Inevitably, and with partial justice, the accuracy with which Styron portrays the blackness of his hero has been challenged. But the vehemently bitter response to the first white wave of critical acclaim has not only attacked *Nat Turner* at a vulnerable point, it has in its single-mindedness distorted the very nature of the novel. As obviously involved with the problems of being a Negro and a revolutionary as Styron in his latest book may be, he is ultimately concerned with the same tensions that have dominated all his work—between freedom and necessity, master and slave, father and child. Styron has not dealt with this theme—for it is a single theme with distinct attributes—statically; its

[1] See especially *William Styron's Nat Turner: Ten Black Writers Respond*, ed. John Henrik Clarke (Boston: Beacon Press, 1968).

implications have been developed from novel to novel in a manner parallel to, though not necessarily dependent on, Dante's *Divine Comedy*. It is the brief tracing of this theme in Styron's earlier work, and a more detailed examination of its culmination in *The Confessions of Nat Turner*, that will form the substance of this essay.

In *Lie Down in Darkness* (1951), whose title and epigraph from Sir Thomas Browne's *Urn Burial* supply appropriate introductions to Styron's infernal vision, the struggle for freedom appears only intermittently in a theological context. Guilty over her behavior toward her youngest daughter, Helen Loftis explains her hatred to Reverend Carey Carr as a product of the devil's temptation. Carey rejects this evasion of responsibility: "The cowardly Puritan, he had always thought, or the cowardly fundamentalist, unwilling to partake of free religious inquiry, uses the devil as a scapegoat to rid himself of the need for positive action."[2] However, the problem does not rest here. Carey is spectacularly unsuccessful in his attempts to understand Helen (or any Loftis); far from the novel's moral center, his simplistic conception of free will ignores the complexities of human experience. More sophisticated is Milton Loftis' father, a ghostly presence hovering throughout the novel on the borders of Milton's consciousness, who less smugly proclaims the importance of exercising free will: "*My son, most people, whether they know it or not . . . get on through life by a sophomoric fatalism. Only poets and thieves can exercise free will, and most of them die young*" (91).

There may be no devil in Styron's world, but in his place exist powerful psychological forces that operate beneath the façade of conscious volition. In this secularized Hell, reminiscent in its mechanics of Sartre's *No Exit*, the needs and desires of individual members of the Loftis family make them psychologically dependent upon one another. Helen, already Puritanical, experiences additional guilt at the birth of Maudie, and, slighting her husband and her younger daughter, Peyton, devotes all energies toward her crippled, retarded child. Milton resents his wife, Peyton her mother; father and daughter are forced together; and Helen, feeling their estrangement from her, becomes even more preoccupied with Maudie. Caught in this circle, none are able to act freely. Peyton, at least figuratively both poet and thief, tries and dies young.

In fact, the novel is shaped by Peyton's futile attempt to escape, like a "poor flightless bird." She is no less a slave than Nat Turner, her journey to the North ultimately no more successful than Hark's. Of course, since she is a woman, the emphases of her relationships with father and mother differ significantly from those of later Styron rebels; but she shares with them a crucial ambivalence toward the father from

[2] *Lie Down in Darkness* (New York: Signet, 1960), p. 113. Subsequent references to this book will be followed by page numbers in parentheses.

whom she must be free, with whom she must be reconciled. Her flight, then, from father, husband, and God is paradoxically a function of her desire to be united with them. And so her suicide, her desperate final grasp at freedom, ironically is the most fully determined action in the novel.

From the Hell of *Lie Down in Darkness* there is no escape short of extinction; the novel isolates the conflict between the wish to be a distinct individual and the overwhelming internal and external pressures against it, but the outcome is never in doubt; the struggle is hopeless. *The Long March* (1953) begins the agonizing task of transforming hopelessness into hope, despair into faith; the torments of this novel are impressive, but, like those of Dante's *Purgatory,* they hold at least the promise of ultimate triumph.

Lacking an actual father-child relationship, *The Long March* nonetheless centers on an archetypal variation on this theme, the conflict between master (Colonel Templeton) and slave (Captain Mannix). Nat Turner's reactions on learning that the freedom promised by Samuel Turner has been revoked by the Reverend Eppes are scarcely more intense than those of Mannix assigned to Templeton, whose name in fact links him to the clergy: "He detested Templeton not because of any slight or injustice, but because Templeton was a lieutenant colonel, because he was a regular, and because he possessed over Mannix—after six years of freedom—an absolute and unquestioned authority."[3] For Nat and for Mannix, whose name seems to suggest everyman, the dangers of tyranny are similar: a loss of individuality, a loss of dignity, a loss of humanity. It is to retain these qualities that Mannix commits himself to his "not symbolic, but individual, therefore hopeless, maybe even absurd" gesture, his decision to force himself and his men, all out of condition, to endure the Colonel's maliciously long march (55–56). Like Peyton, Mannix is doomed to defeat; unlike her, however, he is not destroyed, and has, in fact, "endured and lasted." Closely related to Camus' Sisyphus, Mannix defends an absurd freedom in the face of implacable necessity and creates human values in a world efficiently calculated to dehumanize.

The fire in the passage by John Donne from which the title of *Set This House on Fire* (1960) is derived, is the fire of God, entering and burning clean the human spirit; and in this purgatorial novel, the attempt to survive the considerable burdens of freedom continues in what amounts to a greatly expanded, more complex civilian version of *The Long March.* Culver, center of consciousness of the earlier book, is replaced by Peter Leverett as the observer-participant in a deadly struggle. The symbiotic antagonists are Cass Kinsolving and Mason Flagg, involved in a relationship that has more than a hint of Thomas

[3] *The Long March* (New York: Modern Library, 1956), p. 19. Subsequent references to this book will be followed by page numbers in parentheses.

Mann's *Mario and the Magician*. Here, however, the wealthy Flagg, himself drunk with the exercise of power, uses not hypnosis but rather the drunken desperation of Kinsolving to subjugate and humiliate him. Overwhelmed by visions of darkness and oblivion, Cass had been enveloped in a kind of Sartrean nausea, an inability to find significance in his work, or even to work at all—he is an artist—matched by an equal inability to live without significance, without work. In giving himself over to Flagg, Cass is simply carrying to its logical conclusion the "nothingness" he feels his existence to be. However, because the rape of Francesca is beyond his enduring, Kinsolving—like Mario— frees himself by killing his tormentor. In this act of violence, he carves being out of the void:

But to be truthful, you see, I can only tell you this: that as for being and nothingness, the one thing I did know was that to choose between them was simply to choose being, not for the sake of being, much less the desire to be forever—but in the hope of being what I could be for a time.[4]

The transience of Cass's assertion of being should not be passed over lightly; Cass, as Peter finds him, has become relatively complacent, especially in view of his knowledge that Mason was not Francesca's murderer. But he has at the very least carried Mannix' revolt one step further.

Thematically related to the central struggle for power is the network of tensions between father and son that runs through the book. Peter Leverett's conversation with his father early in the novel, besides anticipating its apocalyptic conclusion, sets its pattern. The relatively uneventful encounter leaves Peter "jaded and depressed," with "a sudden sharp pang of total estrangement, as if my identity had slipped away, leaving me without knowledge of who I was and where I had been and where I was going" (16). Peter's reactions form a gloss on Cass's actions; the unresolved conflict with the father makes being impossible.

We are later introduced to the father of another of the three main characters. Justin Flagg appears with godlike powers to save his Mason, for whom he has the deepest contempt, from the father of a young girl Mason has seduced. Mason, who has always been close to his mother, is finally reduced to tears by the scene. Clearly, his own attitudes toward experience and his own need for the illusion of omnipotence, are a necessary result of his sense of helplessness in the face of his father's awesome strength. His death seems a conspiracy of ironies, not least of which is that in becoming his father he has insured, perhaps willfully, his own destruction.

---

[4] *Set This House on Fire* (New York: Random House, 1960), pp. 500–501. Subsequent references to this book will be followed by page numbers in parentheses.

Of Cass Kinsolving's relations with his father we know little directly, although there may be some relevance to the dissipated artist's appearance at one point "as blind-drunk off of *Oedipus* as I was off booze" (130); it is rather his relation to Flagg that captures our interest. But there is still another archetypal configuration in the novel that commands our attention, that involving the fascist state (master-father) and the policeman Luigi (slave-son). Luigi, claiming that the Italian mind resists ideology, tells Cass he became a fascist partly for expediency, partly because of his hatred of the British. More important, however, is his implicit need to be part of something greater than himself. Luigi has looked into the abyss, has felt the agony of being cut off from the father. Like Eliot in *The Waste Land*, he perceives that we are all "serving our sentences in solitary confinement. . . . Once we were able at least to talk with our Jailer, but now even he has gone away, leaving us with the knowledge of insufferable loss" (497).[5] Still, true to his own claims, Luigi is not easy to pin down. His feelings for the dead Englishwoman, for example, not only cut through his hatred for the British, but for the moment overcome isolation as well. And, as the most effective manipulator of events in the book (when he shields Cass from discovery as Flagg's killer), he is always true to his own values rather than the state's. Luigi suggests a means of coming to terms with reality; and if he is not an untarnished, exemplary hero, then he is at least not unambiguously dissociated from Styron's moral sensibilities.

From a consideration of these relationships we learn that the implications of Styron's Freudian world are existential. Strictly speaking, the deterministic Freudian and open-ended existential views of the universe are not compatible. But by seeing psychological forces as powerful but not final influences on human behavior, Styron has little difficulty merging the two. The Oedipal struggle with the father becomes a manifestation of the conflict between the wish to be free and the wish to escape by submission the abyss that freedom exposes. Cass, frightened by visions of nonbeing, flees to Flagg, a father-dictator; killing him, he chooses being.

Of the characters in William Styron's fiction to date, none has been more deeply immersed in the destructive element than the hero of *The Confessions of Nat Turner* (1967); nor does any emerge so fully and permanently into the realm of being, albeit at the very last moment, as does Nat. As has always been the case in Styron, the philosophical is firmly rooted in the psychological, the abstract in the concrete; and it is here that we must begin. On the other hand, it is necessary to keep in mind that the particular is always in the service of the universal; Nat's relationships with his white masters, and with white women, both of which sets of attitudes have come under heavy

---

[5] See Eliot's note to line 412.

fire by black critics, must finally be traced to Styron's total vision of
reality as well as to his understanding of the Negro slave. That Nat
Turner's revolt against white, slave-holding society should be inter-
twined with the archetypal revolt against the father is at the heart of
Styron's fictive method.

All but one of the father-figures to whom Nat reacts are white; of
his real father, the one exception, Nat has no direct recollection; he is
free to look to the white community for ideals and antagonisms, to
encounter a succession of men in authority who collectively replace the
missing one. But although Nat's real father belongs to the days of
preconsciousness, he continues to exist in his mother's reminiscences.
Significantly, he is drawn for Nat in a posture of defiance. Unjustly
struck by Benjamin Turner, he runs off, refusing to bear the indignity.
Nat's own *non serviam* is finally both more violent and more vengeful,
but in his rebellion against authority he in part becomes the father he
never knew.

Early in his life, a young boy encounters the Oedipal triangle. And
Nat's own earliest recollections are not of his master, Samuel Turner,
but of the Irish overseer who rapes his mother as he watches in horrified fascination. The child's status as slave, coupled with his "father's"
literal omnipotence, magnifies the anxieties inherent in the situation.
But greater than Nat's fear is his wish to emulate his masters. Caught
stealing a book because of his passionate wish to read, Nat becomes a
family pet and is able to resolve all conflicts in an obedience he finds
entirely to his advantage; from the time Samuel Turner decides to
educate him until the departure of Willis, Nat finds as much freedom
as he requires in submission. At this point, all conflict is latent. Appro-
priately, tensions reappear in connection with Nat's awakening sexuality.

The single homosexual encounter between Nat and Willis is
shortly followed by the most shattering of betrayals. Under the guise
of hiring them to work for a neighbor, Turner sells a group of slaves,
including Willis, south. And, since the regular driver is ill, Nat himself
delivers the slaves, only gradually realizing what has happened. Although his master denies—certainly truthfully—all knowledge of Nat's
friendship for Willis, Nat's trust is irrevocably damaged. His lack of
faith is soon justified, as his relationship with his white masters enters
a new phase. Samuel Turner, who has promised to set Nat free after
teaching him a trade, places him in the charge of Reverend Alexander
Eppes, with the understanding that the latter will complete the projected arrangements. Eppes not only breaks the agreement, he unsuc-
cessfully attempts to ravish Nat. The wall between master and slave is
completed, as it was begun, with sexual overtones.

Under Thomas Moore and Joseph Travis, Nat lives in silent
hatred. Although Travis, at least, is a decent man, and affords Nat the
most endurable days since his youth at Turner's, his hatred grows

rapidly in intensity—"the more tolerable and human white people became in their dealings with me the keener was my passion to destroy them."[6] The original passivity with which Nat had chosen to respond to his masters—thematically echoing the homosexual incidents—is transformed into a dream of active violence: the wish to kill the oppressive "father" easily becomes the plan to murder all whites in Southampton County.

This dream is not substantially changed, although it is in one respect modified, by Nat's encounter with still another white figure of authority, Jeremiah Cobb. Aware of the man's "Job-like" afflictions, Nat acknowledges a bond of common humanity forged in suffering by silently vowing to exempt him from the general slaughter. Nat has finally been reconciled with a "father"; but he does not, of course, generalize his sympathies. Rather than being a key to a new morality, the meeting between them remains an isolated incident, ironically concluded when Judge Cobb sentences Nat to "be hung by the neck until you are dead! dead! *dead!*" (106). The progression of whites from the overseer to Cobb achieves a sense of completion, but not of resolution; for that we must look elsewhere.

Parallel to the development of Nat Turner's relation to white masters and crucial to its understanding is his relation to white women. For all his admiration of his mother's strength, Nat invariably associates Negro women with what are for him shameful instincts. He sees his mother first resist, then yield to the Irish overseer; she is essentially no different from the Negro girls the boys take out in the fields. It is in the white community that Nat finds his models of ideal womanhood, first Miss Nell and her daughter Louisa, who spend years "riding their hobby," that is, educating their "smart little tar baby." But just as Nat's fathers disappoint him, so do his women.

Miss Emmeline, the youngest Turner girl, is worshiped by Nat, loved with a "virginal passion," until one night when he is up late fulfilling his duties at a Turner party, he comes upon Emmeline and her cousin rolling in the grass. Linked both to his mother's encounter with the overseer and the Negro girls in the fields, this incident—which reveals Emmeline (who was a whore in Baltimore) as blasphemous as well as promiscuous—alters Nat's entire vision of white women and dominates his masturbatory fantasies. Women for Nat must be virgin or whore, in order to place them either beyond desire or beyond worthiness; only in this way can Nat inhibit his lusting after his father's women, which would incur annihilating wrath.

Accordingly, his feelings toward white women lie dormant for years; but they are roused again by Major Ridley's fiancée, who publicly breaks down and weeps with pity over the wretched state of a

6 *The Confessions of Nat Turner* (New York: Random House, 1967), p. 34. Subsequent references to this book will be followed by page numbers in parentheses.

free Negro, Arnold. Nat is sexually excited, filled with the urge to throw himself upon her. As in his relation with white men, uncomprehending compassion provokes in Nat the desire to kill and violate. It is as if the institution of slavery is tolerable only so long as one side sees the other as something more or less than human; as soon as it is revealed as a relationship between human beings, it becomes unendurable. Under these conditions, pity is a final, most effective, assault on manhood.

In *Nat Turner*, all white women can be seen as adumbrations of Margaret Whitehead, all fantasies of sexual violence as anticipations of her murder. In a work enveloped in ironies, it is conspicuously ironic that she should be the only person, white or black, actually killed by Nat himself. She has always treated Nat not simply with pity, but with respect, and maybe with some love as well. However, unlike Jeremiah Cobb, with whom she has much in common, but whom Nat would have spared, Margaret is naive and uninitiated to the agonies of human experience. The focus of Nat's feelings of love and hate, she becomes the sacrificial victim by means of whom Nat enters and ultimately climbs from the abyss. Not the first of Styron's heroines to die young, Margaret is most closely related to Francesca of *Set This House on Fire*, who is also the innocent victim caught up in an action that transcends the boundaries of her awareness.

The murder of Margaret is the act that finally allows—or rather forces—Nat to plumb the depths of his own soul. He has been in conflict not only with fathers and masters, but with himself as well. Like the various stages of fatherhood, embodied in several characters, Nat's own ambivalent reactions are themselves given concrete form: Hark, easy-going and adaptable to his condition, but who, like Nat, has been betrayed by his master's selling of his loved ones; and Will, filled with pure hatred, with the desire to rape and kill. Literally in the plot of the novel and metaphorically within his own mind, it is Nat's difficult task simultaneously to stir up the hatred latent in Hark and control the unbridled fury of Will. Hark and Will personify the conflict in Nat between the wish to submit to the father and the wish to kill him, a conflict finally resolved far more completely in the direction of Will—who nearly does take command of the entire enterprise—than Nat permits himself to realize; in fact, stripped of the discipline of a religious commitment which grows increasingly cloudy in Nat's mind, he *is* Will.

As I have already suggested, the Oedipal relationships that inform so much of the action of *Nat Turner* provide the groundwork for broader considerations. The symbolic castrating of the slave, the taking away of his independent manhood, has more than sexual implications. Ultimately, it is not masculinity but humanity that is at stake; and it is not only with his own father or with his earthly master that Nat must contend, but with God.

The novel's action begins with the visit of Thomas Gray, a lawyer who seeks the confession that will allay fears of a broad conspiracy, to Nat's cell. Significantly, Gray begins by carefully explaining to Nat the difference between animate and inanimate chattel—Nat being in the former category. The slave is precisely chattel, not a human being but an object to be used. And the chief source of Nat's despair throughout the book is not the *white man's* contempt for the slave—we have already seen that Nat finds pity far more provocative—but rather the slave's own contempt for himself.[7] As an important prelude to his conversation with Jeremiah Cobb, Nat rebukes Hark's obsequiousness: "They is some kind of limit. And you ain't a *man* when you act like that. You ain't a man, you is a fool!" (57). And in the only sermon we hear Nat preach, which occurs immediately after Nathaniel Francis has forced Sam and Will to fight each other, he says: "You is *men*, brothers, *men*, not beasts of the field! You ain't no four-legged dogs! You is *men*, I say! Where oh where, my brothers, is yo' pride?" (307).

In their first meeting, Cobb ironically pretends to be amazed by the fact that Nat "had transcended his sorry state and become not a thing but a *person*" (67). It is for Nat to perform again, and on a large scale, this alchemy; unfortunately, in the slave stripped thoroughly of his identity, Nat has little to conjure with. In his own case, thanks to Turner's plans for his freedom, there is at the very least the possibility of meaningful work. Throughout, a strong contrast is maintained between the obnoxious and demeaning work that Nat is forced to do much of the time, most slaves all the time, and the carpentry at which Nat willingly works extra hours; clearly, work involving skill and responsibility is a partial source of Nat's dignity. However, even for Nat, this in itself falls far short. His conditions at Travis's are "decent," but he is still a slave, only rarely a master of his own actions. And, in comparison with the other slaves, Nat's existence is idyllic.

There is, however, one effective tool at Nat's disposal, and he proceeds to wield it efficiently. It is chiefly through hatred that Nat has managed to become a person—he is brought to self-awareness not by Samuel Turner's kindness but by his betrayal—and it is through hatred that he hopes to awaken the humanity of others. He proposes to channel this emotion into an act of destruction of overwhelming dimensions, into a thorough and final negation: the murder of every white man, woman, and child in the county. The enormity of the project is appropriate to the conditions that have produced it—that is, the thorough and final negation of the black man, who has been reduced to an object dependent upon its user for identity. In this system,

---

[7] In his critique of Herbert Aptheker's *American Negro Slave Revolts*—"Overcome," *New York Review of Books*, I (Sept. 26, 1963), 19—Styron refers to "what must have been the completely traumatizing effect upon the psyche of this uniquely brutal system, which so dehumanized the slave and divested him of honor, moral responsibility, and manhood."

when an occasional Negro is set free, he is not released but destroyed; Arnold, the free Negro whose wretchedness overpowers Ridley's fiancée, is a formless, less than human creature, scarcely able to communicate even with the blacks in the community. Freedom is not enough; the entire dehumanizing hierarchy must be wiped out, the slate must be wiped clean. To become the father, one must first kill him.

Here lies the core of Nat's dilemma. Some critics have seen *Nat Turner* as a conflict between the vengeful God of the Old Testament and the forgiving one of the New;[8] and this is, of course, an important theme in the novel. However, it is also—maybe fundamentally—a struggle between Christ and Antichrist. For Nat, who sees his way prepared by his own John the Baptist (Isham, the free Negro whose child starves to death and who terrifies Thomas Moore with his hatred) and by signs and portents (the eclipse), is trapped by the very grandeur of his vision and its uncompromising nihilism. As Will, his destroying angel becomes stronger and stronger, Nat becomes less and less certain his actions are truly in the service of God. Thus far, Nat has walked hand in hand with Cass Kinsolving, each reaching the point of murder as an assertion of being. Here, however, they part company; Nat alone stays to face the terrifying implications of his actions.

Again, the crucial first section sets the problem. Thomas Gray is, as we have seen, interested in allaying fears, and in settling some—for him—puzzling motives. Nat is not in the least interested in Gray's questions; the passionate intensity he brings to his confessions is provided by his own—why in his revolt against his earthly master has he been cut off from his heavenly Father? Unable to pray since the insurrection, Nat has requested a Bible with which he hopes to reestablish contact with God. Gray, informing Nat that his request has been denied, attempts to console him by attacking Christianity. Beginning with an allusion to the "new science," insisting on the ambiguity of revelation, Gray says: "Here's what Christianity accomplished. Christianity accomplished the mob. The *mob.* It accomplished not only your senseless butchery, the extermination of all those involved in it, black and white, but the horror of lawless retaliation and reprisal" (113).

That Gray has hit home is clear in Nat's last thoughts in Part I: *"Then what I done was wrong, Lord?* I said. *And if what I done was wrong, is there no redemption?"* (115). In breaking the old order, Nat is forced to recreate the world; in moving beyond conventional morality, he is forced to search for new standards. He has the Bible, to be sure. But as Gray points out, what he really has is his *interpretation* of

[8] See Richard Gilman, "Nat Turner Revisited," *New Republic,* CLVIII (April 27, 1968), 25.

the Bible. The responsibility remains Nat's. Appropriate to Nat's dilemma is Kierkegaard's exegesis of the story of Abraham and Isaac:

The paradox of faith is this, that the individual is higher than the universal [human morality], that the individual . . . determines his relation to the universal by his relation to the absolute [God], not his relation to the absolute by his relation to the universal. . . . The tragic hero renounces himself to express the universal, the knight of faith renounces the universal in order to become the individual.[9]

If there can be no direct contact between man and God, then God's values must be worked out experientially, always with the agonizing possibility of error. Either the individual as an individual can stand in an absolute relation to the absolute, or Abraham is a murderer. By Kierkegaard's categories, Nat Turner is a knight of faith rather than a tragic hero; the latter gives up the certain for the still more certain, while the former gives up the certain for the abyss.

There is, of course, a crucial difference between Abraham and Nat Turner. Both have been divinely commanded to commit acts of violence, and both face the possibility of having been tempted by the devil. But while Abraham is tested with an act clearly beyond human morality, the murder of a son who loves him, Nat will destroy the masters who have deprived him and his people of their essential humanity. Even this distinction, however, is blurred when we consider the baby at the Travis home that Nat remembers when his band is leaving and orders killed. However great Nat's righteousness, he is clearly in need of support beyond the purely ethical to sustain him in this action.

But it is not the murder of the child that immobilizes him, although from the very start his leadership is in jeopardy when he repeatedly finds it impossible to deal mortal blows to any of the victims (except Margaret). Nat, in fact, appears to be discovering that his abstractly derived values—which include the right to murder—may not work in terms of his own experience. Yet it is not until his bungling murder of Margaret, who has within the limits of her awareness treated Nat as a person rather than a thing, that Nat is finally cut off from God. And it is undoubtedly in atonement for this act that he knowingly allows to escape the girl that succeeds in spreading the alarm.

The barrier between Nat and God remains until the novel's last pages, until the last moments before his execution. Even then, Nat does not repent of most of what he has done, including the murder of the infant: "Yes, I think just before I turn to greet him, *I would have done it all again. I would have destroyed them all. Yet I would have*

[9] *Fear and Trembling* and *The Sickness Unto Death* (New York: Doubleday Anchor, 1954), pp. 80–86.

spared one. I would have spared her that showed me Him whose presence I had not fathomed or maybe never even known" (428). Although the "her" is unquestionably Margaret, the passage is not without difficulty. Margaret has obviously taught Nat nothing about the Bible or Christian doctrine; linked with Jeremiah Cobb as one who would be spared, she has, in being destroyed by Nat, taught him that his own vision, although reversed, is fully as dehumanizing as the one it replaces. If, as has been suggested above, the novel pits Old Testament against New, then we can see Job-like Cobb as the highest expression of the former—forced to apply the rigors of a law he knows to be inadequate to the full complexities of the situation, by sentencing Nat to death—while Margaret—in the spirit of the latter—is sacrificed so that Nat can come to terms with his condition.

Like Dante's *Divine Comedy*, *The Confessions of Nat Turner* ends with the protagonist seeing God no longer through a glass darkly, but face to face. Styron's work has all along moved toward this culmination, not each novel beginning where the last left off, but rather each new book recapitulating the spirit's long journey and furthering it. Whether Styron has, however, to his final satisfaction explored his vision of man's emergence from the abyss is unlikely; Dante's great poem ends with the certainty of mystical knowing; but Styron's novel, if not its hero, does not escape existential doubt.

William Styron:
An Interim Appraisal

MELVIN J. FRIEDMAN

"FOR IN POINT OF FACT NEITHER THE NOVEL NOR, BY EXTENSION, PROSE fiction in general has *fallen* on bad days; that desolate fancy that assumes that they have has been entertained by too many people—by young writers, needlessly, in self-pity; by a few shallow critics, arrogantly, out of self-satisfaction, not to mention a kind of weird self-promotion." Thus wrote William Styron in his introduction to the 1959 *Best Short Stories from the Paris Review*. This remark explains his position on several of the more controversial literary issues of the

Melvin J. Friedman, "William Styron: An Interim Appraisal," *English Journal*, L (March 1961), 149–158, 192. Copyright © 1961, by the National Council of Teachers of English. Reprinted by permission of the National Council of Teachers of English.

Fifties. It is his answer to the antifiction pronouncements of T. S. Eliot and Yvor Winters who have declared the novel moribund. The "young writers" suffering from "self-pity" have found a kind of champion in Styron who has done his best to rescue them from anonymity by offering them publication in the *Paris Review* (which he has served faithfully as an advisory editor) and by defending them in his infrequent critical statements. The "few shallow critics" have constantly been a target for his attack as Styron has keenly felt the stifling effect of an age dominated by critics.

One can almost map out a three-part program to explain Styron's position: he has tried to prove, mostly from his own example, that the novel is still a plausible art form; he has identified with new movements in fiction and has been especially responsive to the work of the younger creative writers; he has stood out boldly against the crippling influence of established critics who have dominated the literary journals. Most remarkable about all this is that Styron, who recently turned 35, has been conscientiously listened to and been taken seriously both in and out of the university. Robert Gorham Davis, Charles Fenton, and Howard Mumford Jones have applauded him as fervently as Malcolm Cowley, Maxwell Geismar, and Granville Hicks. He has been linked with almost every movement from Naturalism through Existentialism. He has become a kind of messianic figure who has made a miraculous appearance before the literary world offering new hope for the novel form. Charles Fenton has made this point with telling effect: "Styron has undertaken the major effort which American critics have blandly urged on so many other [149/150] skillful craftsmen in the past few years—O'Hara, Steinbeck, Marquand, Wescott—and which so seldom has been realized." (*South Atlantic Quarterly*, Fall 1960, p. 475.)

None of the elaborate formulas dear to the hearts of literary historians can explain Styron's sudden rise to eminence. Before he published *Lie Down in Darkness* in 1951 no one outside of creative writing seminars would have known his name. We were at least prepared for John Updike's *The Poorhouse Fair* and Philip Roth's *Goodbye, Columbus*—mature work by very young men—by their authors' appearances in the *New Yorker*. Before Styron's sudden success his publication had been limited to four short stories, all included in volumes edited by creative writing teachers. His two short stories in *One and Twenty: Duke Narrative and Verse, 1924–1945* suggest very little about his later work. "Autumn" is the account of a fossilized prep school English teacher who has a painful moment of self-recognition. His unyieldingly high principles are compromised by an unhappy confrontation with an arrogant student. This Joycean-type epiphany alerts him to the approach of old age and to the horrors of loneliness. "The Long Dark Road" is the story of a Negro lynching. Styron tests the reaction of the event on a young boy, Dewey Lassiter, who offers a response similar to that of Nick Adams in Hemingway's "Indian Camp." As in the Hemingway story, we are confronted with a boy's amazement at the cruelty and harsh reality of the adult world. The other two stories appeared in *American Vanguard* (1948 and 1950), a collection edited by creative writing teachers at the New School for Social Research in New York for the purpose of introducing "young American authors on the verge of professional recognition."

Styron's earliest work is thus a product of creative writing seminars at Duke University and the New School. The derivative quality of these early stories—which are especially indebted to Hemingway and Faulkner—is evidence of too much time spent in the classroom. But it was at the New School apparently that he was encouraged to go on with the manuscript of *Lie Down in Darkness* which won him the kind of recognition which one never expects from a first novel.

Lie Down in Darkness

Elizabeth Janeway was quick to point out in the January 21, 1952 number of the *New Leader* that the previous year had been unusual for the quality of its first novels. *Lie Down in Darkness*, together with Salinger's *Catcher in the Rye*, both published in 1951, suggested that the young writer of the Fifties might try something significantly new with fiction as a way of ridding it, on the one hand, of too much experimentation, and on the other of a too-rigid traditional form. The Forties had proved exasperatingly pessimistic in failing to come up with anything more hopeful than Mailer's *The Naked and the Dead*. A closely written novel, with a hard core of intellectual and moral direction, reinforced with a formidable structure, was what was finally realized with *Lie Down in Darkness*. [150/151]

It is a handbook for novelists and at the same time a sort of "condemned playground" for critics too fond of influence hunting. Styron proves himself to be the kind of craftsman T. S. Eliot believed had passed out of novel writing with James and Flaubert—both in his careful method and his skillful borrowing and making over of effects from other writers. His reviewers have all suggested that *Lie Down in Darkness* is a very Faulknerian book both in subject and in technique. It offered a field day to commentators who immediately connected Peyton's funeral march with the burial procession in *As I Lay Dying*, Peyton's suicide monologue with Quentin's in *The Sound and the Fury*, and Peyton's lasciviousness with Temple Drake's in *Sanctuary*. It was clear to every reviewer that Styron had read Faulkner and had relied heavily on him. But it was also evident that Styron's type of literary appropriation was creative, and Malcolm Cowley suggested in the October 8, 1951 issue of the *New Republic* that Styron was probably at his best when he was closest to Faulkner. J. D. Scott, writing in the April 19, 1952 *New Statesman and Nation*, even went so far as to say that Styron was perhaps engaging in a subtle form of literary pastiche. Whatever literary term is most appropriate, it should be clear to every reader that *Lie Down in Darkness* is indebted to Faulkner for several of its characters, for its principal symbolic effects, and for its stylistic pace.

It is a novel about Southern degeneracy and the falling apart of an unprincipled world. Milton Loftis received the following Faulknerian heritage from his father which tormented the few non-alcoholic moments in an otherwise dissipated manhood:

My father told me when I went barreling off to the University, "Son," he said, "you don't have to be a camp-follower of reaction but always remember where you came from, the ground is bloody and full of guilt where you were born and you must tread a long narrow path toward your destiny. If the crazy sideroads start to beguile you, son, take at least a backward glance at Monticello." You see . . . (*Lie Down in Darkness*, New York, Signet Books, 1960, pp. 69–70.)

Loftis is, in a sense, the Jamesian "focus of narration" in this novel which abounds in frequent changes in point of view. Events seem to ricochet off his blurred view of a series of occurrences which he only partly understands. While he stands at the structural center of the novel, we do not always see events through his eyes. Styron seems to have learned from the Faulkner of *Absalom, Absalom!* how to have the story filtered through several sensibilities, each in turn advancing the action and clearing up certain of the complications. Loftis' wife Helen, with her unflinching moral sense, gives a puritanical view of the events which her husband would be incapable of. The minister, Carey Carr, with a characteristic "air of cherubic vacancy and bloodlessness," can add detachment to Helen's view and give still another version. All of this is achieved through third-person narrative with an omniscient Styron lending his own presence and dignity to the proceedings. Only once does Styron completely refine [151/152] himself out of existence and that is when Peyton, the wayward daughter, pronounces words of self-destruction in a frantic, illogically ordered suicide monologue. This is the only genuine stream-of-consciousness writing in a novel which is in most ways traditional.

As one reads Peyton's soliloquy, one is struck by J. D. Scott's remark that much of *Lie Down in Darkness* is clever pastiche. As Peyton broods on her clock, one is forcibly reminded of Quentin Compson's obsession with his watch which Faulkner described as "the mausoleum of all hope and desire":

I couldn't think for a minute, thinking that the bank was full of money, my money, but then I remembered: all that which Bunny sent me on my birthday I'd spent, and I remembered the phonograph I had bought, and all the records, and the Benrus clock, my womb all jeweled and safe; it cost $39.95. Too much for a clock but I just knew it had to be a good one, and pretty, with fine turning hands: somewhere in the play someone said the bawdy hand of the hour is on the prick of noon. I peeked into my handbag; Harry's was just right. Once he asked me who took my maidenhead and I said a bicycle seat named Dickie Boy: when we lay down that afternoon I heard Papegeno singing in my sleep and I dreamed of dancers on a green fantastic lawn and sand and pyramids; it was the first time I ever dreamed of birds, they came sedately across the sand, and when we woke up Dickie Boy couldn't get in. I looked; my clock was safe. (p. 329)

Her monologue continues for another forty pages before she makes her suicide leap. The clock recurs with the consistency of a Wagnerian leitmotiv and in some way mirrors Peyton's distrust of time. The passage has no logical unity; it depends on free association. This is stream-of-consciousness writing, but written at a period when it was no longer fashionable to emulate Joyce and Faulkner. One can feel only that Styron is so intrigued with the method that he cannot resist using it; even if he must engage in genial pastiche. Peyton's mind, in the above passage, wanders more erratically than Faulkner's Quentin Compson or than Joyce's Molly Bloom (the two monologuists most frequently mentioned as models for Peyton's soliloquy). Money suggests birthday which recalls the purchase of an expensive clock. The hands on the clock remind Peyton of a line from *Romeo and Juliet* pronounced by Mercutio. This in turn produces several sexual associations which tend to be linked with birds through Mozart's Papageno (misspelled in Peyton's monologue) who made his living by catching birds. The passage ends with a return to the clock. The succession of associations, organized about the purchase of a clock, seems to be experienced by the preconscious—the level of awareness of Peyton's entire fifty-page monologue. There is a kind of poetical arrangement of ingredients organized about a central metaphor which suggests the interplay of imagery in the partly conscious mind. (The whole history of stream-of-consciousness writing has illustrated that the more removed the mind is from consciousness the closer it is to clusters of images and to poetry.) [152/153]

This passage is fairly typical of the entire sequence of Peyton's monologue. The image of the clock recurs as does the reference to birds; the latter is especially evident as the monologue reaches its final crescendo with Peyton preparing her suicide leap:

Perhaps I shall rise at another time, though I lie down in darkness and have my light in ashes. I turn in the room, see them come across the tiles, dimly prancing, fluffing up their wings, I think: my poor flightless birds, have you suffered without soaring on this earth? Come then and fly. And they move on past me through the darkening sands, awkward and gentle, rustling their feathers: come then and fly. And so it happens treading past to touch my boiling skin—one whisper of feathers is all—and so I see them go—oh my Christ!—one by one ascending my flightless birds through the suffocating

night, toward paradise. I am dying, Bunny, dying. *But you must be proper.*
I say, oh pooh. Oh pooh. Must be proper. Oh most proper. Powerful.
    Oh most Powerful.
    Oh must.
(p. 368)

This passage uses many of the ingredients of the other except that here
the central metaphor is the birds. Peyton's mind is also more constant
as it manages to concentrate more completely on the single image. The
reference to sand is also a reminder of the earlier passage. The allitera-
tive note on which this section ends, as Peyton's monologue trails off
before her suicide leap, is further reminder of the poetic qualities of
the mind released from the tensions of thought and depending on
unrelieved impressionism.

The remarkable aspect of Peyton's monologue is its curious sus-
pension in the midst of a novel which is otherwise fairly orthodox.
Styron reverts to third person for the final pages of his novel, using the
additional Faulknerian note of ending it with a Negro Revivalist
gathering. Why this one concession to a method which was widely
used during the Twenties and Thirties and which seemed to disappear
afterwards is difficult to explain. Perhaps *Lie Down in Darkness*, in this
sense, is another *Don Quixote* or *Rape of the Lock*. Tales of chivalry
and heroic poetry, as literary forms, were virtually mocked out of
existence by Cervantes and Pope in the same way that Styron seems
intent on mirroring the exhaustion of the stream-of-consciousness
method. Peyton's monologue does seem out of joint both with the rest
of the novel and with the "new literature" of the Fifties. In Styron's
skillful hands the timepiece or clock, the favorite symbol of the
Bergsonian novel,[1] seems also through its overuse to suggest the end
of a kind of fiction.

Styron and Literary Trends

It is no exaggeration to say that the Fifties ushered in a new kind
of novel. Norman Mailer, in an essay "The White Negro," used the
term American Existentialist to indicate a counterpart to the Sartrean
and Kafkaesque [153/154] novel of disengagement. David Stevenson,
writing in *The Nation*, admirably expressed the same notion: "Struc-
turally their novels exist in the individual intensity of a series of
moments in the lives of their characters rather than in a progression of
events toward a sharply defined denouement."[2] Salinger seems to be

---

[1] Bergson's theory of psychological time has had its literary equivalence in
Proust's "special moments," in Joyce's "epiphanies," in Virginia Woolf's temporaliz-
ing of space, in Faulkner's displacement of chronology. Each of these stream-of-
consciousness writers has made elaborate use of timepieces: witness Big Ben in
Mrs. Dalloway and Quentin's watch in *The Sound and the Fury*.

[2] See "Fiction's Unfamiliar Face," *Nation*, 187 (November 1, 1958), p. 307.

concentrating his efforts on giving us unrelated "moments" in the history of the Glass family—each detached from time. There is none of the saga treatment which the Victorians were fond of giving, nor even the full blown falling apart of a world which Proust chronicled. The French writers of the Fifties, those variously referred to as *Chosistes* and *L'Ecole du Regard,* are also offering a concerted rebellion against the chronicle novel and the stream-of-consciousness novel. Alain Robbe-Grillet, Nathalie Sarraute, Michel Butor—the best known practitioners of the *nouveau roman*—favor a kind of disjointed fiction, loosely structured, with an inverted time scheme. They seem to have emptied the novel of content in the traditional sense and have argued for a new sense of space in fiction. They have used watches and clocks with the same symbolic insistency as Proust, Faulkner, and Virginia Woolf, but somehow the timepieces in their novels are in a state of disrepair. Robbe-Grillet's protagonist in *The Voyeur* is an unsuccessful watch salesman who ironically misses his boat because he has not taken proper account of the time. The detective in his *Les Gommes* operates through most of the novel with a watch which has stopped. Time, in these works, ceases to be the one saving grace in a world of anarchy and chaos which it was in the Bergsonian novel.

This is the literary ambiance which must be acknowledged by anyone writing fiction today. It is clear that Styron has carefully considered the new commitments of the writer both from his occasional critical statements and from the long delay between *Lie Down in Darkness* and his second full-length novel, *Set This House on Fire* (1960). As has been pointed out by Maxwell Geismar and others, Styron's immediate success with *Lie Down in Darkness* did not prompt him to rush into print with just any unpublished literary document which might have been littered with cobwebs in a forsaken attic. He resisted the temptation which Kerouac and Mailer have succumbed to repeatedly in the past few years. What Styron has given us instead of a quasi-literary *Doctor Sax* or *Deer Park* is a long period of calculated waiting which resulted in a timely novella, *The Long March* (1953), occasional critical writings in connection with the *Paris Review,* and several interview statements.

Lie Down in Darkness made him an important enough novelist to command interest in his few published remarks about literature. He has said on several occasions that his working habits demand the patience of a Flaubert; in the *Paris Review* interview, for example, he said: "I average two-and-a-half or three pages a day, longhand on yellow sheets." He insists on the inviolability of technique in the novel: he will accept no substitutes for stylistic integrity, careful structure, and "round" characters. He has set himself up as a spokesman for his own generation of writers. He is [154/155] perhaps a bit too hopeful when he says:

Yes, can and will produce literature equal to that of any other generation, especially that of the twenties. It was probably rash to say, but I don't see any reason to recant. For instance, I think those "signs in the air" are apparent from just three first novels, those being *From Here to Eternity*, *The Naked and the Dead*, and *Other Voices, Other Rooms*.
(*Writers at Work: The Paris Review Interviews*, New York, Viking, 1958, p. 279.)

He has, finally, made abundantly clear his position on literary criticism. He stated his position for the first time in his "Letter to an Editor" which prefaced the first number of the *Paris Review*. He reviewed his claim and reinforced it in an article in *Harper's Bazaar* when he insisted that there is only a limited place for criticism in the *Paris Review*. As he reminisces about the early policy of the magazine, he mentions with telling effect:

Only one major question of policy was settled during these early sessions: that criticism, so long the staple and wearying product of the little magazines, would, if it appeared at all in the *Paris Review*, be placed where it belonged—in the very back.
("The *Paris Review*," *Harper's Bazaar*, 87, August 1953, p. 122.)

But clearly the most important effort of the years between *Lie Down in Darkness* and *Set This House on Fire* is *The Long March* which was originally published in *Discovery No. 1* but has since received more permanent form as a Modern Library paperback. This novella is a contribution to the literature of violence and is comparable in scope, despite its length, to almost any of the more ambitious literary reactions to World War II or Korea. Maxwell Geismar was correct in calling it "a propaganda tale, embodying that 'individual' protest which William Styron believes to be so hopeless today."[3] It concerns a forced march in the Marine Corps, involving mainly reserve personnel called back because of the Korean conflict. Colonel Templeton, a career officer, arranges the "little walk" through the heat of the Carolina summer with the intention "of inculcating a sort of group *esprit*." Lieutenant Culver, the point-of-view character, despite his involuntary status in the Corps, agrees to most of the Colonel's severe measures. But another reserve officer, Captain Mannix, offers a running protest which ends in probable tetanus, insubordination, and a very certain court martial. Captain Mannix interests us most because he offers the extreme reaction, because it is his world which falls apart at the seams. We get a hint that this is meant to be more than a personal tragedy in a Carolina setting in passages such as the following:

[3] See *American Moderns* (New York: Hill and Wang, 1958), pp. 249–250.

In the morbid, comfortless light they were like classical Greek masks, made of chrome or tin, reflecting an almost theatrical disharmony: the Colonel's fleeting grin sculpted cleanly and prettily in the unshadowed air above the Captain's darkened, downcast face where, for a flicker of a second, something outraged and agonized was swiftly graven and swiftly scratched out. (*The Long March*, New York, Random House, 1956, p. 29.) **[155/156]**

The ending reminds one a bit of the final section of *Lie Down in Darkness;* a Negro voice has the final say and seems to reinforce the sense of endurance and survival.[4]

Set This House on Fire

Styron's second big book had all the effect of anticipated surprise when it arrived finally in the spring of 1960. The *New Yorker* which had given *Lie Down in Darkness* a grudging notice in its "Briefly Noted" column offered *Set This House on Fire* the lead review in the June 4 issue and significantly turned it over to one of its company of faithful, Donald Malcolm. *Critique,* a critical journal concerned with modern fiction, devoted one-half of its Summer 1960 number to Styron—with special attention to his new novel.

Set This House on Fire has already, six months after publication, inspired the most opposed kinds of reaction. Richard Foster, writing in *Critique,* speaks of it as an "orgy of commerce," insists on the Hollywood directed "Cineramic shape," and ingeniously connects its characters with a long succession of fictional creatures which includes such unlikely bedfellows as Holden Caulfield, Nick Carraway, and Humbert Humbert. Charles Fenton, writing in the *South Atlantic Quarterly,* on the contrary, is unsparing in his praise: ". . . *Set This House on Fire* is the American novel which most completely delivers the 1950's to us. . . ." The latter appraisal seems to be the more useful, at least as a springboard for further critical speculation.

Set This House on Fire is entirely symptomatic of the urgency for a new type of novel. Styron falls back on the single narrator, Peter Leverett, who seems to represent him in the novel although he does not in any sense have the assured omniscience of the novelist. Leverett gropes as frantically for a solution as the detached observers in Henry James (like Fleda Vetch) who get increasingly drawn into a situation which is not of their making. Leverett's White Protestant, Virginia background does not equip him especially well for the moment of violence in the small Italian town of Sambuco. But he does seek out

---

[4] "Endure" is a key word also for William Faulkner. It is the last word of his appendix to *The Sound and the Fury* and also appears frequently in his 1950 Nobel Prize Address. Styron has used the word in an important context in "The Prevalence of Wonders" (*Nation,* 176, May 2, 1953, p. 371), "One must end a credo on the word 'endure,' but I think we will do just that—Americans and Italians and Frenchmen, in spite of all those who threaten us momentary harm."

evidence and makes criminal inquiries with the relentless insistency of the Simenon detective.

Leverett gets involved with two very different types of Americans. One is a former prep school friend, Mason Flagg, whose profligate ways have caused an unending series of scandals. Leverett reviews in the first half of the novel, with almost clinical consistency, the various misdemeanors of Flagg which would be worthy of any psychiatric case book: rape, veiled incestuous feelings towards his mother, mythomania, exaggerated sexual tendencies, possession of elaborate erotica. Leverett follows his career with undivided interest from their first meeting in a Virginia prep school through Flagg's assault on an Italian girl and his subsequent death. The second half of the novel is the slow, deliberate [156/157] piecing together of the Sambuco episode with the help of the second American, the long-expatriated-recently-repatriated Cass Kinsolving. Cass's story reaffirms the evil of Mason Flagg and explains his own part in the rape and murder.

Each of the two parts of the novel has its characteristic pace and tone. The first section seems to be written with considerable remove from the person of Mason Flagg. Leverett views Flagg with a sense of unreality, almost as if he were part of some mythic framework. His attempts at uncovering the hidden Flagg are much like Theseus' journey through the labyrinth which houses the feared Minotaur. Leverett gives us piecemeal and unchronological glimpses which are always colored with the insubstantial and imagined:

> Maybe you recollect that dream of betrayal which I described early in this story—of the murderous friend who came tapping at my window. Somehow when again I recall that dream and then remember Mason at this moment, I am made conscious of another vision—half-dream, half-fantasy—which has haunted me ever since I left Sambuco.
> It goes like this: I have taken a picture of a friend with one of those Polaroid cameras. While waiting for the required minute to elapse I have wandered into another room, and there I pull out the print all fresh and glossy. "Ha!" or "Well!" or "Look!" I call out expectantly to the other room. Yet as I bend down to examine the picture, I find there, not my friend at all but the face of some baleful and unearthly monster. And there is only silence from the other room.
> (*Set This House on Fire*, New York, Random House, 1960, p. 124.)

Mason Flagg, in this first section, is no more than a succession of fleeting images etched in myth and legend.

The second section is more introspective. We are allowed systematic glimpses into Cass Kinsolving's mind as we follow for sustained periods the workings of his consciousness. The framework is the Faulknerian-type colloquy: the exchange between two people intent on clearing up a complicated problem. Although Leverett retains the titular role of narrator the second part is mostly Kinsolving's own story and in his own words and gestures. Some of his most intimate thoughts are revealed through diary notations which have the truncated quality of stream-of-consciousness writing. (The presence of these notebook jottings, with the clipped, illogically ordered phrasing, seems more natural here than Peyton's monologue did in *Lie Down in Darkness*.)

The structure of *Set This House on Fire*, as several critics have already suggested,[5] is that of the detective story. The solution is judiciously withheld until the end. Peter Leverett dons the inappropriate costume of the amateur sleuth and manages to piece together the details of the rape and murder. The surprise ending that Mason Flagg—inevitably the chief suspect in any tale of sexual excess—is not the "final" rapist and murderer of Francesca has a somewhat false and improbable ring. The village idiot has never been a convincing suspect so when we discover that he is the guilty party we wonder why so much energy has been expended to make us loathe Mason Flagg. Sartre has something to say [157/158] about the improbable nature of what he calls "an anti-novel that reads like a detective story."[6] Perhaps Styron is writing just this kind of novel and *Set This House on Fire* should be linked with the fiction of Nathalie Sarraute, Alain Robbe-Grillet, Michel Butor, and perhaps even Samuel Beckett—which often tends to be, in Sartre's words, "a parody on the novel of 'quest.'" Nathalie Sarraute's "detectives" go through all the appropriate motions but usually discover that the money has not been stolen at all or no crime has been committed; the accustomed detective motifs fall gracefully to pieces in her novels. Alain Robbe-Grillet's characters tend to become implausible murderers because of ironical twists in circumstances. Michel Butor's creatures often piece together ingenious crimes which have more basis in fancy than in fact. Beckett's people are usually involved in some quest or search which inevitably comes to nothing. Although we do have a double murder in *Set This House on Fire*—the village idiot kills Francesca and Cass Kinsolving kills Flagg —the circumstances and solution have a kind of droll, unlikely setting. The Fascist policeman, Luigi, who offers Cass absolution from the murder he committed by declaring Flagg's death to be a suicide, seems almost to be an ironical portrait of the Agatha Christie or Georges Simenon detective who never mixes philosophy and moral sermonizing with murder. In the end, one must think of *Set This House on Fire* as part of this new detective literature devised almost in caricature of the straight, unpretentious murder mystery.[7]

[5] See, for example, Abraham Rothberg's "Styron's Appointment in Sambuco," *New Leader* (July 4–11, 1960), p. 26.

[6] See Jean-Paul Sartre's preface to Nathalie Sarraute's *Portrait of a Man Unknown* (New York: Braziller, 1958), p. viii.

[7] Colin Wilson's recent *Ritual in the Dark* is another attempt at reshaping the conventional detective story. Wilson has recast the Jack the Ripper theme in twentieth century dress. One of the two central characters, Austin Nunne, has a great deal in common with Mason Flagg except that Austin turns out to be the murderer.

Together with this seems to go a certain presentiment about place. Sambuco assumes an eerie importance, almost as if evil things were destined to happen there. It is certainly no accident that Styron should open his novel with a page-long description of the village. Styron's words about it are curiously revealing. He speaks of it as being: "Aloof upon its precipice, remote and beautifully difficult of access, it is a model of invulnerability . . ." and as being "proudly, even unfairly, preserved, like someone fit and sturdy among a group of maimed, wasted veterans." This is the kind of appreciation of landscape which suggests more than just physical appeal. It is somewhat the way Proust spoke of his beloved Balbec and Venice—places which enter his novel with almost the importance of characters. Mason Flagg had committed every variety of sexual excess before he came to Sambuco: the rape during his prep school days; the orgies in Greenwich Village. But he seemed strangely destined to pay for his sins, most of them committed earlier, in this small, idyllically situated Italian town. It was almost as if Sambuco had become the agent of retribution. But more than this, we are made to feel throughout the novel the contrast in place between Sambuco and Leverett's native Port Warwick (which has become Styron's equivalent of [158/192] Faulkner's mythical Yoknapatawpha County). There is no doubt that *Set This House on Fire* is crucially concerned with setting—almost as a moral force on character.

There has been much talk in recent literary criticism on both sides of the Atlantic about "The New Literature." It has been keenly felt that the Fifties has done more systematically than any other decade to transform the shape of the novel and save it from the total extinction which Eliot and Yvor Winters had prophesied for it. William Styron has come to maturity during the period when France introduced its *nouveau roman*, England produced its Angry Young Men, and America retaliated with its own brand of Existentialism. Styron has recognized these movements and seems to be writing the kind of fiction which profits from the work of his contemporaries. But he demands tighter structure for the novel, more concern with style, more completely "rounded" characters. He seems to insist more on a technically perfect novel than on a "new" novel. [192]

4. NAT TURNER AND SLAVERY

Nat Turner's Insurrection

THOMAS WENTWORTH HIGGINSON

DURING THE YEAR 1831, UP TO THE TWENTY-THIRD OF AUGUST, THE Virginia newspapers were absorbed in the momentous problems which then occupied the minds of intelligent American citizens:—What General Jackson should do with the scolds, and what with the disreputables,—Should South Carolina be allowed to nullify? and would the wives of Cabinet Ministers call on Mrs. Eaton? It is an unfailing opiate, to turn over the drowsy files of the "Richmond Enquirer," until the moment when those dry and dusty pages are suddenly kindled into flame by the torch of Nat Turner. Then the terror flares on increasing, until the remotest Southern States are found shuddering at nightly rumors of insurrection,—until far-off European colonies, Antigua, Martinique, Caraccas, Tortola, recognize by some secret sympathy the same epidemic alarms,—until the very boldest words of freedom are reported as uttered in the Virginia House of Delegates with unclosed doors,—until an obscure young man named Garrison is indicted at Common Law in North Carolina, and has a price set upon his head by the Legislature of Georgia. The insurrection revived in one agonizing reminiscence all the distresses of Gabriel's Revolt, thirty years before; and its memory endures still fresh, now that thirty added years have brought the more formidable presence of General Butler. It is by no means impossible that the very children or even confederates of Nat Turner may be included at this moment among the contraband articles of Fort Monroe.

Near the southeastern border of Virginia, in Southampton County, there is a neighborhood known as "The Cross Keys." It lies fifteen miles from Jerusalem, the county-town or "court-house," seventy miles from Norfolk, and about as far from Richmond. It is some ten or fifteen miles from Murfreesboro in North Carolina, and about twenty-five from the Great Dismal Swamp. Up to Sunday, the twenty-first of August, 1831, there was nothing to distinguish it from any other rural,

Thomas Wentworth Higginson, "Nat Turner's Insurrection," *The Atlantic Monthly*, VIII (August 1861), 173–187. Reprinted by permission of *The Atlantic Monthly*.

lethargic, slipshod Virginia neighborhood, with the due allotment of mansion-houses and log-huts, tobacco-fields and "old-fields," horses, dogs, negroes, "poor white folks," so called, and other white folks, poor without being called so. One of these last was Joseph Travis, who had recently married the widow of one Putnam Moore, and had unfortunately wedded to himself her negroes also.

In the woods on the plantation of Joseph Travis, upon the Sunday just named, six slaves met at noon for what is called in the Northern States a picnic and in the Southern a barbecue. The bill of fare was to be simple: one brought a pig, and another some brandy, giving to the meeting an aspect so cheaply convivial that no one would have imagined it to be the final consummation of a conspiracy which had been for six months in preparation. In this plot four of the men had been already initiated,—Henry, Hark or Hercules, Nelson, and Sam. Two others were novices, Will and Jack by name. The party had remained together from twelve to three o'clock, when a seventh man joined them,—a short, stout, powerfully built person, of dark mulatto complexion and strongly-marked African features, but with a face full of expression and resolution. This was Nat Turner.

He was at this time nearly thirty-one years old, having been born on the second of October, 1800. He had belonged originally to Benjamin Turner,—whence his last name, slaves having usually no patronymic,—had then been transferred to Putnam Moore, and then to his present owner. He had, by his own account, felt himself singled out from childhood for some great work; and he had some peculiar marks on his person, which, joined to his great mental precocity, were [173/ 174] enough to occasion, among his youthful companions, a superstitious faith in his gifts and destiny. He had great mechanical ingenuity also, experimentalized very early in making paper, gunpowder, pottery, and in other arts which in later life he was found thoroughly to understand. His moral faculties were very strong, so that white witnesses admitted that he had never been known to swear an oath, to drink a drop of spirits, or to commit a theft. And in general, so marked were his early peculiarities, that people said "he had too much sense to be raised, and if he was, he would never be of any use as a slave." This impression of personal destiny grew with his growth;—he fasted, prayed, preached, read the Bible, heard voices when he walked behind his plough, and communicated his revelations to the awe-struck slaves. They told him in return, that, "if they had his sense, they would not serve any master in the world."

The biographies of slaves can hardly be individualized; they belong to the class. We know bare facts; it is only the general experience of human beings in like condition which can clothe them with life. The outlines are certain, the details are inferential. Thus, for instance, we know that Nat Turner's young wife was a slave; we know that she belonged to a different master from himself; we know little more than this, but this is much. For this is equivalent to saying that by day or by night that husband had no more power to protect her than the man who lies bound upon a plundered vessel's deck has power to protect his wife on board the pirate-schooner disappearing in the horizon; she may be reverenced, she may be outraged; it is in the powerlessness that the agony lies. There is, indeed, one thing more which we do know of this young woman: the Virginia newspapers state that she was tortured under the lash, after her husband's execution, to make her produce his papers: this is all.

What his private experiences and special privileges or wrongs may have been, it is therefore now impossible to say. Travis was declared to be "more humane and fatherly to his slaves than any man in the county"; but it is astonishing how often this phenomenon occurs in the contemporary annals of slave insurrections. The chairman of the county court also stated, in pronouncing sentence, that Nat Turner had spoken of his master as "only too indulgent"; but this, for some reason, does not appear in his printed Confession, which only says, "He was a kind master, and placed the greatest confidence in me." It is very possible that it may have been so, but the printed accounts of Nat Turner's person look suspicious: he is described in Governor Floyd's proclamation as having a scar on one of his temples, also one on the back of his neck, and a large knot on one of the bones of his right arm, produced by a blow; and although these were explained away in Virginia newspapers as being produced by fights with his companions, yet such affrays are entirely foreign to the admitted habits of the man. It must, therefore, remain an open question, whether the scars and the knot were produced by black hands or by white.

Whatever Nat Turner's experiences of slavery might have been, it is certain that his plans were not suddenly adopted, but that he had brooded over them for years. To this day there are traditions among the Virginia slaves of the keen devices of "Prophet Nat." If he was caught with lime and lamp-black in hand, conning over a half-finished county-map on the barn-door, he was always "planning what to do, if he were blind," or "studying how to get to Mr. Francis's house." When he had called a meeting of slaves, and some poor whites came eavesdropping, the poor whites at once became the subjects for discussion; he incidentally mentioned that the masters had been heard threatening to drive them away; one slave had been ordered to shoot Mr. Jones's pigs, another to tear down Mr. Johnson's fences. The poor whites, Johnson and Jones, ran home to see to their homesteads, and were better friends than ever to Prophet Nat. [174/175]

He never was a Baptist preacher, though such vocation has often been attributed to him. The impression arose from his having immersed himself, during one of his periods of special enthusiasm, together with a poor white man named Brantley. "About this time," he says in his Confession, "I told these things to a white man, on whom it had a wonderful effect, and he ceased from his wickedness, and was attacked immediately with a cutaneous eruption, and the blood oozed from the pores of his skin, and after praying and fasting nine days he was healed. And the Spirit appeared to me again, and said, as the Saviour had been baptized, so should we be also; and when the white people would not let us be baptized by the Church, we went down into the water together, in the sight of many who reviled us, and were baptized by the Spirit. After this I rejoiced greatly and gave thanks to God."

The religious hallucinations narrated in his Confession seem to have been as genuine as the average of such things, and are very well expressed. It reads quite like Jacob Behmen. He saw white spirits and black spirits contending in the skies, the sun was darkened, the thunder rolled. "And the Holy Ghost was with me, and said, 'Behold me as I stand in the heavens!' And I looked and saw the forms of men in different attitudes. And there were lights in the sky, to which the children of darkness gave other names than what they really were; for they were the lights of the Saviour's hands, stretched forth from east to west, even as they were extended on the cross on Calvary, for the redemption of sinners." He saw drops of blood on the corn: this was Christ's blood, shed for man. He saw on the leaves in the woods letters and numbers and figures of men,—the same symbols which he had seen in the skies. On May 12, 1828, the Holy Spirit appeared to him and proclaimed that the yoke of Jesus must fall on him, and he must fight against the Serpent when the sign appeared. Then came an eclipse of the sun in February, 1831: this was the sign; then he must arise and prepare himself, and slay his enemies with their own weapons; then also the seal was removed from his lips, and then he confided his plans to four associates.

When he came, therefore, to the barbecue on the appointed Sunday, and found, not these four only, but two others, his first question to the intruders was, How they came thither. To this Will answered manfully, that his life was worth no more than the others, and "his liberty was as dear to him." This admitted him to confidence, and as Jack was known to be entirely under Hark's influence, the strangers were no bar to their discussion. Eleven hours they remained there, in anxious consultation: one can imagine those terrible dusky faces, beneath the funereal woods, and amid the flickering of pine-knot torches, preparing that stern revenge whose shuddering echoes should ring through the land so long. Two things were at last decided: to begin their work that night, and to begin it with a massacre so swift and irresistible as to create in a few days more terror than many battles, and so spare the need of future bloodshed. "It was agreed that we should commence at home on that night, and, until we had armed and equipped ourselves and gained sufficient force, neither age nor sex was to be spared: which was invariably adhered to."

John Brown invaded Virginia with nineteen men, and with the avowed resolution to take no life but in self-defence. Nat Turner attacked Virginia from within, with six men, and with the determination to spare no life until his power was established. John Brown intended to pass rapidly through Virginia, and then retreat to the mountains. Nat Turner intended to "conquer Southampton County as the white men did in the Revolution, and then retreat, if necessary, to the Dismal Swamp." Each plan was deliberately matured; each was in its way practicable; but each was defeated by a single false step, as will soon appear.

We must pass over the details of horror, as they occurred during the next [175/176] twenty-four hours. Swift and stealthy as Indians, the black men passed from house to house,—not pausing, not hesitating, as their terrible work went on. In one thing they were humaner than Indians or than white men fighting against Indians,—there was no gratuitous outrage beyond the death-blow itself, no insult, no mutilation; but in every house they entered, that blow fell on man, woman, and child,—nothing that had a white skin was spared. From every house they took arms and ammunition, and from a few, money; on every plantation they found recruits: those dusky slaves, so obsequious to their master the day before, so prompt to sing and dance before his Northern visitors, were all swift to transform themselves into fiends of retribution now; show them sword or musket and they grasped it, though it were an heirloom from Washington himself. The troop increased from house to house,—first to fifteen, then to forty, then to sixty. Some were armed with muskets, some with axes, some with scythes; some came on their masters' horses. As the numbers increased, they could be divided, and the awful work was carried on more rapidly still. The plan then was for an advanced guard of horsemen to approach each house at a gallop, and surround it till the others came up. Meanwhile what agonies of terror must have taken place within, shared alike by innocent and by guilty! what memories of wrongs inflicted on those dusky creatures, by some,—what innocent participation, by others, in the penance! The outbreak lasted for but forty-eight hours; but during that period fifty-five whites were slain, without the loss of a single slave.

One fear was needless, which to many a husband and father must have intensified the last struggle. These negroes had been systematically brutalized from childhood; they had been allowed no legalized or permanent marriage; they had beheld around them an habitual licentiousness, such as can scarcely exist except in a Slave State; some of them had seen their wives and sisters habitually polluted by the husbands and the brothers of these fair white women who were now absolutely in their power. Yet I have looked through the Virginia newspapers of that time in vain for one charge of an indecent outrage on a woman against these triumphant and terrible slaves. Wherever they went, there went death, and that was all. Compare this with ordinary wars; compare it with the annals of the French Revolution. No one, perhaps, has yet painted the wrongs of the French populace so terribly as Dickens in his "Tale of Two Cities"; yet what man, conversant with slave-biographies, can read that narrative without feeling it weak beside the provocations to which fugitive slaves testify? It is something for human nature that these desperate insurgents revenged such wrongs by death alone. Even that fearful penalty was to be inflicted only till the object was won. It was admitted in the "Richmond Enquirer" of the time, that "indiscriminate massacre was not their intention, after they obtained foothold, and was resorted to in the first instance to strike terror and alarm. Women and children would afterwards have been spared, and men also who ceased to resist."

It is reported by some of the contemporary newspapers, that a portion of this abstinence was the result of deliberate consultation among the insurrectionists; that some of them were resolved on taking the white women for wives, but were overruled by Nat Turner. If so, he is the only American slave-leader of whom we know certainly that he rose above the ordinary level of slave vengeance, and Mrs. Stowe's picture of Dred's purposes is then precisely typical of his. "Whom the Lord saith unto us, 'Smite,' them will we smite. We will not torment them with the scourge and fire, nor defile their women as they have done with ours. But we will slay them utterly, and consume them from off the face of the earth."

When the number of adherents had increased to fifty or sixty, Nat Turner [176/177] judged it time to strike at the county-seat, Jerusalem. Thither a few white fugitives had already fled, and couriers might thence be despatched for aid to Richmond and Petersburg, unless promptly intercepted. Besides, he could there find arms, ammunition, and money; though they had already obtained, it is dubiously reported, from eight hundred to one thousand dollars. On the way it was necessary to pass the plantation of Mr. Parker, three miles from Jerusalem. Some of the men wished to stop here and enlist some of their friends. Nat Turner objected, as the delay might prove dangerous; he yielded at last, and it proved fatal.

He remained at the gate with six or eight men; thirty or forty went to the house, half a mile distant. They remained too long, and he went alone to hasten them. During his absence a party of eighteen white men came up suddenly, dispersing the small guard left at the gate; and when the main body of slaves emerged from the house, they encountered, for the first time, their armed masters. The blacks halted, the whites advanced cautiously within a hundred yards and fired a volley; on its being returned, they broke into disorder, and hurriedly retreated, leaving some wounded on the ground. The retreating whites were pursued, and were saved only by falling in with another band of fresh men from Jerusalem, with whose aid they turned upon the slaves, who in their turn fell into confusion. Turner, Hark, and about twenty men on horseback retreated in some order; the rest were scattered. The leader still planned to reach Jerusalem by a private way, thus evading pursuit; but at last decided to stop for the night, in the hope of enlisting additional recruits.

During the night the number increased again to forty, and they encamped on Major Ridley's plantation. An alarm took place during the darkness,—whether real or imaginary does not appear,—and the men became scattered again. Proceeding to make fresh enlistments with the daylight, they were resisted at Dr. Blunt's house, where his slaves, under his orders, fired upon them, and this, with a later attack from a party of white men near Captain Harris's, so broke up the whole force that they never reunited. The few who remained together agreed to separate for a few hours to see if anything could be done to revive the insurrection, and meet again that evening at their original rendezvous. But they never reached it.

Sadly came Nat Turner at nightfall into those gloomy woods where forty-eight hours before he had revealed the details of his terrible plot to his companions. At the outset all his plans had succeeded; everything was as he predicted: the slaves had come readily at his call, the masters had proved perfectly defenceless. Had he not been persuaded to pause at Parker's plantation, he would have been master before now of the arms and ammunition at Jerusalem; and with these to aid, and the Dismal Swamp for a refuge, he might have sustained himself indefinitely against his pursuers.

Now the blood was shed, the risk was incurred, his friends were killed or captured, and all for what? Lasting memories of terror, to be sure, for his oppressors; but on the other hand, hopeless failure for the insurrection, and certain death for him. What a watch he must have kept that night! To that excited imagination, which had always seen spirits in the sky and blood-drops on the corn and hieroglyphic marks on the dry leaves, how full the lonely forest must have been of signs and solemn warnings! Alone with the fox's bark, the rabbit's rustle, and the screech-owl's scream, the self-appointed prophet brooded over his despair. Once creeping to the edge of the wood, he saw men stealthily approach on horseback. He fancied them some of his companions; but before he dared to whisper their ominous names, "Hark" or "Dred,"— for the latter was the name, since famous, of one of his more recent recruits,—he saw them to be white men, [177/178] and shrank back stealthily beneath his covert.

There he waited two weary days and two melancholy nights,— long enough to satisfy himself that no one would rejoin him, and that the insurrection had hopelessly failed. The determined, desperate spirits who had shared his plans were scattered forever, and longer delay would be destruction for him also. He found a spot which he judged safe, dug a hole under a pile of fence-rails in a field, and lay there for six weeks, only leaving it for a few moments at midnight to obtain water from a neighboring spring. Food he had previously provided, without discovery, from a house near by.

Meanwhile an unbounded variety of rumors went flying through the State. The express which first reached the Governor announced that the militia were retreating before the slaves. An express to Petersburg further fixed the number of militia at three hundred, and of blacks at eight hundred, and invented a convenient shower of rain to explain the dampened ardor of the whites. Later reports described the slaves as making three desperate attempts to cross the bridge over the Nottoway between Cross Keys and Jerusalem, and stated that the leader had been shot in the attempt. Other accounts put the number of negroes at three hundred, all well mounted and armed, with two or three white men as leaders. Their intention was supposed to be to reach the Dismal Swamp, and they must be hemmed in from that side.

Indeed, the most formidable weapon in the hands of slave-insurgents is always this blind panic they create, and the wild exaggerations which follow. The worst being possible, every one takes the worst for granted. Undoubtedly a dozen armed men could have stifled this insurrection, even after it had commenced operations; but it is the fatal weakness of a slaveholding community, that it can never furnish men promptly for such a purpose. "My first intention was," says one of the most intelligent newspaper narrators of the affair, "to have attacked them with thirty or forty men; but those who had families here were strongly opposed to it."

As usual, each man was pinioned to his own hearth-stone. As usual, aid had to be summoned from a distance, and, as usual, the United States troops were the chief reliance. Colonel House, commanding at Fort Monroe, sent at once three companies of artillery under Lieutenant-Colonel Worth, and embarked them on board the steamer Hampton for Suffolk. These were joined by detachments from the United States ships *Warren* and *Natchez,* the whole amounting to nearly eight hundred men. Two volunteer companies went from Richmond, four from Petersburg, one from Norfolk, one from Portsmouth, and several from North Carolina. The militia of Norfolk, Nansemond, and Princess Anne Counties, and the United States troops at Old Point Comfort, were ordered to scour the Dismal Swamp, where it was believed that two or three thousand fugitives were preparing to join the insurgents. It was even proposed to send two companies from New York and one from New London to the same point.

When these various forces reached Southampton County, they found all labor paralyzed and whole plantations abandoned. A letter from Jerusalem, dated August 24th, says, "The oldest inhabitant of our county has never experienced such a distressing time as we have had since Sunday night last. . . . Every house, room, and corner in this place is full of women and children, driven from home, who had to take the woods until they could get to this place." "For many miles around their track," says another, "the county is deserted by women and children." Still another writes, "Jerusalem is full of women, most of them from the other side of the river,—about two hundred at Vix's." Then follow descriptions of the sufferings of these persons, many of whom had lain night after night in the woods. But the immediate danger was at an end, the short-lived insurrection was finished, and now [178/179] the work of vengeance was to begin. In the frank phrase of a North Carolina correspondent,—"The massacre of the whites was over, and the white people had commenced the destruction of the negroes, which was continued after our men got there, from time to time, as they could fall in with them, all day yesterday." A postscript adds, that "passengers by the Fayetteville stage say, that, by the latest accounts, one hundred and twenty negroes had been killed," —this being little more than one day's work.

These murders were defended as Nat Turner defended his: a fearful blow must be struck. In shuddering at the horrors of the insurrection, we have forgotten the far greater horrors of its suppression.

The newspapers of the day contain many indignant protests against the cruelties which took place. "It is with pain," says a correspondent of the "National Intelligencer," September 7, 1831, "that we speak of another feature of the Southampton Rebellion; for we have been most unwilling to have our sympathies for the sufferers diminished or affected by their misconduct. We allude to the slaughter of many blacks without trial and under circumstances of great barbarity. . . . We met with an individual of intelligence who told us that he himself had killed between ten and fifteen. . . . We [the Richmond troop] witnessed with surprise the sanguinary temper of the population, who evinced a strong disposition to inflict immediate death on every prisoner."

There is a remarkable official document from General Eppes, the officer in command, to be found in the "Richmond Enquirer" for September 6, 1831. It is an indignant denunciation of precisely these outrages; and though he refuses to give details, he supplies their place by epithets: "revolting,"—"inhuman and not to be justified,"—"acts of barbarity and cruelty,"—"acts of atrocity,"—"this course of proceeding dignifies the rebel and the assassin with the sanctity of martyrdom." And he ends by threatening martial law upon all future transgressors. Such general orders are not issued except in rather extreme cases. And in the parallel columns of the newspaper the innocent editor prints equally indignant descriptions of Russian atrocities in Lithuania, where the Poles were engaged in active insurrection, amid profuse sympathy from Virginia.

The truth is, it was a Reign of Terror. Volunteer patrols rode in all directions, visiting plantations. "It was with the greatest difficulty," said General Brodnax before the House of Delegates, "and at the hazard of personal popularity and esteem, that the coolest and most judicious among us could exert an influence sufficient to restrain an indiscriminate slaughter of the blacks who were suspected." A letter from the Rev. G. W. Powell declares, "There are thousands of troops searching in every direction, and many negroes are killed every day: the exact number will never be ascertained." Petition after petition was subsequently presented to the legislature, asking compensation for slaves thus assassinated without trial.

Men were tortured to death, burned, maimed, and subjected to nameless atrocities. The overseers were called on to point out any slaves whom they distrusted, and if any tried to escape, they were shot down. Nay, worse than this. "A party of horsemen started from Richmond with the intention of killing every colored person they saw in Southampton County. They stopped opposite the cabin of a free colored man, who was hoeing in his little field. They called out, 'Is this Southampton County?' He replied, 'Yes, Sir, you have just crossed the line, by yonder tree.' They shot him dead and rode on." This is from the narrative of the editor of the "Richmond Whig," who was then on duty in the militia, and protested manfully against these outrages. "Some of these scenes," he adds, "are hardly inferior in barbarity to the atrocities of the insurgents."

These were the masters' stories. If even these conceded so much, it would be interesting to hear what the slaves had to report. I am indebted to my honored friend, Lydia Maria Child, for some vivid [179/180] recollections of this terrible period, as noted down from the lips of an old colored woman, once well known in New York, Charity Bowery. "At the time of the old Prophet Nat," she said, "the colored folks was afraid to pray loud; for the whites threatened to punish 'em dreadfully, if the least noise was heard. The patrols was low drunken whites, and in Nat's time, if they heard any of the colored folks praying or singing a hymn, they would fall upon 'em and abuse 'em, and sometimes kill 'em, afore master or missis could get to 'em. The brightest and best was killed in Nat's time. The whites always suspect such ones. They killed a great many at a place called Duplon. They killed Antonio, a slave of Mr. J. Stanley, whom they shot; then they pointed their guns at him, and told him to confess about the insurrection. He told 'em he didn't know anything about any insurrection. They shot several balls through him, quartered him, and put his head on a pole at the fork of the road leading to the court." (This is no exaggeration, if the Virginia newspapers may be taken as evidence.) "It was there but a short time. He had no trial. They never do. In Nat's time, the patrols would tie up the free colored people, flog 'em, and try to make 'em lie against one another, and often killed them before anybody could interfere. Mr. James Cole, High Sheriff, said, if any of the patrols came on his plantation, he would lose his life in defence of his people. One day he heard a patroller boasting how many niggers he had killed.

Mr. Cole said, 'If you don't pack up, as quick as God Almighty will let you, and get out of this town, and never be seen in it again, I'll put you where dogs won't bark at you.' He went off, and wasn't seen in them parts again."

These outrages were not limited to the colored population; but other instances occurred which strikingly remind one of more recent times. An Englishman, named Robinson, was engaged in selling books at Petersburg. An alarm being given, one night, that five hundred blacks were marching towards the town, he stood guard, with others, on the bridge. After the panic had a little subsided, he happened to remark, that "the blacks, as men, were entitled to their freedom, and ought to be emancipated." This led to great excitement, and he was warned to leave town. He took passage in the stage, but the stage was intercepted. He then fled to a friend's house; the house was broken open, and he was dragged forth. The civil authorities, being applied to, refused to interfere. The mob stripped him, gave him a great number of lashes, and sent him on foot, naked, under a hot sun, to Richmond, whence he with difficulty found a passage to New York.

Of the capture or escape of most of that small band who met with Nat Turner in the woods upon the Travis plantation little can now be known. All appear among the list of convicted, except Henry and Will. General Moore, who occasionally figures as second in command, in the newspaper narratives of that day, was probably the Hark or Hercules before mentioned; as no other of the confederates had belonged to Mrs. Travis, or would have been likely to bear her previous name of Moore. As usual, the newspapers state that most, if not all the slaves, were "the property of kind and indulgent masters." Whether in any case they were also the sons of those masters is a point ignored; but from the fact that three out of the seven were at first reported as being white men by several different witnesses,—the whole number being correctly given, and the statement therefore probably authentic,—one must suppose that there was an admixture of patrician blood in some of these conspirators.

The subordinate insurgents sought safety as they could. A free colored man, named Will Artist, shot himself in the woods, where his hat was found on a stake and his pistol lying by him; another was found drowned; others were traced to the Dismal Swamp; others returned to their homes, and tried to conceal their share in the insurrection, assuring their masters that they had been [180/181] forced, against their will, to join,—the usual defence in such cases. The number shot down at random must, by all accounts, have amounted to many hundreds, but it is past all human registration now. The number who had a formal trial, such as it was, is officially stated at fifty-five; of these, seventeen were convicted and hanged, twelve convicted and transported, twenty acquitted, and four free colored men sent on for further trial and finally acquitted. "Not one of those known to be concerned escaped." Of those executed, one only was a woman: "Lucy, slave of John T. Barrow": that is all her epitaph, shorter even than that of Wordsworth's more famous Lucy;—but whether this one was old or young, pure or wicked, lovely or repulsive, octoroon or negro, a Cassy, an Emily, or a Topsy, no information appears; she was a woman, she was a slave, and she died.

There is one touching story, in connection with these terrible retaliations, which rests on good authority, that of the Rev. M. B. Cox, a Liberian missionary, then in Virginia. In the hunt which followed the massacre, a slaveholder went into the woods, accompanied by a faithful slave, who had been the means of saving his life during the insurrection. When they had reached a retired place in the forest, the man handed his gun to his master, informing him that he could not live a slave any longer, and requesting him either to free him or shoot him on the spot. The master took the gun, in some trepidation, levelled it at the faithful negro, and shot him through the heart. It is probable that this slaveholder was a Dr. Blunt,—his being the only plantation where the slaves were reported as thus defending their masters. "If this be true," said the "Richmond Enquirer," when it first narrated this instance of loyalty, "great will be the desert of these noble-minded Africans." This "noble-minded African," at least, estimated his own desert at a high standard: he demanded freedom,—and obtained it.

Meanwhile the panic of the whites continued; for, though all others might be disposed of, Nat Turner was still at large. We have positive evidence of the extent of the alarm, although great efforts were afterwards made to represent it as a trifling affair. A distinguished citizen of Virginia wrote three months later to the Hon. W. B. Seabrook of South Carolina,—"From all that has come to my knowledge during and since that affair, I am convinced most fully that every black preacher in the country east of the Blue Ridge was in the secret." "There is much reason to believe," says the Governor's message on December 6th, "that the spirit of insurrection was not confined to Southampton. Many convictions have taken place elsewhere, and some few in distant counties." The withdrawal of the United States troops, after some ten days' service, was a signal for fresh excitement, and an address, numerously signed, was presented to the United States Government, imploring their continued stay. More than three weeks after the first alarm, the Governor sent a supply of arms into Prince William, Fauquier, and Orange Counties. "From examinations which have taken place in other counties," says one of the best newspaper historians of the affair, (in the "Richmond Enquirer" of September 6th,) "I fear that the scheme embraced a wider sphere than I at first supposed." Nat Turner himself, intentionally or otherwise, increased the confusion by denying all knowledge of the North Carolina outbreak, and declaring that he had communicated his plans to his four confederates within six months; while, on the other hand, a slave-girl sixteen or seventeen years old, belonging to Solomon Parker, testified that she had heard the subject discussed for eighteen months, and that at a meeting held during the previous May some eight or ten had joined the plot.

It is astonishing to discover, by laborious comparison of newspaper files, how vast was the immediate range of these insurrectionary alarms. Every Southern State seems to have borne its harvest of terror. On the Eastern shore of Maryland great alarm was at once manifested, [181/182] especially in the neighborhood of Easton and Snowhill; and the houses of colored men were searched for arms even in Baltimore. In Delaware, there were similar rumors through Sussex and Dover Counties; there were arrests and executions; and in Somerset County great public meetings were held, to demand additional safeguards. On election-day, in Seaford, Del., some young men, going out to hunt rabbits, discharged their guns in sport; the men being absent, all the women in the vicinity took to flight; the alarm spread like the "Ipswich Fright"; soon Seaford was thronged with armed men; and when the boys returned from hunting, they found cannon drawn out to receive them.

In North Carolina, Raleigh and Fayetteville were put under military defence, and women and children concealed themselves in the swamps for many days. The rebel organization was supposed to include two thousand. Forty-six slaves were imprisoned in Union County, twenty-five in Sampson County, and twenty-three at least in Duplin County, some of whom were executed. The panic also extended into Wayne, New Hanover, and Lenoir Counties. Four men were shot without trial in Wilmington,—Nimrod, Abraham, Prince, and "Dan the Drayman," the latter a man of seventy,—and their heads placed on poles at the four corners of the town. Nearly two months afterwards the trials were still continuing; and at a still later day, the Governor in his proclamation recommended the formation of companies of volunteers in every county.

In South Carolina, General Hayne issued a proclamation "to prove the groundlessness of the existing alarms,"—thus implying that serious alarms existed. In Macon, Georgia, the whole population were roused from their beds at midnight by a report of a large force of armed negroes five miles off. In an hour, every woman and child was deposited in the largest building of the town, and a military force hastily collected in front. The editor of the Macon "Messenger" excused the poor condition of his paper, a few days afterwards, by the absorption of his workmen in patrol duties, and describes "dismay and terror" as the condition of the people, of "all ages and sexes." In Jones, Twiggs, and Monroe Counties, the same alarms were reported; and in one place "several slaves were tied to a tree, while a militia captain hacked at them with his sword."

In Alabama, at Columbus and Fort Michell, a rumor was spread of a joint conspiracy of Indians and negroes. At Claiborne the panic was still greater; the slaves were said to be thoroughly organized through that part of the State, and multitudes were imprisoned; the whole alarm being apparently founded on one stray copy of the "Liberator."

In Tennessee, the Shelbyville "Freeman" announced that an insurrectionary plot had just been discovered, barely in time for its defeat, through the treachery of a female slave. In Louisville, Kentucky, a similar organization was discovered or imagined, and arrests were made in consequence. "The papers, from motives of policy, do not notice the disturbance," wrote one correspondent to the Portland "Courier." "Pity us!" he added.

But the greatest bubble burst in Louisiana. Captain Alexander, an English tourist, arriving in New Orleans at the beginning of September, found the whole city in tumult. Handbills had been issued, appealing to the slaves to rise against their masters, saying that all men were born equal, declaring that Hannibal was a black man, and that they also might have great leaders among them. Twelve hundred stand of weapons were said to have been found in a black man's house; five hundred citizens were under arms, and four companies of regulars were ordered to the city, whose barracks Alexander himself visited.

If such were the alarm in New Orleans, the story, of course, lost nothing by transmission to other Slave States. A rumor reached Frankfort, Kentucky, that the slaves already had possession of the [182/183] coast, both above and below New Orleans. But the most remarkable circumstance is, that all this seems to have been a mere revival of an old terror, once before excited and exploded. The following paragraph had appeared in the Jacksonville (Georgia) "Observer," during the spring previous:—

"FEARFUL DISCOVERY. We were favored, by yesterday's mail, with a letter from New Orleans, of May 1st, in which we find that an important discovery had been made a few days previous in that city. The following is an extract:— 'Four days ago, as some planters were digging under ground, they found a square room containing eleven thousand stand of arms and fifteen thousand cartridges, each of the cartridges containing a bullet.' It is said the negroes intended to rise as soon as the sickly season began, and obtain possession of the city by massacring the white population. The same letter states that the mayor had prohibited the opening of Sunday-schools for the instruction of blacks, under a penalty of five hundred dollars for the first offence, and for the second, death."

Such were the terrors that came back from nine other Slave States, as the echo of the voice of Nat Turner; and when it is also known that the subject was at once taken up by the legislatures of other States, where there was no public panic, as in Missouri and Tennessee,—and when, finally, it is added that reports of insurrection had been arriving all that year from Rio Janeiro, Martinique, St. Jago, Antigua, Caraccas, and Tortola, it is easy to see with what prolonged distress the accumulated terror must have weighed down upon Virginia, during the two months that Nat Turner lay hid.

True, there were a thousand men in arms in Southampton County, to inspire security. But the blow had been struck by only seven men before; and unless there were an armed guard in every house, who could tell but any house might at any moment be the scene of new horrors? They might kill or imprison unresisting negroes by day, but could they resist their avengers by night? "The half cannot be told," wrote a lady from another part of Virginia, at this time, "of the distresses of the people. In Southampton County, the scene of the insurrection, the distress beggars description. A gentleman who has been there says that even here, where there has been great alarm, we have no idea of the situation of those in that county. . . . I do not hesitate to believe that many negroes around us would join in a massacre as horrible as that which has taken place, if an opportunity should offer."

Meanwhile the cause of all this terror was made the object of desperate search. On September 17th the Governor offered a reward of five hundred dollars for his capture, and there were other rewards swelling the amount to eleven hundred dollars,—but in vain. No one could track or trap him. On September 30th a minute account of his capture appeared in the newspapers, but it was wholly false. On October 7th there was another, and on October 18th another; yet all without foundation. Worn out by confinement in his little cave, Nat Turner grew more adventurous, and began to move about stealthily by night, afraid to speak to any human being, but hoping to obtain some information that might aid his escape. Returning regularly to his retreat before daybreak, he might possibly have continued this mode of life until pursuit had ceased, had not a dog succeeded where men had failed. The creature accidentally smelt out the provisions hid in the cave, and finally led thither his masters, two negroes, one of whom was named Nelson. On discovering the terrible fugitive, they fled precipitately, when he hastened to retreat in an opposite direction. This was on October 15th, and from this moment the neighborhood was all alive with excitement, and five or six hundred men undertook the pursuit.

It shows a more than Indian adroitness in Nat Turner to have escaped capture any longer. The cave, the arms, the provisions were found; and lying [183/184] among them the notched stick of this miserable Robinson Crusoe, marked with five weary weeks and six days. But the man was gone. For ten days more he concealed himself among the wheat-stacks on Mr. Francis's plantation, and during this time was reduced almost to despair. Once he decided to surrender himself, and walked by night within two miles of Jerusalem before his purpose failed him. Three times he tried to get out of that neighborhood, but in vain: travelling by day was, of course, out of the question, and by night he found it impossible to elude the patrol. Again and again, therefore, he returned to his hiding-place, and during his whole two months' liberty never went five miles from the Cross Keys. On the 25th of October, he was at last discovered by Mr. Francis, as he was emerging from a stack. A load of buckshot was instantly discharged at him, twelve of which passed through his hat as he fell to the ground. He escaped even then, but his pursuers were rapidly concentrating upon him, and it is perfectly astonishing that he could have eluded them for five days more.

On Sunday, October 30th, a man named Benjamin Phipps, going out for the first time on patrol duty, was passing at noon a clearing in the woods where a number of pine-trees had long since been felled. There was a motion among their boughs; he stopped to watch it; and through a gap in the branches he saw, emerging from a hole in the earth beneath, the face of Nat Turner. Aiming his gun instantly, Phipps called on him to surrender. The fugitive, exhausted with watching and privation, entangled in the branches, armed only with a sword, had nothing to do but to yield; sagaciously reflecting, also, as he afterwards explained, that the woods were full of armed men, and that he had better trust fortune for some later chance of escape, instead of desperately attempting it then. He was correct in the first impression, since there were fifty armed scouts within a circuit of two miles. His insurrection ended where it began; for this spot was only a mile and a half from the house of Joseph Travis.

Torn, emaciated, ragged, "a mere scarecrow," still wearing the hat perforated with buckshot, with his arms bound to his sides, he was driven before the levelled gun to the nearest house, that of a Mr. Edwards. He was confined there that night; but the news had spread so rapidly that within an hour after his arrival a hundred persons had collected, and the excitement became so intense "that it was with difficulty he could be conveyed alive to Jerusalem." The enthusiasm spread instantly through Virginia; Mr. Trezvant, the Jerusalem postmaster, sent notices of it far and near; and Governor Floyd himself wrote a letter to the "Richmond Enquirer" to give official announcement of the momentous capture.

When Nat Turner was asked by Mr. T. R. Gray, the counsel assigned him, whether, although defeated, he still believed in his own Providential mission, he answered, as simply as one who came thirty years after him, "Was not Christ crucified?" In the same spirit, when arraigned before the court, "he answered, 'Not guilty,' saying to his counsel that he did not feel so." But apparently no argument was made in his favor by his counsel, nor were any witnesses called,—he being convicted on the testimony of Levi Waller, and upon his own confession, which was put in by Mr. Gray, and acknowledged by the prisoner before the six justices composing the court, as being "full, free, and voluntary." He was therefore placed in the paradoxical position of conviction by his own confession, under a plea of "Not guilty."

The arrest took place on the thirtieth of October, 1831, the confession
on the first of November, the trial and conviction on the fifth, and the
execution on the following Friday, the eleventh of November, precisely
at noon. He met his death with perfect composure, declined addressing the multitude assembled, and told the sheriff in a firm voice
that he was ready. Another account says that he "betrayed [184/185]
no emotion, and even hurried the executioner in the performance of his
duty." "Not a limb nor a muscle was observed to move. His body, after
his death, was given over to the surgeons for dissection."

This last statement merits remark. There would be no evidence
that this formidable man was not favored during his imprisonment
with that full measure of luxury which slave-jails afford to slaves, but
for a rumor which arose after the execution, that he was compelled to
sell his body in advance, for purposes of dissection, in exchange for
food. But it does not appear probable, from the known habits of
Southern anatomists, that any such bargain could have been needed.
For in the circular of the South Carolina Medical School for that very
year I find this remarkable suggestion:—"Some advantages of a peculiar character are connected with this institution. No place in the
United States affords so great opportunities for the acquisition of
medical knowledge, subjects being obtained among the colored population in sufficient number for every purpose, and proper dissections
carried on without offending any individual." What a convenience, to
possess for scientific purposes a class of population sufficiently human
to be dissected, but not human enough to be supposed to take offence
at it! And as the same arrangement may be supposed to have existed in
Virginia, Nat Turner would hardly have gone through the formality of
selling his body for food to those who claimed its control at any rate.

The Confession of the captive was published under authority of
Mr. Gray, in a pamphlet, at Baltimore. Fifty thousand copies of it are
said to have been printed, and it was "embellished with an accurate
likeness of the brigand, taken by Mr. John Crawley, portrait-painter,
and lithographed by Endicott & Swett, at Baltimore." The newly published "Liberator" said of it, at the time, that it would "only serve to
rouse up other leaders, and hasten other insurrections," and advised
grand juries to indict Mr. Gray. I have never seen a copy of the
original pamphlet, it is not to be found in any of our public libraries,
and I have heard of but one as still existing, although the Confession
itself has been repeatedly reprinted. Another small pamphlet, containing the main features of the outbreak, was published at New York
during the same year, and this is in my possession. But the greater part
of the facts which I have given were gleaned from the contemporary
newspapers.

Who now shall go back thirty years and read the heart of this
extraordinary man, who, by the admission of his captors, "never was
known to swear an oath or drink a drop of spirits,"—who, on the same

authority, "for natural intelligence and quickness of apprehension was surpassed by few men," "with a mind capable of attaining anything,"—who knew no book but his Bible, and that by heart,—who devoted himself soul and body to the cause of his race, without a trace of personal hope or fear,—who laid his plans so shrewdly that they came at last with less warning than any earthquake on the doomed community around,—and who, when that time arrived, took the life of man, woman, and child, without a throb of compunction, a word of exultation, or an act of superfluous outrage? Mrs. Stowe's "Dred" seems dim and melodramatic beside the actual Nat Turner. De Quincey's "Avenger" is his only parallel in imaginative literature: similar wrongs, similar retribution. Mr. Gray, his self-appointed confessor, rises into a sort of bewildered enthusiasm, with the prisoner before him. "I shall not attempt to describe the effect of his narrative, as told and commented on by himself, in the condemned-hole of the prison. The calm, deliberate composure with which he spoke of his late deeds and intentions, the expression of his fiend-like face when excited by enthusiasm, still bearing the stains of the blood of helpless innocence about him, clothed with rags and covered with chains, yet daring to raise his manacled hands to heaven, [185/186] with a spirit soaring above the attributes of man,—I looked on him, and the blood curdled in my veins."

But the more remarkable the personal character of Nat Turner, the greater the amazement felt that he should not have appreciated the extreme felicity of his position as a slave. In all insurrections, the standing wonder seems to be that the slaves most trusted and best used should be most deeply involved. So in this case, as usual, they resorted to the most astonishing theories of the origin of the affair. One attributed it to Free-Masonry, and another to free whiskey,—liberty appearing dangerous, even in these forms. The poor whites charged it upon the free colored people, and urged their expulsion, forgetting that in North Carolina the plot was betrayed by one of this class, and that in Virginia there were but two engaged, both of whom had slave-wives. The slaveholding clergymen traced it to want of knowledge of the Bible, forgetting that Nat Turner knew scarcely anything else. On the other hand, "a distinguished citizen of Virginia" combined in one sweeping denunciation "Northern incendiaries, tracts, Sunday-schools, religion, reading, and writing."

But whether the theories of its origin were wise or foolish, the insurrection made its mark, and the famous band of Virginia emancipationists who all that winter made the House of Delegates ring with unavailing eloquence—till the rise of slave-exportation to new cotton regions stopped their voices—were but the unconscious mouth-pieces of Nat Turner. In January, 1832, in reply to a member who had called the outbreak a "petty affair," the eloquent James McDowell thus described the impression it left behind:—

"Now, Sir, I ask you, I ask gentlemen, in conscience to say, was that a 'petty affair' which startled the feelings of your whole population,—which threw a portion of it into alarm, a portion of it into panic,—which wrung out from an affrighted people the thrilling cry, day after day, conveyed to your executive, *We are in peril of our lives; send us an army for defence*'? Was that a 'petty affair' which drove families from their homes,—which assembled women and children in crowds, without shelter, at places of common refuge, in every condition of weakness and infirmity, under every suffering which want and terror could inflict, yet willing to endure all, willing to meet death from famine, death from climate, death from hardships, preferring anything rather than the horrors of meeting it from a domestic assassin? Was that a 'petty affair' which erected a peaceful and confiding portion of the State into a military camp,—which outlawed from pity the unfortunate beings whose brothers had offended,—which barred every door, penetrated every bosom with fear or suspicion,—which so banished every sense of security from every man's dwelling, that, let but a hoof or horn break upon the silence of the night, and an aching throb would be driven to the heart, the husband would look to his weapon, and the mother would shudder and weep upon her cradle? Was it the fear of Nat Turner, and his deluded, drunken handful of followers, which produced such effects? Was it this that induced distant counties, where the very name of Southampton was strange, to arm and equip for a struggle? No, Sir, it was the suspicion eternally attached to the slave himself,—the suspicion that a Nat Turner might be in every family,—that the same bloody deed might be acted over at any time and in any place,—that the materials for it were spread through the land, and were always ready for a like explosion. Nothing but the force of this withering apprehension,—nothing but the paralyzing and deadening weight with which it falls upon and prostrates the heart of every man who has helpless dependents to protect,—nothing but this could have thrown a brave people into consternation, or could have made any portion of this powerful Commonwealth, for a single instant, to have quailed and trembled." [186/187]

While these things were going on, the enthusiasm for the Polish Revolution was rising to its height. The nation was ringing with a peal of joy, on hearing that at Frankfort the Poles had killed fourteen thousand Russians. "The Southern Religious Telegraph" was publishing an impassioned address to Kosciusko; standards were being consecrated for Poland in the larger cities; heroes, like Skrzynecki, Czartoryski, Rozyski, Kaminski, were choking the trump of Fame with their complicated patronymics. These are all forgotten now; and this poor negro, who did not even possess a name, beyond one abrupt monosyllable,—for even the name of Turner was the master's property,—still lives a memory of terror and a symbol of retribution triumphant. [187]

The Old Dominion

G. P. R. JAMES, ESQ.

OUR WAY LAY THROUGH THE WOODS; AND I MAY NOTICE HERE HOW MUCH more of the land, especially in this state of Virginia, is uncultivated than we generally [273/274] imagine in England. When we talk of a plantation, we think of a wide tract of country, all smoothly laid out in maize, or tobacco, or cotton or rice, and don't comprehend that perhaps two thirds of that plantation will be forest, either the first or second growth. I must remark too that a good deal of the country, especially on the sea-board, has gone back to forest; the earlier colonists having been like prodigals newly come into a fortune, and exhausted their lands, with unvarying crops, principally of tobacco. Thus, what was once, we have every reason to believe very fertile soil, will now only bear pine or other trees of hardy habits.

At length we came to a small open space, between the wood through which we had passed, and another beyond. It could not be more than a hundred and fifty yards wide, but extended on either hand as far as the eye could see, like a long avenue through the forest. The grass with which the ground was covered [274/275] was very green and soft, being sheltered, I suppose, from the heat of the sun by the woods on either side, and fertilized by the moisture which trees invariably draw around them.

"This is a curious interval in the woods," I said, looking up and down. "I should almost be tempted to think a river once flowed down here."

"Oh, no," she answered, "they have a tradition in the country that it was caused by what they call here a *flaw* of wind, which broke clear through the forest, like a hemmed-in warrior cutting his way through his enemies. The trees that the blast overthrew, have long since decayed; but the path that he made for himself, still remains. Man boasts his mighty deeds; but when will king or conqueror leave such permanent traces of his footsteps as are here?"

"And yet, dear Bessy," I answered, "man can occasionally hew for himself ways more magnificent, more indelible than this. The [275/

This novel was published by Thomas Cautley Newby, Publisher, 30 Welbeck Street, Cavendish Square, London, in 1856. It appeared in three volumes. This selection is taken from the final pages of vol. I.

276] forest around may be cut down, the roots rot away, the plough-share pass over where we stand, and not a trace be left. But the mighty human mind, when nobly and vigorously exerted, opens out, for ever-lasting ages, paths which millions follow every day, and which are never blotted out. He who sweeps away the prejudices of a race—he who opens out a wide and noble path for the human mind—he who leads an Exodus from any land of darkness to a land of light, performs a more powerful and more permanent work than the tempest—ay, and one more beneficent."

"True, true," she cried, eagerly, "very true; but such thoughts set my little weak brain whirling. I should like to have been a man, and done some great deeds; but here I am, a mere Virginian girl, no stronger than a butterfly, and fit only for small thoughts, and petty personal adventures. But, talking of adventures, I could make your hair stand on end, if I chose, by a tale of what happened in [276/277] this wood, through which we are going. It has been called 'The Hunter Wood,' ever since."

"And what is it?" I asked.

"No, no," she answered, "I won't tell you now; I should only frighten myself; and in ten minutes, we shall be at Nat Turner's cottage, for this is the boundary of Mr. Travis's property. We will come back the other way, for the sun will then throw the shade more northerly, and that will bring us to the house where uncle Jack, as they call him, pays a visit every year."

"Is that the old man you spoke of yesterday?" I asked.

"Yes; and very old he is," she replied; "how old, nobody knows, exactly, but he must be more than ninety, for he was brought from the coast of Africa, they say, when a good big boy, more than eighty years ago, in one of the last slave-ships that ever came to Virginia." [277/278]

"He is a slave then," I said.

"Oh no," she answered; "he is so very much loved and respected, that several people joined together and purchased his freedom."

"He must indeed be an extraordinary man, to create such feelings in his favour," I remarked.

"The most extraordinary thing of all, perhaps," added she, "is that he has not the slightest touch of the negro pronunciation. I dare say, you must have remarked, cousin Richard, that none of them can ever learn to speak English properly; that there is always a sort of thickness, a difficulty, about their utterance; and some sounds they cannot form at all. But this old man speaks as good English as you do."

"That is indeed extraordinary," I answered; "for so universal is that difficulty of utterance, which you mention, in the African race, whatever language they are speaking, that I imagine it to proceed from a natural defect. I [278/279] have heard they talk both French and Spanish in the same peculiar manner that they talk English."

"Hear this man talk in a dark room, and you would not know him from an American," said Bessy.

But I had soon an opportunity of judging for myself; for shortly after, we came in sight of two or three cabins, with a larger house peeping over the trees at some little distance. Approaching the hut, farthest from us, I knocked at the door on my fair companion's suggestion. We had heard voices speaking within; and, on entering, we found the cabin tenanted by two negroes, who were seated at a small table, with a bowl of milk, and some bread made of Indian corn between them. The first was my friend, Nat Turner, and a powerful, though spare man he was. The other was fully as dark in complexion, and had probably once been as strong in form; but he was now [279/280] an old man, with the wool upon his head as white as snow, and a good many wrinkles in his dingy skin. He was well dressed in black, with very white linen, and a white neck-cloth tied in what I may call clerical style. I should have judged him to have been a man of about seventy, and stout and hale for his age; but, nevertheless, this was Bessy Davenport's negro, Jack; and, I must say, there was something very reverent and prepossessing in his appearance, as he rose and made us a respectful, but not servile, bow.

"Well, Mr. Turner," I said, "I promised to pay you a visit; and Miss Davenport has been kind enough to guide me; otherwise, as a stranger in the land, I might have missed my way."

"You are very welcome, sir," answered Nat. "Pray, Miss Bessy, take dis stool. Here is good uncle Jack, whom you know."

Bessy held out her hand to uncle Jack, who shook it kindly; but he did not miss an [280/281] opportunity of reproof; and looking sadly at Nat Turner, he shook his head, saying—

"Whom callest thou good? There is none good but one—that is God."

"Well, I meant good as this world goes," answered Nat Turner.

"There is so little difference between any two of us," replied the old man, "that no one has a right to claim or receive the title of good; far less to arrogate superiority over other brethren."

"That is an admirable text you have quoted, my friend," I said; "but do you know, I one time heard a man make it an argument against the Divinity of our Saviour?"

"He was very much mistaken," answered uncle Jack, mildly. "The young man to whom he spoke had addressed him as a man, and called him 'Good master,' looking upon him as nothing but a man. Christ reproved him for calling any mere man good, and in so doing, [281/282] spoke of himself in his human character. That man must have been very hard pressed for an argument against a belief that was too powerful for him."

"The case of many a man, I fear," replied I; "but do not let us interrupt your breakfast, Mr. Turner," I continued, turning to Nat.

"It matters not to me when I eat or when I drink," answered Nat

Turner, in what seemed to be a somewhat stilted tone. "The man who wishes to bring the body under the mind, must not care about such things. I have often gone without food for three days."

"I should think that must require some practice and preparation," I observed, somewhat inclined to smile; "and unless it was done from necessity, I do not see the use of it."

"Nor I either," said uncle Jack; "food and drink were given to us for our natural support, and while we reverence God's [282/283] blessings, by using them moderately, we should show our thankfulness for them, by using them as He wills."

"The use was very great," exclaimed Nat Turner, in a more excited tone than before; "and as for preparation, I have accustomed myself to abstinence from my childhood. I knew from my earliest years that I was born for great things. What placed that mark upon my forehead before my birth?" And he laid his finger upon a sort of scar on his brow resembling a cross. But before I could examine it accurately, he went on in the same tone—"Who taught me things which happened before I was born, and which were only known to my mother and my father? If it was God who did this, why did he do so but to show that he intended me to—to—do great things?"

I looked round to uncle Jack, beginning to think that the man was going mad; and the [283/284] old man, taking my glance as a question, answered—

"All the people will tell you it is as he says, sir. But I think Nat lets his mind rest too much upon such things. I fear it may do him harm. He has plenty of strong, good sense, and if he will but continually seek God's grace to use it right, he may, indeed, do great things amongst the poor people who surround him. But the quickest walker goes farthest wrong, when he does not take the right way, and I fear that may be Nat's case."

"No fear, no fear," cried the other. "God, who willed me to be what I am, will teach me to do what I have to do." Then, dropping his voice into an almost sepulchral tone, he added, "He will give me a sign—He has promised it."

Uncle Jack shook his head very gravely, and Bessy Davenport, who had not yet spoken, remarked— [284/285]

"We are often inclined, Nat, to misunderstand signs. Take care that you don't apply to yourself signs that may be intended for the whole world. Don't you remember, when there was an eclipse a little while ago, you said it was a sign sent to you?"

"I don't know what you mean by an eclipse," answered the man, gloomily; "but I know there *was* a sign, and a terrible sign too. However," he continued, in a more cheerful tone, "every one must read such things by the lights he has got, and the Lord will not suffer those whom He favours to mistake. He will direct us," he added, with a sigh, and then seemed inclined to change the conversation.

I tried to keep it in the same course, for I wanted to hear more of his views on such subjects; but, with a great deal of skill—I might almost say, cunning—he avoided it; and I purposely brought up the subject of freedom and slavery. The old preacher spoke upon it frankly and freely enough, and with a degree of liberality [285/286] towards the masters, which greatly surprised me. He said that the great majority were excellent, good, and kind-hearted people, and that, if they were all such, his race would be much more happy under their management, than they could be under their own.

"The great evil of slavery, sir," he continued, "is the possibility of any extent of ill-treatment. Where such a possibility exists, the thing will occur. It is true, I have no opportunity of comparing any other state of society with this; and for aught I know, there may be evils as great, or greater, in all others. I cannot remember my own country at all distinctly. Some vague, general notions I have about it; and, if they be correct, I was a great deal worse off there than I am here; but I cannot be sure whether these notions come from my own recollections, or from what I have read or heard. One thing, however, is certain, slavery has existed in all ages. The Hebrews had their bond-servants, and they themselves [286/287] were hewers of wood and drawers of water to the King of Egypt."

"Ay, but they rose and delivered themselves, and God helped and directed them;" said Nat Turner, with a peculiar flash in his dark eye.

"He is a God of justice and strong to deliver," said a voice at the door, speaking in a very nasal tone; and turning round, to my surprise, I saw the lanky and extraordinary figure of the Rev. Mr. McGrubber.

Nat Turner started forward, and shook him by the hand, and uncle Jack made him a formal and, I thought, somewhat stiff bow. Bessy Davenport gave me a rueful and yet a merry glance; and, judging that we should not profit much by what was likely to follow, I prepared to take my departure.

Nat Turner, however, instantly began the conversation with his visitor, who was evidently an old acquaintance and friend, by calling upon him to tell uncle Jack all that he had been [287/288] telling him the day before. "You will convince him but I can't," cried the man, not heeding a cloud that came over Mr. McGrubber's brow, and a quick sign that he made to him to be silent. "His heart seems as hard as the nether millstone towards his own people."

"My heart is not hard, Nathaniel," answered uncle Jack; "but I love my own people too well to try and make them discontented, with a situation from which they cannot escape, but which may be ameliorated, if they show themselves peaceable, quiet, and faithful. It is my duty to preach peace and good-will, resignation to the will of God and dependence upon His mercy; and not to stimulate men's passions, either in a right or wrong cause, to conduct which may end, God only knows how."

While the two negroes had been speaking, Mr. McGrubber had evidently been upon thorns; though, at the end of uncle Jack's [288/289] reply, he had put on a look of meek and pious resignation.

"Far be it from me, brother," he said, "to stimulate men's passions or induce them to act in any violent and hasty manner. God forbid that I should bring poor people into trouble, or do anything, which is not pointed out by calm reason and religion. But we are told that we shall not spare to speak God's truth; and when I am asked what is right and what is wrong, must I not say what is right? Ay, if any poor soul demands of me, 'Has my fellow-man a right to keep me in bondage?' would'st thou have me reply 'Yea' or 'Nay?' I preach the truth, brother; let the results be what they may. That is in God's hand, not mine."

Uncle Jack shook his head, with a somewhat melancholy look; but merely said, "The Apostle teaches us to be obedient to the powers that are; and again, we are told that servants should obey their masters. He who [289/290] teaches differently, I cannot look upon as speaking by the Holy Spirit, and I fear that evil will come of it."

Thus saying, he left the cabin; and Bessy Davenport and I followed, after having taken leave of Nat Turner. I thought, as I walked away, that I heard the voice of Mr. McGrubber, raised loudly and harshly; and I doubted not that poor Nat was receiving a stout reproof for having betrayed to the ears of others, the nature of the reverend gentleman's communications with himself.

On the whole, my visit had a good deal disappointed me. My first interview with Nat Turner had impressed me with an idea that he was very much more superior to the rest of his race than I found him upon farther acquaintance. That he was superior, there could be no doubt; but I thought I had discovered traits in him that day of almost all the peculiar weaknesses of the African race. That he was cunning, superstitious, and conceited, was very [290/291] clear; and there was something in the expression of his face and the glance of his eye, which inclined me to believe that there might be a certain degree of ruthless cruelty and fierce passion within, though now concealed, if not subdued, by the command he had acquired over himself.

In comparing the two negroes with each other, one thing was very remarkable. In uncle Jack you could not, as Miss Davenport had already indicated, trace the slightest vestige of the African pronunciation. What I may call Virginian-isms he unquestionably had: there was a certain intonation and also a pronunciation of some letters and syllables which in England we do not consider English; for instance, he pronounced the word "to" as we should pronounce "toe"; but nothing at all negro could be detected in it. On the contrary, Nat Turner, though he had evidently a good command of language, and could express [291/292] himself with great fluency and propriety, had that sort of thick and jerking utterance which characterises the African race.

Uncle Jack was walking on slowly before us, and Bessy and I soon overtook him; but the good old man seemed unwilling to enter any farther upon the subjects we had been discussing.

"Mr. McGrubber," he said, "was a very good man, he had no doubt; but he did not think a very discreet one." As to Nat Turner, he remarked, "It was grievous to him to see a man fitted for better things, delude himself by vain imaginations. I believe, Miss Bessy," he continued, looking with a smile at my fair companion, "half the faults of men and women arise from vanity. This poor youth Nat, if he did not believe himself far greater than he is, would be far better than he is. But he is a good young man, and means well to all, I do believe." [292/293]

Soon after, we left him, and went upon our way, discussing between ourselves the characters of those whom we had just left.

"I cannot help thinking," I said, "that Mr. McGrubber is a rather dangerous man in this part of the country."

"He is a very odious one," answered Bessy, in the true woman spirit; for ladies, my dear sister, you must acknowledge, place the agreeable qualities in comparison with the more important ones, higher in estimation than men do.

"He must have been speaking," I continued, "of things he did not wish us to hear, and was evidently in a great fright, when Nat Turner alluded to them."

"Oh, that was quite clear," answered Bessy. "Uncle Jack clearly intimated, I thought, that the man had been trying to instigate the slaves against their masters. He is an abolitionist, we all know; and I have a [293/294] great mind to talk to Mr. Stringer about it, but it may make mischief."

"Every man has a right to his own opinion, of course," I said; "but I can imagine nothing more unpardonable than for a foolish fanatic to come into a state, not his own, and attempt, in his vain self-conceit, to cause a violent change in the relations of the different classes of society without a consideration of all the consequences."

"The consequences would be frightful," exclaimed Bessy. "Were the slaves to get the mastery, imagination itself cannot picture what would be the result. They are so violent in their temper—their passions are so uncontrollable, that the very thought makes one shudder. Did you ever see a negro in a passion, Cousin Richard? It is the most frightful thing you ever beheld. He looks, and acts, and speaks, and, I am sure, feels, more like a demon than a human creature. I recollect when I was [294/295] living with dear Aunt Bab, there was a girl in the house, who had taken a peculiar and sort of irrational fancy for one of the small ornaments on the mantel-piece. Twice she had been detected and stopped in attempting to purloin it; but, at length, one day it was gone. Nobody doubted who had got it; and my aunt ordered the girl's room to be searched. I was present, though quite a little thing;

and I remember her quite well, standing in the middle of the room, silent and motionless, her eyes following the other servants as they made the examination, with an expression I shall never forget. For some time, they found nothing, and she was beginning to look quite triumphant; but, at length, the object of search was discovered hidden away in the most cunning manner—suspended, in fact, by threads underneath the bed. The moment it was disclosed, she burst forth, not with any contrition, but with rage and fury, such as I [295/296] never saw in another human being. She stamped, she raved, she cried, she poured forth words so fast that no one could understand them; and she ended by tearing her clothes to pieces like a mad thing."

"And what did my aunt do?" I asked.

"Just what might be expected of her," answered Bessy. "'Tis rather a sad story; but Aunt Bab was not to blame. She looked at her very gravely, and said—

"'Have you gone mad, Juno? You must remain here till you have recovered yourself, and are able to listen like a reasonable being; and I will then come and talk to you. Now it would be of no use.'

"She then left her, ordering her to be locked in. But we had not been gone five minutes, when one of the servants came running in to say, that Juno had jumped out of the window, and was dreadfully hurt. My aunt would not suffer me to see her, and all I know further [296/297] is, that she lingered for about five weeks, and then died; and Aunt Bab wept very bitterly over the poor misguided creature, as she called her."

"It is a sad picture of human nature, indeed," I said; "and from what I see of the negro population, I am inclined to attribute less power to education and more to race than I once did."

"The more you see of them, the more you will think so," answered Bessy. "Good education might, and I have no doubt does, produce a great deal of improvement; but as no cosmetic that ever was tried will make a black man white, so I don't believe any education will make his mind and character those of a white man. And yet, this good old preacher, uncle Jack, appears to be an extraordinary exception."

"It does not seem to me," I replied, "that that proves anything. The fair test might [297/298] be, to take a certain number of children of different races, and educate them from the earliest period exactly upon the same system, and then judge of the race by the average number of each which you found capable, in a certain time, of arriving at an ascertained point of cultivation. Thus, if out of a hundred Anglo-Saxon children, ten should reach the highest proposed point in ten years, and only one negro, we might conclude that the Anglo-Saxon race was far more susceptible of cultivation than that of the negro. But solitary instances prove nothing. And now, my dear Bessy, let us, for Heaven's sake, talk of some other subjects, for otherwise, we shall both of us sink into philosophers—a degradation for which, I am sure, nature never intended us."

"I suspect you intend to be saucy, Richard," answered my fair companion; "but, in sober sadness, we have had a very grave and [298/299] solemn walk of it—very different from yesterday's."

"And I like yesterday's style best," I said.

But though we changed to lighter tones throughout the rest of the walk homeward, we came upon none of those exciting, perhaps I may say dangerous, topics, in which we had previously indulged. I believe the truth is, with every young man and every young woman while unconscious of danger—unconscious that there is near them what, in common gallantry, I must not call a precipice, but a great leap to be taken or not, at their pleasure, which nevertheless, they may still chance to fall over unawares—they go on sporting up to the very edge of the bank, and then, when finding themselves so near it, they pause and look down with some degree of doubt, and draw a little back and avoid the brink, till resolution comes, and over they go.

Thus our talk on the way homeward, was [299/300] very common-place; and, at about a hundred yards from the house, amongst the peach-trees, we met Mr. Stringer, and with him, to my surprise, my Norfolk friend, Mr. Wheatley. [300]

The Ballad of Nat Turner

ROBERT HAYDEN

Then fled, O brethren, the wicked juba
and wandered wandered far
from curfew joys in the Dismal's night.
Fool of St. Elmo's fire

In scary night I wandered, praying,
Lord God my harshener,
speak to me now or let me die;
speak, Lord, to this mourner.

And came at length to livid trees
where Ibo warriors
hung shadowless, turning in wind
that moaned like Africa,

Their belltongue bodies dead, their eyes
    alive with the anger deep
in my own heart. Is this the sign,
    the sign forepromised me?

The spirits vanished. Afraid and lonely
    I wandered on in blackness.
Speak to me now or let me die.
    Die, whispered the blackness.

And wild things gasped and scuffled in
    the night; seething shapes
of evil frolicked upon the air.
    I reeled with fear, I prayed.

Sudden brightness clove the preying
    darkness, brightness that was
itself a golden darkness, brightness
    so bright that it was darkness.

And there were angels, their faces hidden
    from me, angels at war [72/73]
with one another, angels in dazzling
    combat. And oh the splendor,

The fearful splendor of that warring.
    Hide me, I cried to rock and bramble.
Hide me, the rock, the bramble cried. . . .
    How tell you of that holy battle?

The shock of wing on wing and sword
    on sword was the tumult of
a taken city burning. I cannot
    say how long they strove,

For the wheel in a turning wheel which is time
    in eternity had ceased
its whirling, and owl and moccasin,
    panther and nameless beast

And I were held like creatures fixed
    in flaming, in fiery amber.
But I saw I saw oh many of
    those mighty beings waver,

Waver and fall, go streaking down
    into swamp water, and the water
hissed and steamed and bubbled and locked
    shuddering shuddering over

The fallen and soon was motionless.
    Then that massive light
began a-folding slowly in
    upon itself, and I

Beheld the conqueror faces and, lo,
    they were like mine, I saw
they were like mine and in joy and terror
    wept, praising praising Jehovah. [73/74]

Oh praised my honer, harshener
    till a sleep came over me,
a sleep heavy as death. And when
    I awoke at last free

And purified, I rose and prayed
    and returned after a time
to the blazing fields, to the humbleness.
    And bided my time. [74]

Ol' Prophet Nat

DANIEL PANGER

THIS DAY, FOR PERHAPS THE FIRST TIME IN THE HISTORY OF THE WORLD, black men defeated white men fully armed and on horseback. If other, like battles were won by black men, I never heard of them. Slaves have killed their masters, have fired their fields or houses, but until this day they had not met their masters in true combat. [142/143] The scent of victory filled our noses. Never before had we felt more like men.

    We sat down in an adjoining field to rest—battles are a hard dirty work. Thirty-five of my men were fit to carry on, a number still remained at Mister Parker's place, the rest were wounded or lay dead. I

From Daniel Panger, Ol' Prophet Nat, pp. 142–157 (John F. Blair, Publisher, 1967). Copyright, 1967, by John F. Blair, Publisher. Reprinted by permission. This selection occurs toward the end of the novel.

determined that as soon as we had our breaths back we would strike
out for Jerusalem. I felt certain that we could add to our number along
the way. Hark agreed with my plan and none of the others offered
objection. I again was the leader.

As it turned out we were not to get to Jerusalem that day or any
day. In less than half an hour the white men returned, strengthened by
thirty or more.

We could hear the beat of the horses' hoofs and their shouts as
they galloped up the road. Some of the horsemen moved through the
open fields to avoid being trapped on the narrow road. Some of the
whites hung back, using their muskets to good advantage.

We were ready for them. As soon as their sounds reached us I
placed my men in a line across the field and roadway. Ten men were
held in reserve under Hark. Most of my people had muskets. In addition all carried sharp weapons. I determined to sell our lives dearly. I
turned to my men as the whites came rushing towards us. The slaves'
faces were set and hard. "If we lose this day, we may never have the
chance to win again," I told them. "They are no more than men." I
pointed at the enemy. "Aim for their soft white bellies." I had no
further chance to continue for the whites were upon us.

They shouted and screamed like devils, each trying to encourage
the other. My men did their work in silence with scarcely a grunt to
show the strain they were under. It was a bitter battle. Had our
muskets served us well I am confident we would have [143/144]
triumphed that day. The muskets, gathered in the main from the
houses we had taken, were old and many refused to fire when we
needed them most. They were good for nothing more than use as clubs
while the whites made proper service of their guns, doing us great and
grievous harm.

A good half dozen of my men had fallen, their insides torn by
bullets, when I determined that if we remained where we were, with
the whites separated from us by a hundred paces, we would all lie
dead on the field before another hour had passed. The few muskets we
were able to fire shot wide of their mark. The whites, realizing our
weakness, made bolder and bolder, standing in the open taking careful
aim with no need to have concern for their own safety.

I raged within me at the false weapons that had put us at such a
disadvantage. There was nothing for us but to rush forward where
their guns would no longer be a menace and our sharp arms would
have their chance to draw blood.

I shouted at my men to come on, signaling Hark to join us. We
rushed towards the white men who started falling back. Before we had
a fair chance to show them what our weapons and our manhood could
do, they had mounted their horses and were retreating beyond our
reach.

Again they opened fire, again we rushed forward forcing them back. Each rush cost us several more dead or wounded while the whites lost only two who proved to be overly slow in mounting their horses and were cut down by my men.

We were beaten, at least for that day. I knew that any further fighting would only mean greater losses. I would strengthen my forces and I had faith that the next day would tell a different story. I ordered my men [144/145] to retreat. The whites were glad to let us go; they made no effort to follow or to worry us as we fell back.

The full seriousness of our condition had not reached me while the fighting was in progress. As I counted my men and found there were only nineteen left of the thirty-five who entered battle, my chest tightened with worry. Without good muskets our chances were less than poor, yet the only quantity of sound arms was located in Jerusalem. No matter what the cost, I knew we would have to push on to the town and arm ourselves properly.

I grieved for those of my brave men that lay out in the field. Any that chanced to be alive would be alive no longer after the white men had had their way. We were defeated in battle but still I had faith we would win the war. There were hundreds of slaves in that part of the county. As soon as we were supplied with arms they would join us. I kept telling myself over and over that all was not lost, but my heart grew heavy, for deep inside me I knew—I knew that the delay at Parker's place had turned Old Luck against us.

If my men felt my doubt I knew all would be lost. They looked to me for their strength. If my face showed the anguish I felt, they would cease to follow me. I sent several of the men to gather up the slaves who had remained behind at Parker's place. I sent others to scout the countryside for fresh recruits—men who prized their liberty above their lives. We were to meet at Major Ridley's place after dark. His plantation stood away from the highway and was well protected by trees. No matter how brave the white men were during the day, they would not venture off the highway into the trees to look for us at night. I knew we would be safe until morning. By that time who could tell what our condition might be?

We remained scattered in different places for the [145/146] rest of that day. I could hear shouts and halloos from the white men but they never left the highway. They were not yet ready to chance the knives and sickles of the slaves who lay hidden in the tall grass. All the white man's bravery was confined to places where his guns and horses would be useful. Out in the cornfields or the woods, we were the equal of any of them.

As I lay in a field of tall corn hearing their shouts and curses I felt such a hatred towards the whites that my eyes were filled with burning tears. I picked up the rusted sword I had been carrying and slashed at the stalks all around me—slashing and cutting with all the strength of my arms, calling on the Lord, all the while, to rain His most terrible plagues down on their vile and hateful heads. For twenty minutes my madness boiled out of my body. Had any white men chanced into that field their blood would have served to enrich the ground for the growing corn. Even if our defeat was certain, I determined the whites would pay a heavy price. The thought of their pale sickly skins made my stomach turn and tighten within me.

Later I lay on the ground exhausted, weak, more weary than I ever remembered being. I kept saying to myself, "We will quickly build back our strength and then fight on." I kept calling on the Lord to give me the strength to renew my belief. But all the while I felt the cold water of uncertainty running inside my body. I searched my knowledge of the Bible for portions that might give me comfort. My mind rested on the story of King David. Although little more than a boy, weak and unarmed he slew the giant Goliath, the strongest man in all the world. I studied that portion of the Scriptures for any meaning it might have for me. Was God telling me something by bringing this Bible story back to my mind? David was weak, we were weak; David was unarmed, our condition was no better. [146/147] Goliath was likened to the white men—powerful, well armed, feared by all— yet Goliath fell. I began to feel revived; my faith was returning. David had shown a greater cleverness than the giant. With a leather sling he had hurled a rock at the evil giant, felling him to the ground.

I knew the answer. Like David we would have to rely more on our cleverness than on our strength. Like David we would have to keep our distance, stay hidden, striking at the white men when they least expected, not giving them a chance to use their muskets on us. As long as we remained hidden, in the woods, in the corn fields, in the bushes, we could strike out at any white man that ventured too close. They would not dare to follow us into the field or woods. At night our black skins would hide us, then we could creep up softly to the whites, doing our work with silent knives.

We were not defeated. The battle had been a lesson; I was filled with gladness for the lesson I had learned. We would not fight the whites in their way. We would make them fight in ours. Our black skins would be a shield of safety during the dark night. The day would be for sleeping, the night for killing.

As I lay there in that cornfield I was clothed with the peace of understanding. Even if we did not find any fresh recruits we had men enough to do the tasks I now envisioned. We had men enough, all the whites together with all their guns were not enough. For they had everything to fear, everything to lose. We had nothing to lose and our liberty to gain, and we had black skins, skins that blended into the night.

My thoughts were covered by a blanket of refreshing sleep. I was exhausted to the point where it was a great effort to move a hand or foot. Had the enemy approached as I lay there sleeping, I would have fallen an easy victim. [147/148]

The cool breezes of the night awakened me. I had an unreal

feeling upon opening my eyes. I could not remember where I was. I felt the cornstalks and stubble around me but these did not bring back my memory. As I lay there staring up into the speckled sky I filled with a most terrible, unreasoned fear. I could not remember where I was or how I came to be there. I was overpowered by a freezing, choking feeling. Try as I would, I could not bring my mind to work properly. I was afraid to get up and seek my way out of the field for I did not know in which direction safety lay. So filled was I with that fear, which made my breath catch in my chest, that I didn't have the strength to turn my thoughts to God. Had I been able to do this I am certain all my distress and confusion would have vanished.

I lay there, I do not know how long, trying to find a rope of thought to take hold of. My fear and my confusion suddenly vanished when I heard a whisper nearby. "Nat, where you at, Nat? Nat Turner? Speak out, man." I recognized Sam's voice with a rush of warm relief.

I answered his call by saying his name and he pushed his way through the corn. Sam threw his arms around me, hugging me with all his strength. He started crying, telling me that he feared I was dead or captured and that he, along with the others, had been searching for me since sunset. I was deeply pleased by his tender feelings; that plus my good sleep caused me to be completely refreshed.

Hark, Nelson, Henry and the rest were waiting at Major Ridley's place. The Major and his family had deserted so we had his large house all to ourselves that night. As I came up I was greeted with whispered blessings and my hands were squeezed and kissed over and over again. [148/149]

Forty slaves were there; all but half a dozen had been with me the night before. I was pleased that so large a number remained and felt sure that others would join us as we moved from place to place. Had all my men been rested I would have started out without delay to try and secure arms in Jerusalem. But they were tired, some stiff from bruises or light wounds. The next night under the protection of darkness we would slip into the town.

I spoke to the men about the thoughts that came to me as I lay in the cornfield. About avoiding the white man's way of fighting, about using our black skins to the best advantage. All agreed with me, all saw the merit of fighting silently by night.

The forty slaves gathered around me, together with the good things to eat that were to be found in Major Ridley's house, restored my spirits completely. Given another day or two I felt assured we would be able to make our way to the swamp—once there. . . . Before I had a chance to follow the pleasant thought any further one of the men who had been posted as a guard came running into the house gasping that he had heard the sound of horsemen coming.

I was given no chance to confirm this tale or to give the men my orders; they rushed in panic to the doors and windows, out into the night. In a minute they were scattered in every direction, falling over stones and stumps, cursing and striking out blindly with their weapons. I moved into the shadow of the trees, straining with my ears to hear the horsemen so that I might judge their number.

The only sounds I heard were the footfalls of the running slaves, their curses and the sounds of their weapons slashing at the night. There were no horsemen, but the slaves were too widely scattered to hear my call. I feared chasing after any of the men; my [149/150] coming might be mistaken by them for the sounds of the white men and in their panic I might fall a victim.

The distress I felt at that time is hard for me to write. Things were just beginning to look promising when a baseless panic scattered my forces in every direction, leaving me standing alone. I understood that the men had been under great pressure, that they were unused to being abroad at night. Most had never been away from their own plantation after dark. I understood those things but was filled with bitterness and anger none the less.

There was nothing for it but to make an attempt to bring the men back. I carefully picked my way through the darkness, calling ahead at each step so as not to be mistaken for white and thus set upon by one of the hiding slaves. In this fashion I spent the night. By the time the sky began to show the morning's brightness twelve slaves were back under my command. As it became light several more slipped out of the fields and woods, their heads hanging with shame. Since it would have served no good purpose, I kept my silence about the cowardice they had shown. More than anything else I was glad to see them.

We totaled no more than twenty-one. Nearly half my forces had run too far to return or had had their fill of fighting. It is a hard thing to change from a slave to a free man in one night. It took the children of Israel forty years of wandering before they lost the ways of the slave.

All the disturbances of the night caused my plans to become confused. Hark and the others, the original six, all of whom still remained, urged me to lead them to Doctor Blunt's place which was less than a mile distant. He owned a goodly number of slaves and was known to have a well-stocked smokehouse. I [150/151] remembered Doctor Blunt well for the way he had served Hark and me that time in the past. His slaves were kept under a heavy hand, poorly fed and often whipped. For these reasons I felt they would join us without hesitation. Even if the slaves proved reluctant, Doctor Blunt's smokehouse would be sufficient reward.

I can place the blame for what happened on nobody but myself. Had my mind been fresh and clear I would have thought the whole thing out and remained hidden through the day. Night was the time we could move in safety. But the hours of searching during the night left me weakened so that my intention to move only under cover of darkness was forgotten. All the other white people in these parts had fled when they had learned of our coming; Major Ridley's place had been deserted as had others. We expected Doctor Blunt and his family to be gone also, so we anticipated no resistance.

Without taking the precaution of dividing my forces into two, I marched up to Doctor Blunt's plantation. We had scarcely set foot on his land when we were met by gunfire. Behind the old stone fence were Doctor Blunt and several other white men, with them were ten or more of his slaves all armed with good muskets.

The first shots found their marks in two of my brave men. I ordered the rest to hunch down in the tall grass. More shots were fired. Doctor Blunt's slaves, who had known so much pain, were shooting at other black men instead of turning their guns on their masters. They had been beaten so often that they were no longer human. The whip had made them into willing beasts. I cried out to his slaves, begging them not to fire at us, telling them that we were black men like themselves trying for our liberty. I shouted for them to join us, that together we could conquer the entire county. My [151/152] words were answered with more gunfire. The poor slaves knew not what they were doing.

Our weapons did not stand a chance against the deadly muskets so I ordered my men to retreat. Another of our number was lost as we moved back; we were by then reduced to eighteen, two of whom had suffered painful wounds. Being fired upon by black men left all of us shaken, our spirits badly dampened. I knew that if I showed any sign of weakening all would be over; the men were watching my every move. My face did not show the feelings that were in me. I felt deserted; the Lord had turned his back on me. Most of my men were gone. Slaves with guns had just fired on us, killing three and wounding two others. I was filled with sick tears but my face showed nothing.

As we retreated I studied the situation with care. If we could rest until night, some of the lost slaves might return. Other plantations were close at hand; these might supply new recruits. If all else failed, under the protection of the night we might be able to reach the swamp and join with the escaped slaves that were known to be hiding in that place.

None of those things were to take place. I was leading my men in the direction of Captain Harris' place—there we could find ample enough woods and thickets to hide us—when a party of white men rose up from behind some hedges and attacked. There were seven or eight white men, but surprise was on their side. Besides, they were armed with deadly muskets. We stood still for the space of a minute facing those white men. Several of us made as if to rush them with our poor weapons but the musket balls felled two of my men and I knew with certainty that, in another minute, half or more of us would be lying on the ground with lead shot filling our insides. [152/153]

I turned heel and motioned for my men to do the same. In a moment we were scattered into the fields, each fleeing his own separate way. The sounds of the snapping guns behind me caused me to look to my own safety. Once or twice as I ran I called out to the others that we would meet after dark in the woods by Mister Travis' place; I could not tell if they heard me or no.

When I reached a place that I judged to be safe, I stopped to catch my breath and look around. I was completely alone. I listened, trying to hear the movements of the other slaves, but the only sound which reached my ears was the warm hum of the afternoon. I would have welcomed the comfort of a companion for I was as nearly spent in mind as in body. There was no one to see me so I let my tears run freely down my face. They had been pressing against my eyes too long—now there was no further need to keep them hidden.

I stretched myself on the ground in the high grass, crushing my face against the earth. The sobs that tore out of my mouth pained my entire body. I felt as weak and helpless as I had felt many years before when I hid trembling in the cabin while my poor mother was beaten. If it had been within my power at that moment I would have buried myself in the warm earth, seeking forgetfulness and the peace of death. I kept saying over and over between my sobs, Lord help me, please help me. I said the words but at the same time I was empty of faith.

I lay there I know not how long. My exhaustion must have caused me to sleep for the sun lay low in the heavens when I sat up. All was still in the field but far, far away I could hear the faint sounds of musket fire mixed with shouts. This day would be a grim one for the slaves; I knew that now the whites would take [153/154] a terrible vengeance. We were scattered; they no longer had anything to fear.

My thoughts were clearer after the sleep. There was still a chance, just a chance I might meet up with some of the others. I had not completely abandoned hope. If a few of us banded together, I thought we still might be able to find some slaves willing to cast their lots with us. Seven of us had grown to ten times that number in a few short hours; why could not the same thing happen again? There were certain mistakes that would not be repeated if I were granted a second chance. These thoughts on top of the renewing sleep brought me hope.

With the greatest possible caution I moved through the fields until at last the shadows of Mister Travis' woods swallowed me up. I knew that for a day or two I would be safe, hidden among the trees. The whites would show great caution at first. They had been well bloodied and would not relish falling among groups of armed slaves hidden in the dark woods. Later, as more and more whites joined in the search for me and for my poor fellows, their confidence would grow, but for the next day or two I counted myself safe.

I moved from tree to tree inside the darkening woods, softly calling out the names of my companions. I called Hark's name, then Nelson, Sam, Henry, Will and Jack. I was answered by the rustle of rabbits or by the beat of owls' wings as they made their hungry way through the night air. The barking of foxes caused me to stiffen for a moment. Until my ear grew used to this sound, I mistook it for the bark of dogs signaling the approach of my white hunters.

All night long I eased my way through the trees, saying the dear familiar names over and over. Soon it became just a thing to keep me busy; I knew my calls [154/155] would go unanswered. Towards morning I found a place beneath a tangle of bushes where I could safely rest during the daylight hours. I had passed caring about anything except my need to sleep; all my muscles were begging for a chance to rest. As I closed my eyes, waiting for the sleep to rush over me, I thought perhaps a few of my men might find their way to the wood before nightfall—just a few.

Had my hiding place been discovered, that day they would have taken me without a show of resistance. I slept until the cool winds of evening stirred me awake.

As I think back over the weeks to that time—it must be near six weeks since I waited in the Travis woods for my companions—I remember that upon awakening from my long sleep I knew with an absolute certainty that it was all over. I had failed. My people were still in bondage and would remain so until some other one again struck out for liberty. I tried to study why I failed but it was beyond my understanding.

As I have worked to prepare this account of my life and of the things I have done, my mind has asked the question again and again— why did I fail? I tell myself it was the Lord's will, but it was more than that. He shows us the way but we ourselves must walk along the path, climbing over boulders, striking down the serpents that may bare their venomous fangs as we approach. If I were given another chance, if the Good Lord smiled on me again, I would set fire to all Southampton County. I have learned certain things that would serve me well if I were to be granted another chance.

That second night in the woods I prayed for nothing except for some of my companions to find their way to me. There was still time to strike again. As I thought of the unnumbered poor black people pouring the [155/156] years of their lives into their white master's hands, I was filled, for perhaps the thousandth time, with rage at the unfairness of it all. Why should such things be? I turned my face upwards, searching for the sky among the treetops and asked again, why should these things be? Why must the black man suffer at the hands of the white?

They tore my people from their homes in far-off Africa. They took them against their will to a strange land. They forced us into a slavery more wretched than any ever suffered since the Israelites knew the slavery of Egypt. They have beaten us. They have worked our bodies until they were broken. They have had their way with our women. They have cursed and reviled us. What have we ever done to deserve such treatment? Why have the whites served us in such a terrible fashion—Oh, God, why will they not let us alone? I asked these things that night in the woods and I ask them still.

If I had a second chance, even if I knew it meant certain death, even if I knew I could be free and safe if I ran away right now—if I had a second chance I would strike another blow for my poor people. I would smite the rock with such a force that its sound would reach a thousand miles.

If we wait for the whites to give us our God-given rights, we will wait until the sun grows cold. If we wait until the whites decide to treat black people like human beings, we will wait until the ocean is dry. The black man will only get as much as he is willing to fight for. For a man to be free he must be ready to die for that same freedom.

These thoughts and many others crossed my mind that last night in the woods. I prayed from the deepest place inside me for the safety of my companions. I [156/157] prayed with the taste of my heart's blood in my mouth that they would be able to find their way to these woods. But I knew, I knew it was all over.

All during that day I heard the sounds of horses and men; once I heard a long scream. I tried not to think of what that meant, but again I knew. Soon the white men would start searching the forest; each passing hour made them bolder. As darkness began to fall, protected by my black skin I made my way out of the forest to a place. . . . [157]

Escape from Slavery

FREDERICK DOUGLASS

I NOW COME TO THAT PART OF MY LIFE DURING WHICH I PLANNED, AND finally succeeded in making, my escape from slavery. But before narrating any of the peculiar circumstances, I deem it proper to make known my intention not to state all the facts connected with the transaction. My reasons for pursuing this course may be understood from the following: First, were I to give a minute statement of all the facts,

From *Narrative of the Life of Frederick Douglass An American Slave* (New American Library: Signet Book, 1968), Chapter 11. Originally published at the Anti-Slavery Office, No. 25 Cornhill, Boston, in 1845.

it is not only possible, but quite probable, that others would thereby be involved in the most embarrassing difficulties. Secondly, such a statement would most undoubtedly induce greater vigilance on the part of slaveholders than has existed heretofore among them; which would, of course, be the means of guarding a door whereby some dear brother bondman might escape his galling chains. I deeply regret the necessity that impels me to suppress any thing of importance connected with my experience in slavery. It would afford me great pleasure indeed, as well as materially add to the interest of my narrative, were I at liberty to gratify a curiosity, which I know exists in the minds of many, by an accurate statement of all the facts pertaining to my most fortunate escape. But I must deprive myself of this pleasure, and the curious of the gratification which such a statement would afford. I would allow myself to suffer under the greatest imputations which evil-minded men might suggest, rather than exculpate myself, and thereby run the hazard of closing the slightest avenue by which a [105/106] brother slave might clear himself of the chains and fetters of slavery.

I have never approved of the very public manner in which some of our western friends have conducted what they call the *underground railroad,* but which I think, by their open declarations, has been made most emphatically the *upperground railroad.* I honor those good men and women for their noble daring, and applaud them for willingly subjecting themselves to bloody persecution, by openly avowing their participation in the escape of slaves. I, however, can see very little good resulting from such a course, either to themselves or the slaves escaping; while, upon the other hand, I see and feel assured that those open declarations are a positive evil to the slaves remaining, who are seeking to escape. They do nothing towards enlightening the slave, whilst they do much towards enlightening the master. They stimulate him to greater watchfulness, and enhance his power to capture his slave. We owe something to the slave south of the line as well as to those north of it; and in aiding the latter on their way to freedom, we should be careful to do nothing which would be likely to hinder the former from escaping from slavery. I would keep the merciless slaveholder profoundly ignorant of the means of flight adopted by the slave. I would leave him to imagine himself surrounded by myriads of invisible tormentors, ever ready to snatch from his infernal grasp his trembling prey. Let him be left to feel his way in the dark; let darkness commensurate with his crime hover over him; and let him feel that at every step he takes, in pursuit of the flying bondman, he is running the frightful risk of having his hot brains dashed out by an invisible agency. Let us render the tyrant no aid; let us not hold the light by which he can trace the footprints of our flying brother. But enough of this. I will now proceed to the statement of those facts, connected with my escape, for which I am alone responsible, and for which no one can be made to suffer but myself. [106/107]

In the early part of the year 1838, I became quite restless. I could see no reason why I should, at the end of each week, pour the reward of my toil into the purse of my master. When I carried to him my weekly wages, he would, after counting the money, look me in the face with a robber-like fierceness, and ask, "Is this all?" He was satisfied with nothing less than the last cent. He would, however, when I made him six dollars, sometimes give me six cents, to encourage me. It had the opposite effect. I regarded it as a sort of admission of my right to the whole. The fact that he gave me any part of my wages was proof, to my mind, that he believed me entitled to the whole of them. I always felt worse for having received any thing; for I feared that the giving me a few cents would ease his conscience, and make him feel himself to be a pretty honorable sort of robber. My discontent grew upon me. I was ever on the look-out for means of escape; and, finding no direct means, I determined to try to hire my time, with a view of getting money with which to make my escape. In the spring of 1838, when Master Thomas came to Baltimore to purchase his spring goods, I got an opportunity, and applied to him to allow me to hire my time. He unhesitatingly refused my request, and told me this was another stratagem by which to escape. He told me I could go nowhere but that he could get me; and that, in the event of my running away, he should spare no pains in his efforts to catch me. He exhorted me to content myself, and be obedient. He told me, if I would be happy, I must lay out no plans for the future. He said, if I behaved myself properly, he would take care of me. Indeed, he advised me to complete thoughtlessness of the future, and taught me to depend solely upon him for happiness. He seemed to see fully the pressing necessity of setting aside my intellectual nature, in order to contentment in slavery. But in spite of him, and even in spite of myself, I continued to think, and to think about the injustice of my enslavement, and the means of escape.

About two months after this, I applied to Master [107/108] Hugh for the privilege of hiring my time. He was not acquainted with the fact that I had applied to Master Thomas, and had been refused. He too, at first, seemed disposed to refuse; but, after some reflection, he granted me the privilege, and proposed the following terms: I was to be allowed all my time, make all contracts with those for whom I worked, and find my own employment; and, in return for this liberty, I was to pay him three dollars at the end of each week; find myself in calking tools, and in board and clothing. My board was two dollars and a half per week. This, with the wear and tear of clothing and calking tools, made my regular expenses about six dollars per week. This amount I was compelled to make up, or relinquish the privilege of hiring my time. Rain or shine, work or no work, at the end of each week the money must be forthcoming, or I must give up my privilege. This arrangement, it will be perceived, was decidedly in my master's favor. It relieved him of all need of looking after me. His money was sure. He received all the benefits of slaveholding without its evils; while I endured all the evils of a slave, and suffered all the care and anxiety of a freeman. I found it a hard bargain. But, hard as it was, I thought it better than the old mode of getting along. It was a step towards freedom to be allowed to bear the responsibilities of a free-man, and I was determined to hold on upon it. I bent myself to the work of making money. I was ready to work at night as well as day, and by the most untiring perseverance and industry, I made enough to meet my expenses, and lay up a little money every week. I went on thus from May till August. Master Hugh then refused to allow me to hire my time longer. The ground for his refusal was a failure on my part, one Saturday night, to pay him for my week's time. This failure was occasioned by my attending a camp meeting about ten miles from Baltimore. During the week, I had entered into an engagement with a number of young friends to start from Baltimore to the camp ground early Saturday evening; and being detained by my employer, I was [108/109] unable to get down to Master Hugh's without disappoint-ing the company. I knew that Master Hugh was in no special need of the money that night. I therefore decided to go to camp meeting, and upon my return pay him the three dollars. I stayed at the camp meet-ing one day longer than I intended when I left. But as soon as I returned, I called upon him to pay him what he considered his due. I found him very angry; he could scarce restrain his wrath. He said he had a great mind to give me a severe whipping. He wished to know how I dared go out of the city without asking his permission. I told him I hired my time, and while I paid him the price which he asked for it, I did not know that I was bound to ask him when and where I should go. This reply troubled him; and, after reflecting a few mo-ments, he turned to me, and said I should hire my time no longer; that the next thing he should know of, I would be running away. Upon the same plea, he told me to bring my tools and clothing home forthwith. I did so; but instead of seeking work, as I had been accustomed to do previously to hiring my time, I spent the whole week without the performance of a single stroke of work. I did this in retaliation. Satur-day night, he called upon me as usual for my week's wages. I told him I had no wages; I had done no work that week. Here we were upon the point of coming to blows. He raved, and swore his determination to get hold of me. I did not allow myself a single word; but was resolved, if he laid the weight of his hand upon me, it should be blow for blow. He did not strike me, but told me that he would find me in constant employment in future. I thought the matter over during the next day, Sunday, and finally resolved upon the third day of Septem-ber, as the day upon which I would make a second attempt to secure my freedom. I now had three weeks during which to prepare for my journey. Early on Monday morning, before Master Hugh had time to make any engagement for me, I went out and got employment of Mr.

Butler, at his ship-yard near the drawbridge, upon what is called the City Block, thus making it [109/110] unnecessary for him to seek employment for me. At the end of the week, I brought him between eight and nine dollars. He seemed very well pleased, and asked why I did not do the same the week before. He little knew what my plans were. My object in working steadily was to remove any suspicion he might entertain of my intent to run away; and in this I succeeded admirably. I suppose he thought I was never better satisfied with my condition than at the very time during which I was planning my escape. The second week passed, and again I carried him my full wages; and so well pleased was he, that he gave me twenty-five cents, (quite a large sum for a slaveholder to give a slave,) and bade me to make a good use of it. I told him I would.

Things went on without very smoothly indeed, but within there was trouble. It is impossible for me to describe my feelings as the time of my contemplated start drew near. I had a number of warm-hearted friends in Baltimore,—friends that I loved almost as I did my life,—and the thought of being separated from them forever was painful beyond expression. It is my opinion that thousands would escape from slavery, who now remain, but for the strong cords of affection that bind them to their friends. The thought of leaving my friends was decidedly the most painful thought with which I had to contend. The love of them was my tender point, and shook my decision more than all things else. Besides the pain of separation, the dread and apprehension of a failure exceeded what I had experienced at my first attempt. The appalling defeat I then sustained returned to torment me. I felt assured that, if I failed in this attempt, my case would be a hopeless one—it would seal my fate as a slave forever. I could not hope to get off with any thing less than the severest punishment, and being placed beyond the means of escape. It required no very vivid imagination to depict the most frightful scenes through which I should have to pass, in case I failed. The wretchedness of slavery, and the blessedness of freedom, were perpetually before me. It was life and death with me. But [110/111] I remained firm, and, according to my resolution, on the third day of September, 1838, I left my chains, and succeeded in reaching New York without the slightest interruption of any kind. How I did so,—what means I adopted,—what direction I travelled, and by what mode of conveyance,—I must leave unexplained, for the reasons before mentioned.

I have been frequently asked how I felt when I found myself in a free State. I have never been able to answer the question with any satisfaction to myself. It was a moment of the highest excitement I ever experienced. I suppose I felt as one may imagine the unarmed mariner to feel when he is rescued by a friendly man-of-war from the pursuit of a pirate. In writing to a dear friend, immediately after my arrival at New York, I said I felt like one who had escaped a den of hungry lions. This state of mind, however, very soon subsided; and I was again seized with a feeling of great insecurity and loneliness. I was yet liable to be taken back, and subjected to all the tortures of slavery. This in itself was enough to damp the ardor of my enthusiasm. But the loneliness overcame me. There I was in the midst of thousands, and yet a perfect stranger; without home and without friends, in the midst of thousands of my own brethren—children of a common Father, and yet I dared not to unfold to any of them my sad condition. I was afraid to speak to any one for fear of speaking to the wrong one, and thereby falling into the hands of money-loving kidnappers, whose business it was to lie in wait for the panting fugitive, as the ferocious beasts of the forest lie in wait for their prey. The motto which I adopted when I started from slavery was this—"Trust no man!" I saw in every white man an enemy, and in almost every colored man cause for distrust. It was a most painful situation; and, to understand it, one must needs experience it, or imagine himself in similar circumstances. Let him be a fugitive slave in a strange land—a land given up to be the hunting-ground for slaveholders—whose inhabitants are legalized kidnappers [111/112] —where he is every moment subjected to the terrible liability of being seized upon by his fellowmen, as the hideous crocodile seizes upon his prey!—I say, let him place himself in my situation—without home or friends—without money or credit—wanting shelter, and no one to give it—wanting bread, and no money to buy it,—and at the same time let him feel that he is pursued by merciless men-hunters, and in total darkness as to what to do, where to go, or where to stay,—perfectly helpless both as to the means of defence and means of escape,—in the midst of plenty, yet suffering the terrible gnawings of hunger,—in the midst of houses, yet having no home,—among fellow-men, yet feeling as if in the midst of wild beasts, whose greediness to swallow up the trembling and half-famished fugitive is only equalled by that with which the monsters of the deep swallow up the helpless fish upon which they subsist,—I say, let him be placed in this most trying situation,—the situation in which I was placed,—then, and not till then, will he fully appreciate the hardships of, and know how to sympathize with, the toil-worn and whip-scarred fugitive slave.

Thank Heaven, I remained but a short time in this distressed situation. I was relieved from it by the humane hand of MR. DAVID RUGGLES, whose vigilance, kindness, and perseverance, I shall never forget. I am glad of an opportunity to express, as far as words can, the love and gratitude I bear him. Mr. Ruggles is now afflicted with blindness, and is himself in need of the same kind offices which he was once so forward in the performance of toward others. I had been in New York but a few days, when Mr. Ruggles sought me out, and very kindly took me to his boarding-house at the corner of Church and Lespenard Streets. Mr. Ruggles was then very deeply engaged in the memorable *Darg* case, as well as attending to a number of other fugitive slaves, devising ways and means for their successful escape; and, though watched and hemmed in on almost every side, he seemed to be more than a match for his enemies. [112/113]

Very soon after I went to Mr. Ruggles, he wished to know of me where I wanted to go; as he deemed it unsafe for me to remain in New York. I told him I was a calker, and should like to go where I could get work. I thought of going to Canada; but he decided against it, and in favor of my going to New Bedford, thinking I should be able to get work there at my trade. At this time, Anna,* my intended wife, came on; for I wrote to her immediately after my arrival at New York, (notwithstanding my homeless, houseless, and helpless condition,) informing her of my successful flight, and wishing her to come on forthwith. In a few days after her arrival, Mr. Ruggles called in the Rev. J. W. C. Pennington, who, in the presence of Mr. Ruggles, Mrs. Michaels, and two or three others, performed the marriage ceremony, and gave us a certificate, of which the following is an exact copy:—

This may certify, that I joined together in holy matrimony Frederick Johnson† and Anna Murray, as man and wife, in the presence of Mr. David Ruggles and Mrs. Michaels.

JAMES W. C. PENNINGTON

New York, Sept. 15, 1838.

Upon receiving this certificate, and a five-dollar bill from Mr. Ruggles, I shouldered one part of our baggage, and Anna took up the other, and we set out forthwith to take passage on board of the steamboat John W. Richmond for Newport, on our way to New Bedford. Mr. Ruggles gave me a letter to a Mr. Shaw in Newport, and told me, in case my money did not serve me to New Bedford, to stop in Newport and obtain further assistance, but upon our arrival at Newport, we were so anxious to get to a place of safety, that, notwithstanding we lacked the necessary money to pay [113/114] our fare, we decided to take seats in the stage, and promise to pay when we got to New Bedford. We were encouraged to do this by two excellent gentlemen, residents of New Bedford, whose names I afterward ascertained to be Joseph Ricketson and William C. Taber. They seemed at once to understand our circumstances, and gave us such assurance of their friendliness as put us fully at ease in their presence. It was good indeed to meet with such friends, at such a time. Upon reaching New Bedford, we were directed to the house of Mr. Nathan Johnson, by whom we were kindly received, and hospitably provided for. Both Mr. and Mrs. Johnson took a deep and lively interest in our welfare. They proved themselves quite worthy of the name of abolitionists. When the stage-driver found us unable to pay our fare, he held on upon our

---

* She was free.

† I had changed my name from Frederick *Bailey* to that of *Johnson*.

baggage as security for the debt. I had but to mention the fact to Mr. Johnson, and he forthwith advanced the money.

We now began to feel a degree of safety, and to prepare ourselves for the duties and responsibilities of a life of freedom. On the morning after our arrival at New Bedford, while at the breakfast-table, the question arose as to what name I should be called by. The name given me by my mother was, "Frederick Augustus Washington Bailey." I, however, had dispensed with the two middle names long before I left Maryland so that I was generally known by the name of "Frederick Bailey." I started from Baltimore bearing the name of "Stanley." When I got to New York, I again changed my name to "Frederick Johnson," and thought that would be the last change. But when I got to New Bedford, I found it necessary again to change my name. The reason of this necessity was, that there were so many Johnsons in New Bedford, it was already quite difficult to distinguish between them. I gave Mr. Johnson the privilege of choosing me a name, but told him he must not take from me the name of "Frederick." I must hold on to that, to preserve a sense of my identity. Mr. Johnson had just been reading the "Lady of the [114/115] Lake," and at once suggested that my name be "Douglass." From that time until now I have been called "Frederick Douglass;" and as I am more widely known by that name than by either of the others, I shall continue to use it as my own.

I was quite disappointed at the general appearance of things in New Bedford. The impression which I had received respecting the character and condition of the people of the north, I found to be singularly erroneous. I had very strangely supposed, while in slavery, that few of the comforts, and scarcely any of the luxuries, of life were enjoyed at the north, compared with what were enjoyed by the slaveholders of the south. I probably came to this conclusion from the fact that northern people owned no slaves. I supposed that they were about upon a level with the non-slaveholding population of the south. I knew *they* were exceedingly poor, and I had been accustomed to regard their poverty as the necessary consequence of their being non-slaveholders. I had somehow imbibed the opinion that, in the absence of slaves, there could be no wealth, and very little refinement. And upon coming to the north, I expected to meet with a rough, hard-handed, and uncultivated population, living in the most Spartan-like simplicity, knowing nothing of the ease, luxury, pomp, and grandeur of southern slaveholders. Such being my conjectures, any one acquainted with the appearance of New Bedford may very readily infer how palpably I must have seen my mistake.

In the afternoon of the day when I reached New Bedford, I visited the wharves, to take a view of the shipping. Here I found myself surrounded with the strongest proofs of wealth. Lying at the wharves, and riding in the stream, I saw many ships of the finest model, in the best order, and of the largest size. Upon the right and left, I was walled in by granite warehouses of the widest dimensions, stowed to their utmost capacity with the necessaries and comforts of life. Added to this, almost every body seemed to be at work, but noiselessly so, compared with what I had [115/116] been accustomed to in Baltimore. There were no loud songs heard from those engaged in loading and unloading ships. I heard no deep oaths or horrid curses on the laborer. I saw no whipping of men; but all seemed to go smoothly on. Every man appeared to understand his work, and went at it with a sober, yet cheerful earnestness, which betokened the deep interest which he felt in what he was doing, as well as a sense of his own dignity as a man. To me this looked exceedingly strange. From the wharves I strolled around and over the town, gazing with wonder and admiration at the splendid churches, beautiful dwellings, and finely-cultivated gardens; evincing an amount of wealth, comfort, taste, and refinement, such as I had never seen in any part of slave-holding Maryland.

Every thing looked clean, new, and beautiful. I saw few or no dilapidated houses, with poverty-stricken inmates; no half-naked children and bare-footed women, such as I had been accustomed to see in Hillsborough, Easton, St. Michael's, and Baltimore. The people looked more able, stronger, healthier, and happier, than those of Maryland. I was for once made glad by a view of extreme wealth, without being saddened by seeing extreme poverty. But the most astonishing as well as the most interesting thing to me was the condition of the colored people, a great many of whom, like myself, had escaped thither as a refuge from the hunters of men. I found many, who had not been seven years out of their chains, living in finer houses, and evidently enjoying more of the comforts of life, than the average of slaveholders in Maryland. I will venture to assert, that my friend Mr. Nathan Johnson (of whom I can say with a grateful heart, "I was hungry, and he gave me meat; I was thirsty, and he gave me drink; I was a stranger, and he took me in") lived in a neater house; dined at a better table; took, paid for, and read, more newspapers; better understood the moral, religious, and political character of the nation,—than nine tenths of the slaveholders in Talbot county Maryland. Yet Mr. Johnson was a [116/117] working man. His hands were hardened by toil, and not his alone, but those also of Mrs. Johnson. I found the colored people much more spirited than I had supposed they would be. I found among them a determination to protect each other from the blood-thirsty kidnapper, at all hazards. Soon after my arrival, I was told of a circumstance which illustrated their spirit. A colored man and a fugitive slave were on unfriendly terms. The former was heard to threaten the latter with informing his master of his whereabouts. Straightway a meeting was called among the colored people, under the stereotyped notice, "Business of importance!" The betrayer was invited to attend. The people came at the appointed hour, and organized the meeting by appointing a very religious old gentleman as president, who, I believe, made a prayer, after which he addressed the meeting as follows: *"Friends, we have got him here, and I would recommend that you young men just take him outside the door, and kill him!"* With this, a number of them bolted at him; but they were intercepted by some more timid than themselves, and the betrayer escaped their vengeance, and has not been seen in New Bedford since. I believe there have been no more such threats, and should there be hereafter, I doubt not that death would be the consequence.

I found employment, the third day after my arrival, in stowing a sloop with a load of oil. It was new, dirty, and hard work for me; but I went at it with a glad heart and a willing hand. I was now my own master. It was a happy moment, the rapture of which can be understood only by those who have been slaves. It was the first work, the reward of which was to be entirely my own. There was no Master Hugh standing ready, the moment I earned the money, to rob me of it. I worked that day with a pleasure I had never before experienced. I was at work for myself and newly married wife. It was to me the starting-point of a new existence. When I got through with that job, I went in pursuit of a job of calking; but such was the strength of prejudice against color, among the white calkers, [117/118] that they refused to work with me, and of course I could get no employment.*
Finding my trade of no immediate benefit, I threw off my calking habiliments, and prepared myself to do any kind of work I could get to do. Mr. Johnson kindly let me have his woodhorse and saw, and I very soon found myself a plenty of work. There was no work too hard— none too dirty. I was ready to saw wood, shovel coal, carry wood, sweep the chimney, or roll oil casks,—all of which I did for nearly three years in New Bedford, before I became known to the anti-slavery world.

In about four months after I went to New Bedford, there came a young man to me, and inquired if I did not wish to take the "Liberator." I told him I did; but, just having made my escape from slavery, I remarked that I was unable to pay for it then. I, however, finally became a subscriber to it. The paper came, and I read it from week to week with such feelings as it would be quite idle for me to attempt to describe. The paper became my meat and my drink. My soul was set all on fire. Its sympathy for my brethren in bonds—its scathing denunciations of slaveholders—its faithful exposures of slavery—and its powerful attacks upon the upholders of the institution—sent a thrill of joy through my soul, such as I had never felt before!

I had not long been a reader of the "Liberator," before I got a pretty correct idea of the principles, measures and spirit of the anti-

---

* I am told that colored persons can now get employment at calking in New Bedford—a result of anti-slavery effort.

slavery reform. I took right hold of the cause. I could do but little; but what I could, I did with a joyful heart, and never felt happier than when in an anti-slavery meeting. I seldom had much to say at the meetings, because what I wanted to say was said so much better by others. But, while attending an anti-slavery convention at Nantucket, on the 11th of August, 1841, I felt strongly moved to speak, and was at the same time much urged to do so by Mr. William C. Coffin, a gentleman who had heard [118/119] me speak in the colored people's meeting at New Bedford. It was a severe cross, and I took it up reluctantly. The truth was, I felt myself a slave, and the idea of speaking to white people weighed me down. I spoke but a few moments, when I felt a degree of freedom, and said what I desired with considerable ease. From that time until now, I have been engaged in pleading the cause of my brethren—with what success, and with what devotion, I leave those acquainted with my labors to decide. [119]

The Seaboard Slave States

FREDERICK LAW OLMSTED

THE LABOR OF THIS FARM WAS ENTIRELY PERFORMED BY SLAVES. I DID not inquire their number, but I judged there were from twenty to forty. Their "quarters" lined the approach-road to the mansion, and were well-made and comfortable log-cabins, about thirty feet long by twenty wide, and eight feet tall, with a high loft and shingle roof. Each, divided in the middle, and having a brick chimney outside the wall at each end, was intended to be occupied by two families. There were square windows, closed by wooden ports, having a single pane of glass in the centre. The house-servants were neatly dressed, but the field-hands wore very coarse and ragged garments. [47/48]

During three hours, or more, in which I was in company with the proprietor, I do not think there were ten consecutive minutes uninterrupted by some of the slaves requiring his personal direction or assistance. He was even obliged, three times, to leave the dinner-table.

"You see," said he, smiling, as he came in the last time, "a farmer's life, in this country, is no sinecure." This turning the conversation to Slavery, he observed, in answer to a remark of mine, "I only wish your

From Frederick Law Olmsted, *A Journey in the Seaboard Slave States in the Years 1853–1854 With Remarks on Their Economy* (G. P. Putnam's Sons: The Knickerbocker Press, 1904). Originally published in 1856. The book is published in two volumes. This selection is from chapter 2 of vol. I.

philanthropists would contrive some satisfactory plan to relieve us of it; the trouble and the responsibility of properly taking care of our negroes, you may judge, from what you see yourself here, is anything but enviable. But what can we do that is better? Our free negroes—and, I believe it is the same at the North as it is here—are a miserable set of vagabonds, drunken, vicious, worse off, it is my honest opinion, than those who are retained in slavery. I am satisfied, too, that our slaves are better off, as they are, than the majority of your free laboring classes at the North."

I expressed my doubts.

"Well, they certainly are better off than the English agricultural laborers or, I believe, those of any other Christian country. Free labor might be more profitable to us: I am inclined to think it would be. The slaves are excessively careless and wasteful, and, in various ways—which, without you lived among them, you could hardly be made to understand—subject us to very annoying losses. [48/49]

"To make anything by farming, here, a man has got to live a hard life. You see how constantly I am called upon—and, often, it is about as bad at night as by day. Last night I did not sleep a wink till near morning; I am quite worn out with it, and my wife's health is failing. But I cannot rid myself of it."

I asked why he did not employ an overseer.

"Because I do not think it right to trust to such men as we have to use, if we use any, for overseers."

"Is the general character of overseers bad?"

"They are the curse of this country, sir; the worst men in the community. . . . But lately, I had another sort of fellow offer—a fellow like a dancing-master, with kid gloves, and wrist-bands turned up over his coat-sleeves, and all so nice, that I was almost ashamed to talk to him in my old coat and slouched hat. Half a bushel of recommendations he had with him, too. Well, he was not the man for me—not half the gentleman, with all his airs, that Ned here is"—(a black servant, who was bursting with suppressed laughter, behind his chair).

"Oh, they are interesting creatures, sir," he continued, "and, with all their faults, have many beautiful traits. I can't help being attached to them, and I am sure they love us." In his own case, at least, I did not doubt it; his manner towards them was paternal—familiar and kind; and they came to him like children who have been given some task, and constantly are wanting to be encouraged and guided, simply and confidently. At dinner, he frequently addressed the [49/50] servant familiarly, and drew him into our conversation as if he were a family friend, better informed, on some local and domestic points, than himself.

He informed me that able-bodied field-hands were hired out, in this vicinity, at the rate of one hundred dollars a year, and their board and clothing. Four able-bodied men, that I have employed the last year, on my farm in New York, I pay, on an average, one hundred and five dollars each, and board them; they clothe themselves at an expense, I think, of twenty dollars a year;—probably, slaves' clothing costs twice that. They constitute all the force of my farm, hired by the year (except a boy, who goes to school in Winter), and, in my absence, have no overseer except one of themselves, whom I appoint. I pay the fair wages of the market, more than any of my neighbors, I believe, and these are no lower than the average of what I have paid for the last five years. It is difficult to measure the labor performed in a day by one, with that of the other, on account of undefined differences in the soil, and in the bulk and weight of articles operated upon. But, here, I am shown tools that no man in his senses, with us, would allow a laborer, to whom he was paying wages, to be encumbered with; and the excessive weight and clumsiness of which, I would judge, would make work at least ten per cent greater than those ordinarily used with us. And I am assured that, in the careless and clumsy way they must be used by the slaves, anything lighter or less rude could not be furnished them with good economy, and that such tools [50/51] as we constantly give our laborers, and find our profit in giving them, would not last out a day in a Virginia corn-field—much lighter and more free from stones though it be than ours.

So, too, when I ask why mules are so universally substituted for horses on the farm, the first reason given, and confessedly the most conclusive one, is, that horses cannot bear the treatment that they always *must* get from negroes; horses are always soon foundered or crippled by them, while mules will bear cudgelling, and lose a meal or two now and then, and not be materially injured, and they do not take cold or get sick if neglected or overworked. But I do not need to go further than to the window of the room in which I am writing, to see, at almost any time, treatment of cattle that would insure the immediate discharge of the driver, by almost any farmer owning them at the North.

Yesterday I visited a coal-pit: the majority of the mining laborers are slaves, and uncommonly athletic and fine-looking negroes; but a considerable number of white hands are also employed, and they occupy all the responsible posts. The slaves are, some of them, owned by the Mining Company; but the most are hired of their owners, at from $120 to $200 a year, the company boarding and clothing them. (I have the impression that I heard it was customary to give them a certain allowance of money and let them find their own board.)

The white hands are mostly English or Welchmen. [51/52] One of them, with whom I conversed, told me that he had been here several years; he had previously lived some years at the North. He got better wages here than he had earned at the North, but he was not contented, and did not intend to remain. On pressing him for the reason of his discontent, he said, after some hesitation, that he had rather live where he could be more free; a man had to be too *"discreet"* here: if one happened to say anything that gave offense, they thought no more of drawing a pistol or a knife upon him, than they would of kicking a dog that was in their way. Not long since, a young English fellow came to the pit, and was put to work along with a gang of negroes. One morning, about a week afterwards, twenty or thirty men called on him, and told him that they would allow him fifteen minutes to get out of sight, and if they ever saw him in those parts again, they would "give him hell." They were all armed, and there was nothing for the young fellow to do but to move "right off."

"What reason did they give him for it?"

"They did not give him any reason."

"But what had he done?"

"Why I believe they thought he had been too free with the niggers; he wasn't used to them, you see, sir, and he talked to 'em free like, and they thought he'd make 'em think too much of themselves."

He said the slaves were very well fed, and well treated—not worked over hard. They were employed night and day, in relays. [52/53]

The coal from these beds is of special value for gas manufacture, and is shipped, for that purpose, to all the large towns on the Atlantic sea-board, even to beyond Boston. It is delivered to shipping at Richmond, at fifteen cents a bushel: about thirty bushels go to a ton.

The hotel at which I am staying, "the American," Milberger Smith, from New York, proprietor, is a very capital one. I have never, this side the Atlantic, had my comforts provided for better, in my private room, with so little annoyance from the servants. The chamber-servants are negroes, and are accomplished in their business; (the dining-room servants are Irish). A man and a woman attend together upon a few assigned rooms, in the hall adjoining which they are constantly in waiting; your bell is answered immediately, your orders are quickly and quietly followed, and your particular personal wants anticipated as much as possible, and provided for, as well as the usual offices performed, when you are out. The man becomes your servant while you are in your room; he asks, at night, when he comes to request your boots, at what time he shall come in the morning, and then, without being very exactly punctual, he comes quietly in, makes your fire, sets the boots before it, brushes and arranges your clothes, lays out your linen, arranges your washing and dressing gear, asks if you want anything else of him before breakfast, opens the shutters, and goes off to the next room. I took occasion to speak well of him to my neighbor one day, that I might judge whether I was particularly favored. [53/54]

"Oh yes," he said, "Henry was a very good boy, very—valuable servant—quite so—would be worth two thousand dollars, if he was a little younger—easy."

At dinner, a respectable looking, gray-headed man asked another:

"Niggers are going high now, ain't they?"

"Yes, sir."

"What would you consider a fair price for a woman thirty years old, with a young-one two years old?"

"Depends altogether on her physical condition, you know.—Has she any other children?"

"*Yes; four.*"

"——Well—I reckon about seven to eight hundred."

"I bought one yesterday—gave six hundred and fifty."

"Well, sir, if she's tolerable likely, you did well."

What is most remarkable in the appearance of the people of the better class, is their invariably *high-dressed* condition; look down the opposite side of the table, even at breakfast, and you will probably see thirty men drinking coffee, all in full funeral dress, not an easy coat amongst them. It is the same in the street, and the same with ladies as with gentlemen; silk and satin, under umbrellas, rustle along the sidewalk, or skip across it between carriages and the shops, as if they were going to a dinner-party, at eleven o'clock in the morning. The last is only New York repeated, to be sure, but the gentlemen carry it further than in New York, and seem never to indulge in undress. [54/55]

I have rarely seen a finer assemblage of people than filled the theatre one night, at the benefit of the Bateman children, who are especial favorites of the public here. As the Legislature is in session, I presume there was a fair representation of the Virginians of all parts of the State. A remarkable proportion of the men were very tall and of animated expression—and of the women, fair, refined, and serene. The men, however, were very deficient in robustness, and the women, though graceful and attractive, had none of that dignity and stateliness for which the dames of Virginia were formerly much distinguished.

In *manners*, I notice that, between man and man, more ceremony and form is sustained, in familiar conversation, than well-bred people commonly use at the North.

Among the people you see in the streets, full half, I should think, are more or less of negro blood, and a very decent, civil people these seem, in general, to be; more so than the laboring class of whites, among which there are many very ruffianly looking fellows. There is a considerable population of foreign origin, generally of the least valuable class; very dirty German Jews, especially, abound, and their characteristic shops (with their characteristic smells, quite as bad as in Cologne), are thickly set in the narrowest and meanest streets, which seem to be otherwise inhabited mainly by negroes.

Immense wagons, drawn by six mules each, the teamster always riding on the back of the near-wheeler, [55/56] are a characteristic feature of the streets. Another is the wood-carts; small trucks loaded with about a cord of pine wood, drawn by three mules or horses, one in shafts, and two others, abreast, before him, a negro always riding the shaft-horse and guiding the leaders with a single rein, one pull to turn them to the right, and two to the left, with a great deal of the whip whichever way they go. The same guiding apparatus, a single line, with branches to each bit, is used altogether upon the long wagon teams. On the canal, a long, narrow, canoe-like boat, perhaps fifty feet long and six wide, and drawing but a foot or two of water, is nearly as common as the ordinary large boats, such as are used on our canals. They come out of some of the small, narrow, crooked streams, connected with the canals, in which a difficult navigation is effected by poling. They are loaded with tobacco, flour, and a great variety of raw country produce. The canal boatmen of Virginia seem to be quite as rude, insolent, and riotous a class as those of New York, and every facility is evidently afforded them, at Richmond, for indulging their peculiar appetites and tastes. A great many low eating, and, I should think, drinking shops are frequented chiefly by the negroes. Dancing and other amusements are carried on in these at night.

From reading the comments of Southern statesmen and newspapers on the crime and misery which sometimes result from the accumulation of poor and ignorant people, with no intelligent masters to take care of them, in our Northern towns, one might get the impression [56/57] that Southern towns—especially those not demoralized by foreign commerce—were comparatively free from a low and licentious population. From what I have seen, however, I should be now led to think that there was at least as much vice, and of what we call rowdyism, in Richmond, as in any Northern town of its size.[1]

The train was advertised to leave at 3.30 P.M. At that hour the cars were crowded with passengers, and the engineer, punctually at the minute, gave notice that he was at his post, by a long, loud whistle of the locomotive. Five minutes afterwards he gave us an impatient jerk; ten minutes afterwards we advanced three rods; twelve minutes afterwards, returned to first position: continued, "backing and filling" upon the bridge over the rapids of the James river, for half an hour. At precisely four o'clock, crossed the bridge and fairly started for Petersburg.

Ran twenty miles in exactly an hour and thirty minutes, (thirteen miles an hour; mail train, especially recommended by advertisement as "fast"). Brakes on, three times, for cattle on the track; twenty minutes spent at way-stations. Flat rail. Locomotive built at Philadelphia. I am informed that most of those used [57/58] on the road—perhaps all those of the *slow* trains—are made at Petersburg.

At one of the stoppages, smoke was to be seen issuing from the

---

[1] SAD PICTURE.—A gentleman informs the *Richmond* (Va.) *Dispatch* that, while taking a stroll on one of the islands in James river, not far from Mayo's Bridge, last Sunday morning, he counted as many as twenty-two boys, from ten to fifteen years of age, engaged in gaming with cards and dice for money. In some of the parties he saw grown men and small boys playing bluff, and cursing, swearing, and drinking.—*Southern Newspaper.*

truck of a car. The conductor, on having his attention called to it, nodded his head sagely, took a morsel of tobacco, put his hands in his pocket, looked at the truck as if he would mesmerize it, spat upon it, and then stept upon the platform and shouted "All right! Go ahead!" At the next stoppage, the smoking was furious; conductor bent himself over it with an evidently strong exercise of his will, but not succeeding to tranquilize the subject at all, he suddenly relinquished the attempt, and, deserting Mesmer for Preisnitz, shouted, "Ho! boy! bring me some water here." A negro soon brought a quart of water in a tin vessel.

"Hain't got no oil, Columbus?"

"No, sir."

"Hum—go ask Mr. Smith for some: this yer's a screaking so, I durstn't go on. You Scott! get some salt. And look here, some of you boys, get me some more water. D'ye hear?"

Salt, oil, and water, were crowded into the box, and, after five minutes longer delay, we went on, the truck still smoking, and the water and oil boiling in the box, until we reached Petersburg. The heat was the result, I suppose, of a neglect of sufficient or timely oiling. While waiting, in a carriage, for the driver to get my baggage, I saw a negro oiling all the trucks of the train; as he proceeded from one to the other, he did [58/59] not give himself the trouble to elevate the outlet of his oiler, so that a stream of oil, costing probably a dollar and a half a gallon, was poured out upon the ground the whole length of the train.

While on the bridge at Richmond, the car in which I was seated was over-full—several persons standing; among them, one considerably "excited," who informed the company that he was a Member of the House of Delegates, and that he would take advantage of this opportune collection of the people, to expose an atrocious attempt, on the part of the minority, to jump a Bill through the Legislature, which was not in accordance with true Democratic principles. He continued for some time to address them in most violent, absurd, profane, and meaningless language; the main point of his oration being, to demand the popular gratitude for himself, for having had the sagacity and courage to prevent the accomplishment of the nefarious design. He afterwards attempted to pass into the ladies' car, but was dissuaded from doing so by the conductor, who prevailed on a young man to give him his seat. Having taken it, he immediately lifted his feet upon the back of the seat before him, resting them upon the shoulders of its occupant. This gentleman turning his head, he begged his pardon; but, hoping it would not occasion him inconvenience, he said he would prefer to keep them there, and did so; soon afterwards falling asleep.

There were, in the train, two first-class passenger cars, and two freight cars. The latter were occupied [59/60] by about forty negroes, most of them belonging to traders who were sending them to the cotton States to be sold. Such kind of evidence of activity in the slave trade of Virginia is to be seen every day; but particulars and statistics of it are not to be obtained by a stranger here. Most gentlemen of character seem to have a special disinclination to converse on the subject; and it is denied, with feeling, that slaves are often reared, as is supposed by the Abolitionists, with the intention of selling them to the traders. It appears to me evident, however, from the manner in which I hear the traffic spoken of incidentally, that the cash value of a slave for sale, above the cost of raising it from infancy to the age at which it commands the highest price, is generally considered among the surest elements of a planter's wealth. Such a nigger is worth such a price, and such another is too old to learn to pick cotton, and such another will bring so much, when it has grown a little more, I have frequently heard people say, in the street, or the public-houses. That a slave woman is commonly esteemed least for her laboring qualities, most for those qualities which give value to a broodmare is, also, constantly made apparent.[2]

By comparing the average decennial ratio of slave [60/61] increase in all the States with the difference in the number of the actual slave-population of the slave-breeding States, as ascertained by the census, it is apparent that the number of slaves exported to the cotton States is considerably more than twenty thousand a year.

While calling on a gentleman occupying an honorable official position at Richmond, I noticed upon his table a copy of Professor Johnson's Agricultural Tour in the United States. Referring to a paragraph in it, where some statistics of the value of the slaves raised and annually exported from Virginia were given, I asked if he knew how these had been obtained, and whether they were reliable. "No," he replied; "I don't know anything about it; but if they are anything unfavorable to the institution of slavery, you may be sure they are false." This is but an illustration, in extreme, of the manner in which I find a desire to obtain more correct but *definite* information, on the subject of slavery, is usually met, by gentlemen otherwise of enlarged mind and generous qualities.

A gentleman, who was a member of the "Union Safety Committee" of New York, during the excitement which attended the discussion of the Fugitive Slave Act of 1850, told me that, as he was passing through Virginia this winter, a man entered the car in which he was

---

[2] A slaveholder writing to me with regard to my cautious statements on this subject, made in the *Daily Times*, says:—"In the States of Maryland, Virginia, North Carolina, Kentucky, Tennessee, and Missouri, as much attention is paid to the breeding and growth of negroes as to that of horses and mules. Further South, we raise them both for use and for market. Planters command their girls and women (married or unmarried) to have children; and I have known a great many negro girls to be sold off, because they did not have children. A breeding woman is worth from one-sixth to one-fourth more than one that does not breed."

seated, leading in a negro girl, whose manner and expression of face indicated dread and [61/62] grief. Thinking she was a criminal, he asked the man what she had done:

"Done? Nothing."

"What are you going to do with her?"

"I'm taking her down to Richmond, to be sold."

"Does she belong to you?"

"No; she belongs to——; he raised her."

"Why does he sell her—has she done anything wrong?"

"Done anything? No: she's no fault, I reckon."

"Then, what does he want to sell for?"

"Sell her for! Why shouldn't he sell her? He sells one or two every year; wants the money for 'em, I reckon."

The irritated tone and severe stare with which this was said, my friend took as a caution not to pursue his investigation.

A gentleman, with whom I was conversing on the subject of the cost of slave labor, in answer to an inquiry—what proportion of all the stock of slaves of an old plantation might be reckoned upon to do full work?—answered, that he owned ninety-six negroes; of these, only thirty-five were field-hands, the rest being either too young or too old for hard work. He reckoned his whole force as only equal to twenty-one strong men, or "*prime* field-hands." But this proportion was somewhat smaller than usual, he added, "because his women were uncommonly good breeders; he did not suppose there was a lot of women anywhere that bred faster than his; he never heard of babies coming so fast [62/63] as they did on his plantation; it was perfectly surprising; and every one of them, in his estimation, was worth two hundred dollars, as negroes were selling now, the moment it drew breath."

I asked what he thought might be the usual proportion of workers to slaves, supported on plantations, throughout the South. On the large cotton and sugar plantations of the more Southern States, it was very high, he replied; because their hands were nearly all bought and *picked for work;* he supposed, on these, it would be about one-half; but, on any old plantation, where the stock of slaves had been an inheritance, and none had been bought or sold, he thought the working force would rarely be more than one-third, at most, of the whole number.

This gentleman was out of health, and told me, with frankness, that such was the trouble and annoyance his negroes occasioned him—although he had an overseer—and so wearisome did he find the lonely life he led on his plantation, that he could not remain upon it; and, as he knew everything would go to the dogs if he did not, he was seriously contemplating to sell out, retaining only his foster-mother and a body-servant. He thought of taking them to Louisiana and Texas, for sale; but, if he should learn that there was much probability that Lower California would be made a slave State, he supposed it would pay him to wait, as probably, if that should occur, he could take them there and sell them for twice as much as they would now bring in New Orleans. He knew very well, he [63/64] said, that, as they were, raising corn and tobacco, they were paying nothing at all like a fair interest on their value.[3]

Some of his best hands he now rented out, to work in a furnace, and for the best of these he had been offered, for next year, two hundred dollars. He did not know whether he ought to let them go, though. They were worked hard, and had too much liberty, and were acquiring bad habits. They earned money, by overwork, and spent it for whiskey, and got a habit of roaming about and *taking care of themselves;* because, when they were not at work in the furnace, nobody looked out for them.

I begin to suspect that the great trouble and anxiety of Southern gentlemen is:—How, without quite destroying the capabilities of the negro for any work at all, to prevent him from learning to take care of himself. [64]

[3] Mr. Wise is reported to have stated, in his electioneering tour, when candidate for Governor, in 1855, that, if slavery were permitted in California, negroes would sell for $5,000 apiece.

The Irrepressible Conflict

FRANK LAWRENCE OWSLEY

SLAVERY WAS NO SIMPLE QUESTION OF ETHICS; IT CUT ACROSS THE CATE-gories of human thought like a giant question mark. It was a moral, an economic, a religious, a social, a philosophical, and above all a political question. It was no essential part of the agrarian civilization of the South—though the Southerners under attack assumed that it was. Without slavery the economic and social life of the South would have not been radically different. Perhaps the plantation life would not have been as pronounced without it, yet the South would long have remained agricultural—as it still [76/77] is after sixty-five years of "freedom"! Certainly the South would have developed its political philosophy very much as it did. Yet the slavery question furnished more

Pages 76–84 of "The Irrepressible Conflict" by Frank Lawrence Owsley, from *I'll Take My Stand* by Twelve Southerners. Copyright 1930 by Harper & Brothers; renewed 1958 by Donald Davidson. Reprinted by permission of Harper & Row, Publishers.

fuel to sectional conflict and created more bitterness than any or all the other elements of the two groups.

Slavery had been practically forced upon the country by England—over the protest of colonial assemblies. During the eighteenth century it had ceased to be profitable, and colonial moral indignation rose correspondingly. However, when the Revolution came and the Southern colonies gained their independence, they did not free the negroes. The eternal race question had reared itself. Negroes had come into the Southern Colonies in such numbers that people feared for the integrity of the white race. For the negroes were cannibals and barbarians, and therefore dangerous. No white man who had any contact with slavery was willing to free the slaves and allow them to dwell among the whites. Slaves were a peril, at least a risk, but free blacks were considered a menace too great to be hazarded. Even if no race wars occurred, there was dread of being submerged and absorbed by the black race. Accordingly, all slaveholders and non-slaveholders who objected to slavery, objected even more to the presence of the free negro. They argued that the slaves could never be freed unless they could be deported back to Africa or to the West Indies. This conviction became more fervent when the terrifying negro insurrections in Santo Domingo and Hayti destroyed the white population and civilizations almost completely and submerged the remainder under barbarian control. All early abolitionists—which meant most [77/78] of the Southern people up until around 1800—were abolitionists only on condition of colonization. As a result there were organized many colonization societies, mostly in the South during this period.

But colonization was futile. It was soon realized by all practical slaveholders that the negroes could not be deported successfully. Deportation was cruel and expensive. Few of the black people wished to leave the South. The Southern whites shrugged their shoulders and deplored the necessity of continuing the negroes in bondage as the only alternative to chaos and destruction.

Then the invention of the cotton gin and the opening of the cotton lands in the Southwest, 1810–36, made the negro slave an economic instrument of great advantage. With the aid of the fresh cheap lands and the negro slave vast fortunes were made in a few years. Both North and South having now conceded that emancipation was impossible, the Southern planters made the most of their new cotton kingdom with a fairly easy conscience. They had considered emancipation honestly and fairly and had found it out of the question. Their skirts were clear. Let the blood of slavery rest upon the heads of those who had forced it upon the South.

But the opening of the "cotton kingdom" gave dynamic power to the agrarian section, and new lands were desired by the West and South. The now industrial East saw its interest threatened if the South should colonize the territories to the West, including those gained and to be gained. With the tremendous impetus given to the expansion of the Southern system by the growth of the cotton industry [78/79] and culture, the North became uneasy and began to show opposition to the continued balance of power. This first became manifest in the struggle which resulted in the Missouri Compromise of 1822. Up to this point the objection to slavery was always tempered by the acknowledgment on the part of the North that the South was a victim of the system of slavery and ought to be sympathized with, rather than the instigator of the system, who ought to be condemned as a criminal.

But in 1831 a voice was raised which was drowned only in the roar of battle in 1861-5. It was the cry of William Lloyd Garrison that slavery was a crime and the slaveholders were criminals. He established the famous *Liberator*, which preached unremitting and ruthless war upon slavery and the slaveholder. He knew no moderation. He had no balance or sense of consequence. His was the typical "radical" mind which demands that things be done at once, which tries to force nature, which wants to tear up by the roots. Although he was completely ignorant of the South and of negro slavery, he dogmatically assumed an omniscient power of judgment over the section and the institution. In the *Liberator* or in the anti-slavery tracts fostered by the anti-slavery societies which he aided or instigated, he set no bounds of accusation and denunciation. The slave master, said Garrison, debauched his women slaves, had children by them, and in turn defiled his own children and sold them into the slave market; the slave plantation was primarily a gigantic harem for the master and his sons. The handsome octoroon coachmen shared the bed of the mistress when the master was away from home, and the [79/80] daughters were frequently away in some secluded nook to rid themselves of undesirable negro offspring. Ministers of the gospel who owned or sanctioned slavery were included in his sweeping indictment of miscegenation and prostitution. In short, Garrison and the anti-slavery societies which he launched, followed soon by Northern churchmen, stigmatized the South as a black brothel. This was not all! The Southern slaveowners were not merely moral lepers; they were cruel and brooding tyrants, who drove their slaves till they dropped and died, who starved them to save food, let them go cold and almost naked to save clothing, let them dwell in filthy pole pens rather than build them comfortable cottages, beat them unmercifully with leather thongs filled with spikes, dragged cats over their bodies and faces, trailed them with bloodhounds which rent and chewed them,—then sprinkled their wounds with salt and red pepper. Infants were torn from their mothers' breasts and sold to Simon Legrees; families were separated and scattered to the four winds. This brutal treatment of the slaves reacted upon the masters and made them brutal and cruel in their dealings with their fellow whites. Such charges, printed in millions upon millions of pamphlets, were sent out all over the world. Sooner or later, much of it was accepted as true in the North.

In the South this abolition war begot Nat Turner's rebellion, in which negro slaves in Virginia under the leadership of Nat Turner, a freedman, massacred their masters, including women and children. The new situation, in turn, begot a revolution in Southern attitudes. Struck almost out of a clear sky by the Garrisonian blasts and the Nat Turner [80/81] rebellion, Southern leaders were dazed. They discussed momentarily the expedient of freeing the slaves, then closed forever their minds upon the subject as too dangerous to undertake. Then came a counter-blast of fierce resentment, denying all accusations. The South threw up a defense mechanism. The ministers searched the Scriptures by day and night and found written, in language which could not be misunderstood, a biblical sanction of slavery. Abraham, Moses, the prophets, Jesus, and the disciples on many occasions had approved slavery. History from its dawn had seen slavery almost everywhere. A scriptural and historical justification was called in to meet the general indictment of the wrongfulness of slavery in the abstract. Partly as a result of this searching of the Scriptures there took place a religious revival in the South, which had tended heretofore to incline to Jeffersonian liberalism of the deistic type. The South became devoutly orthodox and literal in its theology. But the abolitionists were not willing to accept scriptural justification of slavery. There was an attempt to prove the wrongfulness of slavery by the same sacred book, but, finding this impossible, many abolitionists repudiated the Scriptures as of divine origin. Partly as a result, the North lost confidence in orthodoxy and tended to become deistic as the South had been. One could almost hear Puritan New England creaking upon its theological hinges as it swung away from its old position.

But there were philosophers and thinkers at work in the South who would meet the abolitionists upon their own grounds. Hammond, Fitzhugh, John C. Calhoun, Chancellor Harper, Thomas R. Dew, either because they felt [81/82] that scriptural justification of slavery was inadequate or because they realized the necessity of getting away from the theological grounds in order that they might combat the abolitionists upon common ground, approached slavery from the social and economic standpoint. Their general conclusions were that two races of different culture and color cannot live together on terms of equality. One will dominate or destroy the other. There was no middle ground. It had ever been thus. They contended that the negro was of a backward, inferior race. Certainly his culture was inferior. He must either rule or be ruled. If he ruled, the white race would be destroyed or submerged and its civilization wiped out. For the Southern people there was no choice; the negro must be ruled, and the only way he could be controlled, they believed, was by some form of slavery. In other words, Calhoun, Fitzhugh, and the "philosophers of slavery" justified slavery upon the grounds of the "race question"—which U. B. Phillips has called the theme of Southern history, before and after the Civil War. Aside from the scriptural and social justification, these men defended slavery as an economic necessity. They contended that the culture of rice, tobacco, sugar cane, and especially cotton upon which the world depended could not be carried on without slaves. The South, including the up-country and the mountains, accepted the scriptural justification of slavery, to a great extent. The up-country did not accept the economics of slavery, but slavery, in its aspect as a race question, was universally approved in valleys, plains and mountains. It found, in fact, its strongest supporters among the poor whites and the non-slaveholding small landowners. [82/83] Their race prejudice and fears were the stronger because they knew nothing of the better side of the negro and regarded him as a vicious and dangerous animal whose freedom meant war to the knife and knife to the death. It was the old fear which we have spoken of, common to all in the days of the Revolution and in the days when Jefferson and Washington were advocating emancipation only on condition that the freedman be sent from the country. Outside of the common agrarianism of the multitudinous sections of the South which acted as a common tie, the race question which underlay slavery, magnified and aggravated by the abolition crusade, was the hoop of steel which held men together in the South in the great final argument of arms.

This abolition crusade on the part of the North and justification of slavery by the South were principally outside of the realm of politics in the beginning. The abolitionists, in fact, had a tendency to abjure politics and demand "direct action," as some of our recent radicals do. But the leaven soon spread, and slavery became a burning political issue. The political leaders of the North, especially the Whigs, after the dynamic growth of the South in the first quarter of the nineteenth century, became fixed in their determination that the agrarian section should have its metes and bounds definitely limited. Industrialism, which had undergone an even greater development than had cotton-growing, declared that the balance of power between agrarian and industrial sections must go. Because slave-holding was the acid test as to whether a state would remain agrarian or become eventually industrial, the [83/84] Northern leaders wished that no more slave states should be carved from the Western territories. Between 1836, when the annexation of slaveholding Texas was advocated by the South, and 1860, when Lincoln was elected upon a platform which declared that no more territory was open to slavery, the major issues in national politics were the struggles between North and South over the admission or exclusion of slavery from the national territories. That is, it was a question whether the territories would be equally open to both sections or whether the North should have an exclusive right in these territories to found its own states and system and thereby destroy the balance of power and control the federal government in the interest of its own economic and social system. Unfortunately for the South, the leaders of the North were able to borrow the language of the abolitionists and clothed the struggle in a moral garb. It was good politics, it was noble and convenient, to speak of it as a struggle for freedom when it was essentially a struggle for the balance of power.

So to the bitter war of the abolitionists and the bitter resentment of the South was added the fight over the balance of power in the form of the extension of slavery into the common territories. [84]

QUESTIONS FOR STUDY AND DISCUSSION

Although the questions below force the student to think about the relationship between *The Confessions of Nat Turner* and the historical and literary works which are essential to an understanding of it, he should turn to additional sources for longer papers.

On the subject of slavery he may consult Herbert Aptheker's *American Negro Slave Revolts* (International Publishers, 1963), Ulrich B. Phillips' *American Negro Slavery* (D. Appleton & Co., 1918), Stanley M. Elkins' *Slavery* (University of Chicago Press, 2nd edition, 1968), Kenneth M. Stampp's *The Peculiar Institution* (Knopf, 1956), Gunnar Myrdal's *An American Dilemma: The Negro Problem and Modern Democracy* (Harper, 1944), Frank Tannenbaum's *Slave and Citizen* (Knopf, 1947), Herbert S. Klein's *Slavery in the Americas: A Comparative Study of Cuba and Virginia* (University of Chicago Press, 1967), John Hope Franklin's *The Militant South, 1800–1861* (Harvard University Press, 1956), Eugene D. Genovese's *The Political Economy of Slavery: Studies in the Economy and Society of the Slave South* (Pantheon, 1965). These are some of the classics in the field and represent almost all the varieties of opinion on the subject.

The most reliable and up-to-date historical study of Nat Turner is Herbert Aptheker's *Nat Turner's Slave Rebellion* (Grove Press, 1968); this volume contains the full text of the original *Confessions of Nat Turner* as well as an excellent critical bibliography.

In a new series, "The American Negro: His History and Literature," Arno Press and the New York Times have combined to bring out an impressive number of documents concerned with slavery, retaining the essentials of the original editions. This series should prove indispensable for source material.

The advanced student may also want to acquaint himself with other literary applications of Nat Turner. He should begin by reading the complete texts of G. P. R. James's *The Old Dominion,* Daniel Panger's *Ol' Prophet Nat,* and Paul Peters' *Nat Turner.* Harriet Beecher Stowe's *Dred: A Tale of the Great Dismal Swamp* should also be consulted. (Ernest Kaiser's essay in Part 2 of this collection is a mine of bibliographical information on this subject and related ones.)

251

Background

1. *The Original Confessions of Nat Turner:* What is the purpose of the public notice which precedes the confessions? How do Nat Turner's childhood experiences affect his adult life? Discuss his biblical influences. What are the qualities of his language? Explore Gray's reactions. In what ways does the "real" Nat Turner differ from Styron's? Are the original confessions a fiction?

2. Styron: *This Quiet Dust.* When did Styron first read of Nat Turner? What does he mean by the remark that Southern whites cannot *know* blacks? Explore his treatment of sexual myths. Why does Styron refer to *Young Man Luther?* Can we find in this essay any clues to his treatment of Nat Turner's psychology? How is Dan Seward presented? What are the implications of the Emily Dickinson lines?

3. Plimpton: *William Styron: A Shared Ordeal.* Discuss the meanings of Hiram Haydn's remark. Can the reference to *The Stranger* be elaborated so that a more complete comparison between it and Styron's novel may be made? Is Styron correct in implying that he is the first white American to assume a black persona? What is a *literary* style? Why does Styron call Nat Turner a traditional revolutionary? Explore his characterization of Margaret Whitehead. Relate the last paragraph to ideas advanced by Gilman, Aptheker, and Malin.

4. Sokolov: *Into the Mind of Nat Turner.* How deeply does Sokolov penetrate into the mind of Nat Turner? What biographical details about Styron does he offer? What details of Virginia life does he dwell upon? Explore the reference to *Benito Cereno.* Why is James Baldwin mentioned at length? Trace the implications of the last sentence (quoted from Baldwin). Is this essay written for the average reader? Is it propagandistic?

5. Lewis and Woodward: *Slavery in the First Person.* Why is the John Brown reference helpful? How does Styron justify his "meditation on history?" Explore the "haunting structure" idea. Contrast the Old and New Testament influences in *The Confessions of Nat Turner.* Does Styron change his view toward Margaret in this interview from the views he expressed in the Sokolov and Plimpton pieces? Explore the father-image in *The Confessions.* Herbert Aptheker, in one of the following reviews, accuses Styron of accepting "Sambo" psychology; does this interview bear out such a charge?

Reviews

1. Sheed: *The Slave Who Became a Man.* What is the meaning of the remark that Styron's novel "can hardly be read as an exercise in pure esthetics"? Do Sheed's attempted ironies annoy the reader? Is the historical novel always a "clumsy method of investigation"? Would Sheed agree with Gilman? Is Sheed unfair to Styron's avowed purpose of writing a "meditation on history"? How does Kaiser characterize this essay? Is he right?

2. Friedman: *Nat Turner: A "Meditation on History."* Explore implications of the title. Is it helpful to see Styron as Proustian? Contrast *The Fall* and *The Confessions.* Does the "comparative literature" approach used by Friedman enlarge our view of Styron and his novel? Is this essay a necessary, worthwhile corrective to Sheed's?

3. Rubin: *William Styron and Human Bondage.* Should Rubin discuss the critical reception of *Set This House on Fire*? How does he characterize that novel? Is he concerned with the historical reality of Nat Turner? Would he quarrel with Duberman or Aptheker? Does Rubin say anything new about Nat as narrator? Why does he see *The Confessions* as a *traditional* novel? What do we expect from "traditional" novels?

4. Malin: *Nat's Confessions.* How does Malin contrast the "official" and "private" language of Styron's novel? Is he correct in stressing the biblical tone? Trace at greater length the three recurring symbols. Why should Malin quote Styron's long passage in his last paragraph? Is his analysis exclusively literary? Is it cold?

5. Aptheker: *A Note on the History.* Can a historian be a literary critic? Does Aptheker really look at Styron's novel or does he neglect it for the sake of historical "fact"? Is he helpful in forcing us to read the *original* confessions with great care? Does Styron really believe in "Sambo" psychology?

6. Kaiser: *The Failure of William Styron.* Does Kaiser analyze the validity of Finkelstein's view? Why should he mention that Styron borrowed Aptheker's 1936 thesis? Is "This Quiet Dust" a simple "throwback to . . . racism and paternalism"? How effectively does Kaiser attack the liberal white press? Why is James Baldwin brought into the discussion? Is it for the same purpose as Sokolov's reference to him?

7. Gilman: *Nat Turner Revisited.* Why does Gilman characterize Styron as a writer of "big" novels? Explore the statement: "But we

cannot trace history through literature and bring it down to go on any leash." Can *The Confessions of Nat Turner*'s "historical truth" be validated? Is the novel a "failed religious drama"? Explain why Gilman praises the two narrative passages. Are they completely different from the passages he condemns?

8. Duberman: *Historical Fictions*. Contrast Duberman's remark about the "superlative history" of Styron's novel with those of Gilman, Sheed, and Aptheker. Do the four critics have the same view of history? Explore the charges of the black writers cited in relation to the novel and to Duberman's own analysis. Is Styron "a better historian than any of his critics" because he will not "bury unpleasant evidence"? What exactly should be the role of an historian?

The Worlds of William Styron

1. Styron: *The Long Dark Road*. Are there any reminders of the Hemingway of the Nick Adams stories in this early Styron story? What are they? In what ways does this story reveal its creative-writing-workshop origins? Through whose eyes do we see the events? Would you consider this story to be a useful introduction to *The Confessions of Nat Turner*? Are there signs that the same writer wrote both works? Could this story have been written in 1967? How well do we know the three principal characters: Dewey, his father, and Roy? Is the conflict between Dewey and Roy convincingly realized?

2. Hoffman: *William Styron: The Metaphysical Hurt*. In what way is *Lie Down in Darkness*, according to Hoffman, a representative novel of the fifties and sixties? What is the significance of the "fact of death" in *Lie Down in Darkness*? What does Hoffman believe to be the extent of Styron's indebtedness to Faulkner? What does Hoffman mean when he says, "for Styron's contemporaries, style actually *does* function to qualify life"? Does Hoffman take the relationship between *Set This House on Fire* and F. Scott Fitzgerald more seriously than he does that between *Lie Down in Darkness* and William Faulkner?

3. Hassan: *Encounter with Necessity*. Are the categories of social, domestic, and private useful in uncovering Peyton's position in *Lie Down in Darkness*? Would they work equally well for Styron's Nat Turner? What use does Hassan make of time and space in his analysis of the novel? Is he correct in suggesting that *Lie Down in Darkness* is "narrow in space and diffuse in time"? Do you agree with Hassan's estimate that *Lie Down in Darkness* is "a brilliant formal accomplishment"? Does he give sufficient evidence? What would be Swanson's

probable reaction to this statement? Would Hoffman and Friedman agree or disagree?

4. Swanson: *William Styron's Clown Show*. On what grounds can Styron be accused of failure in his fictional works? Give an account of the dog imagery in Styron's work. What are some of the other images that he develops? Comment on Styron's existentialism. Do you agree with Friedman's view of Styron's timing (in his essay in Part 2) or that expressed by Swanson here? Are they mutually exclusive or can they be reconciled? Are the enthusiasms of Hoffman, Hassan, Malkoff, and Friedman irreconcilable with Swanson's distaste for Styron?

5. Malkoff: *William Styron's Divine Comedy*. What does Malkoff mean by the "secularized Hell" in *Lie Down in Darkness*? Explain the importance of the father figure in Styron's novels. Do you believe that he is as central to Styron's fiction as Malkoff does? Do you believe, as Malkoff does, that Nat Turner has more of the "destructive element" than any of Styron's other characters? Do you agree that the barrier between Nat Turner and God remains "until the last moments before his execution"? Do you believe that *The Confessions of Nat Turner* "pits Old Testament against New"? Please explain. Do you find the parallel with Dante useful? Does it help explain Styron's development as a novelist? What use does Malkoff make of Kierkegaard? How does it compare with Hoffman's use of Kierkegaard?

6. Friedman: *William Styron: An Interim Appraisal*. Explain how Styron uses pastiche in *Lie Down in Darkness*. Does it detract from the quality of the novel? Is it clear from this essay, from Friedman's essay on *Nat Turner* in Part 2, from Hoffman's essay, and from the various interviews with Styron that Styron is aware of tendencies in modern French fiction? What evidence do we have? Which French writers seem especially to have influenced him? In what way is *Set This House on Fire* a mock-detective novel? Can you give other examples of the genre? What evidence do we have that *Set This House on Fire* received a great deal more attention than Styron's earlier work? How did its reception compare with that of *The Confessions of Nat Turner*? Would Friedman agree with Hoffman on the matter of Faulkner's influence on Styron?

Nat Turner and Slavery

1. Higginson: *Nat Turner's Insurrection*. What narrative devices does Higginson use to distinguish his writing from pure journalism or reportage? Are there evidences that Higginson was a novelist? What does Higginson tell us about Nat Turner's wife? Is his account similar

to Styron's? To what extent does Higginson seem to rely on the original 1831 text of the confessions of Nat Turner? To what extent on contemporary newspapers? What comparisons does Higginson make between the John Brown and Nat Turner insurrections? Does Styron's account agree with this remark of Higginson, "Yet I have looked through the Virginia newspapers of that time in vain for one charge of an indecent outrage on a woman against these triumphant and terrible slaves."? Does Higginson take sides in his account of the insurrection? Do you consider it an unfair account? Is Higginson widely read? If so, what evidence do we have for this assumption? Does Higginson describe the details of Nat's capture dramatically?

2. James: *The Old Dominion.* Even though this is only a small segment of a three-volume novel, do we see enough of the characters to form positive notions about them? What do we know of the narrator, for example? What prejudices does Bessy Davenport reveal towards Negroes? Compare G. P. R. James's Nat Turner with William Styron's. What are the essential differences between them? What effect does Uncle Jack have on Nat Turner? In what way do their views on slavery differ? What evidence do we have of Uncle Jack's knowledge of the Old Testament? of the New Testament? What are the narrator's first impressions of Nat Turner? What differences in speech and language does the narrator discern between Nat and Uncle Jack? Is the final exchange between Bessy and the narrator one likely to occur today or is it peculiarly ante-bellum?

3. Hayden: *The Ballad of Nat Turner.* Can you imagine Styron's Nat Turner pronouncing this poem? Do its sentiments at all correspond with his? Aside from its interest for students of Nat Turner do you consider "The Ballad of Nat Turner" a good poem? Please explain in detail. Does the poem end on an affirmative note? Do you agree with Vincent Harding's remark (from his essay in *William Styron's Nat Turner: Ten Black Writers Respond*): "There is nothing in any way equal [in Styron's *The Confessions of Nat Turner*] to the terse power found in Robert Hayden's poem, 'Ballad of Nat Turner' "? What kind of imagery predominates in the poem? Do you find anything biblical in the tone of the poem?

4. Panger: *Ol' Prophet Nat. Ol' Prophet Nat* appeared the same year as Styron's *Nat Turner.* From the short excerpt of Panger's novel reprinted here, what differences do you find? what similarities? What are the differences in the narrative voice between *Ol' Prophet Nat* and *The Confessions of Nat Turner*? Does the same Nat Turner seem to be telling both stories? Do you think that the contributors to *William Styron's Nat Turner: Ten Black Writers Respond* would find this first-person as offensive as that of Styron's novel? What parallels does the David-Goliath story offer Nat? Are they reassuring? What is the significance of this paragraph: "If we wait for the whites to give us our God-given rights, we will wait until the sun grows cold. If we wait

until the whites decide to treat black people like human beings, we will wait until the ocean is dry. The black man will only get as much as he is willing to fight for. For a man to be free he must be ready to die for that same freedom."? Is it timely? Which black leaders of today would be likely to approve of it? Which would dissent?

5. Douglass: *Escape from Slavery*. Why does Frederick Douglass not reveal all the details connected with his escape? What are Douglass' first reactions to New Bedford? Is he disappointed with what he sees? What are Douglass' anti-slavery activities? Read Robert Hayden's poem "Frederick Douglass" (found in his *Selected Poems*). Compare it to Hayden's "The Ballad of Nat Turner." What kind of view of Douglass does it present?

6. Olmsted: *The Seaboard Slave States*. What indication is there that Olmsted is a Northerner (born in Hartford, Connecticut)? Is his view of the Virginia slave economy different from that expected of a Southerner? What is the proprietor's views of the overseer? Would you consider this proprietor an enlightened slaveholder (if such is possible)? What is Olmsted's view of German Jews? Does he seem generally uncomfortable with foreigners? Does Olmsted consistently maintain his vantage point of onlooker or does he occasionally involve himself? Do we generally know what his reactions are to a given situation?

7. Owsley: *The Irrepressible Conflict*. Is Owsley's history of American slavery reliable? What is Owsley's view of William Lloyd Garrison? Is Owsley correct in calling Nat Turner a "freedman"? Does Owsley seem to believe in "a biblical sanction of slavery"? The twelve contributors to *I'll Take My Stand* have often been called Agrarians. What evidence is there in this essay that Frank Owsley holds the Agrarian position?

William Styron:
A Bibliography

JACKSON R. BRYER AND MARC NEWMAN

This bibliography supplements and updates previous listings by Harold W. Schneider (*Critique*, Summer 1960), David D. Galloway (*The Absurd Hero in American Fiction*), and August J. Nigro (*Configuration Critique de William Styron*). The area in which the present listing adds most substantially to these earlier ones is in material surrounding the publication of *The Confessions of Nat Turner*—i.e., reviews of the novel; interviews with Styron concerning it; reactions to it by Negro critics, most notably John H. Clarke's *William Styron's "Nat Turner": Ten Black Writers Respond;* and, finally and inevitably, reactions to the Negro reaction, in the form of reviews of and comments on the Clarke collection.

The book review section has also been expanded by the addition of numerous newspaper reviews of *Set This House on Fire*. These notices, as well as the local reviews of *Nat Turner*, were located in the files of Random House, to whose publicity department we are most grateful. Reviews of particularly noteworthy substance are marked with an asterisk. We also owe a debt of thanks to Lewis Lawson for his comments and advice, and to Susan Robinson for research assistance.

I. Works by Styron

A. NOVELS

Lie Down in Darkness. Indianapolis, Ind.: Bobbs-Merrill, 1951; London: Hamish Hamilton, 1952.

Set This House on Fire. New York: Random House, 1960; London: Hamish Hamilton, 1961.

The Long March. London: Mayflower, 1961; New York: Vintage, 1962.

The Confessions of Nat Turner. New York: Random House, 1967; London: Jonathan Cape, 1968.

B. SHORT FICTION

"Autumn." In William M. Blackburn, ed. *One and Twenty: Duke Narrative and Verse, 1924–1945.* Durham, N.C.: Duke University Press, 1945. Pp. 36–53.

"The Long Dark Road." In William M. Blackburn, ed. *One and Twenty: Duke Narrative and Verse, 1924–1945.* Durham, N.C.: Duke University Press, 1945. Pp. 266–280.

"A Moment in Trieste." In Don Wolfe, ed. *American Vanguard.* Ithaca, N.Y.: Cornell University Press, 1948. Pp. 241–247.

Reprinted: *New Voices: American Writing Today,* Don Wolfe, ed. Garden City, N.Y.: Doubleday, 1953.

"The Enormous Window." In Charles I. Glicksberg, ed. *1950 American Vanguard.* New York: New School for Social Research, 1950. Pp. 71–89.

"The Long March." In John W. Aldridge and Vance Bourjaily, eds. *Discovery No. 1.* New York: Pocket Books, 1953. Pp. 221–283. Collected as *The Long March.*

Reprinted: *The Best Short Stories of World War II: An American Anthology,* Charles Fenton, ed. New York: Viking Press, 1957. Pp. 361–421.

"The McCabes," *Paris Review,* XXII (Autumn-Winter 1959–1960), 12–28. Incorporated into *Set This House on Fire.*

"Works in Progress," *Esquire,* LX (July 1963), 50–51, 105. Incorporated into *The Confessions of Nat Turner.*

"Virginia: 1831," *Paris Review,* IX (Winter 1966), 13–45. Incorporated into *The Confessions of Nat Turner.*

"Runaway," *Partisan Review,* XXXII (Fall 1966), 574–582.

"The Confessions of Nat Turner," *Harper's,* CCXXXV (September 1967), 51–102. Incorporated into *The Confessions of Nat Turner.*

"Novel's Climax: The Night of the Honed Axes," *Life,* LXIII (October 13, 1967), 54–60. Incorporated into *The Confessions of Nat Turner.*

C. ARTICLES

"Letter to an Editor," *Paris Review,* I (Spring 1953), 9–16.

"Prevalence of Wonders," *The Nation,* CLXXVI (May 2, 1953), 370–371.

"*The Paris Review,*" *Harper's Bazaar,* LXXXVII (August 1953), 122, 173.

"What's Wrong With the American Novel?" *American Scholar,* XXIV (Autumn 1955), 464–503 [Roundtable discussion with Ralph Ellison, Hiram Haydn, *et al.*].

"If You Write for Television . . . ," *New Republic,* CXLVI (April 6, 1959), 16.

"Introduction." In *Best Short Stories From "The Paris Review."* New York: E. P. Dutton, 1959. Pp. 9–16.

"Mrs. Aadland's Little Girl, Beverly," *Esquire*, LVI (November 1961), 142, 189–191.

Reprinted: *First Person Singular: Essays for the Sixties,* Herbert Gold, ed. New York: Dial Press, 1963. Pp. 209–216.

Reprinted: *Esquire's World of Humor.* New York: Esquire, 1964. P. 210 [as "True Confessions"].

"The Death-in-Life of Benjamin Reid," *Esquire*, LVII (February 1962), 114, 141–145.

Reprinted: *An Approach to Literature,* 4th ed., Cleanth Brooks, John Thibaut Purser, and Robert Penn Warren, eds. New York: Appleton-Century-Crofts, 1964. Pp. 496–503.

"As He Lay Dead, A Bitter Grief," *Life*, LIII (July 20, 1962), 39–42.

"Aftermath of Benjamin Reid," *Esquire*, LVIII (November 1962), 79.

"Writers Under Twenty-five." In William M. Blackburn, ed. *Under Twenty-five: Duke Narrative and Verse, 1945–1962.* Durham, N.C.: Duke University Press, 1963. Pp. 3–8.

"Two Writers Talk It Over," *Esquire*, LX (July 1963), 57–59 [Discussion with James Jones].

"This Quiet Dust," *Harper's*, CCXXX (April 1965), 135–146.

Reprinted: *Best Magazine Articles of the Year 1966,* Gerald Walker, ed. New York: Crown Publishers, 1966. Pp. 1–18.

"Truth and Nat Turner: An Exchange—William Styron Replies," *The Nation*, CCVI (April 22, 1968), 544–547.

"Oldest America," *McCalls*, XCV (July 1968), 94, 123.

"Symposium: Violence in Literature," *American Scholar*, XXXVII (Summer 1968), 482–496 [Roundtable with Robert Penn Warren, Theodore Solotaroff, Robert Coles, and Styron].

"In the Jungle," *New York Review of Books*, XI (September 26, 1968), 11–13.

"My Generation," *Esquire*, LXX (October 1968), 123–124.

"On Creativity," *Playboy*, XV (December 1968). [Styron's statement appears on p. 138.]

"The Uses of Historical Fiction," *Southern Literary Journal* I (Spring 1969), 57–90 [Discussion with Ralph Ellison, Robert Penn Warren, C. Vann Woodward, and Styron].

D. BOOK REVIEWS AND RECORD REVIEW

"New Editions," *New York Review of Books*, I (Special Issue 1963), 43 [*Slave and Citizen: The Negro in the Americas*, by Frank Tannenbaum].

"Overcome," *New York Review of Books*, I (September 26, 1963), 18–19 [*American Negro Slave Revolts*, by Herbert Aptheker].

"An Elegy for F. Scott Fitzgerald," *New York Review of Books*, I (November 28, 1963), 1–3 [*The Letters of F. Scott Fitzgerald*, Andrew Turnbull, ed.].

"The Habit," *New York Review of Books*, I (December 26, 1963), 13–14 [*The Consumers Union Report on Smoking and the Public Interest*, Ruth and Edward Brecher, eds.].

"A Southern Conscience," *New York Review of Books*, II (April 2, 1964), 3 [*A Southern Prophecy*, by Lewis H. Blair].

"Tootsie Rolls," *New York Review of Books*, II (May 14, 1964), 8–9 [*Candy*, by Terry Southern and Mason Hoffenberg].

"MacArthur," *New York Review of Books*, II (October 8, 1964), 3–5 [*Reminiscences*, by Douglas MacArthur].

"John Fitzgerald Kennedy . . . as we remember him," *High Fidelity*, XVI (January 1966), 38. ["John Fitzgerald Kennedy . . . as we remember him," by Charles Kuralt: Columbia Recording L2L:1017].

"The Vice That Has No Name," *Harper's*, CCXXXVI (February 1968), 97–100 [*Light on Dark Corners* . . . , by B. G. Jefferis and J. L. Nichols].

"The Shade of Thomas Wolfe," *Harper's*, CCXXXVI (April 1968), 96, 98–104 [*Thomas Wolfe*, by Andrew Turnbull].

II. Works about Styron

A. BOOKS

Aldridge, John W. "The Society of Three Novels." In his *In Search of Heresy*. New York: McGraw-Hill, 1956. Pp. 126–148 [*Lie Down in Darkness*].

———. "William Styron and the Derivative Imagination." In his *Time to Murder and Create: The Contemporary Novel in Crisis*. New York: McKay, 1966. Pp. 30–51 [*Set This House on Fire*].

Allen, Walter. *The Modern Novel in Britain and the United States*. New York: E. P. Dutton, 1964. Pp. 305–307. [*Lie Down in Darkness*].

Baumbach, Jonathan. "Paradise Lost: *Lie Down in Darkness* by William Styron." In his *The Landscape of Nightmare: Studies in the Contemporary Novel*. New York: New York University Press, 1965. Pp. 123–137.

Bradbury, John M. *Renaissance in the South: A Critical History of the Literature, 1920–1960*. Chapel Hill: University of North Carolina Press, 1963. Pp. 122–123 and *passim*.

Butor, Michel. "Préface." *La Proie des Flammes*, tr. M.-E. Coindreau. Paris: Gallimard, 1962. Pp. vii–xx.

Chapsal, Madeleine. *Quinze Écrivains*. Paris: Julliard, 1963. Pp. 173–181.

Clarke, John H., ed. *William Styron's "Nat Turner": Ten Black Writers Respond*. Boston: Beacon Press, 1968.

Lerone Bennett, Jr., "Nat's Last White Man," pp. 3–16.

Alvin F. Poussaint, *"The Confessions of Nat Turner* and the Dilemma of William Styron," pp. 17–22.

Vincent Harding, "You've Taken My Nat and Gone," pp. 23–33.

John O. Killens, "The Confessions of Willie Styron," pp. 34–44.

John A. Williams, "The Manipulation of History and of Fact: An Ex-Southerner's Apologist Tract for Slavery and the Life of Nat Turner; or William Styron's Faked Confessions," pp. 45–49.

Ernest Kaiser, "The Failure of William Styron," pp. 50–65.

Loyle Hairston, "William Styron's Nat Turner—Rogue-Nigger," pp. 66–72.

Charles V. Hamilton, "Our Nat Turner and William Styron's Creation," pp. 73–78.

Mike Thelwell, "Back With the Wind: Mr. Styron and the Reverend Turner," pp. 79–91.

Davis, Robert Gorham. "The American Individualist Tradition: Bellow and Styron." In Nona Balakian and Charles Simmons, eds. *The Creative Present: Notes on Contemporary Fiction.* Garden City, N.Y.: Doubleday, 1963. Pp. 111–141.

Detweiler, Robert. "William Styron and the Courage to Be." In his *Four Spiritual Crises in Mid-Century American Fiction.* Gainesville: University of Florida Press, 1964. Pp. 6–13.

Finkelstein, Sidney. "Cold War, Religious Revival, and Family Alienation: William Styron, J. D. Salinger, and Edward Albee." In his *Existentialism and Alienation in American Literature.* New York: International Publishers, 1965. Pp. 211–242.

Fossum, Robert H. *William Styron: A Critical Essay.* Grand Rapids, Mich.: Eerdmans, 1968.

Friedman, Melvin J., and August J. Nigro, eds. *Configuration Critique de William Styron.* Paris: Minard, 1967.

Melvin J. Friedman, "Préface," pp. 7–31.

Frederick J. Hoffman, "La Thérapeutique du Néant: Les Romans de William Styron," pp. 33–56.

David L. Stevenson, "L'Individu, Le Milieu et La Liberté Dans Les Romans de William Styron," pp. 57–71.

Roger Asselineau, "En Suivant *La Marche de Nuit,*" pp. 73–83.

Melvin J. Friedman, "William Styron et Le Nouveau Roman," pp. 85–109.

August J. Nigro, "Mûrir à Sambuco," pp. 111–121.

James Boatwright, "Réflexions sur Styron, Ses Critiques et Ses Sources," pp. 123–135.

August J. Nigro, "William Styron: Sélection Bibliographique," pp. 137–151.

Fuller, Edmund. *Books with Men behind Them.* New York: Random House, 1962. Pp. 9–10.

Galloway, David D. "The Absurd Man as Tragic Hero" and "A William Styron Checklist." In his *The Absurd Hero in American Fiction.* Austin: University of Texas Press, 1966. Pp. 51–81 and 203–210.

Geismar, Maxwell. "William Styron: The End of Innocence." In his

American Moderns from Rebellion to Conformity. New York: Hill and Wang, 1958. Pp. 239–250.

Gossett, Louise Y. "The Cost of Freedom: William Styron." In her *Violence in Recent Southern Fiction.* Durham, N.C.: Duke University Press, 1965. Pp. 117–130.

Hartt, Julian. *The Lost Image of Man.* Baton Rouge: Louisiana State University Press, 1963. Pp. 60–63, 130.

Hassan, Ihab. "Encounter with Necessity: Three Novels by Styron, Swados, and Mailer." In his *Radical Innocence: Studies in the Contemporary American Novel.* Princeton, N.J.: Princeton University Press, 1961. Pp. 124–152 [*Lie Down in Darkness*]. Reprinted in Richard Kostelanetz, ed. *On Contemporary Literature.* New York: Avon Books, 1964. Pp. 597–606.

Hoffman, Frederick. "The Sense of Place." In Louis D. Rubin and Robert D. Jacobs, eds. *South: Modern Southern Literature in Its Cultural Setting.* Garden City, N.Y.: Doubleday Dolphin Books, 1961. Pp. 76–94 [*Lie Down in Darkness*].

———. "William Styron: The Metaphysical Hurt." In his *The Art of Southern Fiction: A Study of Some Modern Novelists.* Carbondale: Southern Illinois University Press, 1967. Pp. 144–161. Reprinted (in French) in Melvin J. Friedman and August J. Nigro, eds. *Configuration Critique de William Styron.* Paris: Minard, 1967. Pp. 33–56.

Kazin, Alfred. "The Alone Generation." In his *Contemporaries.* Boston: Little, Brown, 1962. Pp. 214–216.

Ludwig, Jack. *Recent American Novelists.* Minneapolis: University of Minnesota Press, 1962. Pp. 31–34.

Mackin, Cooper R. *William Styron.* Austin, Tex.: Steck-Vaughn, 1969.

Mailer, Norman. *Advertisements for Myself.* New York: New American Library, 1960. Pp. 415–416.

Matthiessen, Peter, and George Plimpton. "William Styron." In Malcolm Cowley, ed. *Writers at Work: The "Paris Review" Interviews.* New York: Viking Press, 1959. Pp. 267–282 [Reprinted interview].

Meeker, Richard K. "The Youngest Generation of Southern Fiction Writers." In R. C. Simonini, Jr., ed. *Southern Writers: Appraisals in Our Time.* Charlottesville: University of Virginia Press, 1961. Pp. 162–191.

Mohrt, Michel. *Le Nouveau Roman Américain.* Paris: Gallimard, 1955. Pp. 171–174.

O'Connor, William Van. "John Updike and William Styron: The Burden of Talent." In Harry T. Moore, ed. *Contemporary American Novelists.* Carbondale: Southern Illinois University Press, 1964. Pp. 205–221.

Podhoretz, Norman. "The Gloom of Philip Roth." In his *Doings and Undoings.* New York: Farrar, Straus, 1964. Pp. 236–243.

Rubin, Louis D., Jr. *The Curious Death of the Novel: Essays in American Literature.* Baton Rouge: Louisiana State University Press, 1967. Pp. 4, 9, 10, 20–22, 146–147, 277, 280, 286, 292.

————, Katherine Anne Porter, Flannery O'Connor, Caroline Gordon, and Madison Jones. *Recent Southern Fiction*. Macon, Ga.: Wesleyan College, 1960.

————. "William Styron: Notes on a Southern Writer in Our Time." In his *The Faraway Country: Writers of the Modern South*. Seattle: University of Washington Press, 1963. Pp. 185–230.

Stevenson, David L. "Novelists of Distinction." In Nona Balakian and Charles Simmons, eds. *The Creative Present*. Garden City, N.Y.: Doubleday, 1963. Pp. 195–212.

————. "William Styron and the Fiction of the Fifties." In Joseph L. Waldmeir, ed. *Recent American Fiction: Some Critical Views*. Boston: Houghton Mifflin, 1963. Pp. 265–274.

Urang, Gunnar. "The Voices of Tragedy in the Novels of William Styron." In Nathan A. Scott, Jr., ed. *Adversity and Grace: Studies in Recent American Literature*. Chicago: University of Chicago Press, 1968. Pp. 183–209.

"William Styron." In Dorothy Nyren, ed. *A Library of Literary Criticism: Modern American Literature*. New York: Frederick Ungar, 1960. Pp. 473–476.

B. PERIODICALS

Aldridge, John W. "Highbrow Authors and Middlebrow Books," *Playboy*, XI (April 1964), 173–174.

Aptheker, Herbert, "A Note on the History," *The Nation*, CCV (October 16, 1967), 375. [On *Nat Turner*]

————. "Styron's Turner vs. Nat Turner," *New South Student*, May 1968, pp. 3–7.

————. "Truth and Nat Turner: An Exchange," *The Nation*, CCVI (April 22, 1968), 543–544.

Arnavon, Cyrille. "Les Romans de William Styron," *Europe*, XLI (septembre 1963), 54–66.

Baumbach, Jonathan. "Paradise Lost: The Novels of William Styron," *South Atlantic Quarterly*, LXIII (Spring 1964), 207–217. Reprinted in his *The Landscape of Nightmare* (See II, A).

Benson, Alice R. "Techniques in the Twentieth Century Novel for Relating the Particular to the Universal: *Set This House on Fire*," *Papers of the Michigan Academy of Science, Arts and Letters*, XLVII (1962), 587–594.

"Biographical Sketches of Persons Selected for the Pulitzer Prizes for 1968," New York *Times*, May 7, 1968, p. 34.

Bonnichon, André. "William Styron et le Second Oedipe," *Études*, CCCXV (octobre 1962), 94–103. [*Set This House on Fire*]

Briere, Annie. "La Proie des Critiques," *Nouvelles Littéraires*, XL (22 mars 1962), 8. [Interview by M.-E. Coindreau and Michel Butor]

Bryant, Jerry H. "The Hopeful Stoicism of William Styron," *South Atlantic Quarterly,* LXII (Autumn 1963), 539–550.

Cambon, Glauco. "Faulkner fa scoula," *La Fiera Letteraria,* March 7, 1954, p. 5.

Canzoneri, Robert, and Page Stegner. "An Interview with William Styron," *Per/Se,* I (Summer 1966), 37–44.

Carver, Wayne. "The Grand Inquisitor's Long March," *Denver Quarterly,* I (Summer 1966), 37–64. [Dostoevsky's *The Legend of the Grand Inquisitor* and *The Long March*]

Chapsal, Madeleine. "Entretien," *L'Express,* No. 560 (8 mars 1962), 26–27. [Interview]

Cheyer, A. H. "WLB Biography: William Styron," *Wilson Library Bulletin,* XXXVI (April 1962), 691.

Cowley, Malcolm. "American Novels Since the War," *New Republic,* CXXIX (December 28, 1953), 16–18.

Davis, Richard Beale. "Spadework, American Literature and the Southern Mind: Opportunities," *South Atlantic Bulletin,* XXVI (March 1966), 1–4.

Davis, Robert Gorham. "In a Ravelled World Love Endures," *New York Times Book Review,* December 26, 1954, pp. 1, 13.

———. "Styron and the Students," *Critique,* III (Summer 1960), 37–46.

Dempsey, David. "Talk with William Styron," *New York Times Book Review,* September 9, 1951, p. 27.

Doar, Harriet. "Interview with William Styron," *Red Clay Reader,* 1964, pp. 26–30.

Dommergues, Pierre. "L'Ambiguité de l'Innocence," *Langues Modernes,* LIX (mars-avril 1965), 54–59.

Duberman, Martin. "Historical Fictions," *New York Times Book Review,* August 11, 1968, pp. 1, 26–27. [Review of Clarke's *William Styron's "Nat Turner"*]

Duffer, Ken. "Now Nat Turner as He Might Have Written It," Winston-Salem (N.C.) *Journal and Sentinel,* December 17, 1967, Sec. D, p. 6. [Review of *Ol' Prophet Nat,* by Daniel Panger]

Durden, Robert F. "William Styron and His Black Critics," *South Atlantic Quarterly,* LXVIII (Spring 1969), 181–187. [Review of Clarke's *William Styron's "Nat Turner"*]

Farrell, James T. "Literary Note," *American Book Collector,* XVII (May 1967), 6.

Foster, Richard. "An Orgy of Commerce: William Styron's *Set This House on Fire,*" *Critique,* III (Summer 1960), 59–70.

Fraisse, Simone. "Une Tragédie de Notre Temps: *La Proie des Flammes* de William Styron," *Esprit,* octobre 1963, pp. 483–488.

Fremont-Smith, Eliot. "Nat Turner I: The Controversy," *New York Times,* August 1, 1968, p. 29. [Review of Clarke's *William Styron's "Nat Turner"*]

———. "Nat Turner II: What Myth Will Serve?" *New York Times,*

August 2, 1968, p. 31. [Review of Clarke's *William Styron's "Nat Turner"*]

Friedman, Joseph. "Non-Conformity and the Writer," *Venture,* XX (Winter 1957), 23–31.

Friedman, Melvin J. "William Styron: An Interim Appraisal," *English Journal,* L (March 1961), 149–158, 192. Reprinted (revised) as "Préface" in Friedman and Nigro, eds. *Configuration Critique de William Styron* (See II, A).

Galloway, David D. "The Absurd Man as Tragic Hero: The Novels of William Styron," *Texas Studies in Literature and Language,* VI (Winter 1965), 512–534. Reprinted in his *The Absurd Hero in American Fiction* (See II, A).

Geismar, Maxwell. "The American Short Story Today," *Studies on the Left,* IV (Spring 1964), 21–27.

———. "The Post-War Generation in Arts and Letters," *Saturday Review of Literature,* XXXIV (March 14, 1953), 11–12.

Genovese, Eugene D. "An Exchange on 'Nat Turner,'" *New York Review of Books,* XI (November 7, 1968), 34–36.

———. "The Nat Turner Case," *New York Review of Books,* XI (September 12, 1968), 34–37. [Review of Clarke's *William Styron's "Nat Turner"*]

Gresset, Michel. "Sur William Styron," *Mercure de France,* CCCL (février 1964), 297–303.

H., E. P. "On Author," *Saturday Review of Literature,* XXXIV (September 15, 1951), 12.

Hamilton, Charles V. "Nat Turner Reconsidered: The Fiction and the Reality," *Saturday Review,* LI (June 22, 1968), 22–23. [Review of Clarke's *William Styron's "Nat Turner"*]

Harding, Vincent. "An Exchange on 'Nat Turner,'" *New York Review of Books,* XI (November 7, 1968), 31–33.

Hassan, Ihab. "The Avant-Garde: Which Way Is Forward?" *The Nation,* CXCII (November 18, 1961), 396–399.

———. "The Character of Post-War Fiction in America," *English Journal,* LI (January 1962), 1–8.

———. "The Novel of Outrage: A Minority Voice in Postwar American Fiction," *American Scholar,* XXXIV (Spring 1965), 239–253.

———. "The Way Down and Out," *Virginia Quarterly Review,* XXXIX (Winter 1963), 81–93.

Hays, Peter L. "The Nature of Rebellion in *The Long March,*" *Critique,* VIII (Winter 1965–1966), 70–74.

Hazard, E. P. "Eight Fiction Finds," *Saturday Review of Literature,* XXXV (February 16, 1952), 17.

———. "William Styron," *Saturday Review of Literature,* XXXIV (September 15, 1951), 12.

Holder, Alan. "Styron's Slave: *The Confessions of Nat Turner,*" *South Atlantic Quarterly,* LXVIII (Spring 1969), 167–180.

"Howe and Styron to Write Book Column for *Harper's*," New York *Times*, October 26, 1967, p. 40.

Hutchens, John K. "William Styron," *New York Herald Tribune Book Review*, September 9, 1951, p. 2.

Johansson, Eric. "Lettres: Les Sortiléges de la Mauvaise Conscience," *Démocratie*, 27 juin 1963, p. 10.

Juin, Hubert. "Rencontre avec William Styron," *Lettres Françaises*, ler-8 mars 1962, p. 5.

Kazin, Alfred. "The Alone Generation," *Harper's* (Special Supplement), CCXIX (October 1959), 127–131. Reprinted in his *Contemporaries* (See II, A).

Kihss, Peter. "Pulitzer to Styron Novel; No Prize Given for Drama," New York *Times*, May 7, 1968, pp. 1, 34.

Klotz, Marvin. "The Triumph Over Time: Narrative Form in William Faulkner and William Styron," *Mississippi Quarterly*, XVII (Winter 1963–64), 9–20.

Kostelanetz, Richard. "The Bad Criticism of This Age," *Minnesota Review*, IV (Spring 1964), 389–414.

Las Vergnas, Raymond. "Étoiles Anglo-Américaines: Nathanael West, William Styron, Robert Penn Warren, Carson McCullers, V. Sackville-West," *Les Annales*, août 1962, p. 33.

Lawson, John Howard. "William Styron: Darkness and Fire in the Modern Novel," *Mainstream*, XIII (October 1960), 9–18. [*Set This House on Fire*]

Lawson, Lewis. "Cass Kinsolving: Kierkegaardian Man of Despair," *Wisconsin Studies in Contemporary Literature*, III (Fall 1962), 54–66.

Le Clec'h, Guy. "Un 'Grand' de la Nouvelle Vague Américaine: William Styron," *Figaro Littéraire*, 24 février 1962, p. 3. [Interview centered on *Set This House on Fire*]

Lehan, Richard. "Existentialism in Recent American Fiction: The Demonic Quest," *Texas Studies in Literature and Language*, I (Summer 1959), 181–202.

Lewis, R. W. B. "American Letters: A Projection," *Yale Review*, LI (December 1961), 211–226.

Lichtenstein, G. "The Exiles," *New Statesman and Nation*, LV (September 6, 1958), 320.

McNamara, Eugene. "The Post-Modern American Novel," *Queen's Quarterly*, LXIX (Summer 1962), 265–275.

———. "William Styron's *Long March*: Absurdity and Authority," *Western Humanities Review*, XV (Summer 1961), 267–272.

Mailer, Norman. "Norman Mailer vs. Nine Writers," *Esquire*, LX (July 1963), 63–69, 105.

Mason, Robert. "Teacher Guided, Publisher Fired Him—Encouragement and a Kick Made Bill Styron a Writer," Norfolk *Virginian-Pilot*, September 9, 1951, Part 5, p. 5. [Detailed biographical sketch, based on interview with W.S.'s father]

Matthiessen, Peter, and George Plimpton. "William Styron," *Paris Review*, V (Spring 1954), 42–47. Reprinted in Cowley, ed. *Writers at Work* (See II, A). [Interview]

Meras, Phyllis. "The Author," *Saturday Review*, L (October 7, 1967), 30.

Mitchell, Richard. "An Age of Issues and a Literature of Troubles," *Western Humanities Review*, XVII (Autumn 1963), 349–360.

Mizener, Arthur. "Some People of Our Time," *New York Times Book Review*, June 5, 1960, pp. 5, 26.

Mohrt, Michel. "Interview de William Styron," *Nouveau Candide*, No. 70 (29 août 1962), 70.

———. "Michel Mohrt Présente la Première Révélation du Roman Américain Depuis la Guerre: J'ai Vécu Avec William Styron la Dolce Vita," *Arts*, No. 786 (7–13 septembre 1960), 3.

———. "Les Trois Obsessions de William Styron: Le Péché, Le Désespoir, Le Désir d'Évasion," *Arts*, No. 858 (28 février–8 mars 1962), 3.

Monaghan, Charles. "Portrait of a Man Reading," *Book World*, October 27, 1968, p. 8. [Interview]

Moore, L. Hugh. "Robert Penn Warren, William Styron, and the Use of Greek Myth," *Critique*, VIII (Winter 1965–1966), 75–87.

"Movies," *Newsweek*, LXIII (March 9, 1964), 59. [On influence of movies on Styron's technique]

Moyano, Maria Clara. "Speaking Volumes—The Confessions of William Styron," *Book World*, October 1, 1967, p. 6.

Mudrick, Marvin. "Mailer and Styron: Guests of the Establishment," *Hudson Review*, XVII (Autumn 1964), 346–366.

"Nat Turner Saga to be Filmed," Cleveland *Plain Dealer*, February 18, 1968, Sec. G, p. 5.

Nigro, August. "*The Long March:* The Expansive Hero in a Closed World," *Critique*, IX (No. 3, 1967), 103–112.

Noggle, Burt. "Variety and Ambiguity," *Mississippi Quarterly*, XVII (Winter 1963–64), 33.

Nye, Russel. "Le Roman Américain Contemporain," *Revue des Lettres Modernes*, VIII (Spring 1961), 3–16.

O'Connell, Shaun. "Expense of Spirit: The Vision of William Styron," *Critique*, VIII (Winter 1965–1966), 20–33.

———. "Styron's Nat Turner . . . ," *The Nation*, CCV (October 16, 1967), 373–374.

O'Rourke, Elizabeth. "*Best Short Stories from 'The Paris Review,'*" *Best Sellers*, XIX (November 1, 1959), 259.

Phillips, John. "Styron Unlocked," *Vogue*, CL (December 1967), 216–217, 267–271, 278.

Ragan, Sam. "Southern Accent," Raleigh (N.C.) *News and Observer*, September 16, 1951, Sec. IV, p. 5. [WS and the reception of *Lie Down in Darkness*]

Robb, Kenneth A. "William Styron's Don Juan," *Critique,* VIII (Winter 1965–1966), 34–46.

Rosenthal, Jean. "William Styron," *Informations et Documents,* No. 158 (15 mars 1962), 24.

Roth, Philip. "Writing American Fiction," *Commentary,* XXXI (March 1961), 222–233.

Rubin, Louis D., Jr. "The Curious Death of the Novel: Or What to Do about Tired Literary Critics," *Kenyon Review,* XXVIII (June 1966), 305–325. Reprinted in his *The Curious Death of the Novel* (See II, A).

————. "Notes on the Literary Scene: Their (Southerners') Own Language," *Harper's,* CCXXX (April 1965), 173–175.

————. "The South and the Faraway Country," *Virginia Quarterly Review,* XXXVIII (Summer 1962), 444–459. Reprinted in his *The Faraway Country* (See II, A).

Sachs, Viola. "Contemporary American Fiction and Some Nineteenth Century Patterns," *Kwartalnik Neofilogiczny,* XIII (First Quarter 1966), 3–29.

Saint-Phalle, Therese de. "William Styron (Héritier Littéraire de Faulkner): 'Je ne Veux pas Être Appelé un Écrivain du Sud,'" *Figaro Littéraire,* 1–7 juillet 1965, p. 16.

Schickel, Richard. "The Old Critics and the New Novel," *Wisconsin Studies in Contemporary Literature,* V (Winter–Spring 1964), 26–36.

Schneider, Harold W. "Two Bibliographies: Saul Bellow, William Styron," *Critique,* III (Summer 1960), 71–91.

Shepard, Richard F. "Stage and Literary Names Enlist for Candidates," *New York Times,* August 14, 1968, p. 40.

Slavitt, David. "Poetry, Novels, and Critics: A Reply," *Yale Review,* LI (March 1962), 502–504.

Stevenson, David L. "The Activists," *Daedalus,* XCII (Spring 1963), 238–249.

————. "Fiction's Unfamiliar Face," *The Nation,* CLXXXVII (November 1, 1958), 307–309.

————. "Styron and the Fiction of the Fifties," *Critique,* III (Summer 1960), 47–58. Reprinted in Waldmeir, ed. *Recent American Fiction* (See II, A).

Sullivan, Walter. "The Decline of Regionalism in Southern Fiction," *Georgia Review,* XVIII (Fall 1964), 300–308.

Talese, Gay. "Looking for Hemingway," *Esquire,* LX (July 1963), 44–47.

Taylor, Robert. "The Controversions of William Styron," Washington (D.C.) *Post,* May 11, 1969, p. B5. [Interview reprinted from Boston *Globe* on *Nat Turner*]

Thelwell, Mike. "An Exchange on 'Nat Turner,'" *New York Review of Books,* XI (November 7, 1968), 34.

———. "Mr. William Styron and the Rev. Turner," *Massachusetts Review*, IX (Winter 1968), 7–29. Reprinted in Clarke, ed. *William Styron's "Nat Turner"* (See II, A).

Thomas, Emory E. "Ten Views of the Man Who Would Not Die," *Saturday Review*, LI (August 17, 1968), 23–24. [Review of Clarke's *William Styron's "Nat Turner"*]

Thorp, Willard. "The Southern Mode," *South Atlantic Quarterly*, LXIII (Autumn 1964), 576–582.

Times Literary Supplement (London), August 5, 1955, pp. II–III.

Urang, Gunnar. "The Broader Vision: William Styron's *Set This House on Fire*," *Critique*, VIII (Winter 1965–1966), 47–69.

"W. S. Writes PW about His New Novel," *Publishers' Weekly*, CLXXVII (May 30, 1960), 54–55.

Waldmeir, Joseph. "Quest Without Faith," *The Nation*, CXCIII (November 18, 1961), 390–396.

Warren, Robert Penn. "William Styron," *Book-of-the-Month-Club News*, October 1967, pp. 6–7, 14.

Wells, Anne Mary. "An Exchange on 'Nat Turner,'" *New York Review of Books*, XI (November 7, 1968), 31.

Whitman, Alden. "William Styron Examines the Negro Upheaval," New York *Times*, August 5, 1967, p. 13.

Winner, Anthony. "Adjustment, Tragic Humanism, and Italy," *Studi Americani*, VII (1961), 311–361.

C. DOCTORAL DISSERTATIONS

Baumbach, Jonathan. "The Theme of Guilt and Redemption in the Post Second World War Novel," Stanford University, 1961.

Galloway, David D. "The Absurd Hero in Contemporary Fiction: The Works of John Updike, William Styron, Saul Bellow, and J. D. Salinger," University of Buffalo, 1962.

Hux, Samuel H. "American Myth and Existential Vision: The Indigenous Existentialism of Mailer, Bellow, Styron, and Ellison," University of Connecticut, 1966.

Nigro, August. "William Styron and the Adamic Tradition," University of Maryland, 1964.

Scott, James B. "The Individual and Society: Norman Mailer versus William Styron," Syracuse University, 1964.

D. BOOK REVIEWS

Lie Down in Darkness

Aldridge, John W. "In a Place Where Love Is a Stranger," *New York Times Book Review*, September 9, 1951, p. 5.

Bedell, W. D. "William Styron—Bitter Story Hits Home," Houston *Post*, September 9, 1951, Sec. 1, p. 22.

Breit, Harvey. "Dissolution of a Family," *Atlantic Monthly*, CLXXXVIII (October 1951), 78–80.

Byam, Milton S. *Library Journal*, LXXVI (September 15, 1951), 1423–1424.

Cady, Ernest. "Books—Impressive First Novel Surmounts Handicap of Overworked Theme," Columbus (Ohio) *Dispatch*, September 9, 1951, p. F-7.

Chapin, Ruth. "Twilight of the South," *Christian Science Monitor*, October 4, 1951, p. 11.

Cowley, Malcolm. "The Faulkner Pattern," *New Republic*, CXXV (October 8, 1951), 19–20.

Crume, Paul. "Strong Novel of Virginia Tragedy," Dallas *Morning News*, September 9, 1951, Part VI, p. 7.

"Dark Misery," *Newsweek*, XXXVIII (September 10, 1951), 106–107.

Davis, Robert Gorham. "A Grasp of Moral Realities," *American Scholar*, XXI (Winter 1951–1952), 114, 116.

Derleth, August. "Idea Is Good But It Needs a Little Editing," *Chicago Sunday Tribune Magazine of Books*, September 9, 1951, p. 3.

Downing, Francis. "The Young: A Lost Generation," *Commonweal*, LIV (October 5, 1951), 620.

Elwood, Irene. "Family Has Everything, Loses All," Los Angeles *Times*, September 16, 1951, Part IV, p. 5.

Geismar, Maxwell. "Domestic Tragedy in Virginia," *Saturday Review of Literature*, XXXIV (September 15, 1951), 12–13.

Govan, Christine Noble. "Story of Weak Family Is Plea For More Maturity in Adults," Chattanooga *Times*, September 16, 1951, p. 19.

Grove, Lee. "Memorable First Novel Demolishes a Family," Washington (D.C.) *Post*, September 9, 1951, p. 6B.

Heth, Edward Harris. "A Torrential New Talent," Milwaukee *Journal*, September 16, 1951, Sec. V, p. 5.

Janeway, Elizabeth. "Private Emotions Privately Felt," *New Leader*, XXXV (January 21, 1952), 25.

Jones, Carter Brooke. "Work of Virginia's William Styron Hailed as Extraordinary 1st Novel," Washington (D.C.) *Sunday Star*, September 9, 1951, p. C-3.

Jones, Howard Mumford. "A Rich, Moving Novel Introduces a Young Writer of Great Talent," *New York Herald Tribune Book Review*, September 9, 1951, p. 3.

Kelley, James E. "Promising First Novel—Violence of Love and Hate," Denver *Post*, September 9, 1951, p. 6E.

Kirby, John Pendy. *Virginia Quarterly Review*, XXVIII (Winter 1952), 129–130.

L[aycock], E[dward] A. "An Exciting Discovery—William Styron

Writes Magnificent First Novel About a Tragic Family," Boston *Sunday Globe*, September 9, 1951, p. A-27.

Mason, Robert. "Story of the Spirit Is Rich in Poetry and Insight— William Styron of Newport News, 26, Is Suddenly a Major Novelist," Norfolk *Virginian-Pilot*, September 9, 1951, Part 5, p. 4.

New Yorker, XXVII (September 29, 1951), 118–119.

O'Brien, Alfred, Jr. *"Lie Down in Darkness," Commonweal*, LV (October 19, 1951), 43–44.

O'Leary, Theodore M. "Styron's Remarkable First Novel," Kansas City (Mo.) *Star*, September 29, 1951, p. 16.

Pasley, Gertrude. "Unhappy People," Newark (N.J.) *Sunday News*, September 16, 1951, Sec. IV, p. 88.

Prescott, Orville. "Books of The Times," New York *Times*, September 10, 1951, p. 19.

Ragan, Majorie. "A New Southern Author Shows Literary Promise," Raleigh (N.C.) *News and Observer*, September 16, 1951, Sec. IV, p. 5.

Rubin, Louis D., Jr. "What To Do About Chaos," *Hopkins Review*, V (Fall 1951), 65–68.

S., A. *Canadian Forum*, XXXI (January 1952), 239.

Scott, Eleanor M. Providence (R.I.) *Sunday Journal*, September 9, 1951, Sec. VI, p. 8.

Scott, J. D. "New Novels," *New Statesman and Nation*, XLIII (April 19, 1952), 472–473.

Sessler, Betty. Richmond (Va.) *Times-Dispatch*, September 16, 1951, p. 8-A.

Sherman, John K. "First Novel Stamps Young Writer as Great," Minneapolis (Minn.) *Sunday Tribune*, September 30, 1951, Feature-News Section, p. 6.

Smith, Harrison. "Young Writer Depicts Trials of Human Soul," Buffalo (N.Y.) *Evening News*, September 8, 1951, Magazine Section, p. 7. See also Charlotte (N.C.) *Observer*, September 9, 1951, p. 14D; Philadelphia *Sunday Bulletin*, September 9, 1951, Magazine Section, p. 6.

Snyder, Marjorie B. "Love, Hate, Passion All in His Book," Boston *Sunday Herald*, September 9, 1951, Sec. I, p. 6.

Stix, Frederick W. Cincinnati *Enquirer*, September 9, 1951, Sec. 3, p. 13.

Swados, Harvey. "First Novel," *The Nation*, CCLXXII (November 24, 1951), 453.

"The Unbeautiful and Damned," *Time*, LVIII (September 10, 1951), 106, 108.

Wallace, Margaret. "Of a Nobel Laureate and Other Novelists," *Independent Woman*, XXX (November 1951), 325.

Ziegner, Edward. "Here's a First, Not a Last, We Hope," Indianapolis (Ind.) *News*, September 8, 1951, p. 2.

Set This House on Fire

Adams, Phoebe. *Atlantic Monthly*, CCVI (July 1960), 97–98.

Baro, Gene. "Styron's New Novel: Search for the Meaning of Evil," *New York Herald Tribune Book Review*, June 5, 1960, pp. 1, 12.

Betts, Doris. "Serious Violent Novel," Houston *Post*, June 12, 1960, Houston Now Section, p. 36.

Borklund, Elmer. "Fiction of Violence and Pain," *Commentary*, XXX (November 1960), 452–454.

Bourg, Gene. "Italy Is Scene of American Drama," New Orleans *Times-Picayune*, June 19, 1960, Sec. II, p. 3.

Bradley, Van Allen. "Second Styron Novel Close to a Masterpiece," Chicago *Daily News*, June 4, 1960, p. 13.

Breit, Harvey. "A Second Novel," *Partisan Review*, XXVIII (Summer 1960), 561–563.

Bryden, Ronald. "Near Amalfi," *Spectator*, No. 6921 (February 17, 1961), 232–233.

Cheney, Frances Neel. "Rich, Sensitive Prose—Eye for Detail," Nashville (Tenn.) *Banner*, June 3, 1960, p. 24.

Covici, Pascal, Jr. "Powerful Vision for Our Time," Dallas *Morning News*, June 5, 1960, Sec. V, p. 6.

Creed, Howard. "Styron Doesn't Set Reviewer on Fire," Birmingham (Ala.) *News*, August 21, 1960, Sec. E, p. 8.

Culligan, Glendy. "Styron Returns—Jury Still Hung," Washington (D.C.) *Post*, June 5, 1960, Sec. E, p. 6.

Cunningham, Bill. San Antonio *Express and News*, July 10, 1960, Sec. G, p. 5.

*Curley, Thomas F. "The Quarrel With Time in American Fiction," *American Scholar*, XXIX (Autumn 1960), 552–560.

Dahms, Joseph G. *America*, CIII (June 18, 1960), 380–381.

Daniels, N. A. "The Identity of Opposites," San Francisco *People's World*, July 9, 1960, p. 6.

Dawkins, Cecil. "Our Man in Italy—A Study of Evil and Its Expiation," Milwaukee *Journal*, June 5, 1960, Sec. 5, p. 4.

Dwight, Ogden G. "In 'Set This House on Fire' Styron Has Quite a Blaze," Des Moines (Iowa) *Register*, July 3, 1960, Sec. G, p. 11.

"Empty Soul Blues," *Time*, LXXIV (June 6, 1960), 98.

*Fenton, Charles A. "William Styron and the Age of the Slob," *South Atlantic Quarterly*, LIX (Autumn 1960), 469–476.

Fuller, Edmund. "A Picture of Hell By a Writer of Maturing Vision," *Chicago Sunday Tribune Magazine of Books*, June 5, 1960, p. 3.

Gentry, Curt. "Styron's Superb Third Novel," San Francisco *Sunday Chronicle*, June 5, 1960, This World Section, p. 22.

Griffin, Lloyd W. *Library Journal*, LXXXV (June 15, 1960), 2458.

Hayes, E. Nelson. "Novels by Styron and Fifield," Providence (R.I.) *Journal*, June 5, 1960, Sec. W, p. 20.

Hicks, Granville. "After the Fury, a Time of Peace," *Saturday Review of Literature*, XLIII (June 4, 1960), 13.

Highet, Gilbert. *Book-of-the-Month-Club News*, June 1960, p. 7.

Hill, Susan. *Time and Tide*, XLII (February 24, 1961), 285.

Hollander, John. *Yale Review*, L (Fall 1960), 152–153.

Hunter, Anna C. "Styron Fulfills Promise with Explosive New Novel," Savannah (Ga.) *Morning News*, June 5, 1960, Magazine, p. 14.

Hutchens, John K. New York *Herald Tribune*, June 3, 1960, p. 11.

Jones, Carter B. "Mr. Styron's New Novel Is a Disappointment," Washington (D.C.) *Sunday Star*, June 5, 1960, Sec. C, p. 11.

"Just Out: A Kind of Tenderness," *Newsweek*, LV (June 6, 1960), 117–118.

Kaufman, Clarence. "Second Styron Novel Proof of Major Talent," Lincoln (Neb.) *Sunday Journal and Star*, June 5, 1960, Sec. B, p. 12.

Kenney, Herbert, Jr. "Moralizing Binge Spoils Styron Talent," Indianapolis *News*, August 6, 1960, p. 2.

Kirsch, Robert R. "Styron's 'House' Nears Greatness," Los Angeles *Times*, June 5, 1960, Sec. C, p. 7.

Kohn, Sherwood. "Styron . . . An Heir of Camus?" Louisville (Ky.) *Times*, June 15, 1960, p. 11.

L., E. A. "American Spoiled Boy—Styron's Third Novel Shocking, Powerful Picture of Degradation," Boston *Sunday Globe*, June 5, 1960, Sec. A, p. 7.

L., E. H. "New Book Plenty Hot—It Deserves to Burn," Salt Lake *Tribune*, August 14, 1960, Sec. W, p. 15.

Layton, Mike. "Critics Predictions Fulfilled by Styron," Olympia (Wash.) *Sunday Olympian*, June 12, 1960, p. 22.

Lea, George. "New Novel Won't Set House on Fire," Chicago *Sun-Times*, July 10, 1960, Sec. III, p. 5.

"Life, Death of Sadistic Millionaire," Miami *Herald*, June 12, 1960, Sec. J, p. 14.

Lindau, Betsy. Asheville (N.C.) *Citizen-Times*, June 5, 1960, Sec. D, p. 3.

Lowman, Ann. "Too Much Retrospect Mars Styron's Second," Columbus (Ohio) *Sunday Dispatch*, June 26, 1960, TAB Section, p. 12.

McDermott, Stephanie. "Arty People Flounder in Own Morass," St. Louis *Globe Democrat*, June 5, 1960, Sec. F, p. 4.

McManis, John. Detroit *News*, June 5, 1960, Sec. F, p. 3.

Malcolm, Donald. "False Alarms," *New Yorker*, XXXVI (June 4, 1960), 152–154.

Mason, Robert. "Characters Clash in Heroic Conflict," *Virginian Pilot and Portsmouth Star*, June 5, 1960, Sec. F, p. 8.

Miller, Nolan. *Antioch Review*, XX (Summer 1960), 256.

Mizener, Arthur. "Some People of Our Time," *New York Times Book Review,* June 5, 1960, pp. 5, 26.

Monaghan, Charles. "Styronic Manner," *Commonweal,* LXXII (July 22, 1960), 380.

Mooney, Harry, Jr. "Styron Raises Issues, Faces Them Squarely, But Novel Is Seriously Marred by Author's Undisciplined Rhetoric," Pittsburgh *Press,* June 5, 1960, Sec. V, p. 14.

Murray, James G. *The Critic,* XIX (August–September 1960), 37.

"Must Books," *Kirkus,* XXVIII (April 15, 1960), 333.

Newberry, Mike. "Shock of Recognition," *Mainstream,* XIII (September 1960), 61–63.

New Mexico Quarterly, XXX (Winter 1960–1961), 412.

Nichols, Luther. "Styron's Literary Shock Treatment," San Francisco *Examiner,* May 29, 1960, Highlight Section, p. 6.

O'Leary, Theodore M. "All the Elements of Greatness," Kansas City (Mo.) *Star,* June 4, 1960, p. 18.

Peckham, Stanton. "Styron's Second Novel Fulfills Promise," Denver *Sunday Post,* June 5, 1960, Roundup Section, p. 9.

Perkin, Robert L. "Important Fiction," *Rocky Mountain News* (Denver), June 26, 1960, Sec. A, p. 14.

Pickrel, Paul. "Heroic Proportions," *Harper's,* CCXXI (July 1960), 93.

Prescott, Orville. New York *Times,* June 3, 1960, p. 29.

Price, Emerson. "Magnificent Novel Portrays Man Trapped by His Own Folly," Cleveland *Press,* June 7, 1960, p. 28.

Price, R. G. *Punch,* CCXL (March 15, 1961), 441–442.

Ragan, Marjorie. "A Brilliant Fire of Tragedy," Raleigh (N.C.) *News and Observer,* June 5, 1960, Sec. III, p. 5.

Rogers, W. G. "Killing in Italy Theme of New Styron Novel," Cleveland *Plain Dealer,* June 12, 1960, Sec. H, p. 8.

*Rothberg, Abraham. "Styron's Appointment in Sambuco," *New Leader,* XLIII (July 4–11, 1960), 24–27.

*Rubin, Louis D., Jr. "An Artist in Bonds," *Sewanee Review,* LXIX (Winter 1961), 174–179.

———. Baltimore *Evening Sun,* June 3, 1960, p. 30.

Scott, Paul. *New Statesman and Nation,* LXI (February 17, 1961), 270–271.

Sherman, John K. "Melodrama of Good and Evil Probes Human Undercurrents," Minneapolis *Tribune,* June 12, 1960, Sec. E, p. 6.

Sinclair, Reid B. "Prodigious Effort by a Virginian," Richmond *Times Dispatch,* June 26, 1960, Sec. L, p. 10.

Southern, Terry. *The Nation,* CXCII (November 19, 1960), 382.

Virginia Quarterly Review, XXXVI (Autumn 1960), civ.

Watts, Harold H. "Assembly of Horrors," St. Louis *Post-Dispatch,* June 19, 1960, Sec. B, p. 4.

"What Happened at Sambuco," (London) *Times Literary Supplement,* February 17, 1961, p. 101.

The Confessions of Nat Turner

America, CXVII (November 25, 1967), 666.

America, CXVIII (February 24, 1968), 269.

American (Chicago), October 8, 1967, Sec. III, p. 5.

Ancrum, Calhoun. "Novel by Styron Gets Rave Notices," Charlestown (W.Va.) *News Courier*, December 31, 1967, Sec. D, p. 2.

Barkham, John. "60 Whites Were Killed in 1831 Slave Riots," Youngstown (Ohio) *Vindicator*, October 8, 1967, Sec. B, p. 2. See also Woodland (Cal.) *Democrat*, October 18, 1967; Lewiston (Idaho) *Tribune*, October 15, 1967; Albany (N.Y.) *Times-Union*, October 8, 1967.

Bernstein, Victor. "Black Power, 1831," *Hadassah Magazine* (November 1967), 16, 37.

Billings, Claude. "Confessions Bares Negro Slave Revolt," Indianapolis *Star*, December 17, 1967, Sec. VIII, p. 7.

Birlchaui, John. "Nat Turner's Rampage Told," Tucson (Ariz.) *Daily Citizen*, December 2, 1967, Ole Magazine, p. 7.

Booklist, LXIV (December 1, 1967), 425.

Bradley, Van Allen. "Styron Tells Slave's Saga," Memphis *Commercial Appeal*, October 15, 1967, Sec. V, p. 6. See also Birmingham (Ala.) *News*, October 15, 1967.

Brown, Cecil M. *Negro Digest*, XVII (February 1968), 51–52, 89–91.

Bryden, Ronald. "Slave Rising," *New Statesman*, LXXV (May 3, 1968), 586–587.

Buckmaster, Henrietta. "Racism, 1831: The Fire Last Time," *Christian Science Monitor*, October 12, 1967, p. 5.

Bunke, Joan. "Styron Novel Is Powerful as Fiction and Sermon," Des Moines (Iowa) *Register*, October 15, 1967, Sec. T, p. 7.

Callanan, Kathleen B. "Curl Up and Read," *Seventeen* (January 1968), 116.

Choice, V (March 1968), 54.

Clemons, Joel. "Author Dramatizes Event Masterfully," Charlestown *News Courier*, December 31, 1967, Sec. D, p. 2.

*Coles, Robert. "Blacklash," *Partisan Review*, XXXV (Winter 1968), 128–133.

Collier, Peter. "Saga of Rebellion," *The Progressive*, (December 1967), 41–42.

"Confessions of Nat Turner Condemned as Racist Book," Los Angeles *Free Press*, March 29, 1968, p. 8.

*Cooke, Michael. "Nat Turner's Revolt," *Yale Review*, LVII (Winter 1968), 273–278.

*Core, George. "*Nat Turner* and the Final Reckoning of Things," *Southern Review*, n.s. IV (July 1968), 745–751.

Cunningham, Dick. "Styron Writes of Negro with Inside-Out View," Minneapolis *Tribune*, October 8, 1967, Sec. E, p. 6.

Currie, Edward. "Author William Styron—Era's Clarion," *Rocky Mountain News* (Denver), October 22, 1967, Startime Section, p. 19.

Delany, Lloyd Tom. "A Psychologist Looks at *The Confessions of Nat Turner*," *Psychology Today* I (January 1968), 11–14.

Driver, Tom F. "Black Consciousness Through a White Scrim," *Motive*, XXVII (February 1968), 56–58.

*Duberman, Martin. *Village Voice*, December 14, 1967, pp. 8–9, 16.

Duffer, Ken. "Nat Turner: Slave to a Terrible Vision," Winston-Salem (N.C.) *Journal and Sentinel*, October 8, 1967, Sec. D, p. 6.

Fadiman, Clifton. *Book-of-the-Month-Club News*, October 1967, pp. 2–5.

Ferguson, Charles A. "Styron Revises Story of Slave Revolt of 1831," New Orleans *Times Picayune*, October 29, 1967, p. 12.

Fremont-Smith, Eliot. "A Sword Is Sharpened," New York *Times*, October 3, 1967, p. 45.

———. "'The Confessions of Nat Turner'—II," New York *Times*, October 4, 1967, p. 45.

*Friedman, Melvin J. "*The Confessions of Nat Turner:* The Convergence of 'Nonfiction Novel' and 'Meditation on History,'" *Journal of Popular Culture*, I (Fall 1967), 166–175. See also *The University of Wisconsin at Milwaukee Magazine*, Spring 1968, pp. 3–7 (abridged).

Fuller, Edmund. "Power and Eloquence in New Styron Novel," *Wall Street Journal*, October 4, 1967, p. 16.

*Gilman, Richard. "Nat Turner Revisited," *New Republic*, CLVIII (April 27, 1968), 23–26, 28, 32.

Goodheart, Eugene. "When Slaves Revolt," *Midstream*, XIV (January 1968), 69–72.

Greenwood, Walter B. "Nat Turner's Revolt a Tragic Comment on Slavery's Evils," Buffalo (N.Y.) *Evening News*, October 14, 1967, Sec. B, p. 12.

Griffin, Lloyd W. *Library Journal*, XCII (October 1, 1967), 3448–3449.

Grimes, Roy. "Books and Things—*The Confessions of Nat Turner*," Victoria (B.C.) *Advocate*, October 15, 1967, p. 10.

H., S. "Novel of Slave Revolt Eloquent," San Antonio *Express*, October 8, 1967, Sec. H, p. 3.

Hall, Joan Joffe. "Jehovah's Rebel Slave," Houston *Post*, October 22, 1967, Spotlight Section, p. 12.

*Harnack, Curtis. "The Quidities of Detail," *Kenyon Review*, XXX (Winter 1968), 125–132.

Heise, Kenan. *Extension*, LXII (December 1967), 54.

Herman, Dick. "Is Grim Message of Slavery Just Beginning to Be Felt?" Lincoln (Neb.) *Journal and Star*, October 15, 1967, Sec. F, p. 15.

Hicks, Granville. "Race Riot, 1831," *Saturday Review*, L (October 7, 1967), 29–31.

————. "Five for Year's End," *Saturday Review*, L. (December 30, 1967), 19.

Hicks, Walter J. "The Futile Insurrection," Baltimore *Sunday Sun*, October 15, 1967, Sec. D, p. 5.

Hogan, William. "William Styron's American Tragedy," San Francisco *Chronicle*, October 9, 1967, p. 43.

————. "Further Thoughts on the Styron Novel," San Francisco *Chronicle*, October 10, 1967, p. 39.

Hurt, Richard L. "Slavery's Quiet Resistance," Boston *Globe*, October 8, 1967, Sec. A, p. 43.

"The Idea of Hope," *Time*, XC (October 13, 1967), 110, 113.

Ingle, H. L. "Meditation on History," Chattanooga (Tenn.) *Times*, November 12, 1967, p. 30.

*Kauffmann, Stanley. "Styron's Unwritten Novel," *Hudson Review*, XX (Winter 1967–1968), 675–679.

*Kazin, Alfred. "Instinct for Tragedy: A Message in Black and White," *Book World*, October 8, 1967, pp. 1, 22.

Kincaid, Anne. *Library Journal*, XCII (November 15, 1967), 4274.

Kirkus, XXXV (August 1, 1967), 905.

Kirsch, Robert. "The Virginia Slave Revolt," Los Angeles *Times*, October 8, 1967, p. 36.

Krupat, Arnold. "The Shock of Nat Turner," *Catholic World*, CCVI (February 1968), 226–228.

LaHaye, Judson. *Best Sellers*, XXVII (November 1, 1967), 308.

Layton, Mike. "A Negro Slave Revolt and What It Tells Us," Olympia (Wash.) *Sunday Olympian*, October 28, 1967, p. 27.

Lehan, Richard. *Contemporary Literature*, IX (Autumn 1968), 540–542.

Lewis, Claude. "Slavery, Murder, and God," Philadelphia *Sunday Bulletin*, October 15, 1967, Books and Art Section, p. 3.

Long, James. *Oregon Journal* (Portland), November 11, 1967, Sec. J, p. 6.

McCormick, Jay. "An American Tragedy—Lessons That the Gallows Failed to Teach," Detroit *News*, October 8, 1967, Sec. E, p. 3.

McGroaty, Rev. Joseph G. "'Nat Turner': A Racial Tract for Our Times," *The Tablet*, LX (November 16, 1967), 13.

McNeill, Robert. *Presbyterian Survey*, LVIII (February 1968), 26–27.

McPherson, James Lowell. "America's Slave Revolt," *Dissent*, XV (January–February 1968), 86–89.

Mason, Robert. "A Brilliant 'Meditation on History'—Nat Turner, From Birth to Rebellion," *Virginian Pilot and Portsmouth Star*, October 8, 1967, Sec. C, p. 6.

Meyer, June. "Spokesmen for the Blacks," *The Nation*, CCV (December 4, 1967), 597.

Miller, William Lee. "The Meditations of William Styron," *The Reporter*, XXXVII (November 16, 1967), 42–46.

Moody, Minnie Hite. "Documentary Novel Is Pegged to 1831 Revolt," Columbus (Ohio) *Dispatch*, October 22, 1967, TAB Section, p. 14.

Murray, Albert. "A Troublesome Property," *New Leader*, X (December 4, 1967), 18–20.

"Nat Turner's No Longer Unknown—1831 Insurrection Gets a Timely Revival in 'Confessions,'" Grand Rapids (Mich.) *Press*, October 8, 1967, p. 39.

Nolte, William H. "Fact Novel of Revolt in Hot Summer of 1831," St. Louis *Sunday Post-Dispatch*, October 8, 1967, Sec. D, p. 4.

Parker, Roy, Jr. "Styron's 'Nat Turner'—Fact Transmuted into Art," Raleigh (N.C.) *News and Observer*, October 30, 1967, Sec. III, p. 3.

Penne, Leo. "Out From the Vicious Circle," Seattle *Post-Intelligencer*, October 22, 1967, Northwest Today Section, p. 4.

Platt, Gerald M. "A Sociologist Looks at *The Confessions of Nat Turner*," *Psychology Today*, I (January 1968), 14–15.

Q., G. "Revolt of Negro Slaves Echoes Over the Years," Waco (Texas) *Tribune-Herald*, November 5, 1967, Sec. D, p. 13.

*Rahv, Phillip. "Through the Midst of Jerusalem," *New York Review of Books*, IX (October 26, 1967), 6, 8, 10.

Redding, Saunders. "A Fateful Lightning in the Southern Sky," Providence (R.I.) *Journal*, October 29, 1967, Sec. W, p. 18.

Richter, David H. *Chicago Literary Review* (October 1967), 1, 10–11.

Robertson, Don. "One View: Styron Is a Brave Failure," Cleveland *Plain Dealer*, October 15, 1967, Sec. H, p. 8.

Rubin, Louis D., Jr. "Books—Eloquent Story of a Slave Rebellion," Washington (D.C.) *Sunday Star*, October 8, 1967, Sec. G, p. 14.

*———. "William Styron and Human Bondage: *The Confessions of Nat Turner*," *Hollins Critic*, IV (December 1967), 1–12.

Schaap, Dick. "Framework for Confessions," San Francisco *Sunday Examiner and Chronicle*, October 15, 1967, This World Section, pp. 39, 46.

Schlueter, Paul. "Soul Torment," *Christian Century*, LXXXV (February 21, 1968), 234–235.

Schroth, Raymond A. "Nat Turner's Sword," *America*, CXVII (October 14, 1967), 416.

Schwartz, Joseph. "Negro Revolt of 1831 Flares Again in a 'Big' Novel of Fall," Milwaukee *Journal*, October 8, 1967, Sec. V, p. 4.

Shaw, Russell. *The Sign*, XLVII (January 1968), 63.

*Sheed, Wilfrid. "The Slave Who Became a Man," *New York Times Book Review*, October 8, 1967, pp. 1–3, 30, 32, 34.

Sherman, John K. "Portrays Negro View—Novel Illuminates History of Slavery," Minneapolis *Star*, October 10, 1967, Sec. E, p. 4.

Smith, Miles A. "Slave Revolt of 1831 Is Recounted," Indianapolis *News*, October 21, 1967, p. 30. See also St. Louis *Globe Democrat*, October 21, 1967, Sec. F, p. 5.

Sokolov, Raymond A. "Into the Mind of Nat Turner," *Newsweek,* LXX (October 16, 1967), 65–69.

Steiner, George. "Books—The Fire Last Time," *New Yorker,* XLIII (November 25, 1967), 236.

Thomas, Sidney. "Slave Broke His Chains," Atlanta *Journal and Constitution,* November 12, 1967, Sec. D, p. 10.

*Thompson, John. "Rise and Slay!" *Commentary,* XLIV (November 1967), 81–85.

Tucker, Martin. *Commonweal,* LXXXVII (December 22, 1967), 338–339.

Turney, Charles. "Virginian's Novel Seeks 'Meditation on History,'" Richmond (Va.) *Times-Dispatch,* October 15, 1967, Sec. F, p. 5.

"Unslavish Fidelity: The Confessions of William Styron," (London) *Times Literary Supplement,* May 9, 1968, p. 480.

Virginia Quarterly Review, XLIV (Winter 1968), viii.

W., B. "The Negro Fury: A Vital Insight," Long Beach (Cal.) *Independent Press-Telegram,* November 18, 1967, Sec. A, p. 6.

Wade, Gerald. "The Only Effective U.S. Negro Revolt," Omaha (Neb.) *World-Herald,* October 29, 1967, Sec. I, p. 36.

Weber, R. B. "Styron's Power Creates a Real Being," Louisville (Ky.) *Times,* October 13, 1967, Sec. A, p. 11.

Weeks, Edward. *Atlantic,* CCXX (November 1967), 130.

Winfrey, Lee. "When a Negro Slave Rebelled," Detroit *Free Press,* October 8, 1967, Sec. B, p. 5.

Wolff, Geoffrey A. "Slavery Intersects Present," Washington (D.C.) *Post,* October 24, 1967, Sec. A, p. 16.

*Woodward, C. Vann. "Confessions of a Rebel: 1831," *New Republic,* CLVII (October 7, 1967), 25–28.

Wright, Giles E. "Life of Real Slave Treated in Top Novel," Los Angeles *Herald Examiner,* October 8, 1967, Sec. J, p. 4.

Yardley, Jonathan. "Mr. Styron's Monumental 'Meditation on History,'" Greensboro (N.C.) *Daily News,* October 8, 1967, Sec. D, p. 3.